CANARIES IN THE MINESHAFT

Also by Renata Adler

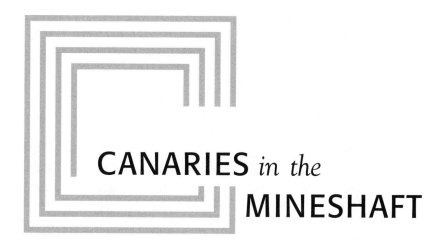

CANARIES *in the* MINESHAFT

ESSAYS ON POLITICS AND MEDIA

RENATA ADLER

ST. MARTIN'S PRESS   NEW YORK

www.stmartins.com

Design by Susan Walsh
Index by Peter Rooney

Many of the essays in this book were previously published, in slightly different form, in other publications. Copyright acknowledgments appear on page 381.

Library of Congress Cataloging-in-Publication Data

Adler, Renata.
    Canaries in the mineshaft : essays on politics and media / Renata Adler.—1st ed.
        p.   cm.
    Includes index.
    ISBN 0-312-27520-X
    1. United States—Politics and government—1945–1989.   2. United States—Politics and government—1989–   3. Press and politics—United States.   I. Title.

E839.5 .A35 2001
973.92—dc21

                                                                    2001019173

First Edition: August 2001

10 9 8 7 6 5 4 3 2 1

For Stephen

CONTENTS

The turning point at the paper, as it happened, was the introduction of the byline. There had always been bylines, of course, but only on rare stories and those of the highest importance. Sometime in the seventies the paper began to put bylines on nearly all stories, by everyone. No one could have predicted where this would take us. It seemed, at first, a step in the direction of truth, of frankness. Part of every story had always been, after all, says who? But the outcome, in retrospect, was this. From anonymous reporters quoting, as a matter of the highest professionalism and with only the rarest exceptions, from named and specific sources, we moved gradually, then rapidly, to the reverse: named reporters, with famous bylines, quoting persons, sources, who remained anonymous. There were several results. The reporter himself, with his celebrity, his byline, became in many cases the most powerful character, politically and otherwise, in his own story. The "sources" lapsed, became sometimes highly placed officials floating as facts rumors to which, like pollsters, they wanted to test a reaction, sometimes disenchanted employees or rivals, trying to exact a revenge, or undermine a policy, or gain an advantage, sometimes "composites," a euphemism for a more or less fictional character introduced for some purpose of the reporter's own; finally, perhaps inevitably, absolute fictions. . . .

—Pitch Dark

INTRODUCTION

Along with every other viewer of television during Operation Desert Storm, the Gulf War of 1991, I believed that I saw, time after time, American Patriot missiles knocking Iraqi Scuds out of the sky. Every major television reporter obviously shared this belief, along with a certainty that these Patriots were offering protection to the population of Israel—which the Desert Storm alliance, for political reasons, had kept from active participation in the war. Commentators actually cheered, with exclamations like "Bull's-eye! No more Scud!" at each such interception by a Patriot of a Scud. Weeks earlier, I had read newspaper accounts of testimony before a committee of the Congress by a tearful young woman who claimed to have witnessed Iraqi soldiers enter Kuwaiti hospitals, take babies out of their incubators, hurl the newborns to the floor, and steal the incubators. I believed this, too.

Only much later did I learn that hardly a single Patriot effectively hit a single Scud. The scenes on television were in fact repetitions of images from one film, made by the Pentagon in order to persuade Congress to allocate more money to the Patriot, an almost thirty-year-old weapon designed, in any case, not to destroy missiles but to intercept airplanes. In his exuberance, a high military official announced that Patriots had even managed to destroy "eighty-one Scud launchers"—interesting not only because the total number of Scud launchers previously ascribed to Iraq was fifty, but also because there is and was no such thing as a "Scud launcher." The vehicles in question were old trucks, which had broken down.

What was at issue, in other words, was not even pro-American propaganda, which could be justified in time of war. It was domestic advertising for a product—not just harmlessly deceptive advertising, either.

The Patriots, as it turned out, did more damage to the allied forces, and to Israel, than if they had not been used at all. The weeping young woman who had testified about the incubator thefts turned out to be the fifteen-year-old daughter of the Kuwaiti ambassador to Washington; she had not, obviously, witnessed any such event. Whatever else the Iraqi invaders and occupiers may have done, this particular incident was a fabrication—invented by an American public relations firm in the employ of the Kuwaiti government.

During Operation Desert Storm itself, the American press corps, as it also turns out, accepted an arrangement with the U.S. military, whereby only a "pool" of journalists would be permitted to cover the war directly. That pool went wherever the American military press officer chose to take it. Nowhere near the front, if there was a front. Somehow, the pool and its military press guides often got lost. When other reporters, trying to get independent information, set out on their own, members of the pool actually berated them for jeopardizing the entire news-gathering arrangement.

It would have been difficult to learn all this, or any of it, from the press. I learned it from a very carefully researched and documented book, *Second Front: Censorship and Propaganda in the Gulf War*, by John R. MacArthur. The book, published in 1992, was well enough reviewed. But it was neither prominently reviewed nor treated as "news" or even information. A review, after all, is regarded only as a cultural and not a real—least of all a journalistic—event. It was not surprising that the Pentagon, after its experience in Vietnam, should want to keep the press at the greatest possible distance from any war. It was not surprising, either, that reporters, having after all not that much choice, should submit so readily to being confined to a pool, or even that reporters in that pool should resent any competitor who tried to work outside it. This is the position of a favored collaborator in any bureaucratic and coercive enterprise.

What was, if not surprising, a disturbing matter, and a symptom of what was to come, was this: The press did not report the utter failure of the Patriot, nor did it report the degree to which the press itself, and then its audience and readership, had been misled. This is not to suggest that the press, out of patriotism or for any other reason, printed propaganda to serve the purposes of the government—or even that it would be unworthy to do so. But millions of Americans surely still believe that Patriots destroyed the Scuds, and in the process saved, or at least defended, Israel. There seemed, in this instance, no reason why the press, any more than any person or other institution, should be eager to report failures of its own.

Almost all the pieces in this book have to do, in one way or another, with what I regard as misrepresentation, coercion, and abuse of public process, and, to a degree, the journalist's role in it. At the time of the Vietnam War, it could be argued that the press had become too reflexively adversarial and skeptical of the policies of government. Now I believe the reverse is true. All bureaucracies have certain interests in common: self-perpetuation, ritual, dogma, a reluctance to take responsibility for their actions, a determination to eradicate dissent, a commitment to a notion of infallibility. As I write this, the Supreme Court has, in spite of eloquent and highly principled dissents, so far and so cynically exceeded any conceivable exercise of its constitutional powers as to choose, by one vote, its own preferred candidate for President. Some reporters, notably Linda Greenhouse of the *New York Times*, have written intelligently and admirably about this. For the most part, however, the press itself has become a bureaucracy, quasi-governmental, and, far from calling attention to the collapse of public process, in particular to prosecutorial abuses, it has become an instrument of intimidation, an instrumentality even of the police function of the state.

Let us begin by acknowledging that, in our public life, this has been a period of unaccountable bitterness and absurdity. To begin with the attempts to impeach President Clinton. There is no question that the two sets of allegations, regarding Paula Jones and regarding Whitewater, with which the process began could not, as a matter of fact or law or for any other reason, constitute grounds for impeachment. Whatever they were, they preceded his presidency, and no President can be impeached for his prior acts. That was that. Then the Supreme Court, in what was certainly one of the silliest decisions in its history, ruled that the civil lawsuit by Paula Jones could proceed without delay because, in spite of the acknowledged importance of the President's office, it appeared "highly unlikely to occupy any substantial amount of his time." In 1994 a Special Prosecutor (for some reason, this office is still called the Independent Counsel) was appointed to investigate Whitewater—a press-generated inquiry, which could not possibly be material for a Special Prosecutor, no matter how defined, since it had nothing whatever to do with presidential conduct. Nonetheless, the first Special Prosecutor, Robert Fiske, investigated and found nothing. A three-judge panel, appointed, under the Independent Counsel statute, by Chief Justice William Rehnquist, fired Fiske. As head of the three-judge panel, Rehnquist had passed over several more senior judges, to choose Judge David Bryan Sentelle.

Judge Sentelle consulted at lunch with two ultra-right-wing senators from his own home state of North Carolina: Lauch Faircloth, who was convinced, among other things, that Vincent Foster, a White House counsel, had been murdered; and Jesse Helms, whose beliefs and powers would not be described by anyone as moderate. Judge Sentelle appointed as Fiske's successor Kenneth W. Starr. North Carolina is, of course, a tobacco-growing state. Kenneth Starr had been, and remained virtually throughout his tenure as Special Prosecutor, a major, and very highly paid, attorney for the tobacco companies. He had also once drafted a pro bono amicus brief on behalf of Paula Jones.

The Office of Special Prosecutor—true conservatives said this from the first—had always been a constitutional abomination. To begin with, it impermissibly straddled the three branches of government. If President Nixon had not been in dire straits, he would never have permitted such an office, in the person of Archibald Cox, to exist. If President Clinton had not been sure of his innocence and—far more dangerously—overly certain of his charm, he would never have consented to such an appointment.

The press, however, loves Special Prosecutors. They can generate stories for each other. That something did not happen is not a story. That something does not matter is not a story. That an anecdote or an accusation is unfounded is not a story. There is this further commonality of interest. Leaks, anonymous sources, informers, agents, rumormongers, appear to offer stories—and possibilities for offers, pressures, threats, rewards. The journalist's exchange of an attractive portrayal for a good story. There we are. The reporter and the prosecutor (the Special Prosecutor, that is; not as often the genuine prosecutor) are in each other's pockets.

Starr did not find anything, either. Certainly no crime. He sent his

staff to Little Rock, generated enormous legal expenses for people interviewed there, threw one unobliging witness (Susan McDougal) into jail
for well over a year, indicted others (Webster Hubbell, for example) for
offenses unrelated to the Clintons, convicted and jailed witnesses in
hopes of getting testimony damaging to President Clinton, tried, after
the release of those witnesses, to jail them again to get such testimony.
Still no crime. So his people tried to generate one. This is not unusual
behavior on the part of prosecutors going after hardened criminals: stings,
indictments of racketeers and murderers for income tax offenses. But here
was something new. Starr's staff, for a time, counted heavily on sexual
embarrassment: philandering, Monica Lewinsky. They even had a source,
Linda Tripp. Ms. Tripp had testified for Special Prosecutor Fiske and
later for Starr. She had testified in response to questions from her sympathetic interlocutor Senator Lauch Faircloth before Senator D'Amato's
Whitewater Committee. She had testified to agents of the FBI right in
the Special Prosecutor's office at least as early as April 12, 1994. An
ultra-right-wing Republican herself, she not only believed White House
Counsel Vincent Foster was murdered, she claimed to fear for her own
life. She somehow had on the wall above her desk at the Pentagon, where
her desk adjoined Monica Lewinsky's, huge posters of President Clinton—which, perhaps not utterly surprisingly, drew Ms. Lewinsky's attention. Somehow, in the fall of 1996 Ms. Tripp found herself eliciting, and
taping, confidences from Ms. Lewinsky. In January of 1997, Ms. Tripp—
who by her own account had previously abetted another White House
volunteer, Kathleen Willey, in making sexual overtures to President
Clinton—counseled Ms. Lewinsky to try again to visit President Clinton.
By the end of February 1997, Ms. Lewinsky, who had not seen the President in more than eleven months, managed to arrange such a visit.
Somehow, that visit was the only one in which she persuaded the President to ejaculate. Somehow, adept as Ms. Lewinsky claimed to be at
fellatio, semen found its way onto her dress. Somehow, Ms. Tripp persuaded Ms. Lewinsky, who perhaps did not require much persuasion, to
save that dress. Somehow, the Special Prosecutor got the dress. And
somehow (absurdity of absurdities), there was the spectacle of the Special
Prosecutor's agents taking blood from the President to match the DNA
on a dress.

Now, whatever other mistakes President Clinton may have made, in this or any other matter, he, too, had made utterly absurd mistakes of constitutional proportions. He had no obligation at all to go before the grand jury. It was a violation of the separation of powers and a mistake. Once again, he may have overestimated his charm. Charm gets you nowhere with prosecutors' questions, answered before a grand jury under oath. And of course, Mr. Starr had managed to arrange questions—illegally, disingenuously, at the absolute last minute—which were calculated to make the President testify falsely at his deposition in the case of Paula Jones. Whether or not the President did testify falsely, the notion that "perjury" or even "obstruction of justice" in such a case could rise to the level of "Treason, Bribery or other high Crimes and Misdemeanors," the sole constitutional grounds for impeachment, had no basis in history or in law.

One need not dwell on every aspect of the matter to realize this much: As sanctimonious as lawyers, congressmen, and even judges may be, most legal cases are simply not decided on arcane legal grounds. Most turn on conflicting evidence, conflicting *testimony*. And this conflict cannot, surely, in every case or even in most cases, be ascribed either to Rashomon phenomena or to memory lapses. In most cases—there is no other way to put it—one litigant or the other, and usually both, are lying. If this were to be treated as "perjury" or "obstruction of justice," then, alas, most losers in litigation would be subject to indictment. Anyone who has studied grounds for impeachment at all knows that "high Crimes and Misdemeanors" refers, in any event, only to crimes committed in the President's official capacity and in the actual conduct of his office.

And now the press. Perhaps the most curious phenomenon in the recent affinity of the press with prosecutors has been a reversal, an inversion so acute that it passes any question of "blaming the victim." It actually consists in casting persecutors as victims, and vilifying victims as persecutors. The *New York Times* is not alone in this, but it has been, until recently, the most respected of newspapers, and it has been, of late, the prime offender. A series of recent events there gives an indication of what is at stake.

In a retreat in Tarrytown, in mid-September, Joseph Lelyveld—in his time a distinguished reporter, now executive editor of the *Times*—gave a speech to eighty assembled *Times* newsroom editors, plus two editors

of other publications, *The New Yorker* and *Newsday*. The ostensible subject of the retreat was "Competition." Mr. Lelyveld's purpose, he said,
was to point out "imperfections in what I proudly believe to be the best
New York Times ever—the best written, most consistent, and ambitious
newspaper *Times* readers have ever had." This was, in itself, an extraordinary assertion. It might have been just a mollifying tribute, a prelude
to criticism of some kind. And so it was.

"I'm just driven by all the big stuff we've accomplished in recent
years—our strong enterprise reporting, our competitive edge, our successful recruiting, our multimedia forays, our sheer ambition," Lelyveld
went on, "to worry" about "the small stuff," particularly "the really big
small stuff." "I especially want to talk to you," he said, "about corrections,
and in particular, the malignancy of misspelled names, which, if you
haven't noticed, has become one of the great themes of our Corrections
column."

He might have been joking, but he wasn't. "Did you know we've misspelled Katharine Graham's name fourteen times? Or that we've misspelled the Madeleine in Madeleine Albright forty-nine times—even
while running three corrections on each? . . . So far this year . . . there
have been a hundred and ninety-eight corrections for misspelled given
names and surnames, the overwhelming majority easily checkable on the
Internet. . . . I want to argue that our commitment to being excellent
and reliable in these matters is as vital to the impression we leave on
readers, and the service we perform for them, as the brilliant things we
accomplish most days on our front page and on our section-front displays."

Lelyveld recalled the time, thirty years ago, when he had first come
to the newspaper (a better paper, as it happens, an incomparably better
paper, under his predecessors, whom present members of the staff tend
to demonize). "Just about everything else we do today, it seems to me,
we do better than they did then." But, in view of "the brilliant things
we accomplish most days" ("We don't just claim to be a team. We don't
just aspire to be a team. Finally, I think we can say, we function as a
team. We are a team"), he did want to talk about what he regarded as
a matter of some importance: "Finally . . . there's the matter of corrections (I almost said the 'festering matter' of corrections). As I see it, this
is really big small stuff."

A recent correction about a photo confusing monarch and queen butterflies, he said, might seem amusing—"amusing if you don't much mind the fact that scores of lepidopterists are now likely to mistrust us on areas outside their specialty."

And that, alas, turned out to be the point. This parody, this misplaced punctiliousness, was meant to reassure readers—lepidopterists, whomever—that whatever else appeared in the newspaper could be trusted and was true. Correction of "malignant" misspellings, of "given names and surnames," middle initials, captions, headlines, the "overwhelming majority" of which, as Lelyveld put it, would have been "easily checkable on the Internet" was the *Times*' substitute for conscience, and the basis of its assurance to readers that in every other respect it was an accurate paper, better than it had ever been, more worthy of their trust. Stendhal, for instance, had recently been misspelled, misidentified, and given a first name: Robert. "A visit to Amazon.com, just a couple of clicks away, could have cleared up the confusion." Maybe so.

The trivial, as it happens often truly comic, corrections, persist, in quantity. The deep and consequential errors, inevitable in any enterprise, particularly those with deadlines, go unacknowledged. By this pedantic travesty of good faith, which is, in fact, a classic method of deception, the *Times* conceals not just every important error it makes but that it makes errors at all. It wants that poor trusting lepidopterist to think that, with the exception of this little lapse (now corrected), the paper is conscientious and infallible.

There exists, to this end, a wonderful set of locutions, euphemisms, conventions, codes, and explanations: "misspelled," "misstated," "referred imprecisely," "referred incorrectly," and recently—in some ways most mystifyingly—"paraphrase."

> On September 19, 2000, "An article on September 17 about a program of intellectual seminars organized by Mayor Jerry Brown of Oakland, California, referred imprecisely to some criticisms of the series. The terms 'Jerrification' and 'pointy-headed table talk' were the article's paraphrase of local critics, not the words of Willa White, president of the Jack London Association."

> On October 5, 2000, "A news analysis yesterday about the performances of Vice President Al Gore and Gov. George W.

Bush of Texas in their first debate referred imprecisely in some copies to a criticism of the candidates. The observation that they 'took too much time niggling over details' was a paraphrase of comments by former Mayor Pete Flaherty of Pittsburgh, not a quotation."

On November 9, 2000, "An article on Sunday about the campaign for the Senate in Missouri said the Governor had 'wondered' about the decision of the late candidate's wife to run for the Senate. But he did not use the words 'I'm bothered somewhat by the idea of voting for a dead person's wife, simply because she is a widow.' That was a paraphrase of Mr. Wilson's views and should not have appeared in quotation marks."

On December 16, 2000, "Because of an editing error, an article yesterday referred erroneously to a comment by a board member," about a recount. " 'A man has to do what a man has to do' was a paraphrase of Mr. Torre's views and should not have appeared in quotation marks."

Apart from the obvious questions—What is the *Times*' idea of "paraphrase"? What were the actual words being paraphrased? What can "Jerrification," "pointy-headed table talk," "niggling," and even "A man has to do what a man has to do" possibly be paraphrases *of*—what purpose is served by these corrections? Is the implication that all other words, in the *Times*, attributed in quotation marks to speakers are accurate, verbatim quotations? I'm afraid the implication is inescapably that. That such an implication is preposterous is revealed by the very nature of these corrections. There is no quotation of which "Jerrification" and the rest can *possibly* be a paraphrase. Nor can the reporter have simply misheard anything that was actually said, nor can the result be characterized as having "referred imprecisely" or "referred erroneously," let alone be the result of "an editing error."

It cannot be. What is at issue in these miniscule corrections is the *Times*' notion of what matters, its professionalism, its good faith, even its perception of what constitute accuracy and the truth. The over-riding value is, after all, to allay the mistrust of readers, lepidopterists, colleagues. Within the newspaper, this sense of itself—trust us, the only errors we make are essentially typos, and we correct them; we never even misquote, we paraphrase—appears even in its columns.

In a column published in the *Times* on July 20, 2000, Martin Arnold of the Arts/Culture desk, for example, wrote unhesitatingly that, compared with book publishing, "Journalism has a more rigorous standard: What is printed is believed to be true, not merely unsuspected of being false. The first rule of journalism," he wrote, "is don't invent."

"Except in the most scholarly work," Mr. Arnold went on, "no such absolutes apply to book publishing. . . . A book writer is . . . not subject to the same discipline as a news reporter, for instance, who is an employee and whose integrity is a condition of his employment . . . a newspaper . . . is a brand name, and the reader knows exactly what to expect from the brand." If book publishers, Mr. Arnold concluded, "seem lethargic" about "whether a book is right or wrong, it maybe [sic] because readers will cut books slack they don't give their favorite newspaper."

In this wonderful piece of self-regarding fatuity, Mr. Arnold has expressed the essence of the "team's" view of its claim: The *Times* requires no "slack." It readily makes its own corrections:

> The Making Books column yesterday misspelled the name of the television host. . . . She is Oprah Winfrey, not Opra.

> An article about Oprah Winfrey's interview with Al Gore used a misspelled name and a non-existent name for the author of *The Red and the Black*. . . . The pen name is Stendhal, not Stendahl; Robert is not part of it.

> The Advertising column in Business on Friday misspelled the surname of a singer and actress. . . . She is Lena Horne, not Horn.

> An article about an accident in which a brick fell from a construction site atop the YMCA building on West 63rd Street, slightly injuring a woman, included an erroneous address from the police for the building near which she was standing. It was 25 Central Park West. (There is no No. 35).

> Because of an editing error, the Making Books column on
> Thursday . . . misstated the name of the publisher of a thriller
> by Tom Clancy. It is G. P. Putnam, not G. F.

> An article on Monday about charges that Kathleen Hagen
> murdered her parents, Idella and James Hagen, at their home
> in Chatham Township, N.J., misspelled the street where they
> lived. It is Fairmount Avenue, not Fairmont.

And so on. Endlessly.

What is the reasoning, the intelligence, behind this daily travesty of concern for what is truthful? Mr. Arnold has the cant just about right. "Don't invent." (Pointy-headed table talk? Jerrification? Niggling? Paraphrase?) "Discipline"? "Integrity"? "Rigorous standard"? Not in a long time. "A newspaper is a brand name, and the reader knows exactly what to expect from the brand." Well, there is the problem. Part of it is the delusion of punctilio. But there is something more. Every acknowledgment of an inconsequential error (and they are never identified as reporting errors, only errors of "editing," or "production," or "transmission," and so forth), in the absence of acknowledgment of any *major* error, creates at best a newspaper that is closed to genuine inquiry. It declines responsibility for real errors, and creates as well an affinity for all orthodoxies. And when there is a subject genuinely suited to its professional skills and obligations, it abdicates. It almost reflexively shuns responsibility and delegates it to another institution.

Within a few weeks of its small retreat at Tarrytown, the *Times*, on two separate occasions, so seriously failed in its fundamental journalistic obligations as to call into question not just its judgment and good faith but whether it is still a newspaper at all. The first occasion returns in a way to the subject with which this introduction began: a pool.

On election night, television, it was generally acknowledged, had made an enormous error by delegating to a single consortium, the Voter News Service, the responsibility for both voter exit polls and calling the election results. The very existence of such a consortium of broadcasters raised questions in anti-trust, and VNS called its results wrongly, but that was not the point. The point was that the value of a free press in our society was always held to lie in competition. By a healthy competition among reporters, from media of every political point of view, the public would have access to reliable information, and a real basis on which to choose. A single monolithic, unitary voice, on the other hand, is anathema to any democractic society. It becomes the voice of every oppressive or totalitarian system of government.

The *Times* duly reported, and in its own way deplored, the results of the VNS debacle. Then, along with colleagues in the press (the *Washington Post,* CNN, the *Wall Street Journal,* ABC, AP, the Tribune Company), it promptly emulated it. This new consortium hired an organization called the National Opinion Research Center to undertake, on its behalf, a manual recount of Florida ballots for the presidential election. The *Miami Herald,* which had already been counting the votes for several weeks, was apparently the only publication to exercise its function as an independent newspaper. It refused to join the consortium. It had already hired an excellent accounting firm, BDO Seidman, to assist its examination of the ballots. NORC, by contrast, was not even an auditing firm but a survey group, much of whose work is for government projects.

The *Times* justified its (there seems no other word for it) hiding, along with seven collegial bureaucracies, behind a single entity, NORC, on economic grounds. Proceeding independently, it said, would have cost between $500,000 and $1 million. The *Times,* it may be noted, had put fifteen of its reporters to work for a solid year on a series called "Living Race in America." If it had devoted just some of those resources and that cost to a genuine, even historic, issue of fact, it would have exercised its independent competitive function in a free society and produced something of value. There seems no question that is what the *Times* under any previous publisher or editors would have done.

In refusing to join the consortium, the *Miami Herald* said the recount was taking place, after all, "in our own back yard." It was, of course, America's backyard, and hardly any other members of the press could be troubled with their own resources and staff to enter it.

The second failure of judgment and good faith was in some ways more egregious. In late September of 2000 there was the *Times'* appraisal of its coverage (more accurately, the *Times'* response to other people's reaction to its coverage) of the case of Wen Ho Lee.

For some days, there had been rumors that the *Times* was going to address in some way its coverage of the case of Wen Ho Lee, a sixty-year-old nuclear scientist at Los Alamos who had been held, shackled and without bail, in solitary confinement, for nine months—on the basis, in part, of testimony, which an FBI agent had since admitted to be false, that Lee had passed American nuclear secrets to China; and testimony, also false, that he had flunked a lie detector test about the matter; and testimony, false and in some ways most egregious, that granting him bail would constitute a "grave threat" to "hundreds of millions of lives" and the "nuclear balance" of the world. As part of a plea bargain, in which Lee acknowledged a minor offense, the government, on September 14, 2000, withdrew fifty-eight of its fifty-nine original charges. The Federal District Judge, James A. Parker, a Reagan appointee, apologized to Lee for the prosecutorial conduct of the government.

The *Times* had broken the story of the alleged espionage on March 6 of 1999, and pursued it both editorially and in its news columns for seventeen months. A correction, perhaps even an apology, was expected to appear in the Week in Review section, on Sunday, September 24, 2000. Two *Times* reporters flew up from Washington to register objections. The piece, whatever it had been originally, was edited and postponed until the following Tuesday. (The Sunday *Times* has nearly twice the readership of the daily paper.) Readers of the Week in Review section of Sunday, September 24, 2000, however, did find a correction. It was this:

> An Ideas & Trends article last Sunday about a trend toward increasing size of women's breasts referred incorrectly to the actress Demi Moore. She underwent breast augmentation surgery, but has not had the implants removed.

In the meantime, however, on Friday, September 22, 2000, there appeared an op-ed piece, "No One Won the Whitewater Case," by James B. Stewart, in which the paper's affinity with prosecution—in particular the Special Prosecutor—and the writer's solidarity with the *Times* reporters most attuned to leaks from government accusers found almost bizarre expression. Stewart, a Pulitzer Prize–winning journalist and the author of *Blood Sport*, wrote of Washington, during the Clinton administration, as a "culture of mutual political destruction." In what sense the "destruction" could be deemed "mutual" was not entirely clear. Mr. Stewart praised an article about Whitewater, on March 8, 1992, written by Jeff Gerth (one of the original writers of the Wen Ho Lee pieces) as "a model of investigative reporting." He wrote of "rabid Clinton haters" who believed that Vincent Foster was "murdered, preferably by Hillary

Clinton herself "; he added, however, the Clintons "continued to stone-wall," providing "ample fodder for those opposed to the President."

"The Independent Counsel's mission," he wrote, "was to get to the bottom of the morass." No, it wasn't. What morass? Then came this formulation:

> Kenneth Starr and his top deputies were not instinctive politicians, and they became caught up in a political war for which they were woefully unprepared and ill-suited. The White House and its allies relentlessly attacked the Independent Counsel for what they thought were both illegal and unprincipled tactics, like intimidating witnesses and leaking to the press. Mr. Starr has been vindicated in the courts in nearly every instance, and he and his allies were maligned to a degree that will someday be seen as grossly unfair.

One's heart of course goes out to these people incarcerating Susan McDougal; illegally detaining and threatening Monica Lewinsky; threatening a witness who refused to lie for them, by implying that her adoption of a small child was illegal; misleading the courts, the grand jury, the press, the witnesses about their actions. Persecuted victims, these prosecutors—"caught up," "woefully unprepared," "relentlessly attacked," "maligned."

> The investigation unfolded with inexorable logic that made sense at every turn, yet lost all sight of the public purpose it was meant to serve. Mr. Starr's failure was not one of logic or law but of simple common sense.

Quite apart from whatever he means by "public purpose," what could Mr. Stewart possibly mean by "common sense"?

> From early on, it should have been apparent that a criminal case could never be made against the Clintons. Who would testify against them?

Who indeed? Countless people, as the *Times* checkers, if it had any, might have told him—alleging rape, murder, threats, blackmail, drug abuse, bribery, and abductions of pet cats.

"The investigation does not clear the Clintons in all respects," Mr. Stewart wrote, as though clearing people, especially in all respects, were the purpose of prosecutions. "The Independent Counsel law is already a casualty of Whitewater and its excesses." What? What can this possibly mean? What "it," for example, precedes "its excesses"? *Whitewater's* excesses?

> But as long as a culture of mutual political destruction reigns in Washington, the need for some independent resolution of charges against top officials, especially the President, will not go away. [A reigning culture of mutual destruction evidently needs another Special Prosecutor, to make charges go away.] After all, we did get something for our nearly $60 million. The charges against the Clintons were credibly resolved.

An extraordinary piece, certainly. Four days later, on Tuesday, September 26, 2000, the *Times* ran its long-awaited assessment, "From the Editors." It was entitled "The Times and Wen Ho Lee."

Certainly, the paper had never before published anything like this assessment. A break with tradition, however, is not an apology. What the *Times* did was to apportion blame elsewhere, endorse its own work, and cast itself as essentially a victim, having "attracted criticism" from three categories of persons: "competing journalists," "media critics," and "defenders of Dr. Lee." Though there may, in hindsight, have been "flaws"—for example, a few other lines of investigation the *Times* might have pursued, "to humanize" Dr. Lee—the editors seemed basically to think they had produced what Mr. Stewart, in his op-ed piece, might have characterized as "a model of investigative reporting." Other journalists interpreted this piece one way and another, but to a reader of ordinary intelligence and understanding there was no contrition in it. That evidently left the *Times*, however, with a variant of what might be called the underlying corrections problem: the lepidopterist and his trust. "Accusations leveled at this newspaper," the editors wrote, "may have left many readers with questions about our coverage. That confusion—and the stakes involved, a man's liberty and reputation—convince us that a public accounting is warranted." The readers' "confusion" is the issue. The "stakes," in dashes, are an afterthought.

"On the whole," the public accounting said, "we remain proud of work that brought into the open a major national security problem. Our review found careful reporting that included extensive cross-checking and vetting of multiple sources, despite enormous obstacles of official secrecy and government efforts to identify the *Times*' sources."

And right there is the nub of it, one nub of it anyway: the "efforts to identify the *Times*' sources." Because in this case, the sources were precisely governmental—the FBI, for example, in its attempt to intimidate Wen Ho Lee. The rest of the piece, with a few unconvincing afterthoughts about what the paper might have done differently, is self-serving and even overtly deceptive. "The *Times* stories—echoed and often oversimplified by politicians and other news organizations—touched off a fierce public debate"; "Now the *Times* neither imagined the security breach nor initiated the prosecution of Wen Ho Lee"; "That concern had previously been reported in the *Wall Street Journal*, but without the details provided by the *Times* in a painstaking narrative"; "Nothing in this experience undermines our faith in any of our reporters, who remained persistent and fair-minded in their news-gathering in the face of some fierce attacks."

And there it is again: Wen Ho Lee in jail, alone, shackled, without bail—and yet it is the *Times* that is subject to "accusations," *Times* reporters who were subjected to those "fierce attacks."

The editors did express a reservation about their "tone." "In place of a tone of journalistic detachment," they wrote, they had perhaps echoed the alarmism of their sources. Anyone who has read the *Times* in recent years—let alone been a subject of its pieces—knows that "a tone of journalistic detachment" in the paper is almost entirely a thing of the past. What is so remarkable, however, is not only how completely the *Times* identifies with the prosecution, but also how clearly the inversion of hunter and prey has taken hold. The injustice, the editors clearly feel, has been done not to Dr. Lee (although they say at one point that they may not have given him, imagine, "the full benefit of the doubt") but to the reporters, and the editors, and the institution itself.

Two days later, the editorial section checked in, with "An Overview: The Wen Ho Lee Case." Some of it, oddly enough, was another attack on Wen Ho Lee, whose activities it described as "suspicious and ultimately illegal," "beyond reasonable dispute." It described the director of the FBI, Louis Freeh, and Attorney General Janet Reno as being under "sharp attack." The editorial was not free of self-justification; it was not open about its own contribution to the damage; it did seem concerned with "racial profiling"—a frequent preoccupation of the editorial page, in any case. The oddest sentences were these: "Moreover, transfer of technology to China and nuclear weapons security had been constant government concerns throughout this period. To withhold this information from readers is an unthinkable violation of the fundamental contract between a newspaper and its audience." It had previously used a similar construction, for the prosecutors: "For the F.B.I. . . . not to react to Dr. Lee's [conduct] would have been a dereliction of duty." But the question was not *whether* the FBI should react (or not) but *how*, within our system, legally, ethically, constitutionally, to do so. And no one was asking the *Times* to "withhold information" about "government concerns," least of all regarding alleged "transfer of technology to China" or "nuclear weapons security." If the *Times* were asked to do anything in this matter, it might be to refrain from passing on, and repeating, and scolding, and generally presenting as "investigative reporting" what were in fact malign and exceedingly improper allegations, by "anonymous sources" with prosecutorial agendas, against virtually defenseless individuals.

There was—perhaps this goes without saying—no apology whatever to Wen Ho Lee. "The unthinkable violation of the fundamental contract between a newspaper and its audience" did not, obviously, extend to him. Lelyveld, too, had referred to a Corrections policy "to make our contract with readers more enforceable." What "contract"? To rectify malignant misspelling of names? This concern, too, was not with facts, or substance, or subject, but to sustain, without earning or reciprocating, the trust of "readers." The basis of "trust" was evidently quite tenuous. What had increased, perhaps in its stead, was this sense of being misunderstood, unfairly maligned, along with those other victims: FBI agents, informers, and all manner of prosecutors. No sympathy, no apology, certainly, for the man whom many, including in the end the judge, considered a victim—not least a victim of the *Times*.

That *Times* editors are by no means incapable of apology became clear on September 28, 2000, the same day as the editorial Overview. On that day, Bill Keller, the managing editor of the *Times*, posted a "Memorandum to the Staff," which he sent as well to "media critics," and which he said all staff members were "free to share outside the paper."

It was an apology, and it was abject. "When we published our appraisal of our Wen Ho Lee coverage," it said, "we anticipated that some people would misread it, and we figured that misreading was beyond our control. But one misreading is so agonizing to me that it requires a follow-up."

"Through most of its many drafts," Keller continued, the message had contained the words "of us" in a place where any reader of ordinary intelligence and understanding, one would have thought, would have known what was meant, since the words "to us" appear later in the same sentence. "Somewhere in the multiple scrubbings of this document," however,

> the words "of us" got lost. And that has led some people on the staff to a notion that never occurred to me—that the note meant to single out Steve Engelberg, who managed this coverage so masterfully, as the scapegoat for the shortcomings we acknowledged.
>
> My reaction the first time I heard this theory was to laugh it off as preposterous. Joe and I tried to make clear in meetings with staff . . . that the paragraph referred to ourselves. . . . In the very specific sense that we laid our hands on these articles, and we overlooked some opportunities in our own direction of the coverage. We went to some lengths to assure that no one would take our message as a repudiation of our reporters, but I'm heartsick to discover that we failed to make the same clear point about one of the finest editors I know. Let the record show that we stand behind Steve and the other editors who played roles in developing this coverage. Coverage, as the message to readers said, of which we remain proud.

Bureaucracy at its purest. Reporters, editors, "masterfully directed" coverage, at worst some "opportunities" "overlooked." The buck stops nowhere. "We remain proud" of the coverage in question, only "agonized" and "heartsick" at having been understood to fail to exonerate a member of this staff. The only man characterized as "the scapegoat" in the whole matter is—this is hardly worth remarking—one of the directors of the coverage, some might say the hounding, of Wen Ho Lee.

Something is obviously wrong here. Howell Raines, the editor of the editorial page (and the writer of the Overview) was, like Joe Lelyveld, a distinguished reporter. Editing and reporting are, of course, by no means the same. But one difficulty, perhaps with Keller as well, is that in an editing hierarchy, unqualified loyalty to staff, along with many other manifestations of the wish to be liked, can become a failing—intellectual, professional, moral. It may be that the editors' wish for popularity with the staff has caused the perceptible and perhaps irreversible decline in the paper. There is, I think, something more profoundly wrong—not just the contrast between its utter solidarity, its self-regard, its sense of victimization and tender sympathy with its own, and its unconsciousness of its own weight as an institution, in the stories it claims to cover. Something else, perhaps more important, two developments actually—the emergence of the print reporter as celebrity and the proliferation of the anonymous source. There is an indication of where this has led us even in the *Times* editors' own listing, among the "enormous obstacles" its reporters faced, of "government efforts to identify the *Times*' sources." The "sources" in question were, of course, precisely governmental. The *Times* should never have relied upon them, not just because they were, as they turned out to be, false, but because they were prosecutorial—and they were turning the *Times* into their instrument.

In an earlier day, the *Times* would have had a safeguard against its own misreporting, including its "accounting" and its Overview of its coverage of the case of Wen Ho Lee. The paper used to publish in its pages long, unedited transcripts of important documents. The transcript of the FBI's interrogation of Dr. Lee—on March 7, 1999, the day after the first of the *Times* articles appeared—exists. It runs to thirty-seven pages. Three agents have summoned Dr. Lee to their offices in "a cleared building facility." They have refused him not only the presence of anybody known to him but permission to have lunch. They keep talking ominously of a "package" they have, and telephone calls they have been making about it to Washington. The contents of the package includes yesterday's *New York Times*. They allude to it more than fifty times:

> "You read that and it's on the next page as well, Wen Ho. And let me call Washington real quick while you read that."

> "The important part is that, uh, basically that is indicating that there is a person at the laboratory that's committed espionage and that points to you."

> "You, you read it. It's not good, Wen Ho."

"You know, this is, this is a big problem, but uh-mm, I think you need to read this article. Take a couple of minutes and, and read this article because there's some things that have been raised by Washington that we've got to get resolved."

And they resume:

"It might not even be a classified issue. . . . but Washington right now is under the impression that you're a spy. And this newspaper article is, is doing everything except for coming out with your name . . . everything points to you. People in the community and people at the laboratory tomorrow are going to know. That this article is referring to you. . . ."

The agents tell him he is going to be fired (he is fired two days later), that his wages will be garnished, that he will lose his retirement, his clearance, his chance for other employment, his friends, his freedom. The only thing they mention more frequently than the article in the *Times* is his polygraph, and every mention of it is something they know to be false: that he "failed" it. They tell him this lie more than thirty times. Sometimes they mention it in conjunction with the *Times* article:

"You know, Wen Ho, this, it's bad. I mean look at this newspaper article! I mean, 'China Stole Secrets for Bombs.' It all but says your name in here. The polygraph reports all say you're failing. . . . Pretty soon you're going to have reporters knocking on your door."

Then they get to the Rosenbergs:

"The Rosenbergs are the only people that never cooperated with the federal government in an espionage case. You know what happened to them? They electrocuted them, Wen Ho."

"You know Aldrich Ames? He's going to rot in jail! . . . He's going to spend his dying days in jail."

"Okay? Do you want to go down in history? Whether you're professing your innocence like the Rosenbergs to the day they take you to the electric chair? . . ."

Dr. Lee pleads with them, several times, not to interrupt him when he is trying to answer a question: "You want me, you want to listen two minutes from my explanation?" Not a chance:

> "No, you stop a minute, Wen Ho. . . . Compared to what's going to happen to you with this newspaper article . . ."
> "The Rosenbergs are dead."
> "This is what's going to do you more damage than anything. . . . Do you think the press prints everything that's true? Do you think that everything that's in this article is true? . . . The press doesn't care."

Now, it may be that the editors of the *Times* do not find this newsworthy, or that they believe their readers would have no interest in the fact that the FBI conducts its interrogations in this way. The *Times* might also, fairly, claim that it has no responsibility for the uses to which its front-page articles may be put, by the FBI or any other agency of government. Except for this. In both the editorial Overview and the "Note from the Editors," as in Mr. Stewart's op-ed piece, the *Times'* sympathies are clearly with the forces of prosecution and the FBI. "Dr. Lee had already taken a lie detector test," the editors write, for example, in their assessment, and "F.B.I. investigators believed that it showed deception when he was asked whether he had leaked secrets."

In the days when the *Times* still published transcripts, the reader could have judged for himself. Nothing could be clearer than that the FBI investigators believed nothing of the kind. As they knew, Dr. Lee had, on the contrary, passed his polygraph—which is why, in his interrogation, they try so obsessively to convince him that he failed it. Even the editorial Overview, shorter and perhaps for that reason less misleading, shows where the *Times'* sense of who is victimized resides. After two paragraphs of describing various activities of Dr. Lee's as "improper and illegal," "beyond reasonable dispute," it describes, of all people, Louis Freeh, the director of the FBI (and Janet Reno, the attorney general) as being "under sharp attack." Freeh was FBI director when agents of the Bureau, illegally detaining Monica Lewinsky, were conducting "investigations" of the same sort for the Office of the Independent Counsel. Freeh was also advocating, not just in government but directly to the press, more Special Prosecutors for more matters of all kinds.

But enough. The *Times* feels a responsibility to correct misimpressions it may have generated in readers—how names are spelled, what middle initials are, who is standing miscaptioned on which side of a photograph, which butterfly is which—is satisfied, in an important way, in its corrections. For the rest, it has looked at its coverage and found it good. The underlying fact, however, is this: For years readers have looked in the *Times* for what was once its unsurpassed strength: the uninflected coverage of the news. You can look and look, now, and you will not find it there. Some politically correct series and group therapy reflections on race relations perhaps. These appear harmless. They may even win prizes. Fifteen reporters working for one year might, perhaps, have been more usefully employed on some genuine issue of fact. More egregious, however, and in some ways more malign, was an article that appeared, on November 5, 2000, in the Sunday *Times Magazine*.

The piece was a cover story about Senator Daniel Patrick Moynihan. Everyone makes mistakes. This piece, blandly certain of its intelligence, actually consisted of them. Everything was wrong. At the most trivial level, the piece said Moynihan had held no hearings about President Clinton's health plan and no meetings with him to discuss welfare. (In fact, the senator had held twenty-nine such hearings in committee and many such discussions with the President.) At the level of theory, it misapprehended the history, content, purpose, and fate of Moynihan's proposal for a guaranteed annual income. It would require a book to set right what was wrong in the piece—and in fact, such a book existed, at least about the guaranteed annual income. But what was, in a way, most remarkable about what the *New York Times* has become appeared, once again, in the way it treated its own coverage.

The Sunday *Magazine*'s editors limited themselves to a little self-congratulatory note. The article, they reported, had "prompted a storm of protest." "But many said that we got it right, and that our writer said what had long seemed to be unspeakable." ("Unspeakable" may not be what they mean. Perhaps it was a paraphrase.) They published just one letter, which praised the piece as "incisive."

The Corrections column, however, when it came, was a gem. "An article in the *Times Magazine* last Sunday about the legacy of Senator Daniel Patrick Moynihan," it began, "misidentified a former senator who was an expert on military affairs. He was Richard Russell, not Russell Long."

The "article also," the correction went on, had "referred imprecisely" (a fine way to put it) to the senator's committee hearings on President Clinton's health care. (Not a word about welfare.) But the Corrections column saved for last what the *Times* evidently regarded as most important. "The article also overstated [another fine word] Senator Moynihan's English leanings while he attended the London School of Economics. Bowler, yes. Umbrella, yes. Monocle, no."

No "malignant" misspellings here. But nothing a reader can trust any longer, either. Certainly no reliable, uninflected coverage of anything, least of all the news. The enterprise, whatever else it is, has almost ceased altogether to be a newspaper. It is still a habit. People glance at it and, on Sundays, complain about its weight. For news they must look elsewhere. What can have happened here?

"The turning point at the paper," I once wrote, in a piece of fiction, "was the introduction of the byline." I still believe that to be true. I simply had no idea how radical the consequences of that turning point were going to be. Until the early seventies, it was a mark of professionalism in reporters for newspapers, wire services, newsmagazines, to have their pieces speak, as it were, for themselves, with all the credibility and authority of the publication in which they anonymously appeared. Reviews, essays, regular columns were of course signed. They were expressions of opinion, as distinct from reporting, and readers had to know and evaluate whose opinion it was. But when a reader said of a piece of information, "The *Times* says," or "The *Wall Street Journal* says," he was relying on the credibility of the institution. With very rare exceptions— correspondents, syndicated columnists, or sportswriters whose names were household words, or in attributing a scoop of extraordinary historical importance—the reporter's byline would have seemed intrusive and unprofessional.

In television reporting, of course, every element of the situation was different. It would be absurd to say "CBS (or ABC, NBC, or even CNN) says" or even "I saw it on" one network or another. It had to be Walter Cronkite, later Dan Rather, Diane Sawyer, Tom Brokaw, Peter Jennings—not just because no television network or station had the authority of any favorite and trusted publication, but because seeing and hearing the person who conveyed the news (impossible, obviously, with the printed byline) was precisely the basis, for television viewers, of trust.

Once television reporters became celebrities, it was perhaps inevitable that print reporters would want at least their names known; and there were, especially at first, stories one did well to read on the basis of a trusted byline. There still existed what Mary McCarthy, in another context, called "the last of the tall timber." But the tall timber in journalism is largely gone—replaced, as in many fields, by the phenomenon of celebrity. And gradually, in print journalism, the celebrity of the reporter began to overtake and then to undermine the reliability of pieces. Readers still say, "The *Times* says," or "I read it in the *Post*" (so far as I can tell, except in the special case of gossip columns, readers hardly ever mention, or even notice, bylines), but trust in even once favorite newspapers has almost vanished. One is left with this oddly convoluted paradox: As survey after survey confirms, people generally despise journalists; yet they cite, as a source of information, newspapers. And though they have come, with good reason, to distrust newspapers as a whole, they still tend to believe each individual story *as they read it.* We all do. Though I may know a piece to be downright false, internally contradictory, in some profound and obvious way corrupted, I still, for a moment anyway, believe it. Believe the most obviously manufactured quotes, the slant, the spin, the prose, the argument with no capacity even to frame an issue and no underlying sense of what follows from what.

At the same time, a development in criticism, perhaps especially movie criticism, affected print journalism of every kind. It used to be that the celebrities featured on billboards and foremost in public consciousness were the movie stars themselves. For a while, it became *auteurs*, directors. Then, bizarrely but for a period of many years, it became *critics*, who starred in the discussion of movies. That period seems, fortunately, to have passed. But somehow, the journalist's byline, influenced perhaps by the critic's, began to bring with it a blurring of genres: reporting, essay, memoir, personal statement, anecdote, judgmental or critical review. Most of all, critical review—which is why government officials and citizens alike treat reporters in the same way artists regard most critics—with mixed fear and dismay. It is also why the subjects of news stories read each "news" piece as if it were a review on opening night.

There is no longer even a vestige or pretense, on the part of the print journalist, of any professional commitment to uninflected coverage of the news. The ambition is rather, under their bylines, to express themselves, their writing styles. Days pass without a single piece of what used to be called "hard news." The celebrityhood, or even the aspiration to celebrity, of print reporters, not just in print but also on talk shows, has been perhaps the single most damaging development in the history of print journalism.

The second, less obvious, cause of decline in the very notion of reliable information was the proliferation of the "anonymous source"—especially as embodied, or rather disembodied, in Deep Throat. Many people have speculated about the "identity" of this phantom. Others have shown, more or less conclusively, that at least as described in *All the President's Men*, by Bob Woodward and Carl Bernstein, he did not, in fact could not, exist. Initially introduced as a narrative device, to hold together book and movie, this improbable creature was obviously both a composite, which Woodward, the only one who claims to have known and have consulted him, denies, and an utter fiction, which is denied by both Woodward and Bernstein—the better writer, who had, from the start, a "friend," whose information in almost every significant respect coincides with, and even predates, Deep Throat's. But the influence of this combination, the celebrity reporter and the chimera *to whom the reporter alone has access,* has been incalculable.

The implausibility of the saga of Deep Throat has been frequently pointed out. Virtually every element of the story—the all-night séances in garages; the signals conveyed by moved flowerpots on windowsills and drawings of clocks in newspapers; the notes left by prearrangement on ledges and pipes in those garages; the unidiomatic and essentially uninformative speech—has been demolished. Apart from its inherent impractibilities, for a man requiring secrecy and fearing for his life and the reporter's, the strategy seems less like tradecraft than a series of attention-getting mechanisms. This is by no means to deny that Woodward and Bernstein had "sources," some but far from all of whom preferred to remain anonymous. From the evidence in the book they include at least Fred Buzhardt, Hugh Sloan, John Sears, Mark Felt and other FBI agents, Leonard Garment, and, perhaps above all, the ubiquitous and not infrequently treacherous Alexander Haig. None of these qualify as Deep Throat, nor does anyone, as depicted in the movie or book. Woodward's new rationale is this: the secret of the phantom's name must be kept until the phantom himself reveals it—or else dies. Woodward is prepared, however, to disqualify candidates whom others—most recently Leonard Garment, in an entire book devoted to such speculation—may suggest, by telling, instance by instance, who Deep Throat is *not*. A long list, obviously, which embraces everyone.

It is no wonder that Woodward, having risked the logic of this, would risk as well an account of a mythical visit to the hospital bedside of former CIA Director William Casey, who was dying and who, according to doctors, had lost all power of speech. Casey's hospital room was closely guarded against visits from all but his immediate family. Woodward claims to have entered the hospital room, asked Casey a question, observed him "nod," and quotes him as saying, "I believed."

There is more. Woodward now claims that the "anonymous source" for another book, *The Brethren*, was Justice Potter Stewart. Justice Stewart, perhaps needless to say, is dead. He was a highly respected and distinguished Justice. But that does not satisfactorily resolve the matter, because Justice Stewart can and does bear a sort of witness here. He *wrote* some important opinions. Some of the opinions most seriously misunderstood, misrepresented, and even misquoted in *The Brethren* are Potter Stewart's. And nothing could be more obvious from the book than the fact that, apart from the clerks, Woodward's primary source was in fact Justice Rehnquist.

The ramifications of this cult of the anonymous source—particularly as Deep Throat, this oracle to whom only a single priest, or acolyte, has access, have been, for journalism, enormous. No need any longer to publish long transcripts. Why bother? No need even to read them, or anything—public documents, the novels of Robert Stendahl. Two clicks to Amazon.com will give you spellings. And an "anonymous source" will either provide you with "information" or provide what your editors will accept as "cross-checking" for what you have already said. The celebrity reporter has created, beginning with Deep Throat, what one would have thought a journalistic oxymoron: a *celebrity* anonymous source. More than that: a celebrity anonymous source who *does not even exist*. As late as page 207 of Leonard Garment's book, *In Search of Deep Throat*, Mr. Garment actually writes:

> I was doggedly confident that Woodward, Bernstein, and, above all, their editor . . . would not have put themselves out

on a long limb for a gimmick that would eventually be re-vealed and denounced as a journalistic fraud of historic pro-portions.

Not a gimmick. A device. When Woodward produced the noumenal encounter between the anonymous source and the celebrity reporter, it turns out, a religion was born, which has grown to affect not just jour-nalism but the entire culture. In print journalism, you can usually tell, when such a source exists at all, who it is: the person most kindly treated in the story. And the religion, with all its corollaries, dogmas, and im-plications, has made of reporters not fallible individuals competing for facts and stories in the real world but fellow members of the cult. Whom-ever or whatever they go after—Wen Ho Lee, Whitewater, or "scandals" that did not pan out—or whomever they equally baselessly support— Independent Counsel Kenneth Starr, Chairman Henry Hyde of the House Judiciary Committee, and FBI Director Louis Freeh—they tend to support dogmatically, and as one. Best of all, they like to consult and to write approvingly of one another and even, if need be, themselves. Administrations come and go. Quasi-governmental bureaucracies, with their hierarchies and often interlocking cults and interests, persist.

The convergence of the anonymous source with the celebrity re-porter now has ramifications that could not have been foreseen. A cer-tain journalistic laziness was perhaps predictable—phoning around as a form of "legwork," attributing information to "sources," in quotes, which no one was equipped either to verify or to deny. But the serious result, which no one could have foreseen, is this: The whole purpose of the "anonymous source" has been precisely reversed. The reason there exists a First Amendment protection for journalists' confidential sources has always been to permit citizens—the weak, the vulnerable, the isolated—to be heard publicly, without fear of retaliation by the strong—by their employer, for example, or by the forces of govern-ment. The whistleblower or the innocent accused were to be protected. Instead, almost every "anonymous source" in the press, in recent years, has been an official of some kind, or a person in the course of a vendetta speaking from a position of power.

More disturbing, in spite of what has been at least since Vietnam an almost instinctive press hostility to the elected government (an adversarial position that can be healthy in a free society), the press now has an unmistakable affinity with official accusers, in particular the Special Prosecutors and the FBI. And when *those* powerful institutions are allowed to "leak"—that is, become the press's "anonymous sources"—the press becomes not an adversary but an instrument of all that is most secret and coercive—in attacks, not infrequently, with an elected administration but also with truly nameless individuals, those who have neither power nor celebrity of any kind, and who have no means of access, least of all as "anonymous sources," to the press.

The press, in these matters, has become far more unified. There may be competition among those who will get the first interview of some celebrity or other, or first access to a treasured "anonymous source." But it is the *same* celebrities and the same sources that journalists pursue, not excluding interviews with one another. Even among the apparently most irate and shouting television personalities whom Calvin Trillin has so memorably characterized as "Sabbath gasbags," there is a sameness. Political views are permitted, routinely, along a spectrum from left to right; but the views of each participant, on virtually any subject, can be predicted from week to week.

The worst, however, is the mystique of the "sources." Citizens of a democracy require reliable information. How can they check "sources"? What possible basis is there for relying on them? The word of the celebrity reporter who cannot bring himself to name them? What sort of reliability, what sort of information, what sort of journalism is this? Especially since there seems to be, among "investigative reporters" and the institutions that support them, a stubborn loyalty to and solidarity with sources—even when a source (as in the recent case of Charles Bakaly of the Special Prosecutor's office) *admits* that he is the previously "anonymous source" in question, or, more puzzlingly, when the "source" has demonstrably deceived the reporter himself. In what may be a journalistic variant of the Stockholm syndrome (whereby hostages become extremely loyal to their captors), journalists and their editors defend and protect the anonymity, and even the reliability, of their sources, even when they have been most seriously misled. A sacred covenant, apparently. But what of the trust and "contract" with the reader? Forgotten, secular, a matter of spelling and perhaps the small stuff. There, for instance, is the *Times*, in its "assessment," trying to establish the basis for a now utterly discredited story as "cross-checking sources" and resisting "obstacles" posed by other people's having tried to "identify our sources." Would this not have been the occasion to name at least the sources who deliberately misled them? Are the identities of self-serving liars, and particularly liars of this sort, who use the newspaper story as a weapon of intimidation, to be protected? Four months later, in February of 2001, the *Times* again reappraised its coverage of Wen Ho Lee. The pieces somehow, under a lot of cosmic obfuscation, seemed to have missed their underlying points: (1) that there was no evidence of spying by anyone at Los Alamos; (2) that there was no evidence of any spying by Wen Ho Lee. The suspicion of him rested largely on two incidents: that he had once telephoned a man under suspicion of something undefined and offered to help him, and that he had once entered, uninvited, a meeting at Los Alamos, and hugged a major Chinese scientist there. Typical spy behavior: a phone call and a hug.

If so, then you are speaking inescapably of the instruments of a police state, with secret informers, and the press just one in a set of interlocking and secretive bureaucracies. The alternative, it seems to me, is to proceed in a more diligent way, one by one, in the press, on the street, in the academy, to look for information and try to draw reasonable inferences from it. A combination of research and thinking and consulting, if need be, a genuine source—that is, someone who has information and is willing to impart it. No professional ideologies that paradoxically combine political correctness with self-serving orthodoxies and an affinity for prosecutors. No faith in Delphic utterances from unidentified persons. In spite of what might have affected generations of aspiring reporters, no one is going to contrive an absurd set of signals for you, meet you secretly and regularly and undetected by others in a garage by night and tell you anything worth knowing.

Pools, informers, leaks from prosecutors, celebrity reporters with anonymous sources—all of these are forms simultaneously of consolidation and of hiding, facets of what the enterprise has become. Consider the celebrity reporter, the particular powers of celebrity in a celebrity culture, especially when his nominal profession, after all, is the purveying of information, the dissemination of what the society will know about itself.

Consider the prosecutorial affinity, which is both easy and immensely destructive. Wen Ho Lee, as it turned out, had nearly miraculous access, in the end, to good, pro bono lawyers. Most noncelebrity citizens simply have no such access—either to lawyers or to the press. They are not just truly anonymous. They are plain unheard.

Consider as well the use of pools. Not the imposed pools of the military, but voluntary, self-satisfied, bonded bureaucracies and consortiums. To use saving money as an excuse for not having the independence, the interest, the curiosity and inclination to go out there and see for yourself—it is simply not reconcilable with any notion of the working journalist. Under the First Amendment, the press enjoys special protections so that the public will hear from many competing individual and institutional voices, and so that debate, as Harry Kalven put it, can be "free, robust, and wide open." Journalism has to be competitive or it is nothing. Television's mistake in using its consortium was understandable and should have been instructive. But television that night was in the business of *prediction*. In Florida, where something already existing is in dispute—in a state with sunshine laws specifically making facts available for public information—to send a surrogate institution is indefensible. For one thing, it virtually guarantees that the sunshine laws will atrophy. For another, it guarantees that the public will *never* know what the real count was. In lieu of NORC, it would have been better to send in, if not professional auditors, a group of diligent fourth-grade children who can count.

All monopolists collaborating in restraint of trade say they are cooperating to save everybody money. In this case, another unmistakable and crucial motive has been to hide. That hiding reflects fear. Fear of being alone, fear of being out of step with the prevailing view. Fear even of being right when everyone else is wrong. So hide yourself in an orthodoxy and a group. Let no independent reporters and, lord help us, no independent newspaper in there. Try to co-opt the *Miami Herald*. Let the sociologists from NORC handle it. The administration, the government, will not be offended. At least not with us.

Oddly enough, even the policy of Corrections is a form simultaneously of consolidation of power and of hiding. The orthodoxy is: We are so scrupulous we correct even the smallest thing. Therefore, you can trust us as you would Mao, the Scripture, the Politburo. It is a form of Fundamentalism, it protects the ideology. Nothing more clearly exposed the essence of that Corrections policy than the Editors' Note about Wen Ho

Lee. They misrepresented what they had actually said. They defended, in glowing terms, what they did say. They gave themselves credit for "calling attention to the problem." Much like those charities a few years ago when the child, who had been photographed so movingly and had corresponded so faithfully with its "adopted" parents, who sent ten dollars a month, turned out to have been long dead or not even to exist. The charities, too, said, "We were just calling attention to the problem." If you do a textual analysis of what the *Times* did say, over a period of many months, and how its "accounting" or "assessment" now describes it, you have not just disinformation but an indication of what much of journalism has become. We were first, but we blame it on the *Wall Street Journal*, which was earlier, and on the misrepresentations of others, who came later. On the whole, we are proud. And the only one to whom we genuinely owe an apology is one of our staff, the editor of the series in question, "the scapegoat," whom we must now praise in the most extravagant terms. And about whom we are abject, agonized, heartsick.

I know nothing about the editor in question. I did read, months ago, his irate and patronizing response, defending those very articles, to someone who had ventured, in *Brill's Content*, to criticize them. There is, in general, in newspapers at least, almost no reliable, uninflected coverage of the news. No celebrity journalists seem even to aspire to it. There is opinion, a verdict, an assumption of the role—how to put it?—of *critic* to the day's events. A verdict. We do not need a verdict. We need an account.

That is where the absence of those once long, verbatim transcripts is of great importance. The transcripts permitted none of that judging or tilting or hiding. They were straightforward. They were something that television, for example, with its scheduling and time constraints, could not do. Nor could tabloids.

Consolidating with others and going secret. From the anonymous source, to the prosecutor's office, to the consortium, all are just steps. And correcting—either typos, or misspellings, or things everyone knows already or that matter to no one, or that correct themselves on a daily basis—is just the mask, the surface of the decay. One more indication of moral and factual authority—and, in consequence, another source of power. It may be, it is virtually certain, that newspapers, to regain their honor, will have to relinquish something of their power and think again.

The whole constitutional system had been, for some time, under attack by all three branches of government. There has been the behavior of the executive, as embodied not just by the President in his understanding of his office, but, paradoxically, by the Independent Counsel in his prosecutions. There has been the behavior of the legislature, in its lascivious travesty of the impeachment process. There has been the conduct of the Supreme Court, intruding on the province of the executive, the legislative, the states, and finally on the rights of every citizen. By making its decision in Gore v. Bush, explicitly, unique—to be regarded as having no precedent and setting none—it undermined the whole basis of Anglo Saxon law, which is grounded in the notion that the decisions derive their validity from being built upon, and in turn relied upon, as precedents.

The Supreme Court, in its power of judicial review, is regarded as nearly sacred within the system and beyond appeal—with one exception: the press. Judicial review is trumped by press review. The Justices are highly aware of this. Judges who claimed to be conservatives, even as they struck most radically at the Constitution, the balance of powers, federalism, the fundamental understandings of the society, played to journalists. Virtually the only decisions of this Court upholding freedoms, under the First Amendment, for example, have been decisions in favor of the press. The press seems less aware of this—still describing the most radical judges, obligingly, as "conservatives." Somehow, comfortable and serene as the system still seems to be, and as though political life were still in some sense normal, the whole question of legitimacy seemed to rest on so few public officials—until recently Senator Moynihan, for example, and now Justices Stevens, Ginsburg, Souter, Breyer. There is always the possibility that there will be heroes, or that the system is self-correcting. But it will not do for the press, with very few exceptions, simply to join all other bureaucracies, to correct spellings or give us their impressions about race (there are still "tensions") while, in the ultimate abdication, they miss the factual. Independent journalists have obligations of their own.

—2001

PART 1

SEARCHING FOR THE REAL NIXON SCANDAL:
A LAST INFERENCE

On the weekend of Memorial Day 1976, at John Doar's farm near Millerton, New York, there was a reunion of what had been, in 1974, the
House Judiciary Committee's impeachment inquiry staff. John Doar, who
was Special Counsel for the inquiry, had since become a partner in a
New York law firm, where he was in charge of a major antitrust case.
Other members of the staff had returned for the occasion from their
various jobs. Some had brought tents and sleeping bags. Others had
rooms in the nearby motels and inns. A few were sleeping in the house.
More than a hundred people in all showed up, also several dogs, including a small terrier called Credence and a huge English sheepdog, who
had attended the original staff picnic, on August 15, 1974, in Washington. Thirty-nine former staff members had chartered a plane from Washington to Pittsburgh, where they were picked up by other former
members of the staff. Supper, the first evening, was catered by the local
Grange. People took motorcycle rides into the hills. Small bonfires were
lit around the farm itself. Some of the youngest bounced on a trampoline
or played basketball. From soon after supper until well after midnight,
there was square dancing. A band and a caller had been brought in from
Hartford. Nearly everyone took part in the square sets and in a virtually
endless Virginia reel. In the wildest fantasies of San Clemente, no one
could dream that such an event was taking place. And even in Millerton,
one had the fleeting impression of dancing on a grave.

It was not a grave, of course. President Nixon had only resigned. After
nearly two years, it was no longer clear what that resignation had meant,
or even what the inquiry had had to do with it. Meanwhile, with every
document published by the Senate Select Committee on Government

Operations with Respect to Intelligence Activities (the Church Committee), it was becoming more clear that the case for the impeachment of Richard Nixon, in 1974, had fallen apart.

It all seemed, anyway, long ago, and difficult to remember in detail. In late July 1974, the House Judiciary Committee, under Chairman Peter W. Rodino, had voted to recommend three Articles of Impeachment to the House. Article I was essentially an obstruction of justice charge. Article II charged misuse of the agencies of government. Article III, in effect, charged contempt of Congress, in doctoring and in refusing to produce subpoenaed evidence. In view of the Church Committee's account of the conduct of previous administrations, including violations of law and abuses of power since at least 1936, the first two Articles seemed to dissolve. As for Article III, there had been disagreement about it from the start. Doar himself ultimately did not support it—on the grounds that requiring the President to produce this evidence, and thereby implicate himself in what would obviously become a highly serious criminal case, was reminiscent of the Star Chamber. Others argued that such a view implicitly endorsed claims of executive privilege, the national security, whatever, as camouflaged euphemisms for the Fifth Amendment; that if the President needed, in effect, to take the Fifth, he ought to be obliged, like any other citizen, to come right out and take it; and that a failure to pass Article III would add to all the other powers of the President a new power, to withhold evidence from the only process the Framers had established specifically to override such claims of secrecy: the impeachment process, the "Grand Inquest of the Nation," by which the President could be held, constitutionally, to account.

In any case, it didn't matter. Article III would never have passed, or even existed, without Articles I and II. The problem with all three Articles, and with their accompanying Summary of Information and Final Report, and with the thirty-odd volumes of Statements of Information, which were also published by the House Judiciary Committee, is that, in spite of a valid perception the whole country shared of the integrity of the process at the time, all those volumes never quite made their case, or any case. And one result, which nobody on the staff could possibly have foreseen, was that, in light of the Church Committee report and other documents, what remains of the records of the impeachment inquiry would support not only a claim that Richard Nixon was hounded from office after all, but also, more strangely, the reverse: that the impeachment inquiry itself was just another phase in the continuation of the cover-up.

Neither of these claims, obviously, is right; yet they are not easy to dismiss. As there continue to be revelations of abuses of and by the CIA, the FBI, the IRS, the military, and officials at every level of government and corporate enterprise, in the remote as well as the immediate past, it becomes less and less clear why the Nixon presidency in particular had to end. This summer, the Senate voted overwhelmingly to establish a permanent Office of Special Prosecutor, as though what had seemed, in 1973, an extraordinary crisis, requiring extraordinary measures, was now perceived as a more or less permanent state of affairs in government—and as though such a permanently critical situation could be remedied by the addition of yet another watchman to the constitutionally established existing watchmen in the night. Another indication of the degree to which the specific Nixon case remains still unresolved is implicit in those theories that Nixon was driven from office by a conspiracy within government itself—more specifically, within the CIA. It is as though history already required, in explanation of Nixon's having left the presidency at all, an elaborate plot, in the form of a reconstruction from scraps of inconsistent evidence of an Agency cabal.

It seems certain, though, that the Nixon presidency, far from being continuous with those before, was in fact unprecedented; that, without the supposition of cabals of any sort, Nixon himself did something not only more than any of his predecessors but altogether else. And the reason why no investigation, by Congress, or the press, or in the courts, has so far managed to establish precisely what he did has to do, I think, both with the way the investigations were conducted and with what I now believe to be the very nature of the case. Putting together some of the circumstances of the impeachment inquiry with a few facts in those Church Committee documents—and trying to reconcile these with several, at the time apparently unaccountable, discrepancies and lapses in the conduct of President Nixon, his lawyers, and his aides—I think one does arrive at a bottom line, a plausible, even obvious explanation of why it was that the Nixon presidency had to end. It may have been for a time unthinkable; or we may have known it all along.

I. What Kind of Case?

The inquiry. On the morning of March 27, 1974, Barbara Fletcher, who was in charge of most calls to the impeachment inquiry staff from congressmen and members of the press, received a long-distance call from a young man who claimed that in 1973, as he was walking down Wisconsin Avenue, President Nixon shot at him. For various reasons, few of the logs and records kept by the staff (and now sealed, for the foreseeable future, in the archives of the House Judiciary Committee) are altogether dependable or complete. The files of congressional committees are, in any case, notoriously inaccurate. But because of her diligence and the delicacy of her assignment in dealing with these calls, Miss Fletcher kept scrupulous and exhaustive logs. The young man said he had been wearing a shield. He asked to be given a lie detector test. He left two Milwaukee phone numbers, his mother's and his own. Miss Fletcher noted all this and said she would pass the information on. It was evident from the whole tone of the entry that the young man, like a lot of other callers—like the lady who brought in her garbage as evidence that she was being poisoned; like the many hundreds of people who sent in rocks, with the message that only he who is without sin should cast them—was not well.

But among the innumerable what-ifs of the inquiry, and of Watergate itself, the problem might not have been a minor one. What if the young man had been completely sane and right? The staff would have been unable to investigate his claim. There were no investigators on the staff. And it is far from clear that shooting at a man in the street is contemplated in the phrase "Treason, Bribery, or other high Crimes and Misdemeanors"—the only grounds on which a President can be impeached. Shooting at a political opponent, certainly, would fall within the constitutional standard, as a "political" crime, that is, a crime against the system and the Constitution itself. But an ordinary violation of the criminal statutes, no matter how serious, is probably not contemplated in the phrase. The astonishingly foolish, poorly reasoned, and poorly documented brief submitted by the White House argued that it is: that "other high Crimes and Misdemeanors" simply meant a literal, ordinary (though in deference to that "high," a serious) crime, committed in the President's "public, or official capacity." It was hard to think of any unlawful acts, apart perhaps from adultery or purse-snatching, which a President might commit in his private, or unofficial capacity. The White House brief was intended, of course, to limit to the narrowest criminal terms any definition of the grounds on which a President might be impeached. It went on to say that "high Crimes and Misdemeanors," as a term of art, had a unitary meaning, like "bread and butter issues"—a comparison which, in its peculiar vulgarity, exemplified something both slipshod and condescending in the work of the White House lawyers, under James St. Clair, by whom the President was at the time so oddly, badly served. It was true of the whole brief what one of the youngest members of the inquiry said of subsequent documents submitted for the White House: that sooner or later, at their characteristic level of effectiveness, in general and in detail, these lawyers seemed bound to produce a brief on behalf of their client, President Philip N. Nixon.

One effect of the White House brief on grounds for impeachment, however, was to draw attention from the quality of the brief produced by the impeachment inquiry staff. That brief, our brief, which was published on February 20, 1974, was the first indication of what kind of work would be done by a staff of nearly forty lawyers who came from both political parties and from all parts of the country and who had, or claimed to have, by 1974, when they were hired, no view one way or another about whether President Nixon ought to be impeached. "I will say that every staff member was questioned whether or not they had taken a position on impeachment," Special Counsel Doar told the Judiciary Committee on January 31, 1974, "and if they had, other than that there should be an inquiry, then they were not considered for the job." For seven months, both Doar and Chairman Rodino insisted that no member of the staff take any side whatever on the question. As late as July 23, 1974, when Minority Counsel Sam Garrison suggested that Democrats on the staff might all along have been inclined to favor impeachment, while Republicans might have tended to oppose it, Rodino said that if he had known Garrison took such a view he would have fired him.

While there were strong reasons for maintaining a bipartisan staff with this apparent viewlessness, in the first serious attempt to impeach a President in more than a century, the criterion is not one for putting together a firm of lawyers. It is more suited to selecting jurors—who are meant unprofessionally to weigh, but never to investigate or to assemble a case. Lawyers are advocates. The lawyers Doar hired were bright, loyal, discreet, and highly recommended. They represented as broad a cross section of the country as the congressmen on the committee. They worked under two ironclad admonitions: to maintain absolute confidentiality and to be "fair." At the same time, Doar had to proceed on the assumption that almost no one could be trusted. On January 2, 1974, I asked him how, in that case, he was going to keep perfect confidentiality in so large a staff of lawyers. "You work them very hard," he said, "and you don't tell them anything." The brief produced by such a staff was, predictably, deficient.

So were most of the other inquiry documents. It turned out to be unimportant. What was important was that, through months of tension, crises of morale, and professional frustration, the staff did manage to work hard and to keep silent. What they were working on, or thought they were working on, is another matter. Few of them, at the time or even two years later, seemed to have more than an intimation that, while what they were doing was essential, the only thing essential about it was that they be seen to be doing *something* in secret, day and night, for months. "Some of it was the worst time of my life," one of the junior lawyers said, more than a year after it was over. "What you had for the first few months, you see, was thirty lawyers, treading water." That "treading water" was his insight. That "for the first few months" was an understatement. The fact that underlay the ordeal was that most of the work, almost all the time by almost all the staff, was a charade. A valuable charade, in that a machine was seen to churn, while no circus took place, and the courts, and a smaller group of Doar's, and ultimately the congressmen themselves could do their work. But the machine itself, firmly required to be directionless, produced, naturally enough, no investigation and, in the end, no case. It is commonly said that "the case" is in those thirty-odd staff volumes. Only by people who have not read them; hardly anyone has read them.

Doar himself was working mainly with a smaller group of about seven people, five of whom were old friends who had worked with him before and who were not on the regular staff.[1] Much of what could be salvaged from or written into the lamentable brief on grounds, for instance, was the work at the last minute of these ad hoc irregulars—as was, for good or ill, the conduct of the inquiry, from the ordering of facts and strategies, through compiling the endless Statements of Information, Summary of Information, and Final Report, to the drafting of letters to the White House, of the actual Articles of Impeachment, and even of the statements of Chairman Rodino, from the opening of the inquiry, through the hearings, to the remarks with which he responded, in his living room, to the television broadcast of Richard Nixon's resignation speech.

There was never any doubt among Doar and this small group that, unless there was overwhelming evidence of Nixon's innocence (and the only conceivable circumstance in which, by 1974, there could be such evidence would have been a conspiracy among his aides to frame him, in which case, under a superintendency theory, he might have been impeached for that), the object of the process was that the President must be impeached. Doar had, in fact, been the second nonradical person I knew, and the first Republican, to advocate impeachment—months before he became Special Counsel, long before the inquiry began. There had to be such complete discretion on this point, and such constant, rote repetition of the words "fair," "fairness," "fairly," that there arose a temperamental hazard of inventing pieties and believing in them, against the evidence of your own purposes and your own sense—a hazard to which Nixon had obviously succumbed. Doar customarily spoke, however, in terms of "war" and "the Cause." It had to be so. To exactly the degree that impeachment is warranted, it is no less than urgent. Given the immense, lawful and (since in an impeachment a refusal to observe the restraints of law is precisely the point at issue) unlawful powers of an American President, it would have been unthinkable for Doar to have taken the job as less than an advocate. As late as this summer, 1976, however, most members of the staff and of the Judiciary Committee were still divided in their view of when it was that Doar reached his decision—whether it was in March 1974, as a result of the grand jury presentment, or on the morning of July 19, when, in one of the many completely imaginary stories generated by the inquiry's lore-manufacturing apparatus, Chairman Rodino was supposed to have shouted at Doar to force him to make up his mind.

All this by way of outlining the circumstances in which the inquiry was conducted. Doar, certain from the start that the President must be, under conditions of exemplary fairness, removed from office, could not, he thought, disclose that determination to the congressmen or to his staff. The situation created its own peculiar stresses. Secrecy and loyalty had been the Watergate virtues, after all. Apart from exercising these virtues, staff lawyers were occupied, for instance, in filling out, on the basis of documents already public, those endless and in terms of impeachment entirely useless "chron cards"—the minute-by-minute chronologies, which had been important in the Neshoba County Case of 1967 (in Doar's successful prosecution, as chief of the Justice Department's Civil Rights Division, of the murderers of Andrew Goodman, Michael Schwerner, and James Chaney), but which had no relevance at all to the case at hand. The congressmen, of necessity, became impatient. When the chron cards were replaced by flat, uninflected, numbered Statements of Fact, which Doar proposed that the staff read to the Judiciary Committee for a period of six weeks, beginning in May, the congressmen argued at length whether the statements could properly be designated *fact* at all— whether what was fact was not the sole prerogative of the committee members to determine. In the end what were read to them were called *Statements of Information.* And in the end, having understandably failed to see the point of all these statements (there was hardly any point, except to gain time and to present the committee with a tidy and impressive format), the congressmen's conduct was exemplary—leading to a President's departure from office, without any of the bitterly partisan recriminations which might have divided Congress and the country for many years.

A single episode, however, illustrates the virtual impossibility, at the time, of conducting almost any impeachment research project. It has to do with the 1976 report of the Church Committee. In the context of the 1974 inquiry, there arises the obvious question: If the conduct of past administrations bears, as it so evidently does, on the Nixon case, why did the inquiry not look into these matters and produce some such report? It tried. Doar, aware that such a report would be among the soundest and most obvious defenses for any President against impeachment, knew he had to commission, from outside the staff, a historical account of abuses of presidential power, in anticipation of any report the White House lawyers would produce. As it happens, the White House lawyers never undertook anything of the kind—an error, perhaps of overconfidence, so profound that it still seems hardly credible.

Doar's own report, by scholars under the direction of the distinguished Yale historian C. Vann Woodward, was supposed, like all other inquiry work, to be kept secret. When Congressman Charles Wiggins, for example, insisted that the inquiry's failure to make such a study was unforgivable, he was never told, nor were any other congressmen, that the project was already under way. Committee members, all of whom are lawyers, had already made it clear that they did not want any professors, Yale or other, to advise them on matters of law. In any case, whether secrecy caused the assignment to be phrased unclearly, or for whatever reason, the study was not what would have been required if the White House had produced such a study, which of course it didn't. Professor Woodward ultimately published the work (which does not appear among the inquiry volumes) elsewhere, in paperback.

A footnote to the story of that project concerns Minority Counsel Albert Jenner. As counsel for those Republicans who concurred in the majority vote of the committee, Jenner was a pivotal and historic figure, the pivot of the pivot, in a sense. Had he construed his job differently, had he seriously disagreed with Doar at any point, Jenner could have obstructed the process at every turn. It is by no means clear what the outcome, under those circumstances, would have been. But the fact is, he did not. Another fact is that he was absent a lot of the time, traveling and lecturing. Jenner still remarks, as he did frequently in the course of the inquiry, that Doar is an "administrator," while he, Jenner, is a "litigator." He says he was persuaded of the case against the President in March of 1974, with the grand jury presentment—at the same time, he adds, as Doar. Then, very amiably, he walks over to the shelves of his law office in Chicago, where his inquiry documents are kept. "This will interest you," he says, "although we've kept it top secret. It's something we relied on very heavily." And he removes from the shelf a bound copy of Professor C. Vann Woodward's study. The title is correct. The authorship is attributed to Vance Packard.

That's how things were, broadly, at the inquiry. And in spite of whatever it did accomplish, what it could not accomplish, or even really attempt, was an investigation of the case. What I am concerned with here is establishing a context for a set of initial assumptions, followed by a few facts from various sources, which led me to what I thought were going to be some wild speculations—about why our side, like their side, could not be doing what it appeared to be doing; about what happened and why, although it is all over, it still seems unsettled now; about what a real investigation, if circumstances had permitted one, would have found. It was evidently not a story of the inexorable processes of simple justice; or of their forces of darkness vanquished by our forces of light. Nixon's chosen successor has, after all, for two years held his office. He has retained the former President's unindicted accomplices and aides, and appointed some of the closest of them to positions—the command of NATO, for example—that ought to be unthinkable for men so utterly compromised. Nixon himself carries on as though the investigation never really reached him. And no revelation about him or, these days, any other holder of a public trust has any sense of finality to it. There never seems to be a truth with which it ends. Unless Nixon did something beyond what is known about him, or his men, or any of his predecessors, his departure from office seems random, arbitrary, and even incomplete. What I was left with finally was a set of questions and, I believe, a single inescapable inference—which would account, not so much in the detail of investigative reporting as in the very logic of events, for what I think must be the last fact, the bottom line.

In the early weeks of the inquiry, at about the time the brief on grounds was in the works, Doar considered a number of loose assumptions about what kind of case it was going to be. There was, in general, a Tip of the Iceberg theory: that whatever the inquiry might ultimately reveal, it could only be the small, visible part of what was actually there; the case would have to be made from that small visible part. There was a Narrow Escape theory: that Nixon and his aides, having made what amounted to an extremely radical analysis of the system (namely, that all its processes were meaningless and all its officials essentially corrupt), had begun to supersede the legitimate forms of government in what amounted to a revolutionary coup; the case would have to protect the country from that coup. There was a Robber Baron theory: that certain forms of corruption and violations of the system, like those committed by the robber barons, while they may have been tolerated for years, grow at some historic point beyond the tolerable; the case would have to bring such abuses of the presidency to an end. There was the Pattern of Conduct theory: that, while there may be abuses of power that a President might randomly, and perhaps by mistake commit, a pattern of systematic violations would provide grounds on which he ought to be impeached. And a Higher Standard of Conduct theory: that, since the President alone is required by the Constitution to "take care that the laws be faithfully executed," the Framers intended (as it is clear, from their letters and debates, they did intend) not to grant the President some "executive privilege" outside the law, but on the contrary, to hold him accountable, by some higher standard than any other citizen, to the law itself. There was the Superintendency theory: that the President, like any other civil or corporate officer, has a reasonable obligation to inquire and to inform himself of the acts of his subordinates, and be held accountable for them, particularly when those acts are crimes committed in his name, and solely for his benefit and on his behalf.

It is obvious that these informal assumptions combined hypotheses about the case with strategies for winning it. More directly in the line of strategy was what to look for and to try to prove. There was the Criminal Act under the Statutes theory, the one set forth in the White House brief, which everyone, from distinguished constitutional scholars to students of the problem in any depth at all, rejected. A Tax Fraud and Emoluments theory—which, for various reasons, including questions posed by the financial affairs of previous Presidents and present congressmen, was never seriously investigated by the staff. And there was a sort of nameless theory, which had to do with getting from the constitutional oath, faithfully to execute the office of President, to the unconstitutional acts, by way of the lies. There is nothing, of course, in the law or in the Constitution which requires anybody not to lie, except under oath. But the President, once he is in office, need not submit to being put under oath; he incurs no risk of perjury. He cannot anyway be indicted while in office; nor can there be an effective warrant to search his premises. The question was whether the President, notwithstanding his special constitutional oath, had a limitless power to commit unlawful acts and to conceal them, by means of a limitless right, in effect, to lie. It was some combination of the Oath-to-the-Acts theory with those in the preceding paragraph which led to the ultimate argument for impeachment, and to the form of the Articles themselves.

All these initial formulations and assumptions were, of course, addressed to the difficult question of what "other high Crimes and Misdemeanors" were. In February 1974, however, one of Doar's small group wrote, in a very short memo, "I think you're being too cavalier about bribery." It had been dismissed. In addition to the problems which followed from any Tax Fraud and Emoluments theory, bribery seemed just too difficult to prove. I remember, however, thinking as I read that memo in February that, if bribery was impossible to prove, then at least two parts of the impeachment provision of the Constitution were obsolete. Having so much occasion to read the phrase "Treason, Bribery, or other high Crimes and Misdemeanors," I thought that, as far as the presidency was concerned, there was no longer any circumstance in which treason could apply. With the technology of modern warfare, foreign policy—allying oneself, for example, on the instant, with a foreign power previously considered an enemy—was necessarily a matter of presidential discretion. There seemed to be no conceivable sense in which treason, by any definition, could be committed by a modern President.

II. The Defense

To turn now to those apparently unaccountable White House lapses, discrepancies, things that don't make any sense. I begin with a proposition that is arguable and that I don't at all require: that if Nixon himself had been caught, red-handed, in the Watergate he would not have been impeached. Burglary is a literal crime, as required by the White House brief; and burglary of the offices of a political opponent makes it that "political" crime that would satisfy anybody's brief; but I think he could have explained it away. As for the cover-up, the obstruction of justice, if the President had been caught red-handed and lied about it, he would not have been impeached. There would, of course, have been an outcry. But an outcry is not an impeachment. There had to be many, many outcries, with two years of metaphoric bombshells, and massacres, and smoking guns, before the process was truly under way. The proposition is, anyway, unimportant. At the time of the break-in, President Nixon was at Key Biscayne. It is only to speculate that if he had been involved in the Watergate, personally, unarguably, and directly, he would have fared better than he did. Until November 1972, there was still, of course, the election to think about; there might have been a risk in that election. But not impeachment. Apart from his own acts, it took a lot of time, and people, and institutions, the press, the Special Prosecutor, the Ervin Committee, the courts, before the mechanism was even in place.

It is after he had won the election, however, by an unprecedented margin, that the odd progression of lapses and inconsistencies begins. Why, for instance, immediately or at least soon after the election, did the President not pardon Hunt and the other Watergate burglars and continue to comply with their demands? The money was there. The payments would have continued to be clandestine. There had been, then, no confessions by John Dean or Jeb Magruder, no accusation even by James McCord. There had certainly been no resignation by Attorney General Richard Kleindienst; no appointment of Elliot Richardson, bringing with him the Special Prosecutor, Archibald Cox; no Saturday Night Massacre, triggering resolutions of impeachment. The Ervin Committee hearings had not even begun. At least as late as March 21, 1973, the President could have pardoned all the Watergate defendants (thereby relieving the pressure of impending sentences by Judge Sirica) and simultaneously, vaguely, taken the blame for the whole affair himself. It might have been nothing to impeach him for. And, as we have since had good occasion to know, to pardon is the President's constitutional right.

Precisely because it would have been safe to pay, pardon, take the blame after the election, it may, however, have seemed safer not to. No politician would have been positively eager to take the blame. For a long time, I thought that was explanation enough. To turn, though, to another, more familiar set of whys: the tapes. Why not, when Alexander Butterfield revealed their existence, destroy the tapes? Why turn over to the House Judiciary Committee what were obviously doctored transcripts of tapes, the originals of which the inquiry staff already had? Why not record, and find, and turn over to the committee a single tape on which the President looked good? His defenders, if they had had the wit to do so, could at least have argued that, while there have been grounds to impeach any President, with Nixon there were, on balance, not only extenuating circumstances but strong, good grounds (the opening to China, peace, détente, whatever) to keep him on. Why not, having decided to turn over any tapes at all, simply *flood* the Judiciary Committee with tapes, masses of tapes, U-Haul truck after U-Haul truck? Every time the staff seemed to find incriminating evidence, the President's lawyers would have claimed to find further tapes with exculpatory evidence, all of which, in the name of being "fair," the inquiry staff would have been obliged to examine. That would presumably have drawn out the inquiry until at least November 1974—when, almost certainly, most members of the Judiciary Committee would have been defeated in the congressional elections, their constituents would have been so impatient with how slow they were. In January 1975, the process would have had to begin again and be drawn out—if anyone could bear to continue with it—until President Nixon had served out his term.

Instead of looking separately at those whys, there are two explanations people like to give for all of them: that Nixon was insane; that it was not his nature, as revealed by the whole history of his life, to yield an inch in anything. One problem with these answers is that, even if true, there is really nothing they explain. To account for apparent lapses in the conduct of a man who rose to great power at least twice, and fell from it, by claiming he was just intransigent or mad is to disregard the particular meaning of any of them. Whatever the state of his sanity or his nature, Nixon was doing all right with them until mid-1974. If there needs to be a single abstraction, or at least a sweeping word, to cover the detail of the mistakes made by and for him, I do not think that a word exists, for a middle way that is not only wrong; it is the only way that is wrong, a kind of dark side of the Golden Mean. Anything—more, less, everything, nothing—is sometimes better than that way. With the medium lie, the partial erasure, the half stonewall, the President and his lawyers were always finding their way into it.

But there doesn't need to be an abstraction, a policy or state of character, to explain those whys. Looking again, in terms of the substance of the tapes themselves, at just that initial question of the pardons, specific explanations do suggest themselves. It has always been an anomaly that whatever we know, from tapes or other sources, about the offenses that led to Nixon's departure from office is based, in one way or another, on what was known to John Dean. Although Dean knew a lot (the Huston plan, the burglary of Ellsberg's psychiatrist's office, the seventeen wiretaps, certain events that preceded the Watergate break-in, the essentials of the cover-up), he was, after all, a minor White House lawyer, who did not even have a conversation of substance with the President until September 15, 1972—when Nixon needed to have talked with Dean as a basis for covering him with a claim of executive, and for good measure, attorney-client, privilege. How little Dean was in the President's confidence is clear from the now-famous conversation of March 21, 1973, in which he "informed" Nixon of what Nixon already so well knew. And because that conversation subsequently acquired such importance (in terms of Dean's credibility, of Watergate, and of choices Nixon subsequently made), almost all subpoenas of presidential conversations were addressed to the matter of confirming or failing to confirm what John Dean knew—which, as far as the President was concerned, was confined almost entirely to conversations in the spring of 1973, about Watergate.

Except for September 15, 1972. And looking again at the transcript of that conversation, it becomes obvious why the President could not safely grant Hunt and the other burglars pardons: the House Committee on Banking and Currency, the Patman Committee. The problem was never the burglary of the Watergate. The problem was the source of the cash. As soon as hundred-dollar bills in the possession of the burglars had been traced via Bernard Barker's bank account to Mexico (i.e., within five days of the burglary), the course of events was set. The same account had cleared $89,000 in checks endorsed by a Mexican lawyer, Manuel Ogarrio. And the problem, from the moment the cash was traced to a Mexican bank account, was that the Patman Committee started to look into it—and that committee, unlike any subsequent investigative body, would have known how and where to look. In late 1969 and early 1970, the Patman Committee had held hearings about secret, numbered foreign bank accounts (in Switzerland, the Bahamas, and elsewhere) mainly with a view to the use of such accounts by organized crime. It had not considered their use in a political campaign. By September 1972, it was beginning to look into exactly that. When it was stopped.

Chairman Wright Patman had a list of witnesses concerning cash transactions related to the Watergate. On September 14, 1972, the first of the important witnesses declined to appear. Chairman Patman scheduled another meeting, for October 3, 1972, to proceed with the subpoena power. On October 2, 1972, Assistant Attorney General Henry E. Petersen wrote Patman a letter, hand-delivered, warning that the committee hearings might "not only jeopardize the prosecution" of the Watergate case but also "seriously prejudice" the defendants' rights. If Nixon had granted pardons, that argument would, of course, have fallen apart; hearings can hardly prejudice the rights of defendants when the President has already pardoned them. The Patman investigation could have gone ahead. In his conversation of September 15, 1972, the President wanted to ensure that it would not. He issued instructions that a number of people be sent to contact the committee with that argument from defendants' rights. He considered sending Attorney General Richard Kleindienst. Then he thought of John Connally. He finally settled on sending Congressman Gerald Ford. (President: "What about Ford? . . .

This is, this is, big, big play . . . they can all work out something. But they ought to get off their asses and push it. No use to let Patman have a free ride. . . .")

The Patman hearings were suspended. By October 31, 1972, the committee's staff had made a little headway all the same. Even without subpoena power, the staff had found enormous irregularities in the bookkeeping of, among others, the treasurer of the Finance Committee to Re-Elect the President, Hugh Sloan. And in the records of several banks where CREEP had its accounts. And in statements, written and oral, made to investigators about the sources of the cash, by the chairman of the Finance Committee to Re-Elect, Maurice Stans. The staff had also, almost incidentally, discovered a campaign contribution to CREEP via the Banque Internationale à Luxembourg. There was so much cash and so much irregularity, though, that without the power to subpoena records or to take testimony under oath, the committee lost the trail.

Secret foreign accounts as a source of laundered campaign contributions would not, in and of themselves, be enough to impeach a President, either. To turn then, for a while, to the questions raised by Nixon's treatment of the tapes. There can hardly be any doubt, in the logic of events, that Alexander Butterfield, who disclosed the existence of the taping system to the minority staff of the Ervin Committee and then to the full committee on national television, was a plant. The only question for a time was whose. Ever since he testified, Butterfield has managed to imply that he spoke reluctantly, that a question was put to him in such a way that he had to tell, or perjure himself, or compromise his honor, or whatever. This version—the reluctant witness, the clever investigator—has understandably not been disputed by the Ervin Committee staff. But the record, the only record that staff made of that interview at the time, simply does not bear that out. Butterfield volunteered. "I feel it is something you ought to know about," he said, "in your investigations." Having added, in that initial interview, "This is something I know the President did not want revealed," Butterfield went on to tell the full committee, on national television, that the tapes "are precisely the substance on which the President plans to present his defense." He went to considerable lengths then to emphasize—utterly misleadingly, as it turned out—the particular *clarity* of the tapes, and the care with which they were checked, both in the Executive Office Building and in the

Oval Office. The EOB tapes were, in reality, so bad that the President himself (in his tape of June 4, 1973) complained of how hard it was to understand them; the group that produced the inquiry transcripts spent approximately one man-hour per minute trying to decipher them. I leave aside the question of whether Butterfield was an agent of the CIA—a rumor reported in the *New York Times* and elsewhere, and denied by him. Although his testimony ultimately backfired, it seems certain that Haldeman (and by extension, Nixon) sent him in.

As a character in all these events, Butterfield has never made much sense. Like Hugh Sloan, Earl Silbert, Henry Petersen, Alexander Haig, Fred Buzhardt, and even James St. Clair, he was one of what became an unlikely herd of self-styled victims of deceit, and then self-serving and improbable heroes of Watergate. Butterfield's wife had been Haldeman's wife's best friend at college. The Butterfields and Haldemans were friends. Butterfield's office was placed to control all access, by persons or documents, to President Nixon's office—surely a sign of an earned trust. When Haldeman needed somebody to hide the $350,000 secret White House fund of cash, the man he used was Butterfield. Butterfield subsequently became an informer, the informer, for the impeachment inquiry. But, apart from homey speculations about the Nixon marriage (he was, in every interview, the source of the story that the Nixons were not close), he never really said anything. His initial disclosure of the existence of the tapes was, after all, in the President's interest. Everyone who had spoken to the President was put on notice: No one could feel safe. With the misleading emphasis on clarity, people were warned all the more clearly. It is probable that, in three years of only normally sycophantic conversation with the President, there was not a major figure in government, from all three branches, the military, all the various bureaus, agencies, and departments (not to mention minor White House officials who might, like John Dean, have felt under pressure to testify), who did not feel compromised, or even implicated in a felony, on those tapes. The President had them, and had at the time no reason to think he must disclose any more of them than he cared to. The message in Butterfield's testimony was a perfect threat, at the very least, to every Nixon confidant and appointee.

To take just one domestic constellation: the Department of Justice (in the person of Attorney General Richard Kleindienst) and the two major investigative agencies (in the persons of Acting FBI Director L. Patrick

Gray and CIA Director Richard Helms) were intimately involved with the obstruction of justice on which the case for impeachment came to rest. When Senator Lowell Weicker, of the Ervin Committee, first suggested that the President might have been guilty of "misprision of a felony" in not reporting to any properly constituted authority what John Dean had told him, and when the House Judiciary Committee considered, as part of its argument for impeachment, the same failure to pass the information on, Nixon may have thought his accusers were not sane. There could scarcely be any legal or constitutional obligation to report a crime to people who were in on it—and for whose complicity he thought he had, among other evidence, the tapes.

If the tapes as a veiled and planted threat did not entirely work, the reason may apply to most adversary situations, in public and in private life, in which both parties are lying and at fault. When people lie in concert, a single, simple truth can be impossible to prove—as in the case of finding, among only three suspects, the individual who produced the eighteen-and-a-half-minute gap. But when they lie in conflict, each liar, in indignation about the other, may begin to feel innocent. People who feel *wronged*, in particular, are likely to forget what regrettable thing it is they themselves did or said. It could be that, in their outrage, those people who were compromised on the tapes simply forgot. Or maybe the threat did work, and they did not forget. History, after all, is left with the remarkable fact that, to this day, nobody except John Dean has come out with testimony, borne out by the tapes or otherwise, that implicates President Nixon in any crimes. And here is the status of the tapes themselves: Although Congress has, by special legislation, impounded them (thereby foreclosing Nixon's access to the main weapon he thought he had against others and, simultaneously, precluding access to the best evidence against the man himself), the tapes remain, while the matter is appealed to the Supreme Court, in the EOB. Dr. James Rhodes, the national archivist, has written to Nixon's lawyers and to the White House to request permission to rewind the tapes—which he says are deteriorating because they are loosely wound. Dr. Rhodes has also asked to check which tapes, of what may be as many as five thousand hours of conversation, actually do contain a "signal," i.e., voices—a matter that can be very quickly checked. He has received no reply. It is possible that, among all the parties of interest in the tapes, only the national archivist is concerned with preserving them.

As for why Nixon would submit to the Judiciary Committee doctored transcripts of tapes the staff already had, that nearly worked. The White House released its thick book of doctored transcripts on April 30, 1974. The regular staff, at the time, was in such a daze of fairness that it simply could not find systematic discrepancies between the White House version and the true version of eight conversations that overlapped. When the EOB tapes turned out to be mostly garble, interrupted by hissing, buzzing, and tapping noises, Doar considered abandoning this form of evidence. The lore-manufacturing apparatus, at this point, introduces a blind lady, with miraculously sensitive ears. There was no blind lady. A blind man who listened to the EOB tapes couldn't understand them either. A member of Doar's small group insisted, threatening to resign over the question, that Doar permit him and a tape expert to re-record from originals at the White House, and later (when White House Attorney Fred Buzhardt withdrew access to originals) from the tapes in Judge Sirica's chambers. The tape expert and the member of the group who had threatened to resign found two others to "go into the mud," as they put it, for hundreds of hours, filling out each transcript, word by word. The rest of the small group initiated work on the discrepancies—weeks after the White House transcripts were released.

The grand jury had based its presentment, mainly, on the tape of the March 21, 1973, conversation in the Oval Office between the President and John Dean. St. Clair directed his whole case, such as it was, toward showing that the President had not unequivocally authorized the payment of hush money on that day. But the "I don't give a shit . . . I want you all to stonewall it, let them plead the Fifth Amendment, cover-up or anything else . . . save the plan" conversation, which persuaded Republican congressmen Thomas Railsback and Robert McClory to vote for impeachment, took place on March 22, 1973, in the EOB. It was deleted from the White House transcripts and unintelligible on the Special Prosecutor's. The grand jury never heard it. It is even possible that nobody at the White House ever heard it, that it was always mud. Barely possible. The recopying had just reached the tape of March 22, 1973, when Buzhardt cut off access to the tapes.

In this context, too, there is a particular point about the transcript of June 23, 1972—the tape that was supposed so profoundly to have shocked the President's defenders that it obliged them to persuade him to resign. The few, very few, Nixon associates who have not tried since his resignation to save themselves at his expense claim that both Buzhardt and St. Clair had read in May this transcript which so astounded them in July. Buzhardt has said that he knew all was lost when, in late July 1973, he listened for the first time to the tape of June 23, 1972, and heard the incriminating word "Gemstone." The inquiry's tape expert says it took months for him to be able to decipher that word. In any case, it is certain that both Buzhardt and St. Clair were familiar with the contents of the tape before the Judiciary Committee voted, and did not trouble to let any of the President's defenders on the committee know. Months later, during the trial of *U.S.* v. *Mitchell, et al.*, it became clear that this transcript also had been doctored; neither of Nixon's lawyers had called attention to those excisions in July when they had listened to the tape. When one recalls that the President, in the statement with which he released the transcript, made a special point of admitting that he had concealed it from his attorneys—when one realizes that the worst strangler, dope-pusher, child-molester, finds it unnecessary in adversity to apologize to his own counsel—it seems possible that in this little episode the President was framed. St. Clair felt that, before the case reached the floor of the House, he ought to show Congressman Wiggins, the President's major defender on the committee, that transcript of June 23, 1972. Having received what must have been a considerable shock when Wiggins, enraged, told him the transcript meant the case was lost (and that if the White House did not at once make the transcript public, he, Wiggins, would), St. Clair must have returned to his client with an assurance that the problem was not insuperable—as long as the President's counsel did not resign. St. Clair, however, would feel obliged to resign unless the President stated publicly that he had withheld from his attorneys the knowledge of this tape. The President believed, and did as he was told. And St. Clair was able to tell the press that he was not, after all, the first lawyer whose client had lied to him.

As for not having found and turned over a single tape the President looked good on, it is fairly clear, from the tape of June 4, 1973, that Nixon, with the concurrence of Ziegler and earlier Haldeman (and Haig, with his loving assurance, "Only you. Only you"), was under the impression that he sounded pretty good on most of them. On June 26, 1973, Nixon again listened to himself on tape. Within days, the Ervin

Committee heard from Butterfield. And St. Clair, who liked to insist that he was defending the presidency, when he was actually using the presidency to protect a criminal defendant and then using the President himself to protect the President's lawyer's name, never did give a straightforward reply when members of the committee asked whether he had listened to any tapes at all. He could presumably have asked Buzhardt to find a good tape, but neither of the lawyers seems to have felt a necessity for finding one, they were so preoccupied with the minuscule questions posed by the tape of March 21, 1973. Finally, why not have flooded the committee, as is often done in antitrust cases, with unassimilable evidence? As well ask why the White House lawyers were remiss in almost everything. There was every reason, however, for President Nixon not to want to do it. And the inescapable inference, I think, consists in the explanation why.

III. What's Missing?

A piece last year in *Esquire* raised the question of how it was that the *New York Times* at first missed the story of Watergate. One explanation was that *Times* reporters had been following leads on other stories—drugtaking by a high government official, and so on—stories that did not yield. Many papers ultimately made their contribution. The Washington *Star*, interviewing a gardener, discovered that a recent visitor at San Clemente had been Judge Matthew Byrne, of the Ellsberg trial; that broke the story of the offer to him of the directorship of the FBI. The Providence *Journal* broke the story of Nixon's income tax. The *Los Angeles Times*, Jack Nelson in particular, broke various stories. *Time* revealed the seventeen wiretaps. Other reporters uncovered important stories— as, of course, did the *New York Times*. But the reporting that led most directly to Nixon's departure from office was unquestionably Woodward and Bernstein's in the *Washington Post*. The author of the *Esquire* piece concluded that the *New York Times* had been remiss. It seemed more likely, though, that Watergate, and the important revelations it led to, were not the story. And I don't mean the tip of the iceberg here. I mean that, in spite of all the Watergate cover-up talk on the few known transcripts (out of three years, after all, of recorded conversation), Nixon simply did not think Watergate was the front he was vulnerable on.

If one bears with this line of thought, that Watergate was not the story, then the problem is what was. It is hard to sustain a belief in a conspiracy within his administration against him. It would be unreasonable to expect to drive from office, by means of tapes in his sole possession, the man who had appointed (and who presumably had compromising tapes of) the presumptive heads of any such conspiracy. Moreover, no evidence on a grand enough scale ever came *out* about President Nixon to support a view that the intelligence agencies had conspired to produce such evidence. Finally, it is clear from the Church Committee documents and from more recent, almost daily news reports that the agencies had problems enough with secrets of their own to preclude an interest in the removal from office of a chief executive— when that removal would lead, as it inevitably did, to investigations of the agencies themselves.

Even less convincing are theories that the offenses at the heart of the Nixon administration had to do with a Hughes connection, or with the Bebe Rebozo $100,000. So many people, Republicans and Democrats alike, have had some sort of Hughes connection. As for Rebozo, a memorandum of June 16, 1972, from Gordon Strachan to H. R. Haldeman, does report a complaint from Florida CREEP contributors that they had "already given through Bebe." But, as events in the intervening years, concerning kickbacks and financial-political scandal of all kinds and on all sides, demonstrate—and as the fact that no article of impeachment having to do with taxes or finances was ever passed confirms—the President could not have been impeached simply over money. Vice President Agnew did have to resign over money, but it seems beyond question that this resignation would not have occurred had it not been for Watergate—when the President viewed the prospect of Agnew's resignation as protection for himself.

The minds of assassination theorists run, perhaps, to murder: the shooting of Governor Wallace; or the crash of the plane bearing Mrs. E. Howard Hunt. But it is unlikely that the Nixon scandal had to do with murder—else why not have murdered a few more people, and those more key? One arrives suddenly at the territory of the florid killings, Jimmy Hoffa, Sam Giancana, John Roselli—and at the Church Committee documents—in a most unlikely way. Because what was happening in the name of intelligence activities provided, at least, a context for the way Nixon conducted his administration; and because the Church investigation itself provides an example of not wanting to know too clearly, or to state at all, what your own research unmistakably implies.

IV. Transactions

The Church Committee's report on intelligence activities consists of seven volumes. Like most government documents, they are hard to read. The first volume, *Alleged Assassination Plots Involving Foreign Leaders,* was, politically, the right place to begin. A bipartisan majority of the committee could agree to investigate these matters—past and foreign— precisely and only because they were remote, indifferent, a subject in which nobody had anything politically to lose. If someone had really managed, in the early sixties, to assassinate Fidel Castro, the whole country probably would have been for it. There was, in those days, no Left to speak of. The rest, among investigators, press, citizens at large, was just consensus and hypocrisy. Consensus, because in the matter of old and failed assassinations, all parties could agree to a distraction from the real and serious questions: whether, for instance, the agencies were doing what they were authorized and paid to do, and at what price; whether there was any way to keep them, domestically, within the law. Hypocrisy, because everyone could agree to be outraged that such plots were ever contemplated—when it was, and is, by no means clear that they were not always part of what has been required, from time to time, of an intelligence agency.

One might even have thought naïveté compounded with consensus and hypocrisy, in that people could seriously entertain the idea that foreign interventions of a high and violent order could be undertaken by underlings, without the knowledge of the various Presidents. This would involve a misunderstanding of the presidency so profound that it brings in just the cast of mind that made it difficult to know what Nixon did: a bureaucratic logic of passing the buck downward, of presuming, in the name of "fairness," the ignorance of the man in power, beyond the farthest reaches of common sense. What did the boss know and when did he know it makes sense only as the question of a jury lawyer whose client is the boss. The presumption of innocence is, after all, a practical, moral convention for the conduct of fair trials. It was never meant to go any further, to suggest that truth itself, say, consists in the outcome of a conflict of legal strategies. And certainly not to express the Mafia ethic that the lowest takes the rap.

But when the Mafia itself, literally, was brought into the story, there was something in the details that began to obscure the drift. The collaboration of the CIA and the Mafia in a plan for a foreign assassination had its initial plausibility. The Mafia had had profitable operations in Cuba; it must have longed to have them back. Then, with Sam Giancana, John Roselli, even Judith Campbell Exner, Frank Sinatra, the rococo elements appear—giving rise to at least one speculation, and one certainty. The speculation: that the whole story is backward, that there might have been a White House connection with the Mafia, perhaps accidentally and carelessly. The connection would have come, inevitably, to the attention of J. Edgar Hoover—whose FBI cannot, as it claimed, have been bugging a Mafia phone, but must have been tapping the White House phones for many years, for the FBI director's purposes. There cannot have been any other reason to wait *fifty-four* weeks to bring the Roselli-Giancana matter to President John Kennedy's attention. To exactly the degree that a connection is dangerous to the national security, its termination, too, is presumably no less than urgent; it took Hoover more than a year to feel that urgency. It was obviously just a moment when, for whatever reason, Hoover felt he must deal this card. As for the CIA, when this Mafia connection, by whatever route, came to its attention, the White House might have said—as it said so recently, in the case of the burglary of Ellsberg's psychiatrist's office—Stay away from that. That's national security. The CIA's employment of the Mafia for purposes of assassinating Castro would have become the consensual fiction. Advantage to the Mafia: such private services as having the CIA break into the apartment, years ago, of the singer girlfriend of that jealous lover, Sam Giancana; tax relief; and relief from various other legal pressures, probably.

That would be a speculation. But a certainty is this: that, at some unspecified point in its history, the CIA began to include the investigation and control of narcotics traffic, without mandate or explanation, in its own interpretation of its intelligence work; that, in recent years, virtually every group that has newly claimed the control of narcotics as part of its mission (from Egil Krogh's Plumbers, through the units of John Caulfield and G. Gordon Liddy, when they came from drug-enforcement agencies) has used that claim as a cover for some crime; that the CIA, in the course of the Church Committee hearings, was unable to give any satisfactory account either of its dealings with the opium-running tribes-men of Southeast Asia, or for allegations of drug traffic by its own South-east Asian airline, Air America. A report by the CIA's own inspector general concluded that there was "no evidence that the Agency . . . has ever sanctioned or supported drug trafficking *as a matter of policy*" (italics added). Those words in italics must constitute the weakest disclaimer of criminal activity by a governmental agency ever to be seriously presented in any public forum.

And looking back, then, at the alleged purpose of the association with Giancana and Roselli, there arises at least this question: Does it make sense for the CIA to have enlisted organized crime as an ally in a plan for an assassination of the highest importance, while, at the same time, it claims responsibility for suppressing traffic in narcotics, which is the most highly profitable enterprise for organized crime? Does either half of this proposition, which would make of the secret collaborator in one international enterprise the bitterest conceivable enemy in the other, make any sense? (The fact is, of course, that Castro was not assassinated. Narcotics traffic, on the other hand, has flourished, supporting not only organized crime but all those bureaucracies whose mission is to suppress it.) The reason the questions are not idle is that there is evidence, scat-tered throughout the Church Committee report, that, at least since its demoralization in the Bay of Pigs, the CIA has changed from a band of courageous and patriotic amateurs into another sort of band entirely.

Investigative reporting is not what I intended or what I have done here; my politics, such as they are, tend to be moderate. But one cannot help, in looking at documents which might establish a context for a last inference about the Nixon administration, finding signs, in government in recent years, of something, in economic terms at least, radically amiss—evidence of great improprieties involving immense sums of cash. There are, to take two examples, transactions involving two of the CIA's "proprietaries"—the businesses which the CIA says it must own, as a cover for its intelligence activities. The first is the sale of an airline, Southern Air Transport, which the CIA bought, in 1960, for use in Asia. The CIA bought the airline, which was based in Miami, Florida, for approximately $300,000, and held the shares in the name of a former board member of its other airline, Air America. In 1973, it sold Southern

Air Transport, to its former owner, for approximately $6 million—several million dollars less than its book value at the time, and $2 million less than what had already been offered, in cash, by another buyer. The CIA's explanation for the sale was this: it sought "to avoid a conflict of interest." However complicated other aspects of the transaction may have been, one thing is clear: Selling to former associates, at a price millions of dollars below book value and below a competing cash offer, does not so much *avoid* as it quite openly declares the most direct and glaring conflict of interest.

A second case concerns a $30 million "insurance complex," which the CIA claimed it was obliged to set up abroad, as a result of the death of four agents in the Bay of Pigs. Leaving aside the question of whether it might not have been possible to compensate four surviving families by some means other than an enterprise costing millions, the CIA went on to claim that for reasons of "cover" the insurance complex had to make investments, in foreign and American stocks, and also to keep some "non-interest bearing deposits" in foreign banks. The only "issue" which a section of the report obviously written by the CIA itself could find in the matter of these deposits was that the selection of the banks was "non-competitive"—as though the Agency might have been showing favoritism in its choice of banks, or attempting to influence their policies. That is not, of course, the real issue at all. An "insurance complex," in foreign banks, with a portfolio of foreign and American stocks, and deposits on which it claims to get no interest, is not a necessary or even plausible "cover" for intelligence work but an opportunity—stated with a brazenness that insults the committee which investigates—for fraud on a scale that no private corporation could contemplate. Since the CIA refused, on grounds, it says, of national security, to disclose how much money it has at all, and since Congress has so far indulged that refusal, the Agency continues in its special capacity for making illegal profits and never having to account to anyone for them, or to give any explanation of who or what has that money now.

As for the FBI—as portrayed in the Church Committee report, it seems so locked in obsessions of its own that it hardly bears on the Nixon case. In federal government, it has always been vital interests such as defense (and more recently, medical care) which present special opportunities for impropriety, because of their intense importance to a public that, lacking expertise, is helpless in terms of oversight. All this by way of a cursory outline of situations which existed in government, quite apart from the Nixon administration; and to establish a context for what I think the Nixon scandal itself had to be. It would have to be of an entirely other order than any of these, as it were, more normal scandals; and it required not the most florid and aberrant explanation but the worst and perhaps the most obvious. And here's what I think, inescapably, it has to be.

V. Bottom Line

People are accustomed to speak of the tragedies of Vietnam and Watergate, or of the post-Vietnam post-Watergate morality, as though they were linked only in some abstract, ethical sphere. Then, one looks at those transcripts once again. In his conversation of February 28, 1973, with John Dean, President Nixon discussed an allegation that, in 1968, at President Lyndon Johnson's insistence, the FBI tapped conversations between Agnew, the candidate for Vice President, and Anna Chennault, widow of General Claire Chennault and president of Flying Tiger Airlines. The rationale for this tap was supposed to be that Mrs. Chennault was urging the South Vietnamese to slow down or stop the peace negotiations in Paris, to help assure the election of a Republican administration, under which, she was supposed to be telling the South Vietnamese, they would get better terms.

Mrs. Chennault says she did not even know Spiro Agnew in 1968; but that is not the point. She says she knew Richard Nixon very well. On February 28, 1973, President Nixon was preoccupied only with whether there had been such a tap, not with the rationale behind it. One remembers that, less than a week before the 1968 election, the South Vietnamese did stop the negotiations cold. Less than a week. One remembers, too, the remarkable suddenness and, even for refugees, unprecedented hysteria and chaos with which the war, in March 1975, finally did end; and the apparently real fury and sense of betrayal President Thieu expressed when he so precipitately, and it seemed spitefully, gave up. And one cannot help thinking back on 1968 and believing that, in 1972, there must have been a deal. On October 26, 1972, two weeks before the election, Henry Kissinger said of Vietnam, "Peace is at hand." Peace is at hand. There can and could be no doubt that he sincerely meant it. Within the week, however, Alexander Haig flew to

Vietnam. There was unprecedented bombing and the mining of Haiphong. After all that, in January 1973, when the accords were signed, the terms were in no substantial way different from the ones Henry Kissinger had gotten, months earlier, when he genuinely thought peace was at hand. Then, one remembers we were pouring huge amounts of money into South Vietnam; and that the government there, being famously corrupt, was getting a lot of it. One remembers that President Nixon himself was getting a lot of illicit campaign contributions, from a lot of strange sources, and diverting at least some of them to his personal use. And one can't help thinking that, in 1972, the South Vietnamese administration, not wanting peace to be at hand just yet, used some of the enormous amounts of money we were pouring in there to bribe our administration to stay in.

All right, it is difficult, monstrous; and, of necessity, only an inference, impossible to prove. But one looks back—thinking, not laundered money, foreign money. It is hard to recall the sums and characters, where they came from and where they went. But, early in the Ervin Committee hearings, there is the dim sound of the testimony of CREEP Finance Chairman Maurice Stans. He mentioned a contribution, $30,000 in cash, from a "Philippine national"—a contribution, Stans said at the time, he had been too fastidious to keep. Gordon Liddy's successor as counsel to the Finance Committee to Re-Elect, Stans said, had told him that it would not be legal to accept such money. So Stans had arranged, he said, with Fred Larue, an assistant to John Mitchell at CREEP, to return that $30,000 to its source. "Since then, and this is more irony, Senator," Stans went on, amiably, in the ensuing colloquy, he had learned from a Justice Department official that it would have been "perfectly proper" to accept that money from a foreign national, "so long as he is not an agent of a foreign principal." That is what Stans testified on June 12, 1973.

It would not, as it turns out, have been "perfectly proper" to accept a campaign contribution from a foreign national. It would have been illegal. But the sum itself is so trivial, $30,000. One wonders why Stans testified at such length about it. Hugh Sloan, the Finance Committee treasurer, testified at length about it, too. It is not until *four volumes* later, in the records of the Ervin Committee hearings, that one finds any correspondence that deals with this transaction. It occurs in support of the testimony of Fred Larue, who had paid some of the hush money to the burglars, and who was by then negotiating his plea. Stans had not asked Larue to return any money to any source, it turns out, until May 9, 1973—more than a year after the Finance Committee had accepted it; but less than a month before the Ervin Committee hearings began. And even in his letter of May 9, 1973, Stans did not specify to whom the money was to be returned. Larue simply wanted to return the CREEP money in his possession. His counsel *did* specify, more or less. The $30,000, Stan's attorney finally wrote, in acknowledging a letter dated May 16, 1973, from Larue's attorney, was "paid" to Anna Chennault, for "return to foreign nationals"—nationality, Philippine or other, un-specified.

The only reason this trivial amount, this $30,000, came to light at all was that it was part of $81,000 in cash that Hugh Sloan was stuck with when the source of the cash in the possession of the Watergate burglars had been traced to those checks endorsed by the Mexican lawyer Manuel Ogarrio. And that, one recalls, was the cash that had interested the Patman Committee. At first, Stans had told the committee staff that the money came from Ogarrio; then, that he could not disclose whom it came from, since they were Texans to whom he had promised anonymity; finally, that he did not know who the donors were. The Patman Committee staff, having coincidentally discovered, at about the same time, that $700,000 in cash had come to CREEP, in a suitcase, from an American corporation by way of Mexico, was at first misled into thinking that the story had to do not with contributions by foreign nationals but with donations by American corportions and citizens (illegally and in secret) by way of foreign banks. As it turned out, the story was both: Americans and foreign nationals. But the committee, lacking its subpoena power, never got Stans or any other CREEP official under oath—as the Ervin Committee, so many months later, did. And that petty $30,000, within the $81,000 (which remained of the original Ogarrio $89,000), came back to haunt Stans, Sloan, Larue, CREEP, Mrs. Chennault, and the country as a whole. On June 23, 1972, Stans had instructed Sloan to give the $81,000 to President Nixon's personal attorney, Herbert Kalm-bach, who gave it to Larue, who happened to use it as part of the hush money. And Larue plea-bargained. So, in whatever disjointed form, the $30,000 had to be accounted for. And it was foreign.

And thinking foreign, there are anomalies great and small, everywhere one looks. Hugh Sloan explained to the Ervin Committee that he had been unable to give a proper accounting of CREEP funds between April and July 1972, because Kalmbach had been "abroad." Abroad. There is no reason why the President's personal attorney and principal fund-raiser should not travel abroad. The height of the political campaign just seems an odd time for his holiday. In his own testimony, Kalmbach always insists, and when he does, elicits sympathy, that he was deceived and "used." In the memorandum of June 16, 1972, however, there is Kalmbach, returned from abroad, requesting assignments that are "tough and dangerous." Within days, he was raising, from domestic sources this time, the cash for the hush money. Kalmbach had already raised more than $12 million for the 1972 campaign. A political-matters memorandum as early as October 7, 1971, says, "Kalmbach keeps asking for tough, interesting assignments." On February 1, 1972, he is reported to have declared himself "willing to run the very high risk of violating the criminal provisions" of campaign-spending legislation.

And even in what remains of the records of CREEP itself—on file, as required under post-Watergate law, at the Federal Election Commission—one finds both foreign and domestic oddities. What was still until last year the Committee to Re-Elect the President is now called the 1972 Campaign Liquidation Trust. It reports an interest income of $80,000 a year, with this income annually exceeded by expenses—as might be expected in a fund that wants to liquidate. It is only that campaigns normally end with deficits, and that an interest income of $80,000 reflects a lot of capital—which raises the question of who or what has that money now, and by what right. Some domestic curiosities: Until October 1976 the Campaign Liquidation Trust still had on its books a suit against John Dean and his attorney—for the return of $15,100, paid "on or about April 12, 1973." (The suit was settled with the return of that money to the Trust.) On a single day, May 3, 1973, six months after the President had, after all, been overwhelmingly reelected, the Committee to Re-Elect listed on its books seven separate payments of $3,000 and one of $2,500 to Maurice Stans, as "Salary"—making his salary for that day $23,500; four days later CREEP paid him another salary of $3,000. It paid Stans that sort of salary on a lot of days. More surprisingly, perhaps, CREEP was still paying Hugh Sloan—who made such an issue, before the Ervin Committee and elsewhere, of his resignation on the grounds of conscience, in July 1972, on account of Watergate—considerable sums every month until at least spring 1973. In January 1973, Sloan was still carried on the books as "Treasurer"; but his salary had become "Consulting Fee." By February, his title had become "Consultant." On February 15, 1973, Sloan's consulting fee was $1,320; on February 21, 1973, $1,080, and so on. Unlike John Dean, Sloan was never sued by the Committee to Re-Elect. But Sloan had, after all, handled enormous cash contributions, as treasurer to the Finance Committee, in the 1968 campaign as well; and, unlike Dean, he could be presumed to know in 1972, although he never really told, about the sources of the cash.

In the records of CREEP on file at the Federal Election Commission, there are only slim indications of contributions from any foreign source. On February 27, 1973 (again, months after Nixon's reelection), something called "Committee of United States Citizens in Asia for Nixon" did file a registration form. In answer to question (a) "Will this committee operate in more than one state?" the committee replied, "No— only internationally, outside the U.S." In answer to (d) "Will it support a candidate for President or Vice President in the aggregate amount of $1,000 or more during the calendar year?" the reply was "Yes." For (e) "Does this committee plan to stay in existence beyond the current calendar year?" another "Yes." And in answer to (f) "If so, how long?" there is "Perpetually." Under "Name of bank, repository, etc.," the reply is "None." And "List all reports required to be filed by this committee with states and jurisdictions" elicits another "None." Under a question asking the identity of the committee's "custodian of books and accounts," there is "Marshall Hendricks, Lewis Burridge, Anna Chennault." In its Statement of Affiliated and Connected Organizations, the committee listed "(a) Committee of United States Citizens in Hong Kong for Nixon (b) Committee of United States Citizens in Japan for Nixon (c) Committee of United States Citizens in Korea for Nixon," and so on.

There is, on the surface, no absolutely obvious reason why—in late February after the November in which a President, who is constitutionally precluded from serving more than two terms, has already been elected to his second term—citizens should not establish as many Asian branches for his reelection as they like, even listing no "bank, repository, etc." and with an intention (although this might suggest an echo of the Narrow Escape theory) to remain in existence "perpetually." But within a month—by March 22, 1973, in fact—the Asia Committee of CREEP and its affiliated committees found themselves, all together, unable to

claim contributions in excess of $1,000. Having planned to stay in ex-
istence "perpetually," they nonetheless asked to be allowed to cease to
report. The Asia Committee wrote to the Office of Federal Elections,
seeking "the approval of your office to cease reporting, until such time
in the future as we may have receipts in excess of $1,000." That a Nixon
campaign committee in Asia should reserve to itself the possibility of
such receipts at a "time in the future" raises questions about which one
does not care to speculate.

But it is hardly new that there were irregularities everywhere in the
finances of the 1972 campaign. Detail only obscures the logic of historical
events. In thinking about international political contributions, the logic
has normally gone the other way—contributions by the American government or by American corporations to officials, or parties, or governments abroad. But with the by now almost weekly revelations of
payments by American companies to foreign officials in Europe, Asia,
South America, and the Middle East, it began to seem highly probable
in the very nature of secret cash transactions that some of that money
was going to find its way back, and/or that some foreign interests rich
enough to afford it were going to lobby, with cash, in America. Taking
only defense matters, there was for instance Lockheed: With payments
in Italy, Japan, and the Netherlands, the cash seemed to flow in only
one direction. In June of this year, however, there were signs that it had,
for years, been traveling the other way. The Special Prosecutor's office
revealed that a citizen of Saudi Arabia, having received over the years
more than $100 million from Lockheed for his influence in selling aircraft
to the Saudis, had contributed $50,000 to Nixon's 1968 campaign; in
May and November 1972, the Saudi citizen withdrew $200 million from
his account in Bebe Rebozo's bank. Because of a "burglary" in Las Vegas,
which was reported within a week of the start of the prosecutor's investigation, the Saudi lobbyist could produce no records of how that $200
million was spent. Or Grumman. On September 13, 1976, there was the
former president of Grumman International testifying, under oath, that
in 1972 a White House official had suggested that Grumman contribute
$1 million to CREEP for the President's "assistance," on a forthcoming
trip to Honolulu, in getting Japan to buy Grumman fighter planes. In
April 1972, a Grumman official had visited the White House to discuss
sales of fighter planes to Iran; a month later, on a trip to Iran, Nixon
agreed for the first time to sell Iran virtually any weapon it wanted. Signs,

anyway, of a rich foreign country that could afford to pay to influence an American decision now and then.

Looking further back, however, at the Patman hearings on secret foreign bank accounts, one finds, as early as 1968, premonitions of what I think must have happened in 1972. In 1968, well before Nixon's first inauguration, the Patman Committee already had found "kickbacks by Vietnamese importers to American exporters, involving a huge U.S. corporation. Again, Swiss bank accounts were used." Assistant Attorney General Fred M. Vinson (who, in 1973, was the attorney for Fred Larue in his tractations, over the $30,000 from a foreign national, with Maurice Stans) testified, in 1968, as the Justice Department expert on these illicit foreign deals. But the scale, then, was different, and the purpose was different. No one suggested, in 1968, that the Vietnamese kickbacks, through foreign banks, went into American politics.

As, by 1972, I think they clearly did. Turning away from detail, one is struck by the logic overall. It does not make sense, for example, that the President's fund-raisers would put by far the greatest pressure of any political campaign in our history on so many sources, individual and corporate, and *reject* a contribution from the most logical of them all: the administration of South Vietnam, which had the most to lose if the President's opponent (who had announced a willingness to go, it must be remembered, to Hanoi on his knees for peace) actually won. And although the President might have liked to announce the war's end before any ordinary election, by the time he sent Haig to undo Kissinger's late October accords, he knew he did not need, in 1972, any peace to win. At the same time, Nixon never seems to have felt any diminution of need for campaign contributions. In the fall of 1968, the South Vietnamese had only to dig in their heels and wait, while the war cost Humphrey the election. By the fall of 1972, if they wanted the support of the administration, I think they had to pay.

And even the structure of the underlying proposition had occurred, minus only cash, in another context, at least once before: in the secret bombing of Cambodia. The rationale for lying to the American people, and to their elected officials, about the bombing of Cambodia was, it was said at first, national security. But that made no sense. Since the enemy knew, and certainly the Cambodian people who were being bombed would know, Americans were the only people it was being kept secret from. It was then that the entire logic advanced a step, and the circle closed. Sihanouk, the administration said, had invited or acquiesced in the bombing of Cambodia. In order that he could conceal this complicity from his own people, our administration had to keep it secret, too, from ours. It is the logical substructure that matters here. A pact can be arrived at, secretly and therefore deniably, between our leaders and theirs, which entails the killing of their people, in their own country, in their own ignorance of their leader's consent; and which entails the loss of our pilots' lives, in their country, without our knowledge of our leader's consent. That logic requires only the addition of money, money contributed by South Vietnamese officials to an American President, to explain why peace was not quite at hand in October 1972.

If one accepts, for a moment, the proposition that the awful secret that underlay the Nixon administration was money, from that source and for that reason, there is the question of what would have happened to the money, and how the former President could reach it now. John Wilson, the attorney for Haldeman and Ehrlichman, was the lawyer who, more than twenty years ago, won the major settlement which left the secrecy of Swiss bank accounts inviolable, even if—as in the case of the German investors in I. G. Farben, which became the American company General Aniline—the depositors in those accounts were likely to be former Nazis, who were precluded from access to their investments, under American law. At secret foreign bank accounts, the trail always ends. As for how Nixon could reach the money, however, there are several possibilities. There is, for instance, Rabbi Korff.

Rabbi Korff did not even enter the story until July 1973, when he took out a $5,000 ad in the New York Times in the name of the National Citizens Committee for Fairness to the President. A genuine friend of Nixon's since then, and truly committed to the former President's vindication, Rabbi Korff has been an unusual figure all along. Every few months, Korff holds a press conference to announce that the contributions he has been receiving from all over the country (for what has now become the United States Citizens' Congress and the President Nixon Justice Fund) are great, but not sufficient to cover the former President's legal fees. Then, he journeys to San Clemente, to report on the former President's frame of mind. It stands to reason that, although there may be contributions every time the rabbi calls a news conference (among the largest of them are those of the Dewitt Wallaces of Reader's Digest, and strangely enough, those of Rabbi Korff himself, who is paid a salary by the committee, from which he contributes to the fund), citizens are not racing to send in their checks for the former President's defense. Then one remembers that the argument for those contributions—compassion, *legal fees*—precisely duplicates the cover story for payments to the Watergate burglars. It may be coincidental. It is just a cast of mind.

Whatever else is true, it is clear that Rabbi Korff has access to money, and both the opportunity and the explanation for conveying it to the former President. Korff's background has always been international, not to say swashbuckling. In the early forties, he was, he says, raising money to buy passports in Paraguay for Jewish inmates of Nazi camps and, by means of contacts in Switzerland, paying money to Himmler to get those prisoners out. There follows a period in which, Korff says, he spent a lot of time abroad, raising money for the Stern Gang and the Irgun. When one asks raising money from *whom*, the rabbi becomes vague and laughs. In the fifties and sixties, Korff actually had a congregation, a small one, and wrote a lot of speeches, he says, for Democratic congressmen. He now travels a lot abroad. And it proves, of course, nothing more than that the former President has got a loyal, well-traveled, fund-raising friend, whose declared source of funds—citizens sending in a dollar here, a dollar there—would not amount to much or make much sense. It has also been probable from the first that those "loans" from Robert Abplanalp and Bebe Rebozo were never loans in any normal sense. They were not meant to be paid back. Nor were they gifts. What seems clear if one pursues the records and this line of reasoning is that the money Nixon's friends have "loaned" him is in fact his own, which he cannot, for one reason and another, reach any other way.

But the story, the inference really, is not concerned with now—but with the fall of 1972, in Washington and South Vietnam. As for who would know, the South Vietnamese, of course; but they have their own foreign accounts, and no one would believe them anyway. As for who else—all those international money-raisers, Stans, Kalmbach, Connally, perhaps. And Haig. At about the time of the Nixon pardon, President Ford kept making decisions, and then reversing them, about whether or not former President Nixon would have access to his own presidential papers; in the end, Ford let only one set of the presidential papers leave the White House: the ones belonging to Alexander Haig.

As for Nixon himself, he would, I suppose, have managed to think that he made such a deal on patriotic grounds, in the interests of the free world. And it is not so bad to have been paid to do what one might have done out of conviction anyway. Except for this: that he was President of the United States. And that unlike Watergate, unlike Rebozo, or Hughes, or the CIA, or any previous administration in our history, such a bribe and the taking of it would have cost not just the American taxpayer's money but his sons. And if the South Vietnamese government was bribing an American President, with American money, to keep our investment and our boys there any longer than was necessary, it is not to be borne. And that's what I think they did. Like the underlying thesis of Moses and monotheism, the underlying proposition is what we have all, somehow, shared all along. It explains why all the many volumes produced by the inquiry, as Congressman Wiggins correctly pointed out, don't contain enough of a case to fill a single pamphlet. It explains why, in spite of Nixon's departure, nothing was resolved, or laid to rest. The impeachment inquiry did what it could, and the President was removed. But we were, I think, of legal and political necessity, at the tip of the wrong iceberg. The story that required the end of the Nixon presidency, I think, was not Watergate—or even "other high Crimes and Misdemeanors." It was Treason and Bribery. I don't know what follows from it. I think it is the bottom line. It has brought a disorientation beyond reckoning. People died for it. We are going to have to live, I think, with that.

—1976

REFLECTIONS ON POLITICAL SCANDAL

The complete history of these proceedings cannot be written, for the end is not yet; indeed, such a history probably never will be written.... It was something new to see a knot of adventurers, men of broken fortune, without character and without credit, possess themselves of an artery of commerce ... and make levies upon it, not only for their own emolument, but, through it, upon the whole business of a nation.

... No people can afford to glance at these things in the columns of the daily press, and then dismiss them from memory. For Americans they involve many questions;—they touch very nearly the foundations of common truth and honesty without which that healthy public opinion cannot exist which is the life's breath of our whole political system.

—CHARLES FRANCIS ADAMS, JR.
A Chapter of Erie (1871)

I.

When too many scandals have gone on for too long, uninterrupted and inadequately investigated, they tend to merge. What began as isolated instances of corruption grow toward each other and finally interlock. The nursing home operators, and private garbage collectors, and parking lot owners, and film industry executives, and cable television interests, and vending machine distributors, and recording companies, and casino operators, the Teamsters, the Mafia, and defense contractors, and finally the investigative agencies of government and elected officials up to the highest level begin to have in common not just a general corruption but joint ventures and even personnel.

That is an extremely dangerous moment in public life. It is almost impossible to understand. People with an abstract turn of mind adopt conspiracy theories—when the problem is not a conspiracy but some other link. Investigative reporters, meanwhile, find sources, gather facts. There is a lot of news. But the meaning, the most obvious inferences, in a time of high scandal, are lost in a deluge of trivially depressing information.

The "artery of commerce" to which Charles Francis Adams referred was, of course, the Erie Railway. The reason he and his brother Henry could set forth so convincingly, in A *Chapter of Erie*, the threat which the railroad and gold scandals of the 1860s posed to "our whole political system" was that they understood, perhaps more clearly than any other muckrakers in our history, what the particular high scandal of their time meant. It was not a matter of daily facts and revelations, the sums of money, the ranks of the corrupted; or even of dimension, the size of illegal transactions, the buying of judges to declare them legal and then of legislators to procure the law itself.

What the Adams brothers had, at the end of their investigation, was both a scoop (or, rather, a grand accumulation of scoops) and an intellectual perception of its meaning: The system was threatened by that new entity, the corporation—not just trivially, in that officials could be bought, but fundamentally, in that the general public, "the delight and prey of Wall Street," was tempted by and even implicated in the new corruption. The ordinary citizen, the voter, in his capacity as small investor, could delude himself that "his" corporation was being managed in his interest. Drawn, a bit guiltily, by "the fascination of amassing wealth without labour," he was at best numbed by evidence of apparently universal scandal (with investigators either incompetent or, in their turn, corrupted) to the point where he wanted to hear no more about it; at worst, he thought he had part of the action.

What the Adams brothers feared never quite happened; the republic survived its corporate threat. But that threat had all the elements—in particular, the collaboration of the morally and intellectually disoriented victim—which we have recognized, since Hannah Arendt, as pre-totalitarian. The threat recurs, in other times, in other forms. How close, after all, is the analogy between the present member of any notoriously corrupt union and the Adams brothers' small investor? Every Teamster has for decades had reason to know that his leaders are not only in some remote way criminal, they are stealing his pension. Still, it is "his" union—in precisely the sense in which the robber barons' railroads were the small investor's corporation.

We were singularly unprepared for these times: From World War II until 1959, most of us were taught and accustomed to believe that our public officials, and our neighbors for that matter, were honest—if not in the minutest transactions of their daily lives, at least in general. Certainly, we believed that they lived within the law. Most ideologues, of course, never believed it. They believed the contrary—but ideologues do not really figure in this discussion. They "knew" that the entire system was corrupt. Although it could be argued that events have proved them "right," they were not right in any sense that has to do with investigated and reported fact. What they "knew" was ideology. One result of the division between those who knew doctrinally and those who took their information from the study of events has been an odd division in the expository writing of our time—between professional reporters, uncoverers of news, almost professionally disinclined to think; and generalizers, writers of think pieces, who rarely do investigative reporting of their own and who are often precluded, by an ideological commitment, from doing much real thinking either. The result is a general erosion of the capacity to understand what's going on.

In 1959, we had Charles Van Doren. What Sputnik had done to the country's confidence in its know-how, the quiz show scandals seemed to do to its sense that the world was an honest place. The absurdity of the shock was an indication not only of how unprepared we were to gauge the importance of scandal of any kind but also of a peculiarly complicated hypocrisy. It was of no conceivable significance that a television program based on a proposition as disgusting as that which underlay *The $64,000 Question* should turn out to be fake. But the disillusion was intense and it was national. The "fascination of amassing wealth without labour" was succeeded by a pious recoil out of all proportion to the triviality of its source.

In our own time, it is particularly difficult to distinguish between proliferating, demoralizing hanky-panky, no matter how widespread and apparently outrageous, and high scandal in which the entire system is at stake. It is news, but it probably does not much matter, if a lot of people, at taxpayers' expense, take illegal free rides on airplanes. It may not even matter much if Alexander Haig (as he did in 1975) sends for his *dog* with the taxpayers' airplane. What does matter is that Alexander Haig is still, or that he ever was, commander of NATO. The mass of trivially depressing information (and, in this case, the remarkable ability of the man to ingratiate himself with, among others, reporters) has obscured a truth of some significance. The end, as the Adams brothers would say, is not yet.

When there exist what appear to be high, endlessly interlocking scandals, you try to find a self-evident proposition and begin. To an early question: Who is behind it? there is always a likely answer: Whoever had most to gain. By that standard, or with that approach, it has been clear since shortly after President Nixon's resignation that there had to be two major scandals, which threatened, and which still threaten, the system as a whole. The first one is in origin foreign. It consists in the bribing of American officials by governments of other nations—routinely, but most dangerously in matters of defense.

The little, newsworthy scandal, of the sort we are used to, involves the reverse: an American, perhaps a CIA officer, buying a Japanese politician or an Italian Social Democrat. But there can no longer be any question that, while we were preoccupied with our own interventions abroad, a tide had long started to run the other way. The Koreans have been buying our presence, the Taiwanese our backing, the Iranians (and, in all probability, any other nations that can afford it) our training and weapons—not just outright but with bribes and kickbacks to defense contractors and officials of government.

This phenomenon has several, by no means minor, confusing consequences. One is the situation which arises when a legislator is bribed to do what he would have done in good conscience anyway. The backlash which results when such a bribe has been discovered can actually prevent the execution of sound policy. If, for example, we ought to be in South Korea, it is now quite possible that we will get out of there, not because we should but because we have been bribed to stay. That is when the "foundations of truth and honesty" have been shaken almost beyond repair.

A second confusing consequence is this: When we speak of "other nations that can afford" bribery, we must now include poor nations that we subsidize. The result is that bribes and kickbacks to American contractors and officials are now, inevitably, drawn from the huge sums of American taxpayers' money that this country spends abroad for other purposes. It is news, but it does not much matter, if Lockheed, and each of the other companies that did so, bribes foreign officials, routinely, to buy equipment in preference to a competitor's. The laws now under consideration to prevent this, if there is any way to enforce them, will just make selling abroad a bit cheaper and straighter—and, incidentally, prevent employees from stealing the untraceable cash set aside for these bribes. What does matter is again the reversal of the pattern to which we are accustomed. The money now flows toward us. It is a variation on an old isolationist theme. The threat is not subversion by foreign doctrines, or being overrun by foreign populations, but being bought by foreign governments with money paid illegally to our officials—money which is frequently, in origin, our own.

And it has been apparent, since shortly after Nixon's resignation, that the high scandal that really underlay his administration, and required his removal from office, was the existence of precisely this pattern in Vietnam. That is: the South Vietnamese for a time were using part of the huge sums we spent there to buy our presence, our backing, our training, our weapons, and also, since it was war—and this has been the worst of it so far—our soldiers' lives.

By any inductive route, that is where you come out—and the evidence is everywhere: in the tapes, particularly in the February 28, 1973, reference to Johnson's suspicions, in 1968, that his opponents were using Anna Chennault to remind the South Vietnamese what they stood to gain by a Republican victory of that year; in the relative inattention, on those tapes, to Watergate itself except for protecting the ultimate sources of the cash (some of which, it turned out, in an appendix to the volumes of the Ervin Committee, had to be returned to an Asian "foreign national" by, as it happens, Mrs. Chennault);[1] in the derailing of the Patman Committee (which had traced kickbacks by South Vietnamese to Americans, through foreign banks, as early as 1968).[2]

When it became clear to what extent the scandal of the 1972 campaign was huge, secret, and illegal cash contributions, it should have stood to reason that the most likely illegal contributor to Nixon and his reelection would have been the one with the most to gain. Just before the election of 1972, and right after Henry Kissinger first negotiated a peace which was "at hand," the South Vietnamese government paid the Nixon administration (with what was after all American taxpayers' money) to have American taxpayers' sons fight on a few months, while the officials made their last deals, and stole their last money, and got out. And the only difference between this pattern in Vietnam and in all the other nations where its existence has, previously and subsequently, been disclosed is that no other country has paid kickbacks to have Americans kill and die abroad, in war. It may be that Nixon would have stayed on in Vietnam in good conscience anyway,[3] but if his administration was paid to do it—as it now seems certain that it was—that would be high scandal. It would also be, except by the strictest definition, treason and bribery. And it is the foreign scandal, of which the end is not yet.

II.

The second major scandal, the domestic one, linked in not entirely peripheral ways with the first, has to do with drugs. The "artery of commerce" with which Edward Jay Epstein deals, in *Agency of Fear,* is the illegal narcotics trade. In the Adams tradition, Epstein uncovers facts and draws inferences. The ways in which he approaches his subject are basically two: the first, historical, an account of this domestic scandal and the part it played in bringing the Nixon administration down; the other, in some ways more important, methodological—it consists simultaneously of an account of the way Epstein proceeded and an attack on many of the assumptions which underlie what there is of investigative reporting in our time.

Epstein's historical thesis is this: that the Nixon administration was engaged in trying to centralize its power, in what was essentially a coup d'état; that bureaucracies are, by nature, resistant to such centralization; that Nixon, having tried and failed to take over the investigative agencies (the FBI, the CIA, the investigative arms of the IRS, the Justice Department, Treasury, et al.), tried to create a new agency, under White House control, with personnel drawn from all the agencies he had failed to take over; that the pretext and the cover for what would be, in effect, Nixon's own secret police was, under various names and acronyms, a unit nominally dedicated to the eradication of illegal traffic in narcotic drugs.

Epstein concludes further that the plan was at least twice interrupted, by sheer historic chance. The publication of the Pentagon Papers, for example, not only usurped coverage of one day's important public-relations announcement in the antidrug campaign. It also diverted the attention of members of the new secret unit to Daniel Ellsberg, and to the general problem of keeping the secrets of government. The second historic chance was the discovery of the break-in at the Watergate. The regular Washington bureaucrats, Epstein says, having noticed that the burglars were members of the new force so threatening to their separate fiefdoms, saw their opportunity in what was essentially a coup of their own, and the agencies, in particular the CIA, systematically made sure that the link between the break-in and the White House would become known to the press.

In an earlier piece, Epstein had written of Mark Felt as one of the many informants within the FBI who passed information to reporters—with the limited aim of getting the White House to fire L. Patrick Gray (for not being able to keep the Bureau under control). In this book he says that Robert Foster Bennett, of Mullen and Company, was a major source for Woodward, in directing his attention away from the CIA and toward Charles Colson, who began to plant stories in return. There followed the battle, or the symphony of disclosures, with perhaps the most dangerous to Nixon being the release, by IRS officials to a Rhode Island newspaper, of the President's tax returns. While others have mentioned these sources, Epstein discerns a pattern and a plan: The bureaucrats thereby, with the willing but not fully conscious collaboration of the press, foiled Nixon's coup d'état and brought him down.

There are many arguable elements in this theory and, as is almost inevitable when a journalist is investigating idiosyncratically and virtually alone, there are certain factual inaccuracies as well. But in its main features—the drug unit as a cover for a new secret police, and the determination of the established agencies, through judicious use of the press, to reverse the coup—the theory is right. It is partly through the integrity with which Epstein discloses his own journalistic method that certain inaccuracies along the way are not only revealed but also (and this is the strength of the method) accounted for. Epstein, as a matter of professional and ethical policy, reveals who his sources are. The reasons for this, and the result, are of immeasurable importance to anyone who takes a serious interest in investigative reporting, or in the recent scandals themselves.

To stay, for a moment, however, with the secret unit and the problem of drugs. It would take an ideologist of the wildest sort to come up with an anticapitalist satire which would reflect, quite accurately, the present situation of narcotics and the law. Take a substance which is, in nature, cheap, abundant, and addictive. Its addictive properties make it a seller's dream; its only drawback is its easy availability. There is no profit in it. Pass against the selling, production, cultivation, consumption, or possession of that substance the most stringent laws. Instantly, by virtue of being illegal, the substance becomes rare and expensive. The law itself has created a situation in which there is an enormous, in fact incalculable, profit to be made from getting people, children for example, who would otherwise have no reason even to consider narcotics, hooked.

Even the cigarette manufacturers, anomalous as their situation is— namely, that they make their profit from a substance that is addictive, with the drawback that it kills—are in a very different position. It is *incidental* to the production of cigarettes that they are lethal; manufacturers, preferring longer-lived addicted customers, would presumably prefer that the product were safe. It is of the *essence* of the narcotics traffic that it be criminal—or there would be no profit in it. There is no point in enumerating the interests—some vicious, some self-serving, some misguided, some cowardly, some imbecile—which coincide (not conspire) to perpetuate this unique travesty. But there it is. And the profits are such that as soon as you put someone in the business of suppressing narcotics traffic, you can be almost certain that he will engage in it. As soon as the CIA, for instance, somehow got international drug enforcement as part of its mandate, it became a major runner of drugs. The most unlikely and unholy alliances in this country have been created by the narcotics laws.

To keep the substance illegal, it is necessary to exacerbate, from time to time, the public's fear of it. On the history of the drug laws in this country, and on the subsequent history of their enforcement and public relations, Epstein goes a little off. His focus is on fear of the addict. He links this fear to Prohibition, when specters of a vampire alcoholic were succeeded, in the mind of an obscure fanatic called Richmond Hobson, by specters of a vampire dope fiend. He traces the Nixon administration's exploitation of drugs as a law-and-order issue to a panic, artificially and deviously generated for political reasons by Governor Rockefeller in New York.

But the drug laws arose, not out of Prohibition or from fear of addicts but independently, in reaction to unscrupulous manufacturers of nostrums and patent medicines, who resisted truth in labeling. Many babies died when the nostrums their mothers gave them for colic turned out to be opium. Women who took nostrums for a variety of feminine complaints became addicts in due course. By 1906, the law did require that nostrums containing opiates say so on the label. Prescriptions for narcotic drugs were required by 1914. While the forces behind this legislation were mixed, the only thing they had in common with the sponsors of Prohibition was a battle with the whiskey interests—not over whiskey itself, however, but again over truth in labeling. Distillers were mixing dyes with cheap alcohol and calling the product whiskey. The pure food and drug people wanted the labels right.

As for the fear of addiction and addicts, Nixon did not learn from Rockefeller how to exploit it—and Rockefeller himself did not contrive to create it. By the 1960s, the improbable alliance of drug interests, and the number of young people already alienated by the law itself, made fears for one's children, for example, well-grounded and real. But the *statistics* regarding narcotics were neither well-grounded nor real. And this is where Epstein's particular genius as a reporter takes over. He finds that initial, self-evident proposition, and follows it through to the truth at the end:

> I first became interested in the credibility of the crime estimates reported in the press when William Whitworth, an editor at *The New Yorker* magazine, suggested that *ex-addicts in treatment centers had a strong incentive to exaggerate the size of their habit, and that the operators of these treatment centers had no incentive to dispute their claims* [italics added].

Of course, the minute you see that, you see it is true. From there, Epstein went on to the realization that narcotics investigators had a strong incentive to exaggerate the street value of drugs recovered in any given raid, and that newspaper police reporters had no incentive to dispute their claims. Epstein discovered that if estimates of how much the population of addicts had to steal to support their habit were accurate, they would have to be stealing a great part of the gross national product. And finally, from his own research, and from studies by groups with no institutional interest in exaggerating the dimensions of the problem, Epstein found that nearly all statistics having to do with the number of addicts in this country, and the size of their habits, and their propensity to commit crimes, and whether that propensity grew out of their habit or preceded it, and whether that propensity was decreased, increased, or modified by any known form of treatment; and even whether the rates of crime or drug addiction were in any way affected by any incident or program in the history of law enforcement—in short, nearly every statistic having to do with drug addiction and the law—proved, upon examination, false.

That's quite a scoop. Epstein documents it well. In effect, the drug problem, with the law as it is, is insoluble—although not increasing, as other fabricated statistics would indicate. Nearly everyone who has anything to do with the problem, or the attempted solutions of it, lies—profits and lies. One would not have expected, for example, a public-relations firm in the employ of New York methadone treatment centers to try to discredit a disinterested investigator. One would not have expected the facts to be that methadone is not, as claimed, incompatible with heroin; that it does not, as claimed, reduce crime but rather increases all crimes—with the exception (as might be expected) of such nonviolent crimes as prostitution—directly related to supporting a habit in heroin. One would not expect methadone interests, when confronted with these propositions, to concede that they are true, but to add (in retreating to what Epstein calls the "soft argument") that the claims, though false, were valuable—in "calling attention to the problem," and in drawing the addict into a "social context," namely the treatment center.

Doubtless, *Agency of Fear* exaggerates, although I don't know exactly where. The book presents a problem which, while it is not uniquely posed by Epstein's writing, occurs there with exceptional force. It is the problem of the writer on subjects about which nearly everyone already has a strong opinion—who, almost by virtue of these subjects, either enlists or antagonizes people to the point where they are incapable of reading what he says. Epstein's first book, *Inquest*, was a study of the Warren Commission's investigation of the assassination of President Kennedy. It was solid and meticulous, and it drew the only conclusion it was possible to draw: that the Warren Commission had been insufficiently diligent and thorough in its work. The book was at pains responsibly to ward off what was sure to be a herd of conspiracy sensationalists, charlatans, and profiteers. What we got was a best-seller by Mark Lane.

Epstein's second major piece of reporting concerned "genocide" being committed against the Black Panthers by the police. What Epstein showed was that, of the twenty-eight Panthers reported by the Panthers' lawyer (and uncritically accepted by the press) as having been victims of this campaign, eighteen were either not killed or not Panthers, six of the remaining ten were killed by seriously wounded policemen who had no way of knowing their targets were Panthers, and only two (Fred Hampton and Mark Clark) were unarguably killed in the course of a deliberate anti-Panther raid by the police. Now, while two, or even four, such killings are serious, two or four is neither twenty-eight nor genocide. Epstein's report, moderate in tone, said no more than that. It created, however, an enormous animus—professional, among reporters who felt themselves (in view of deadlines, and so forth) unfairly criticized; and political, among people who seemed to regard the piece as an attack upon the Panthers, or upon the Left. Just to mention the piece was to set off an ideological player piano of beliefs—which would play its program to the end, invulnerable to an actual reading of the piece itself, and assuming that you were just another player piano. There seemed, during the late sixties, few people inclined toward mixed or moderate views.

The trouble with having written such a piece, or with being the sort of writer who would write one (not a crotchety Mencken type, or a humorist or stylist; not a Buchanan, whose talentless sarcasms have their own allies and claques, or a polemicist in any recognized tradition), is that the writer may begin to go a little wild himself, stating his own propositions in the most extreme form, generating new animus, in a kind of reciprocated baiting. For the first time, the writer starts unnecessarily to undermine his argument, by making errors. To take but one example: In trying to show that it is prosecutors, with their subpoena power, and not reporters who unravel cases, Epstein writes as follows:

The revelations of the operations of the Plumbers and the break-in of Dr. Fielding's office did not come from enterprising newsmen (although this is commonly misstated in the press); they came from John Dean . . . who provided this information to federal prosecutors in 1973 in return for a promise of lenient treatment. The prosecutors provided this information to Attorney General Elliot Richardson, who transmitted it to Judge Matt Byrne . . . who in turn revealed it to the press.

Now, there are a lot of things wrong with that passage and its underlying propositions. The key inaccuracy, however, which looks so small it could be anybody's oversight, is that the attorney general in question was not Elliot Richardson but Richard Kleindienst. And with this point, the sentence, the passage, the thought, and a section of the book unravel. Because the federal prosecutors "provided this information" not to Richardson but to Henry Petersen, who relayed it to both the President and the attorney general. And none of these three men did anything so simple as what is implied by "who transmitted it to Judge Matt Byrne." They held it up, for weeks. They would have held it up forever, had it not been for the certainty that John Dean was going to reveal it, at the Ervin Committee hearings, on national television.

Nor was Judge Byrne's role in the matter as simple as "who in turn revealed it to the press" implies. It was the press, a reporter for the Washington *Star* in fact, who, in talking with a gardener at San Clemente, discovered the recent visit there of Judge Byrne. That discovery led in turn to disclosure of the improper offer to Judge Byrne, in the middle of the Ellsberg trial, of the FBI directorship. The disclosure also, incidentally, revealed the judge's own improper failure to refuse to entertain such an offer, or to mention earlier in the trial that the offer had been made. And the federal prosecutors—well, the prosecutors did not, as Epstein implies, elicit the information from Dean in return for an offer of leniency. They did not elicit the information at all. Dean's attorney, Charles Shaffer, had practically to spell out for them that they would be taking part in an obstruction of justice themselves if they did not pass the information on.

These prosecutors, like everyone else high up at the Justice Department, had careers to think about. Attorney General Richard Kleindienst had, after all, been told by Gordon Liddy, at Burning Tree golf course, *on the morning after the Watergate break-in,* whose men the Watergate burglars were. The attorney general, whose portrait now hangs on the wall of the Justice Department, while he explains his close friendships with Teamsters and his most recent deals with their pension fund, turned Liddy away.

That was the pattern. Almost without exception, everyone in the Nixon administration charged with investigation was concerned not with the primary event (e.g., a break-in), which they preferred not to know about, or else already knew about too well, but with the secondary problem—namely who else knew, and how to conceal or distort the information to keep it from reaching the public or the press.

The Watergate federal prosecutors got their promotions. But not on account of any information they elicited from John Dean. And in this matter of the government's own role in the investigation of itself, in errors of detail and in his determination to point out the limitations of the press, Epstein is led again and again unnecessarily to oversimplify his broader argument. Because if the press did not "solve" Watergate, neither did the agencies—which were not nearly as resistant to Nixon's takeover as Epstein believes. Two attorney generals, after all, were directly involved in the burglary, Mitchell in planning it, Kleindienst, at least from that early moment at Burning Tree, in covering it up. The head of the CIA and the acting head of the FBI were in it thoroughly—Richard Helms in helping to cause a crucial delay in the FBI's tracing of the foreign checks; L. Patrick Gray in agreeing to "deep six" evidence, which he then held on to for several months—on account, he says, of moral doubts, but more probably to have something with which to put pressure on the administration to continue to support him for the permanent directorship.

As for the Treasury Department and the IRS, they were neither so pure and intransigent, or even so sluggish, in yielding to the White House as they have managed to appear. Edward Morgan, a lawyer who was an assistant to Egil Krogh of the secret police/drug unit, went on to prepare Nixon's fraudulent tax returns, and ultimately went to jail—but not before he had been appointed assistant secretary for enforcement at Treasury.

As for the IRS, and President Nixon's tax returns, this may be the moment to introduce the question of a contemporary hypocrisy: a pervasive, partly deliberate misunderstanding of the presidency, and of the nature of sycophancy, so profound that it is becoming a kind of national scandal in itself. What it means to be President of the United States, what it means to work for such a man, how his wishes are carried out and are expressed—all this has been romantically obscured by the fact that one recent President was an apparently benign and fatherly returning war hero, another an attractive and promising figure tragically assassinated in the prime of life. The place occupied in the imagination by these two has obscured not just any realistic view of what they were and did but a blunt, prosaic fact: that to be President of the United States is, at the very least, to be obeyed more readily than most men in the carrying out of tawdry schemes—grand schemes, but tawdry schemes as well—by which others might be tempted, but which they are not equipped, by the merest intimation of a wish, to get subordinates to execute.

The whole search for "the smoking pistol," in the Watergate scandal, then, was necessarily a sanctimonious charade—as is the search for any "link" between a modern President and the major acts of his subordinates. The "link," whether to a plan to assassinate a dictator, or to a break-in into political offices, or to the cover-up of such a break-in, or to the drawing up of fraudulent tax returns, lies in the nature of the presidency. The "smoking pistol" (since nobody sits down, writes "We're going to commit an obstruction of justice now," and signs his name) is presumptively, in every case, the President's will. To return, then, to the IRS. While it would have been, under these circumstances, if not unreasonable, at least too harsh, to expect the IRS to inspect to any depth at all the tax returns of an incumbent President, the IRS has been auditing, for example, mine, for several years. It would not seem as clear as it does that the end is not quite yet if the former President's tax returns had been audited since his return to private life.

The point is that the agencies did yield to President Nixon, as of course they must, up to a point. And while it may have been their incompetencies and their leaks that ultimately brought him down, it was also their red wigs, their cameras, their pocket litter, and their personnel that for so long helped him out. What we had for a time at the heart of government was not what Ron Ziegler, in the tapes, so memorably called a Rashomon situation but a scenario from an earlier work. In Chesterton's *The Man Who Was Thursday*, the hero is a man who has been recruited as a police agent in a group of seven anarchists, each of whom has adopted the name of a day of the week. At meeting after meeting, a member of the group is exposed as such an agent. As Friday, Wednesday, and several others are discovered, Thursday fears each time that it is he who has been found out. By the end of the book, it turns out that every single anarchist was really a police agent in disguise. It is, in real life, normal for police and outlaws to be mutually dependent and to share an interest—as prison guards require, for their continued employment, the continued existence of prisoners, and therefore, of crimes. But when they share an *identity*, when the enforcers of narcotics laws are the sellers of narcotics, when the cops are the robbers, and the investigators the coverers-up, the foundations of common truth and honesty are shattered altogether, and society requires a subtle (and lucky) combination of forces to dig itself out.

III.

Oddly enough, or, rather, not at all oddly, Epstein's journalistic method and his argument for that method provide the corrective for any errors of fact or impression he may make along the way. The reason the heads of the agencies appear to him to have been the overturners of the Nixon coup, the reason Kleindienst, Petersen, Silbert, Acree, Krogh, Rossides, and others appear to him men alternately of naïveté and rectitude, is that these were the men who talked to him. They were his sources; and Epstein is meticulous and bold enough to name them, so that we can allow for (and sometimes discount) what he says and what they say. The reason Rockefeller is cast as the demon behind Nixon's law-and-order rhetoric is that Patrick Buchanan, Nixon's speechwriter, persuaded Epstein that he was. The reason Epstein traces to that obscure fanatic, Captain Hobson, and to Prohibition, a contemporary fear of drug addicts is that a colleague, an "offbeat sociologist" at the Drug Abuse Council (from which Epstein subsequently received a fellowship), had collected Hobson's papers and assured Epstein that he "could trace any and all present associations about drug abuse" back to him.

Now, Epstein may be faulted for having accepted these assurances uncritically, or for having fallen under the charm and influence of his sources—but that is precisely why his methodology is right, and as important as it is. Because it is impossible to read Epstein's book, and to give serious consideration to contemporary journalism and recent history (in particular, Watergate), without coming to the conclusion that it should, with the rarest and most well-defined exceptions, be the custom—a point of professionalism and of honor—for a journalist to name his source.

Before addressing this conclusion directly, however, and simply for the sake of calling things by their proper names, we might as well get rid anyway of the journalistic use of that word "source." What is in question are not *sources*—with the whole range of scholarly and scientific associations the word brings to mind. What is meant are now simply unnamed informers—and the kinship is, of course, with spies. The reason this point matters is that, with all the valid and legitimate uses of confidentiality by major reporters in recent years, there has been an erosion of the vocabulary on which journalism itself is based. A whole lexicon of euphemisms, metaphors, and misnomers has slipped into investigative reporting from, of all places, the espionage or—in just such a euphemism—the "intelligence" agencies of government.

The strange uses of "source," "leak," "sensitive," "conduit," "intelligence," "intelligence community," and so on actually blur what the subject of investigation is. Unconscious, outright misnamings—KCIA, for example, for what is simply an instrumentality for passing bribes—begin to blur backward, changing the sense, for example, of what the main purpose of our own CIA is meant to be. When code words are added, as in "highly placed source," to indicate who the source is, the professional lapse is compounded. The technique resembles, and is perhaps derived from, the old-style gossip column—where the unnamed characters in, for example, Earl Wilson's "Secret Stuff," tease the ordinary good-faith reader while they signal only to the cognoscenti in a debased, knowing complicity.

To return, then, to the problem of the naming of informants. Since at least Watergate, it has been evident that in any serious scandal, to the questions Who is behind it? and Who has the most to gain? we must add another, Who wanted it known? This question posed itself, more or less insistently, when, from all directions, we learned that the myths we had been brought up on, concerning detectives, prosecutors, G-men, re-porters, political investigators of any kind—tirelessly pounding the pave-ments, badgering witnesses, finding clues, telephoning, nagging their way to a last clue, inference, and resolution of the case—had almost no basis in reality. Facts under investigation normally become known because somebody wants them known or has some reason to tell. We find that, far from inexorably closing in, compiling clues and information, inves-tigators not only require informers, they often resist, with the most in-credible obtuseness, what has been told, brought, confessed, and virtually proved to them.

Kleindienst, in rebuffing Liddy, and all the Watergate figures turning away information were a special case, in that the higher up the inves-tigator, the deeper his involvement in the crimes. But in investigations of all kinds, criminal and political, there is a tendency actively to resist what the investigator is being told. This may result from simple bungling, lack of diligence, or quite often, since the same *names*—the same Team-sters, crooks, attorneys, interests, gangsters, crooners—appear so often on every side, there may even be a fear that the investigation will lead to oneself or to a friend. At the same time, the mystique of "clues," of real evidence, and of expert testimony has been crumbling. Handwriting ex-perts managed to authenticate as the signature of Howard Hughes the scrawl of Mrs. Clifford Irving. In a recent case in Connecticut a lie detector showed clearly and wrongly that a young man had murdered his mother; the state police resolutely refused to notice, or to draw any in-ference from, somebody else's bloody fingerprint at the murder scene. The police composite sketches of Son of Sam resembled him in no re-spect whatever. From the corner burglary to political scandals examined by commissions at the highest level, this has been an era of failed in-vestigations.

As for witnesses—test after test establishes that they are unreliable in describing, fundamentally and in detail, what they saw moments ago; their accuracy declines with time. Yet an investigative reporter's primary resource is the informing witness. This informant may be honorably con-cerned with truth; or he may have a less than honorable stake in what-ever version of the facts he passes on; or he may, like some advertiser, be testing as fact what is the trial run of a plan; or he may be lying. Whichever it is, the unattributed statement, or the unnamed source, or the blind quote, has spread through journalism. It has begun to lose its value altogether and to become a positive, almost insuperable obstacle to investigation of all kinds.

The situation is now as follows: Something is news, and may be reported as such, if somebody told it to a reporter; the bit of news is regarded as more solid if someone else confirms it—that is, if two people told it to a reporter. These people may be anonymous, and they may be liars, but if their story is not decisively controverted, the newspaper will stand by its reporter, who "stands by" his sources. There is, of course, no way to check an unattributed story at its source. Certainly, in stories where attribution would cause harm—for example, a serious reprisal—a reporter may justifiably conceal who told it to him. Some of the major stories of recent times, including the status of the war in Vietnam, were stories of this sort. But if the harm is merely embarrassment to the source, or the risk to the reporter that this particular informant, or other informants, will refuse in the future to confide in him, then the predicament is very delicate. Because we, the reporters, are suddenly in clandestine collusion with our informants. We are to that degree in each other's pockets; there is an element of corruption. And the *Man Who Was Thursday* situation comes to include the press.

Apart from this problem of, as it were, conspiring with unnamed informers, apart from the problem of the uncheckable word of the unnamable source, the reliance on such sources is turning journalists away from far more important, though less romanticized, sources of inquiry and of fact. The richest such source, with which the fewest reporters seem to bother, are documents already published—in particular documents published by the government itself. They are long, repetitious, unorganized, muddled by the investigators and compilers of them, but they (the Church Committee documents, or the House subcommittee hearings on *Reporting Requirements of the Bank Secrecy Act* come readily to mind) are full of scoop after scoop, practically untouched by the press—except for a superficial, rushed scrutiny on the day they appeared.

The obstacle to a constant and systematic study of such documents is no longer a matter of deadlines, either. The relative utility of informants, as opposed to documents, quite apart from questions of time or diligence, is reflected in three kinds of stories by the distinguished reporter Seymour Hersh. The first kind of story was the My Lai massacre—the tireless pursuit of the human source produced the optimal result. (In the end, in any case, the "sources" were named.) As successful, not in their content but in their political effect, were three long stories, again based on informants, about the CIA. The substance, though thin, triggered the Pike and Church Committee investigations. One of the main objects of investigative journalism, to trigger further investigation, was fulfilled.

Then, as diligently, Hersh spent months applying the same technique to get stories on Stanley Korshak and on Charles Bluhdorn—stories that said, at great length and in essence, that some people had, anonymously, compromising things to say about these men, and that both men had, at some time in their lives, and perhaps still, associated with disreputable people, or people said to be disreputable. It is a case in which "source" journalism could not really work.

A successful, completed piece of investigative reporting usually has one or more of the following effects. It results in (1) a change of personnel; (2) a change of program; (3) an indictment; (4) a saving of money; (5) an allocation of money; (6) a further investigation by the appropriate body (prosecutors, grand juries, legislators, the Church and Pike Committees) where journalism's resources end. Until, with "leaks" from the further investigation, they begin again. Under the rarest circumstances, however, is the understanding of a public situation much enhanced by what anonymous sources say.

Apart from those embedded in public documents—I. F. Stone, as far as I know, was the pioneer at wading through them, followed by too few others, including, however, of late, various reporters of the *New York Times*—the other stories that go uninvestigated, on account of the detective/source mystique, are the ones so obvious that you cannot fail to see them if you are not preoccupied with finding someone to tell you something and somebody else to confirm. Such a story was instantly apparent in something as trivial or significant as the publication of *Roots*. From the first, it was as obvious as the numbers of Americans who go abroad each year in search of some ancestral village, or even heraldic crest, that *Roots* could not, simply could not, be accurate. Practically everyone who thought about it knew it. The cultural phenomenon was that people wanted to believe—that a nation of immigrants, who often cannot with any certainty name their great-grandparents, should want so earnestly to think that this "oral history" was history at all.

This was "source" journalism at its nadir and its apogee. If there was someone (even, paradoxically, somebody nameless) to whom to attribute a story deemed newsworthy, the newspapers would run it. Countless, endless stories about *Roots* were run. But if there was a truth nearly as obvious as an equation, newsworthy as it might be, if it was not in the source convention, the newspapers would deem it speculation and pass it by. So it took another "source," a foreign journalist, to investigate and prove the obvious in detail—whereupon Alex Haley and his adherents retreated to what Epstein would call the "soft" position, namely that the book, though a fabrication, called attention to the problem, and thereby revealed a deeper "truth."

So there are two major kinds of stories that reporters under the spell of the source mystique may miss: the treasures buried in public documents, and the truths so obvious that no one could miss them who was not diverted by some disorientation or misapprehension in the process of investigation itself. There is a third kind of story, derived from the other two, which is most clearly vulnerable to Epstein's reasoning and attack. This is what might be called the Daniel Schorr phenomenon, in which the journalist, unwittingly and in fact contrary to his intention, is induced by the cleverness of his "sources" to close off a subject of investigation for good. In such a case, the journalism itself, in the most confusing way, becomes part of the story. In the Schorr case, it was in the obvious interest of only one party that the Pike Committee report on the CIA should be, prematurely and in its entirety, disclosed. That party was the CIA. The agency's likely object, which was reached to perfection, was to demonstrate that a congressional committee cannot keep a secret—and thereby assure that there would not be created any genuine committee of oversight into the activities of the CIA. And so it went. Congress lost itself in investigating where its own "leak" had come from. The oversight committee was lost as well.

The gist of the report itself was also lost somehow in the controversy over its publication. The otherwise inescapable conclusion to be derived from the report was that the failings of the CIA were basically two: not predominantly violations of the rights of American citizens, or even unjustified intervention in the affairs of foreign nations, but incompetence as an espionage agency and financial impropriety as well. Those were two solid and basic scandals. Schorr inadvertently became the reporter to obscure them. In his refusal to disclose his sources, in his insistence on his right and responsibility to make the report public, in short, in his journalistic piety, he was thoroughly had. The productive line of inquiry came to an end.

A similar gambit was tried with Hersh, in the matter of the Glomar Explorer. Most reporters took the story from an odd side—namely, that when Hersh and the New York Times were asked, on the grounds of national security, to suppress the story, they agreed to do so. But the more ominous transaction occurred much later on—when the CIA, as subsequently reported in the New York Times, decided the publication of the story was in its interest—again to demonstrate the inability of Congress to keep secrets and the irresponsibility of the working press. Suddenly, the relentless discoverer of the Agency's secrets became the inadvertent agent of its propaganda. It is this variant of the Schorr phenomenon (revealed in documents obtained under the Freedom of Information Act) which Epstein's method of disclosing and discussing his sources avoids.

Of course, the question of whether to divulge an informant's name will always be a matter of the reporter's judgment. Some reporters are best at inquiring of people; others at study and reflection. In the range of evidence, from rumor and intuition through document and tape, there is a lot of room. But, at present, the use of the blind quote and the unnamed source has become an unprofessional cover for various journalistic cut corners and evasions. There are the feature writers who return from abroad with a statement from an unnamed high foreign official— when the statement is, in reality, just the writer's own view, an act of ventriloquism attributed in space. There are respected reporters attributing statements to, say, a liberal senator from a New England state— either because they can't remember quite who said it, or can't remember exactly what he did say, or simply because they think he might prefer not to be quoted as having said it in that way. And then, of course, there exists in the weekly magazines, in their articles on "trends," a form of attribution, with a real name, which is so meaningless as to constitute a blind quote. That is, Mrs. Blue in Denver said, and Mrs. Gray in Portland said, and Mrs. Green in Billings said—and there appears to be, all over America, a trend. So there ought to be a rule, I think, not a legal rule obviously, but a matter of professional practice, that sources will be named, unless (1) to name them would cause a considerable harm, or (2) to name them would be, as in the case of Mrs. Green or Blue, a meaningless attribution.

Which returns us to the questions raised by Epstein's book. If one takes it, as I think one must, that Epstein's ratio of right (insight, scoop, whatever) to wrong (bias, error) is no worse than such a ratio for any investigative reporter of stature, then one of the most important elements of his story—and the element one requires to make the critical distinctions—is where he got it, and from whom. He is right that a drug unit was formed, into which vast sums, never properly accounted for, were sunk; and that that unit became, in effect, a private police force under the direct control of the Nixon White House.[4] He is right that what became known about Watergate could not have become known without disaffected and self-serving bureaucrats cooperating with the press. He overrates, on the other hand, the quality of honor in the former high officials who talked to him—as other journalists, in their turn, and in line with his theory, were taken in by the men (Haig, Hugh Sloan, and Fred Buzhardt to name but three at various levels) who talked to them.

But the end is not yet. With every book about the series of events called Watergate, it becomes clearer that the break-in, and its cover-up, though reprehensible, as a crime of state was trivial; and that nothing was or will be added to the story—except bits of color, solving nothing. We are left with our failures of investigation. The railroad scandals of the nineteenth century just somehow subsided. There is a vast new railroad scandal now, of course, in the liquidation of the Penn Central—but it's like the City University of New York scandal, and the Medicare scandal, and all the many other scandals. Nobody has the time or the way to begin to get to the bottom of them.

For a minute, by coincidence, in the Watergate, two immense scandals came together. The burglars who were caught there happened to have in their possession cash which could be traced, by way of foreign banks, to an Asian foreign national—which would have raised an immediate question of what was the nexus between the election, the money, and the war. The burglars happened to be members of a new unit nominally dedicated to the enforcement of the narcotics laws, but actually involved in espionage of various sorts. The burglars were also quite closely connected with the CIA, which had its own involvement in narcotics, and its own questionable foreign bank transactions—which might have raised

an immediate question: what was the nexus between the money, narcotics, and espionage? For a minute, everything stopped at the Watergate.

Then, everyone started covering his tracks in the direction most dangerous to him. A war of great covers and petty disclosures was waged in
the press. The higher scandals never quite made it into print. The casualty was Richard Nixon, with the silliest smoking pistol in the world:
a tape he hadn't really even lied about, exactly. In every respect a bizarre
and unsatisfying story. One underlying human thread, though, is greed—
for weapons, drugs, money. Perhaps the most important public documents, in the next few years, and the real locus for investigative reporting, will be the reports of any government committee of financial
oversight, as covered—for the first time in depth—in the business pages
of newspapers.

—1977

THE JUSTICES AND THE JOURNALISTS

Of all writing in this society, the writing of courts—in particular, the Supreme Court—has the most immediate powers and consequences. Men go to jail or are released, great corporate structures are dissolved or left intact, laws are upheld or overturned, men regulate their future conduct on the basis of what judges write. Most writing, of course, aspires to be or to appear original, to tell something new. This is true in scholarship and art. It is especially true, almost by definition, of journalism, where what is old, self-evident, or well-known is simply not the news. The writing of judges, however, aspires to just the opposite effect. Perhaps because of its unique powers, judicial writing rests very largely on citing precedents, on saying: What we say today is more or less what we have always said, or should have said; it's what our citizens have tacitly agreed; it's what the Constitution meant; it's obvious. Every Court decision clearly contains some new element, or there would be no need to make it. What creativity there is, however, goes mainly into saying why it ought to come as no surprise.

When serious investigative reporters confront the Court, there is thus a profound clash of aspirations. It is compounded, for Bob Woodward and Scott Armstrong in *The Brethren: Inside the Supreme Court,* by another problem. The Court, more than any other public institution, explains itself, identifies its sources. A dictator can say: This is the law because I say it is. A journalist can say: These are the facts and I need not tell who told me so. The Court says: This is the law as applied to facts ascertained in a public forum, and, under our system, we are obliged to tell you why. To attempt, as Woodward and Armstrong have done, to go behind the Court's explanations over a period of six terms (1969 to 1975), and to find insights, or even secrets, of any importance whatsoever is an enormously ambitious undertaking. There are intimations, as early as page one of their introduction, that the authors may not be ideally equipped for it.

"And because its members are not subject to periodic reelection, but are appointed for life," they write, "the Court is less disposed to allow its decision making to become public."

Now, however long you may study that sentence, and whether or not you are a lawyer, you will realize that the connection between its two facts—if they are facts, if there is a connection—cannot be "because." If there were a connection, it would more logically be "although." But there is no connection. And looked at more closely, the two facts linked by that "because" are not quite facts. It is true that all federal judges are normally and constitutionally appointed "for life." The Constitution just happens to phrase it "during good Behavior." This distinction might seem unimportant—were it not that the authors later devote pages to efforts made to impeach Justices Douglas and Fortas. There could have been no such efforts if Justices were so simply and unequivocally appointed not during good Behavior but for life. And, since the "decision making" of Justices is, in the most obvious sense, precisely what *is* public, the authors can be alluding only to the Justices'—and, now, the clerks'—reticence about what goes on in conference (where clerks are not present) or in chambers.

What the authors promise, however, and not just in their subtitle, "Inside the Supreme Court," is revelations per se, disclosure of secrets on a grand, even unprecedented scale. Their information, they claim, is "based on interviews with more than 200 people, including several Justices, more than 170 former law clerks, and several dozen former employees of the Court."

A question immediately suggests itself. The custom of protecting the identity of sources, in daily journalism at least, has become extremely widespread. I happen to believe that, except when actual, identifiable harm would result, to the source or to some other worthy cause or person, that practice can be unprofessional, a serious impediment to journalism of all kinds. It makes stories almost impossible to verify. It suppresses a major element of almost every investigative story: who wanted it known. But even if the identity of sources ought, almost invariably, to be protected, is there any tradition of reporting which requires that their *number* be protected as well? "More than 200 people," "several Justices," "more than 170 law clerks," "several dozen former employees." Well, how many? Two hundred and one people or 299? Three Justices, or five? What in the name of journalism would be compromised if we knew?

By the next page, we learn that the authors had "filled eight file drawers with thousands of pages of documents from the chambers of 11 of the 12 Justices" who served in the period under investigation. Then there is an apotheosis: "In *virtually every* instance [of what, they do not say] we had *at least one, usually two,* and *often three or four* reliable sources in the chambers of each Justice" (italics added). Apart from an occasion to smuggle that word "reliable" into what appears to be a quantitative statement, what can these vague enumerations mean? They mean that, at least as regards number, the authors prefer their own pointless secret (how many) and implications of massiveness to precise statements of simple fact.

A related preference appears in more trivial contexts: " 'No way,' Justice Rehnquist shot back, adding a mild obscenity for emphasis." By this point in the book, page 395, the authors have attributed to one Justice or another almost every obscenity I know. Are the identities of even "mild obscenities" now to be protected? Eight Justices were allegedly in the room when Justice Rehnquist said whatever it was, so there can be no question of needing to protect a source. But again, the authors prefer a knowing-sounding secret to a simple fact.

Most of the facts in this book, however, are far from simple. I have not meant to imply that this is a light or even unimportant work. It is only that, in this first, extended confrontation—at book length, outside an actual lawsuit—between the Court with its secrets, whatever they are, and investigative journalists with their secrets, such as they are, the journalists' own technique seems unexamined, and often very far from sound.

The Brethren, as it happens, contains no scandals and, although the authors clearly do not know it, no revelations that would astonish any lawyer or other student of the Court. Nonlawyers, I think, will find the book extremely hard to read. Since early in this century, most American law students have been taught in what is called the "case method" by textbooks called "Cases and Materials": essentially very heavy compilations of appellate decisions in Contracts, Torts, Procedure, and so on interspersed with some expository matter by the author/compiler, and even a few questions at the chapter ends. Whatever the pedagogic value of these textbooks, every law student would concede that they are among the world's most boring books. *The Brethren* is, in some ways, Woodward and Armstrong, "Cases and Materials on the Supreme Court." The cases, however, are not appellate judgments but journalists', not lawyers', summaries; and the materials are meditations—and an odd form of gossip that the authors seem to regard as investigative scoops.

The gossip most characteristically takes the form of a declarative sentence about a frame of mind. "Burger was furious." "Harlan was furious." "Brennan was furious." Innumerable paragraphs begin with the information that one Justice or another was "furious," "delighted," "upset," "especially upset," "exceedingly upset," "happy," "not happy," "also unhappy," "disturbed," "worried," "pleased," "not pleased," "both pleased and frightened," "glad," "troubled," "tormented," "elated," "despondent," "overjoyed," "shocked," "as usual more amused than shocked," "once again enraged," "crestfallen," "flabbergasted," and so forth.

Not only do the Justices ride these gusts of mood and feeling; all the more, the clerks. My favorite piece of American judicial history may be the news (page 326) that "Marshall's clerks were miffed."

The book also chronicles less subjective states of mind: realizations, for example; also vows. "Burger vowed to himself that he would grasp the reins of power immediately." Since the authors admit that Chief Justice Burger refused all contact with them, it is hard to know how they can write this quite so categorically. Justice Burger may, of course, have confided his vow to someone else, who then anonymously passed on the information that Justice Burger said he had vowed something to himself. But it is precisely the weakness of this kind of journalism that, because there is no way to check almost any of its assertions, the journalists themselves are sooner or later drawn into some piece of irresponsibility or idiocy; and one has to read every one of their assertions, from the most trivial to the most momentous, with the caveat "if true." Justice Burger "vows" again, 312 pages later, this time "to his clerks." The content of that vow: "that he would hold his ground." As for realizations. "When Nixon was informed of the investigation, he realized," they actually write, "that Fortas' actions were perhaps criminal and perhaps not."

In fairness to the authors, one ought to raise the possibility that the above sentence reflects editing by lawyers—not good lawyers certainly, not constitutional lawyers but lawyers who did not think Justice Fortas a "public figure" within the meaning of *New York Times* v. *Sullivan*, and who also thought, rather incredibly, that a libel, if libel there was, would evaporate with the addition of two "perhapses" and one "not." There arises, then, the question of *The Brethren* and the law—which the authors treat confidently, seriously, and at length. In small things and in large, with surprising frequency, they get it wrong. They don't seem to know, for example, the difference between appeal and certiorari, or even what an appeal is. This leads them to major misstatements in their first explanation of the steps by which the Court decides to take a case: "I. The decision to take the case requires that the Court note its jurisdiction or formally grant cert. Under the Court's procedures, the Justices have discretion in selecting which cases they will consider." The second sentence is plain wrong. The Justices have such discretion only when the issue is whether to grant cert; they do not have that discretion when a case comes to them on appeal. The first sentence, of course, does not mention appeal.

There are small matters: Justice Douglas, for example, confined to a hospital bed, asking another Justice to be his *"best friend* [authors' italics] and swear out a writ" to get him out. Now the ancient legal locution happens to be *"next* friend"; the only reason, apart from the knowingness implied by those italics, that this is not just a slip too inconsequential to mention is what it implies about the authors' ear for dialogue. In a journalistic enterprise that relies so heavily on a sort of telephone game—Justice, for example, who confides to clerk, who tells reporter— a demonstrably inaccurate ear may be a handicap. It casts doubt particularly on extended conversations that the authors reconstruct, unqualifiedly, in quotes.

As it happens, the way the Justices treat one another's illnesses, aging, reluctant retirements, death is a genuinely moving subtext of the book. The authors, and especially the clerks—because another serious subtext is the patronizing, self-infatuated trivialization, by recent clerks, of the relation of clerkship—have a tendency to reduce the Justices' concern with mortal fallibility to the news that Justice Douglas smelled, in conference, because he had become incontinent.

There are also large, quite complicated mistakes of law, which should startle and confound lawyer and nonlawyer alike. I'll mention just one, before returning to another sort of gossip, which, finally, constitutes the "Materials" of the book. "Moreover, Stewart felt trapped," they write, "by a phrase Rehnquist had convinced him to add to a 1971 opinion (*Roth v. Bd. of Regents*). Though it had seemed harmless to Stewart at the time, the phrase said that due process should be invoked only for rights specifically created by governments."

Roth v. Bd. of Regents came down in 1972, not 1971; but that is not the point. The point is that if Justice Stewart *had* ever written that "due process should be invoked only for rights specifically created by governments," he would have abrogated the Constitution—letter, spirit, and Preamble. Among the truths which the Framers held to be self-evident, the reader will remember, was that certain, emphatically not government-created rights—life, for instance, and liberty—are inalienable. If Justice Stewart had written a phrase to the effect that citizens could, without due process, be deprived of life or liberty, that would be news indeed. Of course, that is not what he wrote. What he wrote was that due process should not be invoked for *property* rights other than those created by government. That view is problematical, controversial, and probably, in spirit, unconstitutional enough. But nothing like what the authors say.

Their discussion of the abortion cases is also, for its length, remarkably askew and superficial; their summary of *Alexander v. Holmes County*—a wonderful case in which the Court reversed a decision of the heroic Fifth Circuit, to that lower court's eternal credit and surprise—shows they have not even a minimal understanding of civil-rights litigation in the South. The reason they cannot address in any depth even the important questions of which they are aware lies in their unusual preoccupation with a very odd kind of gossip: who voted how and when, and whose vote changed; who thought what about whose earlier drafts; but, above all, who liked or disliked whom.

One would have thought the matter of earlier drafts could have been disposed of in a second. No writer, least of all an investigative reporter working on a book, wants to be held accountable for his early drafts. But, " 'If an associate in my law firm had done this,' Powell told a clerk [of Chief Justice Burger's draft in a busing case], 'I'd fire him.' " "White thought Blackmun's drafts [in the abortion cases] were dreadful." "Stewart told his clerks that the Chief's initial draft of the decision [in the Nixon tapes case] would have got a grade of D in law school." Hardly anyone, I think, would contend that even the final opinions of the Court very often reflect the work of nine, or even any, distinguished draftsmen. To the caveat "if true" about this sort of news, in short, one is inclined to add "So what?" But Woodward and Armstrong endlessly return to who thought what of drafts.

Another subject that fascinates them is shifting votes. Now it must be obvious, on a moment's reflection, that it is desirable—even essential to the judicial process—that the Justices be able sometimes to persuade one another to change their minds. The authors do have evidence in support of two old and interesting rumors. The first, that Chief Justice Burger often reserves (or repeatedly and perhaps disingenuously changes) his vote, in order to retain the prerogative of assigning a majority opinion, is not too serious. The result, most often, is only that he joins in a majority position more liberal than any he would have taken on his own. The second, that the Chief Justice has tried to alter certain traditions of the Court—to assign from the minority even when he is in the majority; or to permit rehearing of a case when no member of the deciding majority has voted to rehear—would strike lawyers as more disturbing. Except that, under protest from other Justices, these efforts failed.

More than drafts, however, more than vote changes, the authors are concerned with the popularity, within the Court, of Justices. Their villain is, beyond doubt, Chief Justice Burger. He is characterized, in terms attributed to other Justices, as "grossly inadequate," "overbearing and offensive," "tasteless," "without substance or integrity," "intellectually dishonest," "abrasive," "asinine," a "blustery braggart," and so on. Other Justices are also characterized in terms attributed to their colleagues: Justice Marshall, for instance, as "petulant"; Justice White as "not particularly likeable," "an enigma" who cheats at basketball. But every Associate Justice, according to this book, has something disagreeable to say about the Chief Justice. This may or may not be true. If true (as everyone who has ever worked in an office with even a beloved boss will know), it may or may not have any meaning. But on page 323, in another apotheosis, there may be a kind of clue. "The Justices found themselves entering the clerks' long-standing debate: Was the Chief evil or stupid?"

"The clerks' long-standing debate." There have been countless other clues on this order: "The language remained Blackmun's; the more rigorous analysis was the work of the clerk." "How, Powell asked his clerks, did Marshall turn out such a masterpiece so quickly? The clerks were frank. Marshall's clerk was first rate. . . ."

"The clerks were frank," to the same effect, it seems, quite often. On page 279, this achieves an almost wonderful fatuity. Justice Rehnquist has allegedly brought to conference an issue of the *National Lampoon,* which depicts all members of the Court in obscene postures: Justice Brennan, for instance, opening his robe in front of two little girls; Justice Blackmun sodomizing a kangaroo. Justice Brennan, the authors say, thought he alone was portrayed as innocent. "His clerks decided they owed it to him to explain 'flashing.'" Justice Blackmun claimed not to know what he was supposed to be doing to the kangaroo: "The clerks drew straws to see who would tell him."

Oddly enough, and for reasons of which the authors seem to have no notion, this is the only "Materials" scoop they have: the fact that clerks spoke to them; the precise number who did; the apparent smugness and foolishness of what they said; and the fact that (although they clearly believed otherwise, else why speak to investigative reporters?) the clerks knew no important secrets at all.

The origins of Supreme Court clerkship are recent—the turn of the century. Justices White, Rehnquist, and Stevens are, in fact, the only former Supreme Court clerks to have become Justices. There used to be one clerk per Justice; even in the late years of the Warren Court, when there were two, the relation was close. A clerk was, for a year, an apprentice, a son, research assistant, ghostwriter, friend. His real importance to the Court, if any, was, as a student recently graduated from law school, to bring the views of law faculties to the attention of Justices. Whatever it was, it was a unique and fine relation. Now, with the mushrooming of clerkships (four to each Justice), there is a possibility that they have become a bureaucracy like any other—with confidences to violate, surely; but with fewer secrets, because the Court explains itself, than others have to tell.

The authors' "Materials" scoop, in other words, would have had to do with what has happened to clerks and the relation of clerkship. Their "Cases" scoop, for not unrelated reasons, would have had to do with Justice Rehnquist and his work. As clearly as Chief Justice Burger is their villain, Justice Rehnquist is very much their man. Their inquiry about how he came to be appointed, compared with their discussion of the appointment of other Justices, is remarkably uninquisitive. Here's how he is characterized, however, as a member of the Court: "jolly," "jovial," "sincere," "thoughtful," "remarkably unstuffy," "good natured," "aware of Burger's faults," of "crisp intellect," "diligence," and "friendliness toward clerks," "hard not to like." "Rehnquist and his clerks," the authors typically write of him, "chuckled quite a bit."

It is true that they also quote other Justices to the effect that Justice Rehnquist is "slow even to correct an outright misstatement," that he "misrepresented the legislative history," "twisted the facts," used "disingenuous scholarship," made "misuse of precedents," tried an "underhanded attempt to slip through a major policy shift." But they seem unaware that these adverse characterizations, if true, are of an entirely different order from any others they have made. Even if the clerks did have a "long-standing debate" as to whether the Chief Justice, for instance, was "evil or stupid," that debate, those adjectives, would have no legal or other substance.

The Court, after all, is an ongoing body, committed to the Constitution and its own history. If the Burger Court had allowed certain critical rights to erode (the right, for example, in all criminal trials to a jury of twelve and to a unanimous verdict), it has also (in the first abortion decisions) made some of the most radical and humane judgments in the history of the Court. Even *Alexander* v. *Holmes County*—in which the *Brown* v. *Board of Education* integration formula, "all deliberate speed," was superseded altogether by "at once . . . now and hereafter"—was hardly ineloquent or unradical. These were, however, questions about which reasonable men, and honorable Justices, might differ. But Justices, whatever their views, are supposed to be committed, in the exercise of their profession, to straight facts and valid precedents in law.

This has nothing to do with ideology. There should, there must, at all times, be conservatives on the Court. But if there were a Justice who did "twist facts," "misrepresent . . . history," "misuse precedents," and so on—if there were a Justice somewhat unconcerned not only with what is humane or just (matters, arguably, of rhetoric) but even with what is *apposite*—such a Justice would be fundamentally unserious. If there were a Justice who had few thoughts or even arguments but only positions and strategies (like a teething Jesuit or Talmudic scholar), such a Justice would represent not the judicial mind at all but the legal mind at its most trivial and base—making, in the name of advocacy, arguments that it is precisely the business of the judiciary to cut through. It is possible that the Court has just such an unprecedented casuist in Justice Rehnquist—not a "constructionist" or even a "conservative" at all, except in caricature.

It sometimes seems that if a genuine conservative, of real distinction, were ever on the Court, one would find Justice Rehnquist in dissent.

The authors' partiality for the youngest Justice makes his influence on their book considerable, as considerable in its way as (and analytically more important than) the influence of the clerks. Their error, for instance, about what Justice Stewart wrote in *Roth*—no due process for non-government-created rights, instead of no due process for non-government-created *property* rights—originates, in all probability, with Justice Rehnquist, who (in consistently eliding liberty and property rights) gradually *has* been trying to obscure precisely the distinction Justice Stewart made. In *Arnett* v. *Kennedy*, which most lawyers would agree was his worst opinion (although the authors cite two others as his "worst"), Rehnquist further managed, by a characteristic piece of analysis, to deprive due process of any meaning—as was noted by his colleagues, including Justices White and Powell, but not by the authors here. In their rapport with the youngest Justice, the authors miss the essence of just such attempts to "slip through a major policy shift."

If the book fails—in its legal analysis, in its efforts to find and disclose important secrets, as an account of the Court in any significant or coherent sense—why is it an important book at all? Because of who the authors are and the very extent of their ambition: *Inside the Supreme Court.*

The relation between the press and the courts, in our society, is rarely devoid of interest. It is an important event in the history of both institutions when highly regarded journalists approach the nation's highest Court. The trouble is, it turns out to be futile to approach the subject in this way. It is not unusual for people to misapprehend the nature of the institution and make more or less misguided approaches to Justices. Chief Justice Burger himself made at least one unjudicial approach, in the matter of the bombing of Cambodia, to President Nixon. This story, however, is not the authors' scoop but Mr. Nixon's, in *RN.*

What does the failure mean? It means that certain techniques, perhaps well suited to investigation of breaking stories of a criminal nature, are entirely unsuited to extended, serious analysis of other matters. The only scoop there could possibly be about an institution as public as the Supreme Court *would* be a revelaton of crime or corruption—of which Woodward and Armstrong, at least, found none. It may be that an analytic mind and an integrating theme—an instinct for which facts have meaning, which are meaningless, and which are not even facts—are more suitable than an investigative reporter's sheer persistence, and obsession with keeping (his own) and breaking (others') secrets, to pursuing certain kinds of stories. Most stories—apart from affairs of the military, of crime, and sometimes of the heart—are not, after all, secrets *as such*. Anticipation of this book was high, in journalistic and in legal circles. The Court, with the possible exception of the relation of clerkship, survives— no more nor less public than it ever was. Investigative reporting, perhaps, might think again.

—1979

THE EXTREME NOMINEE

The words "strict constructionist," "judicial restraint," "judicial deference," "original intent," "laissez-faire," and even "conservative" have acquired in recent years at least three entirely distinct sets of meanings. In
one, which is traditional and legitimate, the words accurately characterize
the views of almost all serious constitutional scholars, and of all honorable and competent federal judges—whose work is, after all, not merely
bound but defined by a solemn oath to uphold and apply the Constitution. In another, the words are mere code or buzzwords, used almost
mindlessly and without meaning but with highly polemical intent; that
is, to characterize the views one holds or wishes to applaud, and to disparage all opposing views with yet another, accusatory buzzword: "judicial
activist." Finally, the same words have been appropriated by holders of
views so extreme, so coercive, so intrusive, and so radically at odds with
tradition, with legal precedent, and with the whole text, history, structure,
and meaning of the Constitution that they serve actively to conceal rather
than to express positions, and have come to mean their precise and
Orwellian opposites. In modern political history, this sort of transformation is not at all unusual. The most extreme agendas and regimes often
adopt the terms of legitimacy and moderation.

When President Reagan announced his nomination of Judge Robert
Bork, of the Court of Appeals for the District of Columbia Circuit, to
the seat on the Supreme Court that had been vacated by Justice Lewis
Powell, news publications and spokesmen of every kind used that vocabulary of "strict constructionism," "judicial restraint," "judicial deference," "original intent," "laissez-faire," and "conservative" as though it
applied especially, or at all, to issues now posed for the Senate by that

nomination. This was not surprising. President Reagan, Attorney General Edwin Meese, and Judge Bork himself had used that vocabulary to characterize the positions of the nominee. They were also trying to frame the terms of the debate for all three constituencies of those words—the legitimate, the polemical, and the ideologically extreme to a degree almost unprecedented in the history of the American federal courts. This left most people who had not actually read Judge Bork's published articles and his opinions, both for the Court and in dissent, uncertain of and not overly worried by which set of meanings was intended.

The Supreme Court for more than two decades has been in no sense and by no stretch of the imagination a radical or a liberal, or even a Democratic, court. On the day Justice Powell announced his resignation, the Court consisted of two Justices appointed by Democrats and seven appointed by Republicans. Justices Powell, William Rehnquist, and Harry Blackmun were appointed by Richard Nixon, Justices Sandra Day O'Connor and Antonin Scalia by Ronald Reagan. Justice John Paul Stevens was appointed by Gerald Ford, Justice William Brennan by Dwight Eisenhower.

Justice Byron White, who was appointed by John Kennedy, has voted so consistently with Justice Rehnquist on what has been until now the right wing of the Court that he is no longer mentioned as a swing, or even a moderate, vote. Justice Thurgood Marshall, who was appointed by Lyndon Johnson, is the sole liberal Democratic appointee.

It is this Court, and its continuity with its predecessors in almost every major decision upholding an individual constitutional right against the powers of the state, over a period of more than thirty years—going back to *Brown* v. *Board of Education* and beyond—that Judge Bork has repeatedly and consistently accused of deciding "lawlessly" and "without principle," and of "creating rights," and of imposing "value choices" and "preferences," and of "lacking candor," and of being "unprincipled," and of producing a line of precedents "as improper" and "as intellectually empty" as *Griswold* v. *Connecticut*—a 1965 case in which the Court upheld a married couple's right to use contraceptives, a decision to which Bork has returned obsessively and scornfully again and again, and one that he would clearly vote to overrule. He has accused the Court, including on major occasions Justices Oliver Wendell Holmes, Louis Brandeis, Felix Frankfurter, Potter Stewart, and Lewis Powell, with whom he prefers on other occasions to be identified, of being, unaccountably but consistently less principled, less competent intellectually, and less committed to the Constitution than Judge Bork believes himself to be.

It goes without saying, although we all seem to feel obliged to say it, that a man who is nominated for the Supreme Court is entitled, like every other citizen, to his views, his judgment, his character, his history, his temperament, his intellectual quality, his personality and predilections. We know of Judge Bork, for instance, that he was a professor of law at Yale; that he was Solicitor General under President Nixon; and that he fired Special Prosecutor Archibald Cox, an act that was subsequently found by a federal court to be unlawful but that he now defends as having saved the "viability" of the Justice Department. We know that he has been a judge on a federal appellate court; that some of his friends regard him as witty; that he smokes, and likes martinis; that he did not pay certain taxes he had owed in New Haven since 1972, but paid them in July 1987, the day before the New Haven *Register* broke the story.

We know that he had been about to resign from the bench and resume private practice (he had hired no new clerks) when President Reagan announced his nomination for the Court. All this seems to leave open the possibility that he is an open-minded man, experienced in legal scholarship and in public office, who might affect the "balance" but would in no way threaten either the continuity, collegiality, and integrity of the Court itself or the entire constitutional structure—the separation of powers, the system of checks and balances—with which the republic was founded, and which has endured and developed over the past two hundred years.

From most of the reaction to his nomination so far, one might think: Well, some blacks oppose him, and some gays oppose him, and some women who oppose sex discrimination and believe in the right to abortion oppose him, and some woolly-headed liberals who believe in a right to privacy, or even believe that the First Amendment protects speech, oppose him, but those groups don't always speak with one voice—or for the whole decent, centrist consensus of the country. On the other hand, the right wing supports him. And even some members of the establishment, including the academy and the press, support him, or at least are reconciled to him. And Roosevelt, after all, had his Court-packing scheme. So unless there is some "smoking gun," the Senate might as well confirm him and get it over with. That's the way the system works.

But that's not how the system works. The Court-packing plan, for instance, failed. It was defeated by the Senate. The vast majority of the House, the Senate, and the electorate, moreover, were of President Roosevelt's party, and supported his social policy, at a time of genuine economic and political disaster. The present House and the Senate, many of whose members were elected as surely as and more recently than the current President, are not of his party. There is no crisis, except in extreme constituencies, and that is a crisis of ideology. But Judge Bork has made it so clear how he would decide nearly all major constitutional cases that have come before the Court, not just in the last thirty years but long before, that certainly for the first time in this century, and perhaps in the history of the republic, the Senate is being asked not to confirm a man but to establish on the Court a doctrine and a set of concrete decisions, most of which are reversals of established law and precedent. And Bork's published work seems to set forth methods, certainties, and positions that, while they may be consistent with what Bork calls "representative democracy," are so radically at odds with the Constitution as to amount to a rigid ideological system of his own.

What Bork has been looking for, and believes he has found, is above all a theory, a simple axiom, or principle, or formula, that the Court can—in fact, must—apply in constitutional adjudication to all cases that come before it. This "theory," developed at length in an article in the *Indiana Law Journal* in the fall of 1971, does not initially acknowledge the existence of "rights" at all but speaks instead of competing "gratifications," "pleasures," "preferences," but repeatedly and above all "gratifications": "Every clash between a minority claiming freedom and a majority claiming power to regulate involves a choice between . . . gratifications," and "There is no principled way to decide that one man's gratifications are more deserving of respect than another's or that one form of gratification is more worthy than another."

The innumerable "lawless," "utterly specious," and "unprincipled" decisions—in fact, the perpetration of "limited" judicial "coups d'état"—that Bork thinks he discerns particularly, but by no means only, in the Warren Court seem to him, however, to "establish the necessity for theory." To be a "principled" judge "means," in fact, to "have and rigorously adhere to a valid and consistent theory." And "the Court's power is legitimate only if it has . . . a valid theory . . . of the respective spheres of majority and minority freedom." Bork believes that, while he does "not offer a complete theory of constitutional interpretation," he has found the best one by far. It is essentially this:

There are two classes of constitutional "rights"—or, rather, claims to "gratification." (He notes in passing, and with disdain, "rhetoric" to the effect that any "rights . . . inhere in humans.") The first class of rights consists of those which are "specified"; namely, those which the "Framers" can be found literally and "actually to have intended," and which are "capable of being translated into principled rules." And the second class consists of "secondary," or "derived," rights, which "are located in the individual *for the sake of a governmental process*" (italics added). "They are given to the individual because his enjoyment of them will lead him to defend them in court and thereby preserve the governmental process." In all other cases, the Court must simply administer the "majoritarian" "will," or "preferences," as these are expressed in law. This Judge Bork believes to be the doctrine of "strict constructionism," "laissez-faire," and "original intent."

There are many difficulties with this theory. In the first place, the constitutional command that the courts consider only specific "cases" or "controversies" has precluded them from proclaiming "theory"—either philosophical or "advisory" or in advance of any set of facts. That is how constitutional adjudication works. The law is discovered in the cases, and not the other way around. That is why Justice Powell, in a long interview in the *Times* after his resignation, took the trouble to say, "I never think of myself as having a judicial philosophy. . . . I try to be careful, to do justice to the particular case, rather than try to write principles that will be new, or original, or whatever."

Secondly, the notion that "rights . . . inhere in humans," which Bork dismisses as some new, modish rhetorical development, was held so firmly by the founders of the republic that the second paragraph of the Declaration with which they proclaimed their independence began, "We hold these truths to be self-evident, that all men are created equal, that they are endowed by their Creator with certain unalienable rights." The Constitution itself was drafted with three clear aims: to create a compact to form a republic, which would unite the separate states; to establish a structure by which that republic would be governed; and to protect precisely the individual rights of citizens against majoritarian intrusion and coercion by the state.

That the Framers regarded these rights as inhering in the individual, and not as in any sense "derived," either from any document or from any trivial, utilitarian "governmental process," is clear, and not just from the Bill of Rights—which Judge Bork, in the same article, brushes aside as a "hastily drafted document upon which little thought was expended." It was thoroughly thought out again, after the Civil War, when the Fourteenth Amendment extended the core of the Bill of Rights, along with due process and equal protection, to the citizens of all the states. But Bork treats this amendment rather dismissively as well, speaking of the "value choice (or, perhaps more accurately, the value impulse) of the Fourteenth Amendment." He writes of the "men who put the amendment in the Constitution" that "many or most of them had not even thought the matter through."

"Courts must accept any value choice the legislature makes unless it clearly runs contrary to a choice made in the framing of the Constitution," Bork writes. And: "It follows, of course, that broad areas of constitutional law ought to be reformulated." And: "The distinction between rights that are inherent and rights that are derived from some other value is one that our society worked out long ago with respect to the economic market place. . . . A right is a form of property. . . . The modern intellectual argues the proper location and definition of property rights according to judgments of utility. . . . As it is with economic property rights, so it should be with constitutional rights relating to governmental processes."

The notion that the individual or his rights exist for the state, and to serve its "judgments of utility," is the basis of Bork's ideology. A notion more antithetical to the whole purpose and structure of the Constitution can hardly be imagined. "There is no principled way in which anyone can define the spheres in which liberty is required and the spheres in which equality is required." But the Constitution does not speak of "spheres," and the founders of the republic discerned so little of the tension that Bork consistently finds between "liberty" and "equality" that the same sentence of the Declaration which speaks of "liberty" as one of men's "unalienable rights" includes the statement "All men are created equal."

"It is emphatically the province and duty of the judicial department," Justice John Marshall said in 1803, in the great case of *Marbury v. Madison*, "to say what the law is." To that end, insulated by life tenure from the majoritarian pressures to which members of the two other branches, and of the state legislatures, were subject, the federal courts were empowered—indeed, obliged—to protect, from the prospect of "tyranny" by any of these majoritarian bodies, individual constitutional rights. The Constitution is complicated, intricate, difficult to understand and apply. That has been part of its continuing vitality. But two hundred years of decisions by the Court have understood ever more clearly that it was the intention of the Framers to make very difficult—to require the state to give fairly compelling justifications for—any attempt to take any of those individual rights away. And the reason Judge Bork's whole formulation is more disturbing than the mere ruminations of an ideologically extreme, revisionist professor is that he misapprehends the nature of "strict construction" in such a way as to compel him, as a "principled" judge, to abdicate the judicial duty "to say," on behalf of the individual constitutional right against the state, or on behalf of one branch of the federal government bringing suit against another, "what the law is." And yet nothing could be more apparent from his writings than that he is and intends to be a highly "activist" Judge, concerned less with theory than with results, and with reaching what he considers certain desirable outcomes.

The consistent form of his activism has so far been repudiation. Sometimes, particularly in congressional hearings, he rather tepidly and ambiguously repudiates prior positions of his own. But when it suits him, and if the result he wishes to reach requires it, he repudiates, without hesitation, the clear text of the Constitution itself. Thus, if the Constitution says explicitly, "Congress shall make no law . . . abridging the freedom of speech," Bork writes, "Laymen may perhaps be forgiven for thinking that the literal words" are what is meant, and that any legislation seeking to censor or repress that speech bears the burden of explaining why an exception should be made. "But what can one say of lawyers who think any such thing? Anyone skilled in reading language should know that the words are not necessarily absolute. . . . We are, then, forced to construct our own theory of the constitutional protection of speech."

Having set aside, in other words, "original intent" as it is expressed in a specific provision of the Constitution, he proceeds to attack also, as "deficient in logic and analysis as well as in history," the "clear and present danger" standard that was first developed by Justices Holmes and Brandeis in the years after World War I. He wishes to overrule all the free-speech cases that elaborated and refined that standard, and then to apply instead the test set forth in his "own theory," which leaves constitutionally protected only what he calls "explicitly political speech," a category that he defines so narrowly as to exclude not only what most people mean by "speech" but also what is generally meant by "political." If Judge Bork's narrow conception of "explicitly political" speech had prevailed against the sermons, marches, boycotts, and sit-ins that advocated violation of what the federal courts eventually found to be bad and lawless state laws, those laws would never have been found unconstitutional, and there would still be Jim Crow in the South.

What he clearly wants, and clearly intends on the Court to vote to achieve, is to overrule as well many other important lines of cases—concerning, for instance, the right of privacy. Bork believes quite simply that no such right exists: that it is a "court-created right"—or, rather, an imposition of the "unprincipled preference" of the judges for the "gratification" of that "minority" which, for instance, wishes, as in *Griswold*, to be free to use contraceptives, over the "gratification" of that majority which wishes to be free not only *not* to use contraceptives but to prevent anyone else from using them. He does not acknowledge, or appear to perceive, a difference in the order of "freedom" embodied by choosing to do or not to do something and "freedom" to prevent anyone else, even in private, from doing or not doing whatever it is. In fact, Bork routinely uses the vocabulary of coercion to describe choices of the private citizen, and the language of "loss of liberty" or "loss of freedom" to describe the position of the majority whose intrusion the private citizen is trying to resist.

In the name of "freedom," he wants to overrule, for instance, *Shelley* v. *Kraemer*, a 1948 decision, thereby allowing states to enforce "a racially restrictive covenant." And to overrule *Skinner* v. *Oklahoma*, a 1942 decision, and thereby uphold the right of the state to sterilize robbers. He thinks that the Supreme Court decision forbidding the poll tax was wrongly decided, since the poll tax in question was "not discriminatory" and was "very small." And so on. There are, of course, cases about which men of good will reasonably disagree—having to do, for example, with capital punishment, with the one-man, one-vote reapportionment cases, and with the "exclusionary rule," which forbids the state to use in criminal trials evidence that was illegally seized. Of the last, he has said in an interview that it seems to him that "the conscience of the court ought to be" at least as much "shaken by the idea of turning a criminal loose upon society" as by the idea of admitting illegally seized evidence.

It might be worth examining by Judge Bork's own reasoning the kind of "majoritarian" statute he would feel compelled to uphold. The only individual right that he finds in the Fourteenth Amendment, albeit "derived," is the right to be protected from state action that enforces "racially invidious classification." So there is nothing to prevent a majoritarian preference from being expressed, for instance, in a statute requiring everyone, of every race, to be blond. And nothing—perhaps this is more serious—to prevent the state from enforcing a majoritarian preference that all single mothers should be sterilized. Or all women with an IQ below 130. Or all mothers under eighteen.

Bork has repeatedly called *Roe* v. *Wade*, the 1973 decision recognizing the right to abortion, "an unconstitutional decision," a "judicial usurpation of state legislative authority." This has a different significance altogether from calling it a mere mistake, which arguments for the continuity and predictability of the Court's decisions could leave undisturbed. If it is "an unconstitutional decision" and a "judicial usurpation," then Justice Bork would be obliged by his constitutional oath not to reaffirm it. And overruling *Roe* v. *Wade* would permit the recriminalization of abortion by the states.

On the other hand, since there is no right of privacy in the matter, one way or the other, there is nothing to prevent a state from *imposing* abortions, as long as that imposition is expressed in a "racially neutral" law.

Bork would doubtless reply that no such statutes could be passed anywhere in this country, and that we should have more faith in "majoritarian" "preferences" than that. But there have been totalitarian states in this century, as "majoritarian" as any in history, which have passed very extreme statutes of that order. For that matter, for decades in the South there were statutes of a related kind.

In a simultaneously impassioned and derisive article published in *The*

New Republic of August 31, 1963, Bork left no doubt of where he stood. What he opposed at the time was "legislation by which the morals of the majority are self-righteously imposed upon a minority." He also said, "The simple argument from morality to law can be a dangerous non-sequitur." He was not writing about *Griswold*, or *Roe* v. *Wade*. The dangerous "majority" in this instance included, among many other individuals and institutions, Congress, then about to pass the Interstate Public Accommodations Act, which became Title II of the Civil Rights Act of 1964.

Bork was so exercised at the prospect of this majoritarian "mob coercing and disturbing other private individuals"—the "mob" presumably composed of Rosa Parks, religious elderly people, schoolchildren, sedate college students at lunch counters, and perhaps even those brave, mostly Republican judges of the Fifth Circuit, Elbert Tuttle, John Minor Wisdom, Richard Rives, John Brown, and others who supported them—that he referred no fewer than four times to the impact of the proposed law on barbers, though barbers were explicitly excluded, in public hearings before Congress, from enterprises covered by the act. Although he warned of "the danger of violence," he gave no indication that he knew which side the violence was on, or was aware that the "private individuals" he described as being "coerced" were really mobs armed with baseball bats and ax handles, and troopers with dogs, clubs, and water hoses, and that though there was "violence"—bombings, beatings, shootings—not one incident of that kind, in all the years of the desegregating transformation of the South, was perpetrated by the people whose conduct he so deplored.

In as recent a case as *Dronenburg* v. *Zech*, 1984, Judge Bork repeated many of the views he had expressed in *The New Republic* in 1963 and the *Indiana Law Journal* in 1971. *Dronenburg* was a case that should have been—and, in a sense, was—decided in a single paragraph, to the effect that there was ample precedent for upholding a policy that permitted the military to discharge an officer for homosexuality. But Judge Bork, speaking for the Court, used the occasion to write one of what have become known as his Ed Opinions, or Ed Notes, or Letters to Attorney General Meese—in effect, job applications, reiterations of commitments he had made concerning what he would do as a member of the Supreme Court.

"The principle of such legislation," Bork once wrote, "is that if I find your behavior ugly by my standards, moral or aesthetic, and if you prove stubborn about adopting my view of the situation, I am justified in having the state coerce you into more righteous paths. That is itself a principle of unsurpassed ugliness." These lines were not part of any opinion having to do with privacy, say, or abortion, or censorship, or freedom of speech. They were written to describe the desegregation provisions embodied in Title II. The "principle of unsurpassed ugliness" that so exercised him was desegregration.

For at least the past thirty years, no American institution has served us better than the federal courts. For almost twenty-five years, Bork has staked his career on repudiating and denouncing the decisions of those courts. He has expressed his views so forcefully, and for so long, that he has become the nominee because of them. A senator faithful to his own constitutional oath cannot lightly or blandly vote to confirm the nomination unless he is prepared to endorse those views.

—1987

COUP AT THE COURT

I.

The unprecedented, increasingly improper, and deceptive campaign by and on behalf of Robert H. Bork for a seat on the Supreme Court is beginning to provide some measure of the degree to which Americans ought to be frightened by that nomination. In an essay "On Lying and Politics," Hannah Arendt long ago pointed out the entirely contemporary dangers in confusing Madison Avenue public relations with genuine politics—the difference between selling an, inherently "defactualized," "image" to a "consumer" and the legitimate political contention among electoral candidates for the decision of the voter, which, in an open society, necessarily involves some ascertainable element of fact.

But we have never had a political "candidate" marketed in this sense for the nation's highest court before. It is astonishing how far the "defactualization" has already gone. A law professor and a judge on a federal appellate court has, one would have thought undeniably, a factual "record." Bork's views on constitutional law, as expressed in his published articles and opinions, exist. Taken together they would amount to no more than a single, small volume or tract. But they are hard to read, cynical, poorly reasoned, and ideologically extreme to a degree that is unusual even on the outermost fringes of our public life. Few people apparently have taken the trouble to wade through them.

Every few days, however, the Bork lobby manages to plant, in the *New York Times* or the *Washington Post* or elsewhere, some story to the effect that, contrary to his record of more than twenty years, Bork is now, or has ever been, a "centrist," or a "moderate," or "open-minded," or anywhere near the "mainstream" of constitutional adjudication, going back more than thirty, and in important lines of cases more than sixty years. Bork himself has repeatedly and stridently denounced that legislation as "lawless," "unprincipled," "improper," and "deficient" in "candor," "logic," and "legitimacy." The resulting stories now unhesitatingly characterize as "liberal" anyone who happens to oppose Bork's nomination. They also promote an image of the nominee, contradicted surprisingly but absolutely by his published work, as a respecter of "original intent" and an advocate or a practitioner of "judicial restraint."

"The man," Bork once wrote, in his long, often-quoted article in the *Indiana Law Journal* in 1971, "who understands the issues and nevertheless insists upon the rightness of the Warren Court's performance . . . occupies an impossible philosophic position." Look at the tone; look at the vocabulary; look particularly at the word "performance." "Such a man"—namely anyone who does not share Bork's own theories and ideological commitments—"prefers results to processes" and "claims for the Supreme Court" a "role as perpetrator of limited coups d'état." Bork went on to say that he could see "no reason" why such a person should not entirely "ignore the Court whenever he can get away with it and overthrow it if he can"—or why this person should not choose to "argue the case to some other group, say the Joint Chiefs of Staff."

The putsch vocabulary of "coups d'état" is characteristic, as is the habit, the mentality, of extreme overstatement disguised as rational argument. And the "performance" of which this revised and repackaged "centrist" wrote with such derision has, of course, been the law of the land for more than thirty years. In some forums the Bork campaign has managed to convey the impression that the nominee has somehow tempered, or even changed, his more rigid and most often reiterated views. But with his real constituents, and outside the mainstream press, Bork leaves no doubt. "I finally worked out a philosophy which is expressed pretty much in that 1971 *Indiana Law Journal* piece," he said in the *Conservative Digest* in late 1985; and in June 1985 in the *District Lawyer*: "My views have remained about what they were." The reason we cannot dismiss much of his published work as instances of a simultaneously ponderous and cutting sarcasm, more refreshing perhaps in academic circles than becoming to a judge, is that it is Bork himself who turns out to prefer "results" to "processes." In fact, when it suits him he manages to set "processes," and the Constitution itself, entirely aside in order to reach his preferred "results."

"Logic has a life of its own," Bork wrote in the *Indiana Law Journal* piece, "and devotion to principle requires that we follow where logic leads." Bork likes the words "logic" and "logical," and categorical statements claiming "neutrality" or labeling themselves "neutral" but phrased in terms of absolutism and excess: "all," "any," "nothing," "no one," "none," "ugly," "offensive," "repugnant," "coerced," "compelled." And, "I would be appalled by many statutes that I am compelled to think would be constitutional."

The five areas in which Bork has been most radically, insistently, and "logically" at variance with constitutional precedent, and in which he would think himself inescapably "compelled" to uphold "many statutes" struck down as unconstitutional in the past six decades by the Court, are these: privacy, equal protection, race, due process, and speech.

Privacy. Bork not only unequivocally denies, he repeatedly and scornfully derides the very notion that such a constitutional right exists. This view has consequences. It means, for instance, that *Roe* v. *Wade* must be overruled. Bork has called it an "unconstitutional decision" and a "wholly unjustified judicial usurpation"—which would require him, under his own constitutional oath, not to leave it in place in deference to stare decisis or to the continuity of the Court, but to overrule it. State legislatures would be empowered, of course, to pass criminal statutes that ban abortions. But since no right of privacy exists, and since a woman has no rights in the matter one way or the other, the states could as readily enact statutes that *impose* abortion—on welfare mothers, say, or on single mothers, or on any group of women defined by any criteria other than "individious racial classification," the only category of discrimination that Bork acknowledges as forbidden by the Fourteenth Amendment. Whether Bork would be "appalled" by such a statute is not clear. "Logic" and "devotion to principle" would oblige him to uphold it.

Equal Protection. Bork explicitly finds in the equal protection clause of the Fourteenth Amendment only "two legitimate meanings": "It *can* require formal procedural equality, and . . . it *does* require that government not discriminate along racial lines" (italics added). "But much more than that cannot properly be read into the clause." This, too, has consequences. Except maybe ("can require") in the strictest "formal procedural" sense, it excludes from constitutional equal protection of the law not only all women, and of course all homosexuals, but any other group or minority not explicitly defined by race. There is no constitutional impediment to enacting into law any community prejudice against groups defined, say, by class, affinity, profession, union, party affiliation, infirmity, age, culture, physical or mental attribute, non-racial physical similarity, or even religious belief.

State legislatures at present seem benign enough not to enact most statutes of that kind. But Bork has not in the past been perceptibly "appalled" by laws or policies that involve, for instance, sterilization. Among many pre–Warren Court cases he has found "improper" and "wrongly decided" was *Skinner v. Oklahoma,* a 1942 decision in which the Court struck down a statute that required sterilization of "habitual criminals." As recently as 1984, in *Oil, Chemical, and Atomic Workers v. American Cyanamid,* he found no difficulty in adopting the language, and sympathizing with the conduct, of a company that "offered" its female employees as an "option" under what it called its "fetal protection policy," the choice between "proof of surgical sterilization" and being fired. If, under the pressures of some not unimaginable or unforeseeable crisis, states were to pass some "racially neutral" statute ranging from discrimination against members of the unprotected groups to relocation or even sterilization of them, Bork would be "compelled" by "logic" and "devotion to principle" to uphold it.

Race. Since Bork finds in the equal protection clause nothing substantive, except that "government [may] not discriminate along racial lines," one might think he would hold firm at least on race. But no, or at least not on the side of equal protection and desegregation. There are not only intemperate and perhaps hastily drafted views: his infelicitous phrase in a 1978 article in the *Wall Street Journal,* for example, which characterized as "hard core racists of reverse discrimination" a group that would include at least four Justices in *Bakke*—and perhaps the main target of Bork's attack in that article, Justice Lewis Powell. Bork's relentless habit of extreme overstatement leads him to find in *any* decision that strikes down state enforcement of racial discrimination an unconscionable intrusion on some right or "freedom" to discriminate on racial grounds. Thus, among the many pre–Warren Court lines of cases that he explicitly states "logic" and "devotion to principle" oblige him to find unconstitutional is *Shelley v. Kraemer,* a 1948 case in which the Court struck down a state court decision to enforce contracts that included "a private, racially restrictive covenant."

"The rule of *Shelley,*" Bork wrote, "would require the Court to deny the freedom of any individual to discriminate in the conduct of any part of his affairs." The "rule" would apply as well to "any situation in which the person claiming freedom in any relationship had a racial motivation." The rhetoric of sheer racist, alarmist demagoguery is not unfamiliar from white segregationist politicians in the South of the early sixties, most of whom came around far sooner and more generously than Bork to the acknowledgment that permitting blacks to exercise certain constitutional rights would not immediately and "logically" infringe upon the "freedom" of whites to discriminate "in *any* relationship."

Bork has written several times that he would uphold *Brown* v. *Board of Education*—though not on the grounds on which the Warren Court decided it, and not with any of the remedies that the Court and Congress itself have used to implement the decision. But if the "rule of *Shelley*," which after all upholds only the right of a willing black buyer to purchase a house from a willing white seller, seems to Bork so drastically to threaten the "freedom" of the individual to discriminate "in any part of his affairs," it is hardly credible that he would have concurred in *Brown*, which required the desegregation of the nation's entire school system. (Lord knows how he would, at the time, have formulated "the rule of *Brown*.") And it is of course how a judge or a justice decides a case *at the time* it comes before him, and not some belated and grudging ac-knowledgment that the law, to which the vast majority has long been reconciled, is workable and should therefore be upheld that defines the exercise of his constitutional duty "to say what the law is."

Due Process. The Court has often used the constitutional guarantee that citizens shall not be deprived of liberty without due process of law to reach the results, particularly in the privacy cases, that Bork most consistently and vituperatively deplores. Thus, Justice John Paul Stevens, in an address on "liberty" before the Eighth Circuit Judicial Confer-ence in July, used the arguments of due process to explain the Court's decisions in several important lines of cases, including specifically *Roe* v. *Wade* and *Griswold* v. *Connecticut* (a 1965 decision that struck down a statute that banned even married couples from using contraceptives), which Bork has always gone out of his way, as recently as his 1984 opinion in *Dronenburg* v. *Zech*, to deride.

In fact the primary target of Bork's attack on Supreme Court prece-dent, and the decision to which he returns most obsessively, is *Griswold*. His analysis of that case is indicative not just of the kind of reasoning he finds persuasive but of the sort of view people who have not actually read him but who are sure of his ideological moderation have simply overlooked. He has repeatedly compared the "right" of married couples, in *Griswold*, to use contraceptives to the "right" of a utility company to generate "smoke pollution." "The majority finds the use of contraceptives immoral. Knowledge that it takes place and that the State makes no effort to inhibit it causes the majority anguish." "The smoke-pollution regulation" causes stockholders of the electric utility company anguish. Smoke pollution, however, can be regulated. The use of contraceptives by one's neighbors should be regulated as well. "The cases," he has written, more than once, "are identical."

Speech. It is on the issue of speech, oddly enough, that Bork's positions, and his possible appointment to the Court, pose the most radical threat to the whole constitutional system, and would set in motion the most immediate and far-reaching transformation of society. Bork has never deviated in any significant respect from what he regards as his insight that the only speech protected by the Constitution is "explicitly and predominantly political speech." For years he excluded from protection all art, all science, all philosophy, education, and literature. He has more recently relented, to include, in protected "political speech," "science" and "normative discussion." Art, literature, and the rest may still, without constitutional protection, be censored, banned, subject to criminal prosecution. Beyond that, Bork specifically removes from his own category of constitutionally protected "political speech" *"any speech advocating the violation of law"* (italics added).

In this he consciously repudiates, as "deficient in logic and analysis as well as in history," the "clear and present danger" standard enunciated more than sixty years ago by Holmes and Brandeis and developed in the intervening decades by the Court. But what he misses entirely, in seeming so innocuously to exclude from protection "any speech advocating the violation of law," is the crucial question of who is to define "advocacy," or "violation," or even "speech." It is clear that if the judiciary, in the form of Justice Bork, refuses to make that determination, then someone else—the police, the neighbors, the prosecutor, at best the state legislatures or the federal executive or legislative branches—will. The Framers' very purpose in protecting speech so nearly absolutely ("Congress shall make no law . . . abridging the freedom of speech") rested on their enlightened perception that "tyranny" resorts immediately to repression by declaring criminal the articulation of unpopular ideas in, precisely political, speech. Since any utterance other than a bland affirmation of the status quo can be construed as political "advocacy" of the unprotected kind, the result can be an intimidated, essentially totalitarian silence—in which the majority is not merely prevented by the absence of speech from deciding what laws it really wants but is finally prevented even from knowing whether it still constitutes a majority.

These are not abstract dangers. Bork's formulation, excluding from constitutional protection "any speech advocating the violation of law," ignores the possibility that there can be—indeed the certainty that there have been—in this century and even in this country, bad, as it turned out unlawful, laws. It was "advocacy" of the "violation" of bad, as it turned out constitutionally unlawful, state "law"—advocacy in the form of boycotts, sit-ins, marches, sermons, peaceful demonstrations—that brought the unlawfulness of those bad laws to the attention of the federal courts, and that obliged first the courageous, honorable, mostly Republican judges on the Fifth Circuit, and then the Justices on the Supreme Court, to "say what the law is," and thereby participate in one of the great periods of constitutional adjudication. If Bork's narrow conception of "explicitly political" speech had been the view of those "advocates" and those judges and that Court, it would have made impossible the whole peaceful and lawful transformation of the South.

As late as 1971, however, Bork could still write of the Framers that "they indicated a value when they say that speech is in some sense special." But they didn't "indicate a value," nor did they say that speech "is in some sense special." They said, "Congress shall make no law." It was only because the plain language of the Constitution made it impossible for Bork to reach his preferred result, a formulation so narrow and repressive that it drained even the words "political" and "speech" of meaning, that he abandoned all pretense of "strict construction" or "judicial restraint" and went on to make laws of his own. In fact, there is a sense in which all issues of law, privacy, equal protection, race, due process, and speech are combined for Bork in a single set of ideological commitments, generally antagonistic to individual liberty, which he commonly expresses in terms of "morals," "public morals," "public morality."

In two recent speeches on law and religion, for example, he ascribed dismissively to John Stuart Mill a notion that "an individual's liberty may not be infringed unless he cause harm to others," and that "material injury" counts as harm but "moral or aesthetic injury does not." "Thus," Bork wrote—as if warning of a particularly ugly and self-evidently untenable proposition—"morality becomes a matter for the individual, not for democratic regulation." Not pausing even to dismiss such a notion, he proceeded toward the "result" he had in mind: "relaxation of currently rigid secularist doctrine" and a few "sensible things to be done," namely the "reintroduction of some religion into public schools" and "some greater religious symbolism in our public life." So much for Supreme Court precedent in school prayer cases and in many matters of church and state.

The ease and frequency with which Bork uses the words "moral," "morality," "public morality"—let alone whatever is meant by "moral or aesthetic injury"—might disturb any judge, senator, or other citizen who is not altogether certain what these words, applied without definition or qualification of any kind to completely private and in no sense violent or criminal conduct, can possibly mean. Bork has used the words most freely to apply, in one way, to matters of sex, where he would impose "public morality" as "majoritarian" and "conclusively valid for that very reason"; and, in an entirely other way, to race, where—in an article published in *The New Republic* as early as August 1963, and developed in many subsequent articles and decisions—he scathingly deplores precisely the "morality of enforcing" majoritarian "morals," and the resulting "loss in a vital area of personal liberty," indeed the "principle of unsurpassed ugliness" embodied in "self-righteously imposing" the degree of "morality" required by the Interstate Public Accommodations Act, which became Title II of the Civil Rights Act of 1964.

In other words, where "morality" seems to him to have to do with sex, he wants to impose it; where it has to do with race, he can think of nothing uglier than imposing "morality."

II.

I have been a registered Republican all my voting life. I had set out, unalarmed, to review William H. Rehnquist's book, *The Supreme Court: How It Was, How It Is.* The book seems at first equable and innocuous, a chatty little memoir of Rehnquist's clerkship in 1952 for Justice Robert H. Jackson, and perhaps a modest civics lesson, which Rehnquist himself describes as a "history of the Court from the time of John Marshall to the middle of the 20th century," and an attempt to "give some idea of how the Court has responded to important developments in the history of our country." The tone is personable, informal—with nothing, for instance, of the aggressive, sarcastic, intellectually shallow, biased, and even dishonest quality that has been characteristic of many of Justice Rehnquist's opinions, particularly in dissent. In a Reagan Court, Rehnquist would be less frequently, if at all, in dissent. The degree of compromise required to enlist four other Justices in a majority for his decisions might seem congenial to the nonconfrontational, nonideological fellow who wrote this apparently not very substantial book. Then the substance emerges with great clarity. The most remarkable thing about this first book about the Supreme Court by a sitting Chief Justice has to do entirely, almost breathtakingly, with what it eradicates and omits.

Rehnquist says he has omitted all cases after 1953, "because I wanted to avoid any discussion of the cases and doctrines in which any of my present colleagues have played a part." He does, however, mention a 1983 case, a 1974 case, and a 1954 case, Brown v. Board of Education—which, it may be recalled, Rehnquist, clerking for Justice Jackson, wrote a controversial memo to oppose. The least important category of omission has to do with this interesting aspect of his clerkship. Rehnquist's 1952 memo in Brown, which was entitled "Memo: A Random Thought on the Segregation Cases," included these words.

> But as I read the history of this Court, it has seldom been out of hot water when attempting to interpret these individual rights. . . . [Brown] quite clearly is not one of those extreme cases which commands intervention from one of any conviction. . . . To the argument made by Thurgood not John Marshall that a majority may not deprive a minority of its constitutional right, the answer must be made that while this is sound in theory, in the long run it is the majority who will determine what the constitutional rights of the minority are [italics added].

And:

> One hundred and fifty years of attempts on the part of this Court to protect minority rights of any kind—whether those of

business, slaveholders, or Jehovah's Witnesses—have all met the same fate. One by one the cases . . . have been sloughed off and crept silently to rest. . . . I realize that it is an unpopular and unhumanitarian position for which I have been excoriated by "liberal" colleagues, but I think *Plessy* v. *Ferguson* was right and should be reaffirmed [italics added].

At his confirmation hearings Rehnquist claimed that the memo, in which the word "I" appears five times, was a draft not of his own views but of Justice Jackson's, in preparation for a "conference of the justices." This account has been disputed, in 1971 and 1986, as "a smear" by Elsie Douglas, Jackson's secretary, who added, "Justice Jackson did not ask law clerks to express his views." It has also been disputed by Jackson's biographer, Dennis J. Hutchinson, whom John A. Jenkins quoted in the *New York Times* of March 3, 1985, as having examined "every box, every detail" and having found no instance of Justice Jackson's ever having asked a law clerk to prepare a memo summarizing the Justice's own views. And Jackson of course was part of a unanimous Court in *Brown*.

The memo was drafted, moreover, in evident ignorance of the fact that Justice Jackson himself had written major decisions "to protect minority rights" in many cases—one of the most eloquent and important of which was *Board of Education* v. *Barnette*, a 1943 decision upholding the rights precisely of Jehovah's Witnesses. And since Justice Jackson had also written, in perhaps his second most famous opinion, one of the major statements on behalf of "minority rights" in the history of the Court (his dissent in 1944 in *Korematsu* v. *U.S.*, the Japanese-American internment case), he would certainly have had no conceivable occasion, at a "conference of the justices" or elsewhere, to describe himself as having been "excoriated by 'liberal' colleagues." It does, in fact, seem inescapable from the very title of the memo, and from its form, style, and manifest content, that the "I" in this memo can be no one other than the clerk whose initials appear at the end of it, Rehnquist himself.

Hutchinson has more recently discovered two other memos drafted by Rehnquist as a clerk. Both opposed what turned out to be the majority opinion in *Terry* v. *Adams* (1953). "It is about time the Court faced the fact," Rehnquist wrote, "that the white people in the South don't like the colored people. . . . Liberals should be the first to realize . . . that it does not do to push blindly through towards one constitutional goal without paying attention to other 'equally desirable values' that are being 'trampled' on in the process." The "one constitutional goal" upheld in *Terry* v. *Adams* (in which Justice Jackson, joining seven other Justices, concurred as he had in *Brown*) was the right of blacks in Texas to vote in a preprimary that was in effect the local election. The "equally desirable value" being "trampled on" was the "right" of whites to exclude blacks from the vote.

It might be understandable that Rehnquist does not want to revive interest in these memos, or for that matter in any substantive issue he might have addressed in his year and a half as clerk. What gives a small clue that there is an element of at least cosmetic "defactualization" in this personal reminiscence is the fact that the author refers three times to Justice Jackson's secretary Elsie Douglas, in breezy, comradely, clerkish terms. A reader would have no indication either that the memos exist, or that there had once been an important case called *Terry* v. *Adams,* or even that this Elsie Douglas has troubled twice to make public distinctly uncomradely statements to the effect that the author is a liar by whom her boss Justice Jackson has been "smeared."

The second, astounding omission from this "history of the Court from the time of John Marshall to the middle of the 20th century," and from this account of "how the Court has responded to important developments in the history of our country," has ideological implications almost as strong as the most extreme positions declared by Bork. Rehnquist has left out, in addition to all the decisions of the Warren Court, in silence and as it were in passing, virtually all the major lines of cases—having to do with privacy; speech, whether political advocacy or other expression; voting rights; racial equality; prior restraint; right to counsel; illegal search and seizure; freedom of religion; and personal liberty—in which the Court has upheld an individual or minority right against the state, dating back through the thirties and forties, under Charles Evans Hughes and Harlan Stone (both of whom Rehnquist professes to admire) and before.

Nothing here of Bork's despised 1948 *Shelley* v. *Kraemer.* Nothing of Holmes' and Brandeis' "clear and present danger" cases of the 1920s. Nothing either of the Scottsboro Boys case in 1932; or even of the case in 1914 in which the Court first upheld the exclusionary rule. Nothing of the free speech victories of the Hughes Court, or of Hughes' eloquent decision in 1931 in *Near* v. *Minnesota* on behalf of freedom of the press.

Nothing particularly of a proposition advanced by Stone, speaking for a unanimous, far from "liberal" Court in 1938, in footnote 4 of *U.S. v. Carolene Products*—the most important footnote in American judicial history. That statement, anathema to Bork and Rehnquist, has been crucial to the evolving doctrine of the Court with respect to the constitutional rights of individuals against the "presumption of constitutionality."

All these omissions—in which the response of the Court precisely to "important developments in the history of our country" has been eradicated—might reflect nothing more alarming than an immense oversight, based perhaps on Rehnquist's lifelong predisposition in favor of assertions of governmental power over individual and minority rights. With the single exception of the 1952 Steel Seizure case, in which the Court upheld a lower-court decision enjoining President Truman from exercising an emergency authority to run the steel companies at the time of the Korean War—a decision Rehnquist explains, perhaps tellingly, as the result of public-relations pressures on the Court—Rehnquist approves, indeed even troubles to mention, only those twentieth-century decisions that uphold the exercise of governmental power.

The result is that the book, far from being a bland civics lesson, turns out to be a work of disinformation. The effect of erasing all that history, namely, the history of the great decisions of the Hughes Court and the Stone Court in the 1930s and the 1940s, and the major opinions of Holmes, Brandeis, even Jackson, is not only to make the Warren Court and the Burger Court of the 1960s and 1970s seem an aberration. It is to leave a blank, a silence as total as that which eliminates from the "histories" of the Soviet Union all persons and events uncongenial to official Soviet "history," and from German and Japanese textbooks all unwelcome references to even the most recent and major events in the history of those countries. And by eradicating from "history" an immense body of constitutional adjudication dating back at least six decades, the book attempts to establish for any act or agenda of a Reagan Court a legitimacy, a continuity with precedent, that can be based only on a "defactualizing" silence of this sweeping kind.

This raises still a third remarkable thing about the Rehnquist book. The work would have no interest, and no chance of publication, except for the position of its author. The phenomenon of the first book about the Supreme Court by a sitting Chief Justice turns out to have ramifications of its own. Normally the people go to the Court for its decisions, not the other way around. What is "public" about the Court is precisely and only those decisions, not some public-relations "image"—least of all any electioneering of the sort that is proper to candidates for political office but not to members of the judicial, tenured branch. For the first time, with this book, as with the Bork campaign, judges, far from exercising "judicial restraint" or "deference" to the other branches, are reaching out, through speeches, books, manipulation of the press and television, to develop a political base of power and *a constituency for themselves*. If they succeed in that, they will become at once, with their life tenure and their last word in constitutional matters, not the least but the most dangerous branch.

In this context, a striking thing about Bork's writings is the political content of the speeches he has been making in recent years throughout the country. He has alluded in scornful, populist terms to the "gentrification" of the "judicial culture"—as though the Framers themselves had not been gentry, as though the values he imputes to that "culture" were not precisely the ones the Framers entrusted to the judiciary, and as though the only nonideological credential he has for the nomination were not that degree of "gentrification" embodied in having taught at the University of Chicago and at Yale. Another striking thing is the fact that the lines of pre–Warren Court cases Rehnquist omits are precisely the ones Bork has described most scornfully and that he would vote to overrule. A third is the degree to which these writings are incompatible with any moderate "image" the public-relations campaign for Bork's confirmation has been trying to promote. And the last is the intense "polarization," the attempt to raise again ugly and divisive issues on which the vast majority of citizens has long been reconciled, that Rehnquist's book and Bork's nomination, in defactualized, "centrist" disguise, bring to the nation's highest Court.

There exist, for example, only two occasions on which Bork has written anything even arguably in support of a First Amendment right: a concurrence in a minor libel case in which the plaintiff was a Marxist, the press defendants were Evans and Novak, and Bork's remarks were widely understood to be part of his lobbying effort, through his judicial opinions, for a position on the Court. Usually, these missives were addressed to Attorney General Edwin Meese; in this single instance, Bork addressed instead a vital instrument of that campaign, the press. The second case was an opinion in which, in direct opposition to the will of

Congress, as expressed in legislation vetoed by the President, Bork opposed the fairness doctrine. (In 1969, in *Red Lion* v. *FCC*, the Supreme Court upheld the fairness doctrine, and Justice White, speaking for a unanimous Court, wrote that the FCC's elaborations of the fairness doctrine "enhance rather than abridge freedoms of speech and press.") There also exists a single decision in which Bork appeared to uphold a plaintiff in an environmental claim. On July 28, 1987, outnumbered eleven to one on an environmental issue, Bork switched his vote and wrote a unanimous decision *en banc* for the D.C. appellate court. The case was described, in the *Times*, as an example of his "collegiality," his "open-mindedness," his "willingness to change his mind," and, of all things, his "ability to build a consensus."

When "defactualization" has reached these proportions, and when the press, and even some members of the political, legal, and academic establishments, acquiesce or even actively promote it, there exists the mentality, and a real danger, of judicial "coups d'état." The Senate is being asked to confirm and perpetuate for years an ideology that has been decisively rejected, most recently in the elections, but really since the founding of the Republic. Rehnquist only omits mention of a vast body of constitutional law. Bork goes much further. His tone is far less amiable. And his published work, in contrast to his "image," makes unmistakable his intention to overrule whatever outcomes do not suit him. The choice is inescapably between the nominee and the Constitution. *The Supreme Court: How It Was, How It Is* leaves off in 1954. "The Supreme Court: How It Is, How It's Going to Be," if the nomination is confirmed, will resume around 1922, and the country will be unrecognizable for it.

—1987

DECODING THE STARR REPORT

The six-volume Report by Kenneth W. Starr to the U.S. House of Representatives—which consists, so far, of the single-volume *Referral* and five volumes of *Appendices and Supplemental Materials*—is, in many ways, an utterly preposterous document: inaccurate, mindless, biased, disorganized, unprofessional, and corrupt. What it is textually is a voluminous work of demented pornography, with many fascinating characters and several largely hidden story lines. What it is politically is an attempt, through its own limitless preoccupation with sexual material, to set aside, even obliterate, the relatively dull requirements of real evidence and constitutional procedure.

Less obvious at first, and then altogether unmistakable, is the author's scorn for the House of Representatives. The power to prosecute an impeachment is the only important power that the Constitution grants solely to the House. Before the *Communication from the Office of the Independent Counsel, Kenneth W. Starr,* as the document is called, it was unthinkable that *any* official, of any branch of government, would presume to set forth, in a document submitted to the House, in the course of an impeachment inquiry, such conclusions as that the President "lied," or "attempted to obstruct justice," or any of the other judgments that the Report presumes to make on the very first page of its introduction—let alone include on its cover and as part of its title the name of its primary author. On the cover of this document the name of Henry J. Hyde, chairman of the House Judiciary Committee, does not appear. The words "United States House of Representatives" appear in letters about half the size of "Kenneth W. Starr."

From the moment Chairman Hyde permitted Mr. Starr thus to interpose his views between the committee and the evidence, and authorized the publication of these documents under the congressional seal, he set in motion an unprecedented process, in which the House is nearly powerless. On October 9, 1998, the chairman said he would permit his committee to call Mr. Starr, but that he saw "no need" to call, for example, Monica Lewinsky. Other members of the panel said they could rely, for the testimony of witnesses, on Mr. Starr's Report. Apart from the obvious implications of a proceeding in which the judge's major witness is the prosecutor—and other witnesses are neither cross-examined nor even called—this decision limits the power of the House to approving or disapproving the recommendations of the Independent Counsel. For the purposes of impeachment, the Independent Counsel has become the House.

There are signs that the document was never intended to be understood, or even read, by anyone. The absence of dates, tables of contents, index, chronology, context, accurate headings, and logic of any sort from the five supplementary volumes is almost the least of it. So are the distortions and misrepresentations in the Report itself of what the record actually shows. Documents published by the Government Printing Office are often a marvel of information and legibility, printed with great speed and under pressure. In the 7,793 pages that constitute just the *Appendices and Supplemental Materials*, however, there are embedded thousands of smaller pages (sometimes four, often six tiny pages, compressed within a single larger page) in type so minuscule that, quite apart from the time constraints on reporters and other citizens, visual constraints—the eyesight, for example, of aging congressmen—absolutely preclude the reading of vast portions of the text.

There are also countless redactions, blackings-out, excisions by the House Judiciary Committee, which add to the general disorder. The dates of birth of all but a few witnesses, for example, are blacked out—an attempt, presumably, to spare these witnesses (whose privacy is not just violated but mocked in these documents by the prosecutors' constant assurances that their testimony is "secret," and that "there are no unauthorized persons present") the embarrassment of having their ages widely known. Other deletions are inexplicable. Names are blacked out in one place only to appear, in precisely the same context, in another. Relatively mild and perfectly obvious four-letter words are blacked out while other words, traditionally regarded as stronger and more offensive, are left in. Variants of the word "shit," for example, are deleted, but Linda Tripp's remark to Monica Lewinsky "You never, ever realized whose dick you were sucking" is unedited.

There are printed invitations to parties, accompanied by the guest lists. The names of the hosts, on the invitations, are blacked out. These might be mere examples of work done innocently or in haste. It soon becomes clear, however, that a fundamental strategy of the authors is unintelligibility.

To submit a massive document in which it is literally impossible to find information by title, date, alphabetical or chronological sequence, or context of any kind makes it difficult to check whether any particular conclusion is warranted—whether there is evidence for the opposite conclusion, or another conclusion altogether. As a series of anecdotes, of prurient gossip raised, for the first time, to the level of constitutional crisis, the story the Office of the Independent Counsel wants to tell is by now widely known. People seem to have made up their minds about it. Underneath that story, however, scattered in almost incomprehensible pieces throughout the text, are at least two other stories, which the authors go to considerable lengths to hide.

The setting is the White House—a peculiar, almost farcically disordered place of rumor, envy, spite, betrayal, birthday parties. Everyone, from the President's secretary, Betty Currie, through the Uniformed Secret Service guards and the stewards in the Oval Office pantry, seems to think nothing of accepting presents—ties, Godiva chocolates, pocket handkerchiefs, body lotions, gift certificates for manicures and pedicures at Georgette Klinger—from Monica Lewinsky, a young woman who is regarded, almost universally and, as it turns out, with astonishing understatement, as a "stalker," a "hall surfer," a "cling on," and a "clutch." One of the pantry stewards, Bayani Nelvis, has dinners with Ms. Lewinsky, exchanges gifts and confidences with her, offers her the President's cigars, and, according to Ms. Lewinsky, calls her from a presidential vacation on Martha's Vineyard to invite her to come and share a house with him. Mr. Nelvis denies the invitation to stay with him on the Vineyard. On many other matters he is mum.

Another staff member, rumored to be a "graduate," or former intimate of the President's, "clomps" through the corridors wearing the President's shoes. Young people offend older staff members by spilling Coke on White House carpets and putting their feet up on White House chairs. The Uniformed Secret Service guards at the White House feel free to spread scurrilous gossip—among themselves and to other people. On one occasion they tell Ms. Lewinsky, who is trying to enter the White House, that the President already has a female visitor in the Oval Office. Ms. Lewinsky flies into a rage—although she has not visited the President in weeks and was not invited this time. She berates Betty Currie for lying to her about the President's whereabouts. Ms. Currie scolds the guards for their indiscretion. The guards are miffed.

In the summer of 1995, Ms. Lewinsky, who frequently describes herself as "insecure," comes to the White House, as an unpaid intern. She repeatedly approaches the President and "introduces" herself. On November 15, 1995, Ms. Lewinsky says, she flashes her thong underwear at him, tells him she has a crush on him, and accompanies him to a secluded corridor. He asks if he may kiss her. Later that evening, when they meet again, she grabs his crotch and performs oral sex on him—an approach she tries to repeat at virtually every subsequent opportunity.

According to the testimony of Ms. Lewinsky—and she is not one to understate—there are, in all, nine incidents of these, as the Report calls them, "in-person" sexual encounters: three in 1995, four in 1996, and two in 1997. In January 1996, Ms. Lewinsky says, she and the President have phone sex. He does not call her for a week. Feeling "a little bit insecure about whether he had liked it or didn't like it" and wondering "if this was sort of developing into some kind of a longer-term relationship than what I thought it initially might have been," she goes to the Oval Office and asks him whether this is "just about sex," or whether he has some interest in trying to get to know her as a person. He assures her that he "cherishes" his time with her.

On February 19, 1996, the President tells Ms. Lewinsky that their physical relationship must end. He does not feel right about it. Their friendship, however, can continue. This is not an entirely unusual thing for one person to say to another. It is not often misunderstood. Ms. Lewinsky perseveres. Wherever the President is—in the Oval Office, at staff birthday parties, jogging, attending church, at fund-raisers, departing on journeys and returning from them—Ms. Lewinsky contrives to "position" herself there. This does not go unremarked.

On April 5, 1996, the Friday before Easter, Ms. Lewinsky learns that she has been dismissed from her White House job and transferred—with a considerable rise in rank and salary—to the Pentagon. On that Sunday, which is Easter, she goes to the President to complain. He tells her that "after the election" he will be able to find her another White House job. Another young woman might have noticed, and been deterred by, the prospect of so long a separation. Not Ms. Lewinsky. She performs oral sex and departs. She renews her efforts, calling, writing, sending presents.

The President now wards off any private visits from her for nearly eleven months—from April 7, 1996, until February 28, 1997. Ms. Lewinsky hates her job at the Pentagon. She is bored by it. The job entails transcription. She has no typing skills and cannot spell. From her desk, by telephone, by E-mail, and in person, she complains. She sends cards, ties, other presents, importuning letters. She harangues Ms. Currie with incessant calls. She wants to talk to the President, in person and by phone. She wants the White House job she feels she has been promised. The President and Ms. Currie say that they will try. Perhaps not surprisingly, there is no White House job for her. She still manages to position herself in the President's path. She keeps informed of his schedule through Betty Currie and the pantry steward Bayani Nelvis.

Finally, on February 28, 1997, she manages to visit the President again. He gives her a hatpin and Walt Whitman's *Leaves of Grass*. "I wanted to perform oral sex on him," Ms. Lewinsky testifies, "and so I did." On every prior occasion the President has insisted that Ms. Lewinsky stop before what she tends to call completion. On this day she persuades the President to let her continue. "It's important to me," she says. Afterward, Ms. Lewinsky finds—perhaps this was always her intention—semen on her dress. On March 29, 1997, according to Ms. Lewinsky, there is a similar event. The in-person sexual encounters are at an end.

On May 24, 1997, the President calls Ms. Lewinsky in. He says again that their affair, such as it is, is over. He tells her that she is "a great person" and that they will still be friends. He is determined to be good. Ms. Lewinsky attributes the breakup to the President's "wanting to do the right thing in God's eyes." Three days later, the Supreme Court announces its decision in the Paula Jones case. The Jones suit, which accuses him of sexual harassment, can proceed while he is still in office—without "distract[ing him] from his public duties." The decision is surely one of the worst in the Court's history. For now it is the law.

Ms. Lewinsky has never been reticent or soft-spoken. Now she becomes ever more implacable and wild. She phones and pages Ms. Currie at all hours, later even visits her at home. It would not be quite accurate to say that this is just a particularly intense love story. Ms. Lewinsky has too many other interests—shopping, M&M's, finding a good job—one that pays well, with a good title, and that will "intrigue" her—new men: an Australian, a "health nut," an employee of the Pentagon, a former lover, married, with whom she resumes an affair and whom she had blackmailed some years before, by threatening to disclose the affair to his wife if he did not see her again.

Meanwhile, Ms. Lewinsky has made friends with a third major character, Linda Tripp—a colleague, who has also been transferred, under murky circumstances, from the White House to the Pentagon. Ms. Tripp says that Ms. Lewinsky did not confide in her about the "affair" until late September or early October 1996. In January 1997, Ms. Tripp begins to advise Ms. Lewinsky about strategies for getting a new White House job and also for regaining the affection of the President. She edits Ms. Lewinsky's letters and helps her compose audiotapes to send to him. Within a month of this collaboration, Ms. Lewinsky manages to visit the President for the first time in a year, and this visit produces Mr. Starr's most famous piece of "evidence," the blue dress.

Sometime in May or June of 1997, Ms. Tripp begins (at Ms. Lewinsky's request, she claims) to keep a notebook of the history of Ms. Lewinsky's encounters with the President—in order, she says, to analyze them, and look for a "pattern." At approximately the same time, Ms. Lewinsky uses her computer at the Pentagon to create (at Ms. Tripp's suggestion, she says) a "matrix," or spreadsheet, detailing her meetings with the President. Ms. Tripp preserves her notebook. Ms. Lewinsky soon becomes as persistent with her new confidante—calling her at all hours, at home and at the office, leaving messages, interrupting meetings, visiting her at her desk several times a day—as she is with Ms. Currie or the President.

In November, Ms. Tripp testifies, she sees, for the second time, the dress in Ms. Lewinsky's closet, the dress Ms. Lewinsky wore during her visit to the President on February 28, 1997. Ms. Tripp is adamant in her insistence that the stain on the dress be preserved.

> MS. TRIPP: Hey, listen, my cousin is a genetic whatchamacall-it. . . . He said that [if a rape victim] has preserved a pinprick size of crusted semen 10 years from that time . . . they can match the DNA. . . .

MS. LEWINSKY: So why can't I scratch that crap off and put it in a plastic bag?

MS. TRIPP: . . . [P]ack it in with your treasures. . . . It could be your only insurance policy down the road.

Tripp told the grand jury: "I wanted some way for there to be proof of what he was doing with Monica." Of course, by the time Ms. Tripp sees the dress, the President has not been "doing" anything with Monica—except trying to avoid her—for more than eight months.

In October 1997, Ms. Tripp, for whatever reason, begins to tape her phone conversations with Ms. Lewinsky. The prosecutors subsequently lead her through a vast amount of testimony, before the grand jury, about her own life and motives, as well as what she claims to know about Ms. Lewinsky. Fairly late in Ms. Tripp's testimony, a juror speaks up. The jury has a question. Nothing could be clearer than that the prosecutors do not want Ms. Tripp to answer it.

A JUROR: Why did you decide to document?

MR. EMMICK [associate independent counsel]: Can I interrupt, ma'am? I'm sorry. Just to clarify.

MR. SUSANIN [associate independent counsel]: So to clarify this grand juror's question—

A JUROR: Hold on. Can I get an answer to my question?

Apparently not.

MR. SUSANIN: Can I ask a question, ma'am. Just to clarify?

Forty confusing lines later, the juror tries again.

A JUROR: Ms. Tripp, why were you documenting?

THE WITNESS: Why was I documenting?

A JUROR: . . . documenting other than the notebook?

THE WITNESS: Oh, the notebook—well, maybe I should say different words so it doesn't sound contradictory at all because it wasn't. The notebook was something Monica asked me to do in my head to understand cause and effect of all the ups and downs of her relationship in intimate detail.

The jurors keep trying to find out why Ms. Tripp was constantly elic-iting and making tapes of Ms. Lewinsky's confidences. None of Ms. Tripp's explanations of why she taped make any sense. To "arm myself with a record" so that she could testify about Monica Lewinsky, truth-fully, under oath in the Jones case, without fear of being defamed, she says, by the President's lawyers or destroyed by others in the White House. She was "scared," she says many times, but her "integrity" required her to tell the truth. There was, however, no reason whatever, during the months when Ms. Tripp was taping, to imagine that she could pos-sibly be subpoenaed in the Paula Jones case. All her testimony would have been inadmissable, as hearsay and on other grounds. It took a great deal of work, on Ms. Tripp's part and the Special Counsel's, to enable her to intrude herself in the case at all.

In March 1997, Michael Isikoff, a reporter from *Newsweek*, came to Ms. Tripp's desk in the Pentagon. He told her that Kathleen Willey claimed that the President had once subjected her to sexual harassment. Mr. Isikoff said Ms. Willey had given him Ms. Tripp's name as a con-firming witness. Ms. Tripp told Mr. Isikoff she recalled the incident in question, but that Ms. Willey had actually solicited, welcomed, and sub-sequently boasted about the President's embrace. In August 1997, *News-week* published Mr. Isikoff's story—citing Ms. Tripp as a source. A lot has since been said—by Ms. Tripp and in the press—about the matter. What has gradually become clear is this: Ms. Tripp tried to persuade Mr. Isikoff to write not about Ms. Willey but about a former White House intern, "M," who was now working at the Pentagon. Ms. Tripp's testi-mony varies about when, and by what means, she conveyed Ms. Lew-insky's full name to Mr. Isikoff. She admits he knew it by October, the month when she began to tape.

And another chronology begins to emerge about Ms. Tripp. She de-scribes herself to the grand jury as having once been a fairly "apolitical" member of the White House staff in the Bush administration, in the department of media affairs. (It was there, she says, that she first came to know Mr. Isikoff.) She stayed on until August 1994 in the Clinton White House. She believes that Hillary Clinton became "cold" to her— perhaps as a result, Ms. Tripp says, of a mistaken idea that Ms. Tripp had a romantic interest in the President—or that the President had a romantic interest in Ms. Tripp. Ms. Tripp was transferred to the office of White House Counsel Bernard W. Nussbaum, where she was, she says, as she had always been, "loyal" and "apolitical." She worked on what she called "sensitive matters," like "the appointment of the special prosecutor." Odd.

As early as 1993, however, Ms. Tripp had been so appalled, she says, by the Clinton White House that a friend, Tony Snow (a right-wing journalist and occasional stand-in for Rush Limbaugh), urged her to write a book. Mr. Snow offered to put her in touch with a literary agent, Lucianne Goldberg. Ms. Tripp declined. In the summer of 1996—perhaps coincidentally after Ms. Lewinsky's first months at the Pentagon—Ms. Tripp changed her mind. She took Mr. Snow up on his offer and met with Ms. Goldberg, who suggested a ghostwriter. Ms. Tripp ultimately abandoned the project. One character whom Ms. Tripp had intended to describe in her book, however, was none other than Kathleen Willey.

Ms. Tripp, it turns out, had known Kathleen Willey since 1993. As Ms. Tripp describes her, Ms. Willey was, at the time, an unpaid White House volunteer, infatuated with the President and determined to have an affair with him. According to Ms. Tripp, Ms. Willey dressed provocatively, would "position" herself in the President's path, sent him notes, and contrived to bump into him. Ms. Tripp soon began to advise her on strategy and to help her edit cards and letters to the President. Ms. Tripp listened to Ms. Willey's confidences and received her frequent phone calls at home. In short, not an altogether unfamiliar story. As Ms. Tripp tells it, however, she harbors at least one trace of bitterness if not of envy. "I was annoyed," she says, because when Ms. Tripp left the White House, Ms. Willey was hired "essentially in my stead."

There is at least one other, rather hidden, element of Ms. Tripp's story. When she began to tape, Ms. Tripp tells the grand jurors in answer to a question, "I had never even thought about the Independent Counsel in my wildest dreams." This is a statement that the prosecutors—if not Ms. Tripp herself—had every obligation to amplify. Because Ms. Tripp had not only thought or dreamed of the Office of the Independent Counsel, she had appeared before it at least twice before—first under Robert Fiske, and then under Kenneth W. Starr.

According to an FBI report—whose very existence is not acknowledged anywhere in the Starr documents—Ms. Tripp appeared on April

12, 1994, at the Office of the Independent Counsel. Among her concerns was the death of Deputy White House Counsel Vincent Foster. She had suspicions about that death. One source of her suspicion, the FBI report says, was Mr. Foster's conduct when Ms. Tripp brought him what turned out to be his last lunch, a hamburger:

> He removed the onions from his hamburger, which struck Tripp as odd in retrospect. She couldn't understand why he would do that if he was planning to commit suicide. It did not make sense to her that he might be worried about his breath if that were the case. The agent adds: "Tripp does not know if Foster likes or dislikes onions."

Whatever her beliefs—or thoughts or dreams—the fact that neither Ms. Tripp in her testimony nor the prosecutors before the grand jury nor the Independent Counsel anywhere in his Report mentions these contacts at least three years previously between Ms. Tripp and the Office of the Independent Counsel suggests that the real reason Ms. Tripp was taping, from the first, was this: The Office of the Independent Counsel asked her to.

During the year or so—November 1996 to October 1997—when Ms. Lewinsky was still haranguing, plotting, and threatening, in her campaign to return to a White House job, Ms. Tripp had encouraged her to believe that this was a simple matter, and that failure to get such a job would appear to confirm her undeserved reputation as a stalker. Ms. Tripp professed to be outraged on Ms. Lewinsky's behalf that a job had not been found. Ms. Lewinsky became increasingly immoderate in her demands and her behavior. She had been "yelling," at the President, and at Ms. Currie. When she could not reach him on September 12, 1997, she had stood for an hour and a half at an entrance to the White House, "screaming."

On October 6, 1997, Ms. Tripp changed her advice to Ms. Lewinsky. She said that, according to "Kate," a friend of Ms. Tripp's at the National Security Council, Ms. Lewinsky would never work at the White House again, that she was, in fact, known and disliked there as a stalker, and that the best thing for her to do would be to get out of town. This had the not unpredictable effect of setting Ms. Lewinsky off on another frenzy of phone calls to the White House—this time, however, to arrange for a job in another city. Ms. Tripp suggested to Ms. Lewinsky that she ask for a job in New York. According to an FBI report, Ms. Tripp also advised Ms. Lewinsky "to find some way to ask for help from Vernon Jordan."

By this time, it seemed the White House was eager to get Ms. Lewinsky a job in New York, encouraging her not to be silent in any legal matter but merely to go away. In early November, Ms. Lewinsky was offered a job at the UN working for Ambassador Bill Richardson. Ms. Tripp found in this offer a new source of outrage. The offer came "too fast," "so they won't have to—so they will consider it settled." It had Ms. Lewinsky "railroaded," "backed into a corner" as to whether she wanted to take it or not. Ms. Lewinsky turned the job down. At this point, no matter what the President or Ms. Currie said or did, it became—for Ms. Tripp and then for Ms. Lewinsky—a fresh source of grievance and invective. Ms. Tripp encouraged Ms. Lewinsky to believe the White House did not appreciate how little trouble Ms. Lewinsky had been.

> MS. LEWINSKY: And I said [to the President], "You [expletive] tell me when I've been—when I've caused you trouble." I said, "You don't know trouble."
> MS. TRIPP: Man, he should be thanking his lucky stars.
> MS. LEWINSKY: No [expletive] shit.
> MS. TRIPP: That you're the farthest thing from trouble he's ever had. . . . I feel very strongly that he should be thanking his lucky stars, left, right, and center, that you are who you are. . . . Most people going through what you've gone through would have said hey, [expletive] you and the horse you rode in on and let me call the *National Enquirer*.
> MS. LEWINSKY: Yeah.

In December 1997, Ms. Tripp says, she became aware that in her home state of Maryland, surreptitiously taping phone conversations was illegal and that, far from being protected by this "insurance policy," this evidence of her truthfulness and integrity, she might actually go to jail. She contacted Ms. Goldberg, who began calling lawyers she knew, at the Chicago branch of Kirkland & Ellis, where Mr. Starr still worked at the time, sensing apparently no conflict of interest between his private practice and his work as Special Prosecutor. Ms. Goldberg also called lawyers at other firms, in Chicago, New York, Washington, and Los Angeles, about making contact on Ms. Tripp's behalf with the Office of the Independent Counsel to obtain immunity for the illegal taping.

It is not clear why Ms. Tripp needed an intermediary to make contact with Mr. Starr's office, since—as we know, but the grand jury and readers of Mr. Starr's Report do not—Ms. Tripp had been in touch with the Independent Counsel for at least three years.

Ms. Tripp and the Independent Counsel's office claim that she came to them for the first time on Monday, January 12, 1998, the day before their agents and the FBI equipped her with a body wire for a last conversation with Ms. Lewinsky. To make such use of Ms. Tripp, the Independent Counsel needed authorization, on an "emergency basis," from Attorney General Janet Reno or the three-judge special division of the U.S. Court of Appeals. They needed a legal basis for drawing Monica Lewinsky into their investigation. This presented some difficulty: The Independent Counsel was explicitly barred from joining his investigation with the work of the attorneys for Paula Jones. If Ms. Tripp could elicit from Ms. Lewinsky some evidence of a conspiracy to break the law— some evidence, for example, that the President had authorized Vernon Jordan to find a job for Ms. Lewinsky as a bribe for her to commit perjury—Mr. Starr would have some sort of argument for the expansion of his jurisdiction. He could make Ms. Lewinsky herself an agent for the Independent Counsel's office. But the deadlines were tight. The President was due to testify in the Jones case on January 17, 1998. So Starr wired Ms. Tripp, two days earlier, before he had any authorization from the attorney general or the appellate court to do so. He had to hope that the evidence Ms. Tripp would elicit, and tape with her body wire, would override this procedural concern.

Here was the situation in the Independent Counsel's office by the time they came to Ms. Lewinsky. Mr. Starr had recruited lawyers with experience prosecuting organized crime. Since at least the days of Robert Kennedy, the custom in organized-crime cases has been to get the suspects, violate their rights, and if you cannot convict them of one crime then somehow indict them for another. From the day in 1994 when Judge Starr offered to write an amicus brief in the Paula Jones case—moreover, through the years when, as Special Counsel, he maintained his lucrative private practice at Kirkland & Ellis—it was clear that he was by no means remarkable for scruple and in no sense averse to conflicts of interest of the most glaring kind. Nothing could be more obvious than his emotional, ideological, even social and professional links to the old case of Paula Jones. He became Special Counsel in 1994. By the 1996 election, he must have been frustrated and humiliated. None of his expensive lines of inquiry had worked out—not the suicide of Vincent Foster, not Travelgate or Filegate, certainly not Whitewater. Susan McDougal, after more than a year in jail for contempt, was still of no use to him. Webster Hubbell, whom he had sent to jail but given a limited grant of immunity in exchange for his testimony, had not really helped him, either. Vernon Jordan, who found money and jobs for Hubbell, was thriving alongside the newly reelected President. The prosecutor had spent millions so far, and he had failed. He would obviously like to find the constellation—a crime committed on the President's behalf by a subordinate, preferably a bribe by Vernon Jordan—somewhere, before the expiration of the President's term. The love life of Monica Lewinsky seems an odd place to look for that configuration. Yet, with a little prosecutorial zeal and creativity, it might be found. Mr. Starr's documents have vestiges of an attempt to show that it is there.

Another case of the jurors pursuing a line of inquiry in spite of the best efforts of the prosecutors occurs near the end of the testimony of Monica Lewinsky. The jurors want to know about her first encounter with the prosecutors from the Office of the Independent Counsel, on January 16, 1998, when Linda Tripp lured her into the midst of the prosecutors and FBI agents, who would detain her for most of the day and night.

"Tell us about that day," a juror says, and then another juror inquires about the encounter between Ms. Lewinsky and all those men from the Office of the Special Prosecutor and the FBI.

"Maybe if I could ask, what areas do you want to get into?" Mr. Emmick asks. "Because there's—you know—many hours of activity." A few lines later:

A JUROR: We want to know about that day.

A JUROR: That day.

A JUROR: The first question.

A JUROR: Yes.

A JUROR: We really want to know about that day.

MR. EMMICK: All right.

The jurors are right to insist on a description of the day. That was the day, January 16, 1998—and the night—when the prosecutors came as close as they have so far to bringing the entire constitutional system down.

Ms. Lewinsky starts to tell about that day. Ms. Lewinsky and Ms. Tripp had arranged to meet at the food court of the Ritz-Carlton in the Pentagon City mall.

> THE WITNESS: She was late. I saw her come down the escalator. And as I—as I walked toward her, she kind of motioned behind her and Agent [blank] and Agent [blank] presented themselves to me. . . . They told me . . . that they wanted to talk to me and give me a chance, I think, to cooperate, maybe. I—to help myself. I told them I wasn't speaking to them without my attorney.

This is the turning point. This is the moment when the investigation begins to reveal itself as what it truly is. There is absolutely no doubt, none whatsoever, that the investigators—prosecutors and FBI agents alike—were obliged by law to stop right there, without another word, until Ms. Lewinsky brought in her attorney. Indeed, they were required, under Title 28 of the Code of Federal Regulations, to have contacted her attorney in the first place. They did nothing of the kind.

> THE WITNESS: They told me . . . I should know I won't be given as much information and won't be able to help myself as much with my attorney there. So I agreed to go. I was so scared. (The witness begins crying.)

Two questions later, she turns to the lead attorney at this grand-jury hearing, Michael Emmick:

> THE WITNESS: Can Karin [Immergut] do the questioning now? This is—can I ask you to step out?
> MR. EMMICK: Sure. Okay. All right. . . .

MS. IMMERGUT: Okay. Did you go to a room with them at the hotel?

A. Yes.

Q. And what did you do then? Did you ever tell them that you wanted to call your mother?

A. I told them I wanted to talk to my attorney. . . . And they told me—Mike [Emmick] came out and introduced himself to me and told me that—that Janet Reno had sanctioned Ken Starr to investigate my actions in the Paula Jones case, that they—that they knew I had signed a false affidavit, they had me on tape saying I had committed perjury, that they were going to—that I could go to jail for twenty-seven years, they were going to charge me with perjury and obstruction of justice and subornation of perjury and witness tampering and something else.

Q. And you're saying "they," at that point, who was talking to you about that stuff?

A. Mike Emmick and the two FBI guys. . . . And I just—I felt so bad.

This is an extraordinary scene. Monica Lewinsky, who has faced hour after hour, day after day of questioning about her most intimate experiences, has quietly drawn the line. She has asked the prosecutor, Michael Emmick, one of the participants in the events of "that day," to leave the room. It is a side of Monica Lewinsky that has not appeared before.

Q. I guess later, just to sort of finish up. I guess . . . was there a time then that you were—you just waited with the prosecutor until your mother came down?

A. No.

Q. Okay.

A. I mean, there was, but they—they told me they wanted me to cooperate. I asked them what cooperating meant, it entailed, and they told me . . . that they had had me on tape saying things from the lunch that I had had with Linda at the Ritz-Carlton . . . then they told me that I—that I'd have to agree to be debriefed and that I'd have to place calls or wear a wire to see—to call Betty and Mr. Jordan and possibly the President. . . .

Q. And did you tell them that you didn't want to do that?

A. Yes. . . . Then I wanted to call my mom and they kept telling me . . . that I couldn't tell anybody about this, they didn't want anyone to find out and . . . that was the reason I couldn't call [her attorney] Mr. Carter, was because they were afraid that he might tell the person who took me to Mr. Carter.

The person who took her to her attorney, Francis Carter, was Vernon Jordan.

So obsessed are the prosecutors with the prospect of getting the President and Vernon Jordan, or rather the President *through* Vernon Jordan, that they fear that *any* attorney she might select would alert Mr. Jordan. They actually propose to Ms. Lewinsky that she call an attorney they have chosen.

A. They told me that I could call this number and get another criminal attorney, but I didn't want that and I didn't trust them. Then I just cried for a long time. . . . They just sat there and then . . . they kept saying there was this time constraint, there was a time constraint. I had to make a decision.

And then, Bruce Udolf [another prosecutor] came in at some point and then—then Jackie Bennett [yet another prosecutor] came in . . . and the room was crowded and he was saying to me, you know, you have to make a decision. I had wanted to call my mom, they weren't going to let me call my attorney, so I just—I wanted to call my mom and they . . . And they had told me before that I could leave whenever I wanted, but . . . I didn't really know. . . . I mean I thought if I left then that they were just going to arrest me.

As all the FBI agents and prosecutors from the Special Counsel's office gathered in that crowded room had every reason to know, they were in flagrant violation of Ms. Lewinsky's rights—and, not incidentally, their own oaths of office.

A. And so then they told me that I should know that they were planning to prosecute my mom for the things that I had said that she had done.

(The witness begins crying.)

A JUROR: So if I understand it, you first met the agents, Agents [blank] and [blank], at around 1:00 and it wasn't until about 11 p.m. that you had an opportunity to talk to a lawyer?

THE WITNESS: Yes.

Ms. Immergut now makes a small attempt to redeem the reputation of her colleagues:

Q. Although you were allowed to—the thing with Frank Carter was that they were afraid he would tell Vernon Jordan? Is that what they expressed to you?

A. Right. And I had—I had—I think that someone said that Frank was a civil attorney and so that he really couldn't help me anyway. So I asked him if at least I could call and ask him for a recommendation for a criminal attorney and they didn't think that was a good idea. . . .

A JUROR: Sounds as though they were actively discouraging you from talking to an attorney.

THE WITNESS: Yes.

Ms. Immergut tries again, with what is in no sense a question:

Q. Well, from Frank Carter.

A. From Frank Carter, who was my only attorney at that point.

MS. IMMERGUT: Right. Right.

THE WITNESS: So I could have called any other attorney but—

A JUROR: You didn't have another attorney.

THE WITNESS: I didn't have another attorney and this was my attorney for this case, so, I mean, this was—

A JUROR: And this is the attorney who had helped you with the affidavit.

THE WITNESS: Yes. And that—the affidavit—well, the affidavit wasn't even filed yet. It was Fed Ex'd out on that day.

This is an altogether remarkable revelation. For all the prosecutors' talk of "time constraint . . . time constraint" and pressure brought by a squad of no fewer than three prosecutors and two agents of the FBI on

Ms. Lewinsky to "make a decision," the entire apparatus of the Independent Counsel's office, with prosecutors and FBI agents, its four-year, $40 million investigation, was now focused on this young woman—when her affidavit had not yet even been filed. It was Friday. The following Monday was Martin Luther King Day, a federal holiday. For all they knew, in spite of anything she had said to Ms. Tripp on any tape—and, as it turned out, she had lied to Ms. Tripp on several matters crucial to the case—Ms. Lewinsky might have changed her mind and filed a truthful affidavit. So at that point, Ms. Lewinsky, contrary to what the prosecutors were telling her and had told the U.S. attorney general and the court, had committed no crime. They had no right whatsoever to detain, let alone mislead her. They wanted her affidavit to arrive, and they wanted it to be false.

On Thursday, right after their taping, the Special Prosecutor's office had applied on an "emergency basis" to the attorney general, Janet Reno, and to the three-judge appellate court panel to extend the prosecutors' jurisdiction to the Jones case and to Ms. Lewinsky. All they had, at this point, was the suggestion—by Ms. Tripp, on Ms. Tripp's tapes—that Vernon Jordan might have asked Ms. Lewinsky to lie on her Paula Jones affidavit in exchange for a job. It is hard to see how, without deceiving Ms. Reno or the judges, the Special Prosecutor could justify his claim. Ms. Tripp, not the President, had come up with the idea of enlisting Mr. Jordan in the job hunt. Ms. Lewinsky had in fact signed her affidavit before she was offered a job (at Revlon) she found acceptable.

It is hard in any case to see how the possibility that someone will commit perjury can constitute an "emergency." The lie, after all, remains in the record. It will last and be detected in due course. A border crossing with drugs, or a conspiracy to murder might require emergency jurisdiction in that the evidence may vanish, or irreversible damage may be done. But it is the height of absurdity to claim an emergency in the loss of an opportunity to catch someone in a lie *that has not yet occurred*. What seems obvious is that the prosecutors were all too aware that the Tripp tapes really proved no crime. Their hope had to be that wiring Ms. Lewinsky, in conversation with Vernon Jordan and the President himself, might provide evidence of something else—a real obstruction of justice, say, or, better yet, evidence of some Whitewater- or Hubbell-related crime. Ms. Lewinsky refused to be wired.

A JUROR: During this time in the hotel with them, did you feel threatened?

THE WITNESS: Yes.

A JUROR: Did you feel that they had set a trap?

THE WITNESS: I—I—I did and I had—I didn't understand . . . why they had to trap me into coming there. . . . I mean this had all been a set-up and that's why I mean that was just so frightening. It was so incredibly frightening. . . . They told me if I partially co-operate, they'll talk to the judge. . . .

A JUROR: So you didn't know what would happen if you left.

THE WITNESS: No.

It is all very well to say that Ms. Lewinsky is being overly dramatic; that she survived; that she did not collaborate in the prosecutors' efforts to make her, like Ms. Tripp, their agent; and that she suffered no adverse consequences. But it is not true.

Quite apart from her eleven-hour ordeal, the interrogation was not without adverse consequences for Ms. Lewinsky. That night, when her mother, Marcia Lewis, arrived by train from New York, one of the prosecutors took Ms. Lewis aside and conferred with her alone. Later, in a phone call, made at Ms. Lewis's insistence, with Ms. Lewinsky's father, in California, the prosecutor said that the matter was "time sensitive." It may be that any family, under these conditions—in which the prosecutors made so clear their aversion to their daughter's attorney—would have thought it wise to fire that attorney. It may be that Ms. Lewinsky's parents thought things would go better for their daughter with another lawyer. Certainly the prosecutors in their time alone with Ms. Lewinsky's mother had ample opportunity to tell her so. And, in fact, that night the Lewinskys decided to fire Francis Carter and hired William Ginsburg—a California attorney specializing in cases of medical malpractice. Whatever else might be said about Mr. Ginsburg, he was not likely to strike fear into the hearts of the prosecutors or to be in any way connected with Vernon Jordan. He was not an expert in constitutional or criminal law, and he did not move to have the case against Ms. Lewinsky thrown out on grounds of prosecutorial abuses. If Ms. Lewinsky had had a constitutional lawyer, the case against her would have been thrown out.

Later, the Lewinskys may have thought that, to avoid further, long and expensive litigation, they needed Beltway attorneys more acceptable still to the forces arrayed against them. Plato Cacheris and Jacob Stein, respected though they are, are also not without political affiliation. (Cacheris's most famous client, at the time of Watergate, was former attorney general John Mitchell. Stein had been the attorney for Kenneth Parkinson, a Watergate defendant acquitted in the case before Judge Sirica.) Ms. Lewinsky would almost certainly have been better off with her original attorney, Francis Carter.

To return to the case. The President's deposition in the Jones case was scheduled for the following day. Paula Jones' attorneys had made it clear to Ms. Tripp that whatever information she had would be useless to them after that date. Having failed to wire Ms. Lewinsky, Kenneth Starr is eager to supply the Jones attorneys with information to formulate questions for which the President will be unprepared, and on which it is virtually impossible for the President, or any other person, to be entirely truthful, not just for the obvious reasons—discretion, family, a reluctance to injure—but because such a line of inquiry never ends. The many people—journalists, government officials—who have expressed their belief that the whole matter would have gone away if only the President had, from the outset, "looked people in the eye and told the truth" seem not to have considered where that sort of testimony would lead. Even in Mr. Starr's documents, the counsel presses on and on, to elicit testimony about "masturbating," for example—which could have no possible relevance in the case. There is the threat of perjury lurking behind every such expression of the prosecutor's salacious appetite. In fact, the volumes the Special Counsel has submitted to Congress show precisely how detailed, ugly, preposterous, ultimately endless, and unconscionable such questions are.

Since the chronology does not support Mr. Starr, the volumes contain no chronology. Since so much of the "evidence" is irrelevant, or contrived, or contradicted, or suspect in other ways, the Report simply buries it in disorganization and sheer mass.

Taking but one example, there are the famous Linda Tripp tapes. Generally no date or context is given when they are cited in the communication. There are two separate lists of them, neither of which prefaces the transcripts. They give the following order: Tape 18, Tape 19, Tape 1, Tape 2, Tape 13, Tape 3, Tape 8, Tape 7, Tape 15, Tape 11, Tape 16, Tape 26, Tape 16, Tape 9, Tape 5, Tape 23, Tape 6, Tape 17, Tape 27, Tape 10, Tape 12, Tape 14, Tape 20, Tape 21, Tape 24, Tape 25, Tape 28.

It does not take a high level of acuity to see that there is something anomalous about this list. It could be just a result of the order of transcription that Tapes 1 and 2 follow 18 and 19, and so on.

Ms. Tripp testifies at length, however, that she had only one tape recorder and that she did not label tapes by date. As soon as each tape was full, or even before it was full, Ms. Tripp says, she put it in a Spode china bowl at some distance from her tape recorder; she was so anxious not to erase or alter anything that she used tapes one after another, never more than once, and often did not even risk turning a tape over to side B.

There seems no plausible explanation, then, for the fact that Tape 16 is said to hold the conversations of November 8, 11, 13, 14, and 16, while Tape 26 contains conversations of November 11. November 11 falls inescapably between November 8 and November 13. Ms. Tripp would have had to remove Tape 16 after she had recorded the conversations of November 8 and 11, used Tape 26 to record more conversations on November 11, and then put in Tape 16 again to record November 13, 14, and 16—not quite the process she describes.

An FBI report, moreover, states that the taping was sometimes affected by "Tripp's cats" having "activated the pause button." Riveting as some of the recorded conversations are, it seems hard to justify a great reliance on them.

In the 1960s, J. Edgar Hoover and his FBI clandestinely made tapes of Martin Luther King Jr. engaged in various sexual acts in hotel bedrooms. The Bureau sent copies of those tapes to several public officials and members of the press, and to Dr. King himself, in order to humiliate him and either drive him to suicide or hound him into retirement. Judge Starr and his staff, in their failure to make a legal case, have resorted in the end to the same strategy. One difference is that their target is the President. Another is that in the 1960s public officials and the press refused to disseminate such tapes. In the late 1990s the press welcomes, broadcasts, and dwells upon them. The House rushes to publish them, with the congressional imprimatur, and to use them as the basis for an impeachment inquiry.

Even in his worst excesses, Senator Joseph McCarthy made at least the claim of constitutional issues: the alleged infiltration and subversion of the American government by a foreign power. In the Nixonian crisis of Watergate, the issue was also constitutional: abuse of power by the President in his official capacity. In 1974 the House Judiciary Committee specifically rejected as an impeachable offense Nixon's cheating (and thereby lying under oath about it), in his private capacity, on his income taxes.

It is not often remarked that the Constitution protects not against the crimes of people against one another but against abuses by the state itself against its citizens. On January 16, 1998—and before and after— Kenneth Starr and his staff became precisely the governmental agents the Constitution guards against.

There is no question that the President was also very much at fault here: failures of judgment, failures of honor, failures of taste. It may be that each of us knows a Monica Lewinsky. Not every temperament finds it easy to escape from her. But Ms. Lewinsky, even if she turns out to have endearing qualities, is an extreme example. In his political life, the President has evidently found it easy to rebuff, even leave, people when he feels he needs to. Somehow, even when Ms. Lewinsky was at her worst—months after he had terminated any physical relations with her, when she would page Ms. Currie late into the night, with threats and abuse, when she would appear at the White House gate and "scream" until somebody (usually Ms. Currie) came and brought her in—he could not seem to say, or enforce, a decisive no. He seemed to have the same difficulty with the special prosecutor and the grand jury. To have a White House, moreover, that cannot control its interns, pantry stewards, guards—cannot control even access to the President's person and his time—is a security risk and an administrative disaster. It seems, on the basis of these volumes, that the President is not only very nearly friendless but that there is something decidedly less than first-rate about the people with whom he surrounds himself. And, in spite of his intelligence, his interest in history, and concern with his "legacy," there is also something fundamentally wrong with his conception of what the presidency is.

The separation of powers, for example, requires the President to insist that the only court before which he will appear is the House in a matter of impeachment. Even the lowliest suspect in a criminal proceeding is not required to appear before a grand jury or submit to a sworn (let alone a videotaped) deposition. The President, as is so often remarked, is not above the law. In this case, he behaved as though he were below it. The very fact that he consented to testify diminished the powers of his office. Let the Independent Counsel come in waving stained dresses as he liked, he has no authority whatever to summon the President, let alone to take an example of his DNA. The House would look pretty silly deliberating over stains on dresses. In a proceeding of this constitutional order, the President cannot prevail with charm, semantics, or persuasion. To any court other than the House in an impeachment inquiry, he must say, as he should have said to Ms. Lewinsky, simply: No.

The grand jurors, in spite of the evident reluctance of the prosecutors, had been able to elicit testimony—to name but one example—from Linda Tripp which the House needs to examine. In reply to the crucial question of why she taped, she answers, at first, relatively calmly, because she was "afraid," because she needed "protection" against the enormous forces that were trying to "destroy her," to push her, in spite of her integrity, into a "felony" and a "perjury trap." A few questions more and she is talking about "the high level of drug use that was rampant in the White House when I was there," which may extend to the President himself, and testifying that there was a "list of forty bodies or something that were associated with the Clinton administration. At that time, I didn't know what that meant. I have since come to see such a list." Surely a list of forty bodies is something that—unlike the rest of the groundless and inadmissible trash he elicited elsewhere—would have been well within the jurisdiction of the Independent Counsel. The House needs to evaluate for itself the testimony of such a witness, along with the wisdom and good faith of an Independent Counsel who would reduce that testimony nearly to the size of a microdot, and not publish it earlier than page 4,277 of the fifth volume of his text.

The more closely one looks, then, at this huge mass of unsorted, often irrelevant and repellent matter, the clearer it becomes that the intent is to confuse, obscure, and intimidate. The facts the prosecutors were hoping to find—a bribe or other financial inducement to a witness to commit perjury, or at least to remain silent about some underlying crime—did not exist. In the case of Ms. Lewinsky, there was no obstruction of justice. In fact, there was no underlying crime. So they tried to create one. They thought they needed perjury from the President, so they set out to make sure he would commit it. They sent their agent Ms. Tripp to brief lawyers in a civil case with the sort of damaging information that would make it virtually impossible for the President to answer truthfully. Even with untruthful answers (which were peculiarly clumsy and inept), they had no crime—still less, a constitutional high crime or misdemeanor. So they just amassed their sludge and hurled it at the President, and hoped to prevail through embarrassment and disgust.

In one respect, the strategy seems to derive not just from Mr. Starr's staff of lawyers schooled in the prosecution of organized crime but also from Mr. Starr's own experience in the field of antitrust litigation. In the 1970s, it became common for huge corporations in antitrust cases simply to overwhelm the opposition with a huge amount of material, in the discovery phase of the trial, in hopes that the opposition could not find its case. The sheer mass of Mr. Starr's volumes goes even further. It nearly conceals that he unleashed not just the legal mechanism entrusted to him but also a process that violates the ethical and legal norms of the society, on the basis of the—unconvincing, often even internally inconsistent—testimony of one embittered and compromised informant, and one unusually persistent, and demonstrably unreliable, woman of twenty-four.

Mr. Starr likes to dwell, with the press, on his reading of the Bible. There is in the Bible, after all, just one commandment that squarely meets the case as it now stands. It has to do with False Witness, and the false witness in question is not perjury. It is False Witness against Thy Neighbor, and these documents, this compendium of partially false and almost entirely scurrilous testimony, with its accompanying report, is a case of false witness so egregious as to set a standard for the millennium.

—1998

ADDENDUM

On December 30, 1998, Charles Bakaly of the Office of the Independent Counsel wrote a letter to *Vanity Fair*, saying that "While we do not habitually correct published misinformation," he must dispute virtually every factual statement in my piece. On the very day the issue of *Vanity Fair* that contained Mr. Bakaly's letter was published—by apparent coincidence—Mr. Bakaly, having improperly "leaked" information to the press, left the OIC. Mr. Bakaly admitted the leak. He was subsequently found innocent of any legal wrongdoing in the matter. In spite of Mr. Bakaly's own admission that he *was* their source, the *Times* continued to protect his "anonymity." The following piece, in any event, was my answer to Mr. Bakaly's letter.

There can be no doubt that Mr. Bakaly and his colleagues at the Office of the Independent Counsel "do not habitually correct published misinformation." Their enterprise consists so precisely in generating misinformation, in such confusing and lurid volume—before the grand jury, the House Judiciary Committee, the courts, the attorney general, and the press—that by the time the truth emerges about any particular matter the news will simply have moved on. The strategy has so far served the Independent Counsel very well. As recently as this morning (February 10, 1999), the *New York Times* is still reporting, for example, that Linda Tripp "found her way to the Office of the Independent Counsel through a group of private lawyers," and that the Independent Counsel "first learned about the Lewinsky matter" on or about January 8, 1998—"four days before Linda R. Tripp contacted Mr. Starr's office." Ms. Tripp had testified that she contacted the OIC on January 12, 1998, and that her intermediary with Mr. Starr's office, as with Paula Jones' attorneys, was Lucianne Goldberg. Mr. Bakaly now repeats Ms. Tripp's claim that Ms. Goldberg was responsible for the (in his words) "decision to start taping" as well.

I don't know about Ms. Tripp's "decision to start taping," or what time Mr. Bakaly means by (in his other carefully chosen phrase) "at that time," but attempts to cast Ms. Goldberg as all-purpose motivator, intermediary, nexus, do not hold up. The fact, as I pointed out in my piece, was that, by January 1998, Ms. Tripp did not need intermediaries—Ms. Goldberg or any "group of private lawyers"—to contact the Office of the

Independent Counsel, or to initiate taping for the OIC. By 1998, she had been Mr. Starr's witness, and before that Robert Fiske's, in various investigations, for almost four years.

Throughout the long volumes of the *Referral*, there is every evidence of a determination to conceal, and even falsify what the Office of the Independent Counsel actually knows about Linda Tripp. Nowhere in the *Referral*'s FBI reports, for example—which set forth, in considerable detail, both Ms. Tripp's own history and her intended testimony before the grand jury—is there any mention whatever of the fact that she has been interviewed at least once before, on April 12, 1994, on behalf of the Independent Counsel, by the FBI. In my piece, I mentioned the FBI's report of that April 12, 1994, interview—which I found, not in the Starr *Referral* but in documents that accompanied transcripts of the D'Amato hearings on Whitewater. Ms. Tripp was an enthusiastic witness. Her most sympathetic interlocutor was Lauch Faircloth, her fellow conspiracy theorist and one of two senators—the other was Jesse Helms—most directly responsible for the appointment of Kenneth Starr as Independent Counsel.

It is inconceivable that the FBI report of this interview is not in the files both of the FBI and of the OIC. In the whole Starr *Referral*, however, there is no mention of any such prior report, interview, or file. The almost inescapable inference is either that the *Referral*'s 1998 FBI reports were laundered to expunge any mention of the 1994 interview, or the FBI agents interviewing Ms. Tripp were instructed to omit any reference to it. An investigation of what became of these files, and why they were concealed from the grand jury, the House, and the Senate is surely overdue.

Similarly, when Ms. Tripp testified that, until January 12, 1998, she had "never even thought about the Independent Counsel in my wildest dreams," and that she needed Ms. Goldberg to contact the OIC, the grand jury was being actively misled. It was the obligation of the prosecutor immediately to disclose to the grand jury that this testimony, as he knew, if not from his own memory, then from his files, was false.

As for Ms. Tripp's tapes—which occupy literally thousands of pages of the *Referral*, but on which Mr. Bakaly now says the *Referral* "places no great reliance"—it is now clear that more than half of them exhibit doctoring (it is not clear by whom), which the OIC chooses to characterize as "duplication." And it is quite untrue that any discrepancy in the sequence is, as Mr. Bakaly claims, "noted in an appendix to our Referral." The pages that Mr. Bakaly cites are simply lists, without any comment whatsoever on the sequence: They are an *instance* of the lack of integrity, and not a notation of it. It is, in any event, not the "tape," but the *conversation* that is out of sequence: An earlier conversation appears between two later ones—a metaphysical impossibility. The very extent of the deception in defense of the tapes, together with the rapidity with which the OIC granted Ms. Tripp immunity for them make it clear whom Ms. Tripp was working for. Could the prosecutors in a single evening, really have reviewed the contents of all those tapes, appraised their reliability, and phrased questions for Ms. Tripp to pose during an interview (at the Ritz-Carlton, with Ms. Lewinsky) the following day? Surely only Ms. Tripp's prior work for the OIC can explain the speed and degree to which they understood and trusted her account, and the alacrity with which (without any legal authority) they wired her.

There can really be no doubt, either, that on the night of January 16, 1998, when the OIC was trying to coerce Monica Lewinsky to cooperate in secret taping, the prosecutors were aware—contrary to the statements in Mr. Bakaly's letter and to sworn testimony, before the House Judiciary Committee, by Kenneth Starr—that Ms. Tripp was going to meet Paula Jones' attorneys that very night. In fact, as Ms. Tripp testified before the grand jury, the terms of her agreement with Jones' attorneys *required* her to brief them "before the President's deposition," which was, of course, the following day. Aside from the certainty that Ms. Tripp, who was by this time incontestably their agent, would have told them, the whole alleged basis of her conversations with them was that *she was about to be a witness in the Jones case.* Moreover (a fact concealed by the prosecutors even in their representations to the court of Judge Norma Holloway Johnson), throughout most of the hours on January 16, 1998, when prosecutors Jackie Bennettt, Michael Emmick, Bruce Udolf, and Stephen Binhak and FBI Special Agents Steven Irons, Patrick Fallon, and "other OIC attorneys and agents present at various times, mostly in an adjoining room" were detaining Ms. Lewinsky in one room of the Ritz-Carlton—one wonders how many prosecutors and FBI agents are required to detain an enemy spy, or a serial killer—Linda Tripp was waiting in another room of the same hotel. When Ms. Lewinsky declined to be wired, and it was clear the OIC would not be able to enlist her in one plan, Ms. Tripp needed to meet her deadline in setting up the President in another. Ms. Tripp left for her pivotal briefing of the Jones attorneys. Far from having "no inkling" where Ms. Tripp was going, the OIC sent one of their agents to drive her there.

The press, including the *Times*, has brought out some of the other extensive, manifestly illegal, contacts between the OIC and the Jones people, by way of partners in Mr. Starr's law firm and of Mr. Starr himself. There is at least one further clue, in the very basis of the interrogation of Ms. Lewinsky, to the degree of collaboration between the Jones attorneys and the OIC. In fact, the incident cannot even accurately be called an "interrogation." There is no evidence that the prosecutors and agents ever *asked* her anything. It was, rather, a protected exercise in threats, bullying, coercion, and intimidation, based not on inquiry but on what the prosecutors told Ms. Lewinsky they already knew. And the question is, How could they possibly have known it?

Ms. Lewinsky's affidavit had been signed, and mailed, but would not arrive until three days later at the court. Ms. Lewinsky, it must be remembered, had actually lied to Ms. Tripp—to the effect that she was taking Ms. Tripp's advice, and that she had not signed a false affidavit in the Jones case, and would not sign such an affidavit, until the President, through Vernon Jordan, had found her a satisfactory job. Ms. Tripp, in other words, *did not know* that the false affidavit was already signed. How, then, did the prosecutors know—not just that it was false but that Ms. Lewinsky had signed it? The answer is this: Francis Carter, Ms. Lewinsky's attorney, had, five days earlier, informed the Jones attorneys, as a courtesy, of the contents of the affidavit. The Jones people told the OIC.

Finally, there is simply no question that, in this eleven-hour detention of Monica Lewinsky, OIC personnel were in flagrant violation of statutory and professional constraints on prosecutorial misconduct and of Ms. Lewinsky's constitutional rights. It is simply untrue that a federal court "summarily rejected" (Mr. Bakaly's phrase) any such claim, or that the court was ever presented a full and honest account of what occurred that night. The issue before Judge Johnson was whether to quash the OIC subpoenas not of Monica Lewinsky but of Francis Carter. Judge Johnson accepted the OIC accounts of what they actually did. Nonetheless, she wrote: "The Court expresses its concern that" the OIC "may have acted improperly." "This Court's supervisory power to control prosecutorial misconduct before grand juries," she also wrote, "is quite limited. However, the Court is extremely disturbed" that the prosecutors might have disrupted Ms. Lewinsky's relationship with her attorney, Mr. Carter. And that she would "consider referring this matter to the Department of Justice Office of Professional Responsibility for investigation."

After a blizzard of affidavits from the prosecutors and FBI agents that there had been no misconduct on their part (and without having received sworn testimony to the contrary, given, at risk of their immunity, by Ms. Lewinsky and her mother), Judge Johnson withdrew her threat of sanctions. None of the allegations was "summarily rejected." Subsequent testimony by Ms. Lewinsky and her mother made it absolutely clear that the prosecutors were in violation not just of the law but of Justice Department guidelines—by which the Office of the Independent Counsel is, in its authorizing statute, bound.

One has only to read the OIC's own affidavits, In Re Sealed Case, before Judge Johnson, about what they did on the night of January 16, 1998. One constitutional standard for such detentions is whether a "reasonable man" would have known that he was free to leave. There were more than seven men, some, according to their affidavits, alternately in the room and "standing in the doorway," while Ms. Lewinsky was alternately sobbing "hysterically" and staring "off into space." They point out that they gave her permission to go to the bathroom and shut the door. They say that Ms. Lewinsky's mother "thanked" them for giving Ms. Lewinsky "permission" (their word) to call her mother. They deceived her for hours with dire descriptions of what they said her legal situation was. Why did there need to be so many of them, if, as Ken Starr told the Judiciary Committee, they did not intend to "overbear"—another constitutional standard—"the will"? No reasonable person would have felt free to leave. Transcripts of the prosecutors' own affidavits are chilling. In time, this conduct of the

OIC will enter history and the law as precisely the conduct, on the part of public officials, that the Constitution was designed to protect citizens against.

—1998

MONICA'S STORY

People lie, certainly. People forget. People make mistakes. One difficulty in following the narrative of the past year's scandal—which is both utterly frivolous and the gravest threat to our constitutional system in living memory—is that the major characters are not, and as it turns out, never have been, President Clinton and Monica Lewinsky. They have always been, it is now clear beyond question, Linda Tripp and Kenneth Starr. Tripp, Starr, and the Office of Independent Counsel have made every effort to conceal this long, intense connection. Lewinsky, perhaps more than most people, thinks she is the main character in any narrative in which she plays a part. As a result, *Monica's Story* by Andrew Morton does not add much to our understanding of it. Morton refers constantly, as does Lewinsky, to her "insecurity," her lack of "self-worth" and "self-esteem," as an explanation for whatever happens to her. What is more credible, and vastly more interesting, is her astonishing force of will, her single-minded, ineluctable, even imperious, determination to get her way. Someone more easily daunted would never have managed, for example, after ten months—during which the President, his secretary, and virtually everyone else in the White House was trying to ward her off—to make her way to the President again. Her sole argument for returning, for constant meetings, conversations, reproaches, and demands, was that in early April 1996, when she was transferred from the White House to the Pentagon, the President had "promised" to bring her back to a White House job "after the election." Never before can the breaking of an alleged campaign promise have had consequences of this kind.

If Lewinsky were more attuned to rejection, less determined to prevail, she would, on the other hand, have detected from Tripp's bored inflections, her bossy and steering remarks disguised as questions, her tolerance for endless (and somewhat scolding) repetition of details Tripp claimed not to remember, that Tripp was an informer. Which, of course, she was, it now seems fairly obvious, from the first. Neither Lewinsky nor Morton makes a connection between Tripp and the Office of Independent Counsel quite that early. Since they think what they have is a love story, they cast Tripp as just an envious, treacherous rival who betrays Lewinsky in the end. On Starr and his deputies, however, they have it right: They add detail to Lewinsky's already powerful testimony, before the grand jury, about the circumstances of her eleven-hour detention, on January 16, 1998, in Room 1012 of the Ritz-Carlton Hotel, by nine prosecutors and FBI agents from the Office of Independent Counsel. It is the only time the book comes to life.

I.

One major strategy of the Office of Independent Counsel has always been to generate misinformation and outright falsehood in such confounding mass and lurid detail that by the time any one instance, large or small, has been detected, the discovery seems pedantic. Who cares? The news, as lascivious as the Independent Counsel manages to keep it, has moved on. Allegations of a rape, for example, once denied under oath, are revived, in response to the now infamous range of inquiries and pressures by the Independent Counsel, and shown in secret to members of Congress, then made public. The recantation (in every possible forum, in the midst of an impeachment) of the earlier sworn denial is said to be "reluctant" and to "have no motive" other than "ending the lies" or setting the record straight. A new inquiry is called for, and so on.

The story with Starr and Tripp at the center is quite different. On January 12, 1998, Tripp was interviewed, at her request, by prosecutors and FBI agents. Until that week, she testified, under oath, before the grand jury, "I had never even thought of the Independent Counsel in my wildest dreams." This, as it happened, and as the prosecutor had every reason to know, was false. By January 1998, Tripp had, in fact, been the Independent Counsel's eager and enthusiastic witness in at least four prior investigations, going back four years. If it seemed plausible that Tripp's testimony on this point was, in some sense, accurate—that, having come forward to testify in Filegate, Travelgate, the Vincent Foster suicide, and Whitewater investigators, some of which were ongoing throughout the period of her contacts with Lewinsky, she somehow never thought of approaching the Special Prosecutor with her concerns about what she heard from Lewinsky. But if she set out, rather, for personal reasons, to do the taping on her own, then the prosecutors had a legal obligation to call that anomaly immediately to the grand jury's attention. The reason they let this testimony pass is not just that no one (least of all, perhaps, the grand jurors) would have believed it for a moment. It is that any explanation would have revealed the long connection between Tripp and the OIC. It would have led as well to the matter of the tapes. Members of the grand jury asked Tripp, time after time, and in spite of constant interruptions and diversions by the prosecutor, what had prompted her to tape Lewinsky. Tripp's answers never quite persuaded them. It was in the course of responding to this line of inquiry that she made the "never in my wildest dreams" reply. If the prosecutors had disclosed, on the spot—as they were legally obliged to—how long and in how many capacities Tripp had been working for them, the grand jurors would have known, as they seemed to suspect, why and for whom she made her tapes.

Another subject the grand jurors tried, in spite of all sorts of diversions by the prosecutor, to explore was the events of January 16, 1998, at the Ritz-Carlton, where Lewinsky was being detained, for all those hours, at the "invitation"—as one of the prosecutors subsequently put it, in a sworn affidavit—of agents of the FBI. There is no question that the events at the Ritz-Carlton marked a turning point. The stories—of Tripp, and Starr, the tapes, and, it turns out, the Paula Jones case—had always overlapped. On that night, the stories openly converged. It became crucial for the Independent Counsel either to secure—by whatever pressures—Lewinsky's cooperation, or to dispatch Tripp to a meeting with the Jones attorneys and risk disclosure of the OIC's long, manifestly illegal and improper, involvement in that case. To understand the events of that night, one must begin somewhat earlier and choose among competing narratives.

II.

If the prosecutors are to be believed, Tripp was a loyal and "apolitical" White House employee under both the Bush and Clinton administrations. In August 1994, she was transferred to the Pentagon, where in

1996 she met Lewinsky. In early 1997, she heard Lewinsky's account of a relationship, nearly a year before, with President Clinton. By October 3, 1997, she had become so disturbed by this account, and so certain that she would be called as a witness in the Paula Jones case to testify about Lewinsky's relationship and so alarmed that a "perjury trap" would await her when she told the truth about that relationship, that she felt she must "arm" herself "to protect my integrity" and tape what Lewinsky said.

Tripp had once testified, before the D'Amato Whitewater hearings in 1995, about her "background in undercover operations." If the prosecutors are to be believed, it was, however, a New York literary agent, Lucianne Goldberg, who introduced her to the whole notion of tape-recording. Goldberg, in fact, seems to appear at every crucial junction of the prosecutor's narrative. When Tripp decided (as Goldberg advised her to) that she ought not to wait for the Paula Jones attorneys to approach her but to get in touch with them herself, it was Goldberg who called this lawyer or that, who in turn called another lawyer, who was a friend of one of the Jones attorneys, who then made contact with Tripp. In January 1998, it was Goldberg, who, by way of her "elves" (a network of apparently timid but self-important right-wing lawyers), learned how to get in touch with the Office of Independent Counsel and imparted this important information to Tripp. In this version of the story, Goldberg appears at times to be running not just Tripp but the Jones case, the OIC, and the press.

If the prosecutors are to be believed, Tripp first got in touch with them on the evening of January 12, 1998. Four prosecutors and agents immediately raced to Tripp's house. Within two hours (between 11:15 P.M. and 1:15 A.M.), they not only learned the contents of an unsorted twenty-four hours' worth of tape recordings but appraised their reliability and knew precisely what information was missing from them. They were thus able, on the spot, to grant Tripp immunity, to equip her, without any apparent legal authorization, with a body wire, and to suggest a line of questioning, to fill in the gaps, in time for a lunch Tripp would have with Lewinsky at the Ritz-Carlton later that day.

They had providently rented a room to monitor the conversation. On the basis of their tape of this conversation, the prosecutors were able within hours to assure both the attorney general and a three-judge appellate court that they had evidence of a pattern of bribery and obstruction of justice on the President's behalf by Vernon Jordan, similar to a pattern that they thought they had detected but failed to prove in a matter related to Webster Hubbell and Whitewater. The urgency of their request (for expanded jurisdiction to include Lewinsky and the Jones case) consisted, they said, in the fact that, essentially because of Goldberg, a reporter, Michael Isikoff of *Newsweek*, had the story. The attorney general, fearful of *Newsweek* and aware that the three-judge appellate court had in any case appointed Starr and remained remarkably supportive of him, yielded. The appellate court granted jurisdiction readily.

The result was Lewinsky's ordeal and her finest hour. Starr testified, under oath, before the House Judiciary Committee and assured the attorney general, the three-judge appellate court, and the press that he had, before January 15, 1998, no contacts with the Paula Jones case. Goldberg herself made similar remarks that caused journalists to pore over minor discrepancies (whether Goldberg called this particular lawyer or that, perhaps a few days earlier) as though there were any degree of separation between the OIC and the Jones case. As it turns out, there was none. Starr also said, under oath, before the House Judiciary Committee, that "it never crossed our minds" that, on the night of January 16, 1998, while his deputies and agents were detaining Lewinsky, Tripp would go straight to a meeting with the Jones attorneys to brief them about the contents of her tapes. One of Starr's deputies, Michael Emmick, even elicited from Tripp—on her last day before the grand jury, when he was trying to clean up his record and his case—testimony that the prosecutors could have had "no inkling" that she would go to such a meeting.

Not only had it not remotely crossed their minds where Tripp might go that night or what she might do there but Starr said that nothing occurred on January 16, 1998, at the Ritz-Carlton that was not sound, lawful prosecutorial practice. The hotel's rooms, he said, were pleasant and "commodious." Lewinsky was free to call her lawyer. There was no violation of any constitutional right or statute, no intent to "overbear the will." One of the prosecutors who filed affidavits in a related matter said that both Lewinsky and her mother had even thanked him for their treatment of Lewinsky. Several of these affidavits by prosecutors and FBI agents contain the sentence "Because I have prepared this affidavit for a limited purpose, I have not included everything I know about matters concerning Monica S. Lewinsky"—which suggests a certain unease.

Basically, if the prosecutors can be believed, however, their behavior with Lewinsky was routine and proper. Their case and the Jones case were distinct. Near midnight, Lewinsky left the Ritz-Carlton, as according to Starr she had been free to do since 11 A.M., when the FBI agents first issued their "invitation" to her. The OIC had simply caught Lewinsky, Starr testified, in the middle of a "serious crime."

In fact, the prosecutors' predicament on January, 16, 1998, when Tripp lured Lewinsky into their midst and they detained her, was this: They had nothing and they knew it. The matter had become extremely urgent. Lewinsky had, it is true, signed an affidavit in the Jones case. Her attorney, Francis Carter, had mailed it. It had not yet arrived, however, and had therefore not yet been filed with the court. She could still withdraw, amend, or change it. Carter, if she were permitted to speak to him, would doubtless have seen to it that she did. Lewinsky, in other words, had not committed any felony. Unless they isolated, misinformed, threatened, and intimidated her, she would not commit one. The President, moreover, had not yet testified in the Jones case. His deposition was scheduled for January 17, 1998, the following day. If he were alerted, it was clear he would be especially careful about what he said.

So the prosecutors from the OIC were left with the alarming possibility that none of their targets would commit even an arguable crime. They kept telling Lewinsky that she and her mother faced jail if Lewinsky did not agree to become their agent, and agree to be wired, for recording conversations with Vernon Jordan, Betty Currie, and the President. They told her, as they had told the attorney general and the three-judge appellate court, that the matter was an emergency, "time sensitive," "a window of opportunity" was closing. When she was not "sobbing" or "staring off into space," Lewinsky kept asking to speak with her attorney. They did not let her call him. They suggested other attorneys. She must make her decision. Their deadline, as it happened, was truly urgent. Contrary to what they had told the attorney general and the appellate court, however, it had nothing to do with Isikoff. It was imposed by a deal Tripp had made with the Jones attorneys, which required that she brief them "before the President's deposition"—in other words, within the next few hours.

If Tripp, by then undeniably their agent, had not told them about that deal, they had another utterly reliable source: the Jones attorneys themselves. Of course, Tripp did tell them. The source of their urgency was in fact the deadline in Tripp's deal. Among other things the officers and agents of the OIC do not mention in their sworn affidavits about the events of that night at the Ritz-Carlton is that they had rented a room for Tripp in that same hotel. As she waited for the outcome of their session with Lewinsky, she had stayed in touch by phone with the Jones attorneys. When Starr said it "never crossed their minds" that Tripp would brief those attorneys, and Emmick said they had "no inkling" she would do so, they were trying to conceal not just that Tripp's arrangement with the Jones attorneys was dictating the OIC's schedule but how close their own contacts with that case already were. There is the question, for instance, of how they even knew that Lewinsky had signed her affidavit. They could not have learned it from the court, since the affidavit had not yet arrived. They could not have learned it from Tripp, either. Lewinsky, as it happened, had *lied* to Tripp—to the effect that, taking Tripp's advice, she had not yet signed an affidavit and would not sign it until the President, through Vernon Jordan, had found her a satisfactory job. Tripp, in other words, *did not know* that the affidavit was already signed. How, then, did the prosecutors know—not just whether it was true or false but that Lewinsky had signed it? The answer is this: Carter, Lewinsky's attorney, had five days earlier informed the Jones attorneys, as a courtesy, of the contents of the affidavit and sent them a copy of it. The Jones people told the Office of the Independent Counsel—with whom they had been working all along.

On the whole, the prosecutors would have much preferred not to have to rely that night on Tripp. The risk that their contacts with the Jones case would come to light was just too great. So they must bully, taunt, threaten, and, not least, crowd Lewinsky. At least four prosecutors and three FBI agents, over a period of eleven hours, in and out and sometimes standing in the doorway of two hotel bedrooms, does reduce the degree to which Lewinsky's accommodations can be described as "commodious." One wonders why there had to be so many prosecutors and agents if they did not intend, as Starr said they did not, to overbear her will. They tried, *in terrorem*, to coerce her into becoming, like Tripp, their agent; they pressured her to record conversations in hopes of gathering evidence of some crime. All this, Starr has publicly, indignantly, and under oath, denied—unaware perhaps that some of his deputies, in sworn affidavits in a sealed court proceeding before Judge Norma Holloway Johnson, had confirmed it. Lewinsky refused to be wired. They had to use Tripp after all. As the deadline of the President's deposition approached, they sent Tripp off to her rendezvous with the Jones attorneys. It did not have to cross their minds "remotely." One of their agents drove her there.

III.

Why does it matter? "You never, ever, ever commit perjury," Starr said in an interview with Diane Sawyer. He spoke at length to her, as he had to the Judiciary Committee, of his devotion to the law and to the truth. Tripp, under oath before the grand jury, spoke repeatedly of her "integrity" and her inability to bring herself to lie. Such is their dedication to the truth. By the time any particular element of their story comes apart, however, there is already another story. In her testimony before the grand jury, for example, Tripp discussed at length her friendship, in 1993, with another employee at the White House, Kathleen Willey. She made it very clear that she was Willey's confidante, that they plotted together to promote Willey's relationship with the President, that they composed notes and selected gifts for him, that Willey solicited and welcomed the President's embrace, and that Tripp and Willey later consulted about where it might be safe for Willey and the President to conduct an affair. In short, the relationship Tripp described was very like her relationship with Lewinsky. For all we know, Tripp was taping even then. But this version does not comport with what Starr's office now wants to present as Willey's story: a coarse and unwelcome embrace, virtually a sexual assault, which Willey, astonished and appalled, resisted. So Starr has indicted for perjury a witness who does not confirm Willey's testimony.[1] When Tripp was asked, in an interview by Larry King, whether Willey's present story is true, she replied, "Absolutely."

The OIC, apparently ready to threaten even Tripp herself, has announced an investigation of what it chooses to characterize as signs of "duplication" in her tapes. In fact, the tapes show signs of extensive doctoring; it is by no means clear by whom. Their integrity in virtually every respect—their content, their sequence, their presentation in the Independent Counsel's own report—is extremely doubtful. But the likelihood is that the prosecutors want to keep Tripp under control. They had always tried to conceal, from the grand jury and from the volumes of their *Communication and Referral*, not just her prior work for the OIC but her real motives and ideological affinities. At one point, when the grand jurors asked again about her motives for taping, Tripp said that she had felt "physically threatened," that there were already "forty bodies," victims of the Clinton administration. "I have seen the list," Tripp said. One might have thought such a list would have led the prosecutors to inquire further. Certainly, it was in their jurisdiction. Perhaps not surprisingly, they let it pass.

Evidence of the virtual eradication of all traces of the OIC's real relationship with Tripp, however, lies elsewhere. In the documents of the Senate Whitewater hearings of 1995, for example, there is an FBI report of an interview with Tripp, on April 12, 1994, in the offices of the OIC. In all the volumes of the *Communication and Referral*, however, including its extensive FBI reports (which cover in considerable detail both her biography and her intended testimony), there is no mention whatever of this, or any other previous OIC report on Linda Tripp. It is inconceivable that the April 12, 1994, report does not exist in the files both of the Independent Counsel and the FBI. In the whole Starr Report, however, there is no mention of any such prior report, interview, or file. The almost inescapable inference is either that the Report's 1998 FBI reports were laundered to expunge any mention of the 1994 interview or that the FBI agents interviewing Tripp were instructed to omit any reference to it. An investigation of what became of these files, and why they were concealed from the grand jury, the House, and the Senate, is surely overdue.

IV.

There was never, there is not now (as Sidney Zion, among others, has pointed out), a credible legal case against Lewinsky. She never required immunity. She never needed to give those volumes of detailed testimony to the grand jury—or even to turn over that dress. Without Lewinsky, the Special Prosecutor had nothing whatsoever. Tripp's tapes proved only that it was Tripp who encouraged Lewinsky to think she could resume her affair with the President and who worked hard on strategies to get her there; Tripp, who suggested that she contact Vernon Jordan for help in finding a New York job (when Lewinsky already had an offer for a job at the United Nations); Tripp who urged her to hold out for a higher position, higher pay, and to refuse to sign an affidavit unless the grade and job were high—Tripp, in short, who did everything to promote relations between Lewinsky and the President and to construct what might, if Lewinsky had taken her advice, have been a genuine obstruction of justice. In one particularly malevolent communication near the end, Tripp told Lewinsky that she had learned, from "Kate," a friend at the National Security Council, that Lewinsky was blacklisted at the White House and would never again get a job there; Lewinsky had better renew and raise her demands for employment in New York. The "Kate" in question denied, under oath, that she had ever heard or said anything of the kind. Before the scandal became public, she said, she had never heard of Monica Lewinsky.

But here one begins to see what is pernicious. One pattern in the Office of Independent Counsel has been to summon witnesses and compel their testimony on matters—like the emotional and sexual lives of other people—of which they can have no personal knowledge and about which prosecutors have no right, under our system, to inquire. Then, the prosecutors threaten these witnesses with charges of perjury if their testimony does not meet prosecutors' needs. Some people are eager to oblige, with endless gossip about friends, neighbors, and associates. Others would resist but do not know how. The legal costs of resistance are very high. In addition, there is sometimes the threat—for which the Office of Independent Counsel is now notorious—to open inquiry on some other front: the legality of an adoption, say, or possible anomalies in billing a partnership or paying income tax. Even the administration of nursing homes has not, after all, in the past, been altogether scandal free. Everyone, in short, is vulnerable to inquiries and pressures of this sort.

To get any sense of the Independent Counsel, who has made so many millions in his private capacity, spent so many millions more in his public capacity, and incurred such enormous expenses for any witnesses he indicts, you have to look at the written record. To get a sense of Tripp, her motives, and her contribution to the plot, you need to hear the actual tapes. (It was precisely to conceal from the grand jurors almost everything about Tripp that the prosecutors did not present the actual tapes but only read, in their own voices, excerpts from them. It must have been extremely odd, perhaps somewhat comic, to hear Tripp's lines and Lewinsky's in the voices of Michael Emmick and Stephen Binhak.) To get a sense of Lewinsky, one has to see her—on television or elsewhere. Her personality, her charm, her occasional savviness either come through or not. One learns nothing about her from the book.

In a story with, so far, no heroes, Lewinsky's signal vindication was to refuse to be wired. The volumes of testimony in the independent counsel's disgraceful *Communication and Referral to the House Judiciary Committee* documents the gross prosecutorial abuses and deliberate violations of statutory and constitutional limits in those eleven hours at the Ritz-Carlton. Morton's book adds to our understanding of that night. When Lewinsky speaks of the "fear" she and her mother experienced, one tends at first to doubt her—particularly since she seems unmistakably to take a certain pleasure, both in the limelight and in the story that she tells. Then it becomes clear that, however melodramatic the expression of that fear may have been, its basis was absolutely genuine. The pernicious aftermath of the entire affair has been this: Not just the obvious undermining of trust, in the presidency, elected officials, and, for that matter, judges. Not even just, through the relentless generation of sensational, and therefore "interesting" misinformation, the subversion of sanity and of caring whether anything is true or not. But this: The notion that it is the business of government to inquire into people's intimate lives, and of citizens to go, whether out of fear or malice or exuberance or for any other reason, to the government with testimony about the intimate lives of other people—even to wire themselves to record conversation for testimony of that kind—has never been the way, in this or in any other free country. American citizens have had, in the past, no reason to fear that their friends or family or intimates or former intimates will—or even can—betray their personal, in no way criminal confidences to prosecutors. The scandal and the danger is that until the Starr ethic is emphatically repudiated, people now have ample reason for that fear.

—1999

PART 2

LETTER FROM BIAFRA

It is almost impossible to fly into Biafra now, or out of it. The relief organizations (Caritas, World Council of Churches, Nord Church Aid, Canadian Air Relief) that still fly to Biafra from the Portuguese island of São Tomé have formed a single operation, Joint Church Aid, which flies about five planes a night, sometimes two flights per plane, sometimes three, depending on the availability of pilots and the condition of planes. Always at night. Ever since a plane of the International Red Cross was shot down on June 5, by day, by Nigeria, and the International Red Cross suspended its relief flights to Biafra entirely, Joint Church Aid has decided not to fly into Biafra with anyone who, if a plane were to be shot down again, might appear to be on a mission other than church relief. The island of Fernando Po, once a base for Red Cross flights, has been closed off by Equatorial Guinea. The French Red Cross still flies a single plane, sometimes once, sometimes twice a night, from Libreville, Gabon, but it, too, is reluctant to take in passengers; and Biafra, worried that observers might spot incoming flights of arms, does not like to issue visas by way of Libreville. Well-meaning eccentrics used to fly to Biafra from time to time (Abie Nathan, the maverick Israeli pilot, who cooked what food he brought in for refugees himself; an anonymous lady who gave one iron pill to every child she met), but journalists and even doctors are now turned back in São Tomé, to catch the twice-weekly flight to mainland Angola and home again. It is possible that the blockade will soon cut off not only food coming in but reports coming out of this unprecedented war.

The population of São Tomé is one-tenth Portuguese police. The other citizens are mostly contract labor, imported not entirely voluntarily from the Cape Verde Islands, farther off the coast of Africa. A Portuguese island is, in any case, an incongruous place to fly to Biafra from, and there is something about the discontinuity of events and the day-to-day reporting of news that always seems to make either too simple or too mystifying the altogether anomalous predicament of Biafra. Meaningless datelines (Owerri, Emekuku, Awomama, Mbano), scarcely mapped and incessantly changing war fronts, strange friends (Haiti, Tanzania, Ivory Coast, Zambia, Gabon), strange enemies (England, Russia, Egypt, Chad), pictures and statistics no longer automatic in their meaning or credibility, the muddy, bungling, endlessly preoccupying catastrophe in Vietnam, even a sense of Africa derived from Kipling and Waugh—the narrative line for Biafra gets lost. Biafrans do not easily fit any stereotype of martyrdom or ideology. I asked a young Biafran just whose children it is who are dying, and he replied quite seriously that it is the children of villagers who are not strong enough to trek nearer the front to buy what food there is more cheaply and trek back to market to sell it more dearly, for a little profit to support their families. It takes a high tolerance for the sheer, bitterly comic ugliness of human suffering to care much for these survivors out of Bertolt Brecht. Editorial writers for the Western press, unlike reporters on the spot, often treat the Biafran position as morally ambiguous, as though the years from 1939 to 1945 had never existed, and as though killing and dying existed on a single plane of atrocity. It is possible that another ethnic population will be decimated before modern intelligence completes its debate about the extent to which the greatest crimes can be said to be the fault of the victims.

The relief flights from São Tomé take off just before dark, fly with lights off in the darkness over Federal Nigeria, and approach Uli Airport (a widened stretch of what was once a road) in the dark. The blue lights of the runway are flashed very briefly, and then turned off again as the planes begin to land. This is the rainy season in Biafra, but Uli, according to James W. Anderson, one of Joint Church Aid's hired pilots (who earn between $4,000 and $5,000 dollars a month), is "the only place in the world you can fly into and you hope the weather's bad." On clear nights, Nigerian planes, flown by Egyptian or East German pilots, attempt to bomb the runway. They have never hit it yet, and it is a disputed question whether they really want to hit Joint Church Aid planes, but even relief flights quite often miss the darkened landing, and take off abruptly to approach again and again. The pilots, whose professional history usually includes assignments like flying personnel to oil fields in ice storms in Alaska, or flying arms to Israel in 1948, seem fairly sanguine about risk. Last month, a Canadian plane crashed when it apparently received signals, by mistake, from another, more camouflaged Biafran airport. A second crew forgot to lower its landing gear and, when landing without wheels jammed the doors, had to slide down from the cockpit by means of emergency ropes. A few weeks ago, Joint Church Aid headquarters in Geneva made a last-minute exception to admit Eric Pace, of the *New York Times*, and since it seemed that two reporters would no more compromise a single relief flight than one, and since bad weather had limited bombings by what is euphemistically called the Intruder, the local church workers decided to let me go in as well.

On Saturday night, Captain Anderson's plane approached the runway at a right angle (a compass was broken), missed twice, and then landed smoothly in lightning and drenching rain. These trips are entirely calm, perhaps because they lack the unspoken agreement on commercial airlines (the meals, the movies, the silence of engines) to pretend that one has been on the ground all the time, or because they fly into a place suspended from one's personal experience so utterly. The plane, an American C-97, was cleared of its cargo of stockfish and corn-soya-milk extract in seven minutes, and took off for two more trips to São Tomé. The crews were planning three flights that night in order to have one less on Sunday, when they were hoping to hold a barbecue at the rather grim hotel where they are based. Stockfish is now Biafra's main source of animal protein. It was popular before the war in the land that is now Biafra; but when the blockade began, consumption of stockfish was so drastically reduced that the currency of Iceland, a major exporter, had to be devalued, until the United States, by purchasing stockfish for Biafran relief, gave the currency some support.

The tons of fish, in burlap bags, were loaded quickly into lorries. A bearded English relief worker named Graham dashed about in the dark and cold rain, which fogged his glasses. He picked up the passengers and their baggage (distinguishable on the runway by dim strips of yellow masking tape), and drove nearly blindly, with dimmed headlights, among a series of checkpoints manned by armed Biafrans and each consisting of a thatched hut and a branch extended across a road to a steel drum.

One of the branches was lifted and the car drove to a building called State House for entry formalities in earth-floored rooms, by the light of four kerosene lamps. An important shipment of something was clearly expected from Libreville, because Arthur Mbanefo, a Biafran government official, and Professor Ben Nwosu, a Biafran nuclear physicist educated in California and now head of the Biafran Directorate of Research and Production, were gathered in the office of a Major Akigabu, who is in charge of immigration at State House, and who was once a teacher of Virgil in secondary school. Major Akigabu, a middle-aged man in battle fatigues, was quoting in near darkness from Book II of the *Aeneid*. "When you read it, you will shed tears," he said. "You have to shed tears."

The sense here is of a people about to die in isolation and pretending not to know it—convinced in any case by their recent history that they have no choice. Victims are seldom pure, or even entirely attractive, and a case can certainly be made against any victim of murder before some higher court of absolute irrelevance. But Biafrans, fighting a war, in a sense, for a position argued in Hannah Arendt's *Eichmann in Jerusalem*, are determined to avoid at least the accusation of passive complicity in their own destruction and resist, trusting their own interpretation of what the risks of capitulation and the costs of survival might be. Once the foremost advocates of Nigerian unity, they have been persuaded by a series, both before and since the war, of broken accords, systematic exclusions, and outright massacres, both total and selective (including the killing of all males over ten years old in a captured Biafran town whose civilians did not leave), that Nigeria intends to eliminate the peoples of the region that is now Biafra, and that the intention of genocide is not one that you test, passively, until the last returns are in. In the massacres of summer 1966, nearly a full year before Biafra's secession from Nigeria, thirty thousand natives of the Biafran region were murdered.

"I have just been reading *Exodus*," Professor Nwosu told a group of friends, some time after his night of waiting at State House. "Before the war, a novel to me was a trivial thing. But I should have known the West would not be impressed by thirty thousand. Some of you literary people should have told me."

In 1966, pressure to withdraw from Nigeria came mainly from the Ibo people, who make up the majority of the population of the Biafran region, and it was the Ibo intellectuals, spread out over Nigeria and the world, who wavered. Now the situation is different. The intellectuals have returned from their jobs in the outside world to Biafra, to extremity, and to a people with whom, in their own worldliness, they were not even entirely familiar. An Ibo civil servant, educated elsewhere in Nigeria, when he is asked the word in Ibo for a sash in which local women carry their babies on their backs, does not know, until it is pointed out to him, what you are talking about. He certainly does not know the word. English has always been Biafra's intertribal language, but conversations even in Ibo are interspersed now with English expressions, and the Biafran fondness for euphemism has a British ring. The war is everywhere referred to as "the crisis," areas of Biafra destroyed or occupied by Nigerian forces are always called "disrupted" or "disturbed."

The elite are leading now, as perhaps in war they always do. But Ibo society is, by tradition, individualistic and ruled by tribal consensus. The leaders and their ministries are unprotected to a degree uncommon in a country at war. If the people did not support their leaders, they could, being armed almost to a man, overthrow them. Biafrans now prefer the bush to the risks of Nigerian occupation, and Nigerian troops entering Biafran towns now find them empty. What defections there are, like that of Dr. Nnamdi Azikiwe, an Ibo who was once president of Federal Nigeria and who recently turned from the Biafran to the Nigerian side, preoccupy Biafrans continually—perhaps because there have been so few of them. A betrayal in 1967, by Brigadier Victor Banjo, who had been put in charge of all Biafran forces in the Midwestern Region, recurs in war-inspired songs all over Biafra. (Dr. Azikiwe's case is complicated by the fact that he had spent several months in London, in a state that his physicians described as "delayed shell shock," before going to Lagos and, when his extensive Nigerian properties had been returned to him, denouncing Biafra.) The favorable reaction in the American press to Dr. Azikiwe's claim that Biafran fears of extinction are a "fairy tale" presumably gave the Nigerians confidence to resume, a few days after the first editorials, their civilian air raids, bombing and strafing an orphanage at Ojoto. Dead: one nurse and fourteen children, miles from the nearest battle zone.

The former Eastern Region of Nigeria, which since May 30, 1967, has called itself Biafra, has always been the most densely populated region in all of Africa—and, in recent times, the most highly developed and educated black country there is. Its present population is about ten million; present size, ten thousand square miles; war dead in two years, one and a half million civilians by air raids and starvation, half a million more soldiers and civilians killed in actual combat zones. There are several hundred thousand refugees in Biafran refugee camps, millions more living with distant relatives in the traditional Ibo stress claim of the "extended family," seven or even twenty persons to a room. Biafran roads, before the bombings the best roads in Nigeria, are pitted now, interrupted by checkpoints and occasional rows of tree stumps to impede enemy landings, eroded further by the intense rains, sometimes hollowed under the tarmac to stop heavy-armored vehicles, but crowded in the late and early hours of darkness by lines of people—trekking, with burdens on their heads, to relatives, to markets, to shelter or hospitals. Kwashiorkor, the ugly, mortal protein-deficiency disease, which had almost been stopped when Red Cross flights were running at strength, is afflicting children again, and the people on the roads include a high proportion of adults damaged, bandaged, or in pain. Because the Biafran government is not recognized by any major country, Biafra is denied legal access on the international market to, among other things, morphine. In terms of statistics, loss of life, displacement of persons, the war has already taken a greater toll than Vietnam; and yet people on the road inevitably return smiles, and life in this enormous ghetto under siege seems determined to proceed almost normally.

As always in war, unless one happens to be at the front and be shot at, or caught in an air raid, there is nothing but a set of symptoms—distortions of peace—to give one a sense of war and its losses. Premature or simply inaccurate Nigerian claims of areas captured have often sent observers to battle zones to find that they are not simply at the front—they *are* it; and four journalists have already been killed while reporting from the Nigerian side. But the strange image-consciousness of Biafrans makes them highly scrupulous about not sending reporters where Biafran soldiers have not arrived. Biafran information officials will try reporters with the strangest evasions, from subjects as knowable and precise as whether there is or is not a Biafran Telex (there is not), or whether there are in fact flights from Libreville, to subjects as hard to know in wartime as the exact population and casualty rate. But they are deeply concerned for the safety of foreigners. "Why do you choose to fly into this volcano?" an Ibo doctor, exhausted with work, asked a foreign visitor. "You have no right or obligation to die here." When the foreigner replied, "I think it is a shared right," the doctor said, "Thank you." There is everywhere this crazed, articulate, sometimes even irritable courtesy, in the face of an absolute desolation closing in.

Foreigners flying into Biafra now bring their own food and, if the pilot permits it, their own gasoline in jerry cans. What fuel there is in Biafra is made in little roadside refineries, which consist of a thatched hut over firewood and an arrangement of pipes and steel drums beside a brook, like a still. A loss of fuel can be as dire in Biafra now as the shortage of food, since the army must be mobile to reach any stress point on the completely encircling front. The symptoms of war are evident in everything from the sound of mortars miles from the front to the fact that all markets have moved under camouflage in the bush and that children at feeding centers can get only one meal a day. Yet one subject Biafrans hardly ever talk about is the front, the actual progress of the war. Asked about this strange reticence, Biafrans will say the front is "irrelevant," or "We have no place to go. They take Owerri, we retake Umuahia. If we lose it all, we will fight without towns, from the bush." Another subject hardly mentioned in ordinary conversation, without laughter, is food, or even the starving of the children. If pressed, a Biafran will say he finds the subject "painful." Genocide, however, comes up again and again, and Biafrans will talk about a friend, a relative, a town, a personal flight from a mob before or in the war with a precise attention to dates and the most gruesome detail. Bombing raids on markets, churches, orphanages, and hospitals are recounted by families and in palm-wine bars with a kind of awe of their modern European quality, as though by dying on purely ethnic grounds Biafrans had established their place in modern history. One thing one hardly sees in Biafra is cemeteries. The dead are buried all over the third of the country that remains.

Nigeria, in what was originally described by the Nigerian government as a "quick surgical police action" that would last forty-eight hours and that has already lasted more than two years and cost more than two million lives, was armed for the war with highly sophisticated equipment by the British, who wanted, as did nearly everyone else at one time, a strong and unified Nigeria. Reporters like Frederick Forsyth in his book *The Biafra Story*, one of the few cogent accounts of what took place, attribute the subsequent disaster to the Labour Government of Harold

Wilson, who took the advice of civil servants that it would all be over quickly, that it was all a question of Ibo intransigence. Most of Nigeria's oil fields are in the Biafran region, and the oil companies had their doubts. They had personnel in the field who knew the people and who had witnessed the events of the preceding years. But the civil servants prevailed, and when it was not all over quickly, the Labour Government vastly increased its shipments of arms to Nigeria, and covered up at home.

When, in August 1968, after thirteen months of war, the extent of the British commitment became clear, there were expressions of outrage in Parliament and in the press. The Government, no longer able to conceal the size of its arms shipments, began to argue that it was more merciful in the long run to let Biafrans starve and be bombed into submission than to remain neutral, that the alternative was a tribal "Balkanization" of all Africa, that the Ibo leaders were, in any case, exaggerating and prolonging the misery of their people in order to nationalize and abscond with the oil and consolidate their own leadership. In 1967, the Russians began sending heavy arms to Nigeria, and it was argued that it was important to compete with Russia in arming Nigeria for the sake of Nigeria's goodwill. It is now likely that Nigeria's debt to Russia is such that if Nigeria wins, the oil will go at least in part to Russia, and Russia will have its first important ally in black Africa. Biafrans claim their own guerrillas will see to it that, in the event of their defeat, no oil will flow at all. It is not clear what will happen to the oil if Biafra wins, although Biafran loyalty to anyone who gives them any help or recognition just now is strong. President Nixon expressed sympathy for Biafra in a campaign speech on September 9, 1968, but nothing as strong since. The only official expression of support from any Western power came last year, from President Charles de Gaulle.

In 1960, when Nigeria became independent, it was the Northern Region that kept threatening secession, and the Eastern Region, now Biafra, that most strongly wanted unity. The North, inhabited by the Muslim Hausa-Furlani, had been ruled by the British through local emirs, who kept the region feudal and underdeveloped. The Western Region, inhabited by the less militantly Muslim Yorubas, was ruled through local tribal chieftains and remained underdeveloped, too. (The Yorubas, traditionally a peaceful people, are now being recruited by the Hausas for the war, which solves some of the internal problems in what remains of

Federal Nigeria.) The Eastern Region, traditionally governed under chiefs by tribal consultation, with chiefdoms often shifting among ruling families by popular agreement, was far more egalitarian and more difficult to rule. The British imposed "warrant chiefs" on the region, but after riots at Aba in 1929, which protested the imposition of rulers, they left the area to the missionaries—mainly the Anglican Church Missionary Society and the Roman Catholics. England's role in the war, as opposed to the support of Catholics in Caritas, has created a crisis of faith among Biafran Protestants, many of whom now attend predawn Mass in Owerri, in an uncompleted Catholic cathedral camouflaged by palm fronds, in the rain. The Ibos, who traditionally believed in one god, and worshiped him through idols, took to Christianity easily, and to Christian education. Communities sent bright children to schools abroad. By secession in 1967, Biafra had more doctors, lawyers, and engineers than any other country in black Africa. Of six hundred Nigerian doctors before the war began, five hundred were Biafrans. The crowded conditions in the Eastern Region, and their own education, sent Ibos all over the rest of Nigeria. They took part in all Nigerian institutions, but their living quarters were segregated, in ghettos called *sabon garis*. As early as 1953 at Kano, they faced pogroms.

Northern animosity toward Easterners, and suspicion of them, was so great well before independence that the North continually threatened secession unless it could dominate the Nigerian legislature. As early as 1947, Mallam Abubakar Tafawa Balewa, a Northerner who was later to become prime minister of Nigeria (and whom the Sardauna of Sokoto, a Hausa ruler, used to refer to as his "lieutenant" in Lagos), opposed unity and independence with the statement "I should like to make it clear to you that if the British quitted Nigeria now at this stage, the Northern people would continue their uninterrupted conquest to the sea."

In the years after independence, there was a series of rigged censuses, rigged elections, and murders of members of the major political party of the Eastern Region by members of the major party of the North. On January 14, 1966, there was a military coup, which killed Prime Minister Balewa and the Sardauna of Sokoto, and which is sometimes described as the Ibo move for domination that started it all. The coup did end with General Johnson Thomas Umunakwe Aguyi-Ironsi, an Ibo, in power. But it killed only twelve officers, three of whom were Ibos; it was joined by Hausa and Yoruba factions of the army; and it was opposed by, among other Ibos, Lieutenant-Colonel Chukwuemeka Odumegwu Ojukwu, now the head of state of Biafra, and General Ironsi himself.

Six months later, the Northerners staged their coup. In view of the present Nigerian claims for a unified Nigeria, the code word that set off the operation is key: *araba,* the Hausa word for "secession." In his first broadcast after the coup, Lieutenant Colonel Yakuba Gowon, the North-erner who is now head of state of Nigeria, said that Nigerian unity could not stand the test of time, that "the base for unity is not there." Three weeks later Gowon was still flying the flag not of Federal Nigeria but of the Northern Region at his headquarters in the garrison at Ikeja. At a constitutional convention in Lagos in September 1966, the Northern delegates insisted on a clause reading "Any member state of the Union should reserve the right to secede completely and unilaterally from the Union."

But the world, including, at that point, the Biafrans, still believed in one Nigeria, and the Northerners who were then in power began to see the advantages of it. The army became uncontrollable. There followed a series of massacres of Ibos and broken agreements with the Eastern Re-gion. Gowon's announcement to the press, for example, of accords be-tween the Eastern and Northern Regions reached in Aburi, Ghana, in January 1967, differs in almost every detail from tape recordings of those accords subsequently released by Ojukwu. The Northerners had agreed to protect Easterners in the other regions on their passage home, to make financial provisions for the homeless refugees, and to give the Eastern Region a degree of autonomy. Gowon did not mention the refugee agree-ments, and denied the accord on autonomy. Over a million Ibos had already fled for their lives to the Eastern Region. In early May 1967, Gowon blockaded all communications to the East. On May 26, the Con-sultative Assembly of Chiefs and Elders gave Ojukwu, who had been for about a year and a half the military governor of the Eastern Region, a mandate to withdraw from Nigeria. The next day, Gowon published a decree that, among other measures, divided the Eastern Region into three small states, with Port Harcourt and the Eastern oil fields to be excised from the Ibo region. (Port Harcourt had been built by Ibos and was inhabited almost entirely by them. The oil fields, which had only begun producing just before Nigerian independence, had not been a factor in the dispute before.) On May 30, Ojukwu issued a Biafran Declaration of

Independence. On July 6, 1967, with the slogan "One Nigeria!" Nigerian forces invaded Biafra, and soon afterward entered the Ibo town of Nsukka, where they set fire to the university and destroyed all its books.

Surprisingly—since most Ibo members of the Nigerian Army had been technical and administrative personnel, and since Biafra was very lightly armed—the Biafrans nearly won their independence in the first three months. Then the heavy British equipment came in. The Biafrans lost the coast and their major towns, although they had considerable success against the heavy equipment with homemade booby traps manufactured in Professor Nwosu's Research and Production Directorate. By April 1968, their agricultural and river areas were cut off, and people began to die of starvation in numbers that, at their peak, were estimated at ten thousand a day. Caritas, the World Council of Churches, and the Red Cross began sending in small amounts of food on Biafran mercenary arms flights. On October 12, Dr. Herman Middelkoop, of the World Council of Churches, sent a telegram to Secretary-General U Thant of the United Nations requesting UN humanitarian aid for Biafra. On October 19, the Secretary-General told the press that the telegram had not arrived and that the war was, in any case, an internal affair, in which the United Nations could not become involved.

In July 1968, the Red Cross asked General Gowon for permission to fly specially marked relief planes into Biafra. Gowon replied that Nigeria would shoot them down. They flew anyway, and the churches, having obtained the code for landing at Uli Airport, flew in, too. In June of this year, after endless negotiations over relief routes, with Nigeria arguing alternately that all relief must pass through Lagos and that there could be no relief, since total siege is a legitimate instrument of war (although the idea of total siege has traditionally been applied to cities and not to an entire ethnic population of ten million), the Red Cross plane was shot down. Since the shooting, it has been argued with increasing insistence that the situation has changed entirely, and that it is only the Biafran leadership that is making impossible, at great cost to its own people, the dream of a peaceful and unified Nigeria. Biafrans have come to argue that there never was a Nigeria, except as defined by the British colonial presence; that if the colonial "nations" of Africa were in fact to break up along tribal lines, not much would be lost except some unstable, colonial boundaries; and that a new force—local, indigenous, tribal, un-aligned—may yet be brought forth into the world. As for defectors and

the charge that the Biafrans are exaggerating their own danger of genocide, Biafrans reply that every ethnic group marked for extinction has
had sincere and misguided collaborators with the enemy. Their own experience of tribal slaughters and world indifference or unconsummated
sympathy has made them determined not to rely to the last man on
Nigeria's new good faith.

On Sunday, at Owerri market, which is now a little cluster of wooden
tables and benches, reached by a thin track of red earth marked by the
imprint of sandals and bare feet, in the bush, a five-year-old girl sat on
the ground meticulously gathering and blowing sand off each seed of
breadfruit she had dropped on the ground. The price of a scruffy, dazed,
and twitching hen was eight pounds (nearly twenty dollars); a leg of
goat, fifteen pounds; a two-inch bony river fish, a bush snail, or a cigarette, nearly half a pound; a third of a cup of salt, or a cup of *garri* (ground
cassava, the only food most Biafrans can get), one pound. The salary of
a soldier or a beginning civil servant is fifteen pounds a month. A woman
was preoccupied with keeping her entire wares, four minuscule bush
snails, from crawling away. No one was buying anything but *garri*, and
very little of that.

Suddenly, a shrieking, giggling band of eleven young men and three
boys passed through the market, as though carried away by some ener-
vating, mocking joke. These were some of the "artillery cases" one sees
all over Biafra—people claiming some local variant of shell shock and
traveling always in packs. They were treated by other citizens with a kind
of care. Three at Owerri market were given a melon seed or a nut, which
sent them into screams of laughter again. Medical comments about them
vary. Dr. Fabian Udekwu, head surgeon at a hospital in Emekuku, insists
that their disorder is genuine. "The reason their voices are so shrill is
that their hearing is impaired," he said. A young military matron at the
Armed Forces Hospital in Nkwerri was less sympathetic. "They are putting it on," she said. Most of the artillery cases are treated at a psychiatric
hospital in Ekwereazu. It takes about two months to cure the symptoms.

At nine-thirty Sunday morning, in a bullet-scarred bungalow of what
was once the Advanced Teachers' Training College in Owerri (Owerri,
fifteen miles from the front, was taken by Nigerian forces last September,
retaken by Biafra in April; it is now Biafra's provisional capital), I asked
Elizabeth Etuk, who is in her twenties, chairman of the Biafra Youth

Front, and a member of the Ibibio, a minority tribe, how many times she had been a refugee since she fled from Lagos just before the war. She began to count.

"Mark you," she said, "I'm now in a village I never heard of before." Miss Etuk, who received her doctorate in child psychology from Columbia University in 1967, gave up her study of "the intellectual development of our children" (almost all Biafran schools have been closed since the crisis) to form the Youth Front, which so far consists of a few thousand young people in about fifty villages, who administer feedings ("lunch, when there was a lunch"), catch lizards, sausage flies, and snails by night for their protein content, process cassava into *garri*, allot the little salt that is brought in by relief flights, perform and compose songs for the refugee camps, and organize play groups for the children who are not too weak with misery or kwashiorkor.

"They always play war games," she said earnestly. "Nobody wants to play the Nigerians. Sometimes the play is violent. It is the strain." She became very cheerful about the new Biafran songs that mix local languages. "The crisis has mixed the country up," she said. "You find refugees shouting when they hear their language, then other refugees in the same camp shouting when they hear their own." Her youth group has brought back some traditional dances that were beginning to die off. "Before the crisis, you know, some of us were very worried," she said. "We knew how to dance the waltz." I asked her whether women had always had much influence in the Eastern Region, and she became quite grimly militant. She described the Ibo women's part in the 1929 riots, and a more recent protest. "A committee went to His Excellency," she said, referring to Ojukwu. "And they told him, 'We are the ones who have lost children. We are the ones who have lost husbands. We are the ones who lost our homes. Some of us are too old to have children again. Ojukwu, give us guns!' When the women start these things, the men know they are not joking. But they were very adamant. They said it had not come to that." A friend tried to distract her with a joke about soups from the Ibibio area of Biafra, and she laughingly told him that, since the population mixup, Ibos would have to acknowledge that Ibibio soups were the best.

At lunchtime, Miss Etuk and her friend having refused to stay, I cooked some canned soup over a kerosene stove in my bungalow in Owerri and then went to a building called the Overseas Press Service, where it turned out two French journalists, who were about to leave

Biafra, had run out of food. They ate in the press cafeteria. The menu, headed "Progress Hotel Umuahia" (Umuahia was captured in April by Nigeria) and restamped "Owerri": Boiled Yam, Mixed Vegetables (apparently a kind of grass), Sliced Pineapple (a quarter of a single slice per guest).

Sunday afternoon, at the Victoria Palace Hotel, a palm-wine bar (Biafra is full of palm-wine bars called, and sometimes serving as, hotels: Hotel de Gabon, Hotel de Tanzania, Hotel de Haiti, Hotel DeGaulle, Hotel Tranquillity), the palm wine, a mildly alcoholic drink with the taste of oiled lemonade, had run out. There was still Biafra Gin, Biafra Sherry, and Biafra Stout Beer (one-half bottle, seven pounds). The place was filled with soldiers, in uniform and armed with pistols made in France. There were also a few civilian women and some artillery cases, who swarmed around the soldiers without shrieking and yet seemed to embarrass them. The aging proprietor of the Victoria Palace said that he had begun, in pre-crisis times, by trading salt, soap, and shoes to accumulate money to buy his hotel but that the "vandals" had looted his hotel when Owerri was disrupted. "Vandals" is the almost universal word in Biafra for Nigerians.

Just after dark on Sunday, in the house of N. U. Akpan, who is Chief Secretary to the Military Government, head of the Biafran civil service, a Presbyterian elder, and a member of the minority Ibibio tribe, the lights went out. The water in Owerri had been shut off some time before. Kerosene lamps were brought in. It was cold, and the rain outside looked bleak. I asked Mr. Akpan whether anyone in Biafra advocated simply giving up. (These questions always seemed to me awful, but Biafrans seemed to mind if they were not asked. Women at markets looked worried if notes were not made of every answer; and one is asked everywhere in Biafra to sign a guestbook, as though simply writing things down—names, comments—would someday give evidence that there had been a Biafra at all.) "If you said that," Mr. Akpan said quietly about giving in, "you would be beaten up. If I said it, I would be lynched."

I asked what the politics of Biafra, whose enemy had been armed after all by both the Russians and the British, might be after the war. Mr. Akpan said it would be unaligned in terms of ideology. "Only let us be unaligned," he said. "Let us look inward." He paused a long time in the near darkness. "The West brought us good tidings, but it wouldn't let us expand on them. Now we are suffering this strange mercy killing at the hands of the British, and it has brought out qualities we did not know we had. Nigeria, you see, has mortgaged its future to the Soviet Union, but we would wish after the crisis that they would be stable. We wouldn't wish a confused and unstable neighbor." He paused again. "Mark you," he said, "when Nixon was campaigning, Nigeria became jittery."

When I asked whether de Gaulle's expression of sympathy might have been a case of enlightened self-interest, he denied it vigorously. "France spoke for us when we had lost the oil, when we were nearly finished," he said. "Some of us, you see, thought last September was the end. But here we are."

At the dinner hour on Sunday, I again saw Elizabeth Etuk, with Austin Ogwumba (head of Biafran Security), Dr. Pius Okigbo (a Biafran economist, and former representative of Nigeria to the European Common Market), and some other guests, at the home of Godwin A. Onyegbula, the former Nigerian charge d'affaires in Washington, now permanent secretary of the Biafran Ministry of Foreign Affairs and Commonwealth Relations. (The word "Commonwealth" in the title of Mr. Onyegbula, who is essentially the Biafran foreign minister, dates from a time when Biafrans still had hopes for the British, but it now refers only to "the commonwealth of nations.") I asked whether Biafrans felt comfortable with recognition by, of all nations, Haiti. François Duvalier went to school with several young Ibos in Michigan, long before he became Papa Doc, when he was still a young liberal medical student. Mr. Onyegbula laughed, averted his eyes, and entered that tangle of reasoning with which Biafrans express their loyalty to any of the strange partners with whom they now find themselves.

"Well, you know, when Haiti recognized us, I began to doubt all the things I had ever heard about it," he said. "I have never been there myself, but, you see, Haiti was, after all, the world's first black republic. Perhaps when your brother is suffering you have a telepathic experience." Mr. Onyegbula seemed relieved to let the subject drop. Conversation turned to the failure of Biafra to capture the imagination of black Americans. "Yes, yes," Dr. Okigbo said. "How can we get to them?" The guests began a very informed discussion about American black leadership, and whether it might be better to have the support of Mrs. Martin Luther King, Julian Bond, and Jesse Jackson or to enlist the "crisis mentality" of black radicals, who now seem to seek their identity with the descendants of Muslim slave traders—most recently at the Pan-African cultural conference in Algiers.

"It doesn't matter," Dr. Okigbo said, laughing. "After all, we are all on the same train without a ticket."

Late Sunday night, a Biafran rock group called the Fractions, who had brought their own generator for their guitars and against the darkness, were playing to a very crowded dance floor in the hall of the Advanced Teachers' Training College. Most of the young people were dancing Western style, some were doing the Highlife, and a few were discussing the news of Dr. Azikiwe's defection in Lagos. "In war, you always have Lord Hawhaw," a bearded young man said. "It doesn't reflect the core, the generality of opinion." Many of the dancers were soldiers. Two were solemn workers from Caritas. After the dance, in a rain that seemed almost total, on the Owerri-Orlu road, among the trekkers, almost all of whom were barefoot and shivering, and many of whom were naked children carrying basins or articles of furniture on their heads, a little boy put a large machete on top of his head to free his hands to rub his eyes. The driver of a State House car, who had already nearly hit a goat and a chicken, almost ran him down.

On Monday, at 9 A.M., in Owerri, the High Court of Biafra was in session in what was once a school, under Chief Justice Sir Louis Mbanefo, a former judge of the World Court, who as an Ibo justice in Nigeria in 1962 had reduced the sentence, for treason, of Chief Anthony Enahoro, whom he faced again last year in unsuccessful negotiations for peace in Biafra. All the judges and attorneys wore black robes and curled, yellowing wigs. On the table nearest the attorneys was a gray volume, *Reports of the High Court of the Federal Territory of Lagos.* The steps by which messengers climbed to the justices' bench consisted of rusted mortar containers, still marked "Explosives/UK." On the docket was an appeal of a sentence of murder (*Chief Amagwara Achonye* v. *the State*), but the case under discussion was a complicated one, which had already passed through native and higher courts, concerning the right of a man to build on the communal land of his family. The appellant had been in possession of the land since 1921, planted fruit trees and constructed a fence, but there were legal issues that entailed a distinction between "possession" and "ownership," and also issues of tribal law, which elicited phrases like "By native custom, My Lord, a man may not build on the ruins of his father's house unless the line has become extinct" and "If a man should have a house, My Lord, and what is commonly called a yard. . . ." The appellant and members of his family were in attendance, but silent. At one point, Justice Mbanefo asked one of the attorneys, a bearded young man with a severe cold and with thumbprints on his glasses, whether the case might be adjourned until Wednesday. "I don't know, My Lord," he replied. "I have to come all the way from Ihiala for these appeals. The problem of transportation will be—that is, unless my learned friend can . . ." Finally, the court did adjourn. An usher cried, "Court!" Everyone rose, and the justices left the room.

Later, in his office, in what had once been a little classroom, the chief justice remarked that the case should have been tried in 1967, "but the land in question, you see, was disturbed until now. So the matter of ownership was for some time academic." I asked Justice Mbanefo about the accommodation of British and native law. "We are still in the process of sorting it out," he said. "Mark you, the native courts consist of local men of impeccable integrity. We would not reverse the ruling of the customary courts unless it was patently against good conscience, equity, and justice." I asked Justice Mbanefo about the strange history of his two encounters with Chief Enahoro of Nigeria. "Ah, you see, under other circumstances it might have been different," he said, and he pointed out that a brother of Chief Enahoro is now in exile in Norway, where he makes fervent speeches on behalf of Biafra. "Mind you," he said, "only yesterday one of my own nephews, who was commanding a company, found some supplies left by Nigerian forces in retreat. Some of the company drank the beer left behind, and it was full of arsenic. Four men are dead. It is tragic, the loss of life. I don't think the British are acting in this out of a desire to see Biafrans killed. They are like all good imperialists. Human lives don't matter. Political expediency—this, I think, is really behind it."

Mr. Onyegbula came in to ask Justice Mbanefo, who is also an official of the Biafran Petroleum Commission, for an allotment of fuel for the Foreign Ministry. Justice Mbanefo could only give him half of what he asked. "I believe the Nigerian soldiers are fighting for the spoils," the justice said quietly. "You see, our refugees leave everything behind. We are fighting for our homes. With us, oil was never an issue. But now, of course"—he paused and nodded to himself several times—"you cannot ignore it."

On Monday afternoon, Chinua Achebe, the Biafran novelist (author of *Things Fall Apart* and *No Longer at Ease*), arrived in Owerri several hours late for an appointment because of a broken axle on the road from Oguta, where, having been five times a refugee from a series of disturbed areas, he now lives. Mr. Achebe is chairman of the Biafra National Guidance Committee, a group of Biafran intellectuals who go out and interview the people in the countryside to keep the government in touch with what the people are saying. Ordinary Biafrans speak freely of the Guidance Committee, and freely register their grievances at its meetings, but the government (presumably for fear the committee might acquire an image of repressive interrogation) is extremely reticent about it. The sun was out briefly in Owerri. I asked Mr. Achebe, whose novels are preoccupied with problems of the modern breakdown in Ibo tradition, about Ibo relations with the minority tribes—the Efiks, Ibibios, Ijaws, Annangs, Ogojas, and Cross River people (most of them Christians)— who comprise a bit less than half of Biafra's population and about half of the Consultative Assembly of Chiefs and Elders. The assembly consists of ten men, six elected and four appointed by the government, from each of the more than thirty districts of pre-crisis Biafra, and it includes, among representatives of labor, business, professional, and women's groups, such local elders as the Amanyanagbo of Kalabari, the Amanyanagbo of Bonny, Chief J. Mpi of Ikwerre, Douglas Colonel Jaja of Opobo, the Obi of Onitsha, Uyo Clan Head of Okwu Itu-Itam, the Onyiba Enyi of Ohaozara in Abakaliki, and the ninth Eze Dara of Uli. Members of Eastern minority tribes have often been killed along with Ibos, and many of the minorities who once chose to remain in disturbed areas and risk Nigerian occupation have since taken refuge in Biafra. General Ojukwu has frequently asked for a plebiscite, under international supervision, to determine the minority tribes' view of Biafran independence. "The crisis has now thrown everyone together," Mr. Achebe said. "It seems a very curious way to forge a nation."

On Monday evening, Patience Nwokedi, a twenty-two-year-old nurse in the Red Cross hospital at Awomama, hitchhiked the fifteen miles to Owerri to spend her one day off a week with her husband, Ralph, a twenty-eight-year-old civil servant, to whom she has been married for six months. They were going to wait until after the crisis to marry, but after two years decided not to wait. Mr. Nwokedi, who was educated at the Ibo university at Nsukka, used to write advertising for Federal Nigeria, which appeared in newspaper supplements abroad. In Biafra now, he supports his wife's mother, who was recently caught for some days in the bush behind enemy lines ("We are recuperating her," he said), his own mother, his own sixty-six-year-old father and his stepmother and their five children, who live in Nimo, two miles from the front, and a friend and five brothers and sisters who now all live in Mr. Nwokedi's two-room house with him. In good times, he can afford about a cup of *garri* per person per meal. He has four brothers in the army who help. "For a young man not to have served in the army, even if he is on essential services, is very painful to him," he said. "But without me my poor old dad would starve."

Ralph and Patience Nwokedi, who are Protestants, found a car for a visit to an old friend, Father Michael Conniff, at the Caritas mission for the Owerri diocese. Father Conniff, like most white men who have served in Biafra since the crisis, has a frantic, nearly crazed look about his bloodshot eyes. There are thirty-one parishes in the Owerri diocese. With the reduced relief flights, Caritas receives a shipment of food only every other night. "We don't know what we are getting," Father Conniff said. "Often we have to wonder, Is this worth dividing into thirty-one places? We cater for seven hospitals. The Red Cross used to cater for sixty-four. West German relief has fallen off ninety percent since the Biafran Air Force bombed an oil installation in the Midwest. All day long we are worried by wounded soldiers. Now they have nothing to eat. What are we to do?"

I asked him whether the diocese feeds only Catholic children.

"We take every child that comes," he said. "The only distinction is a special diet for the sicker ones." Three children had died in one of his sick bays the night before. Father Conniff patted a mongrel dog named Buster, fed on whatever leaks out of the burlap sacks of fish. "This is not a place everybody would want to come to," he said, in a voice that was by now cracking. "There are a lot of things to kind of scare a fellow from living here. When the area was retaken, there were a lot of bodies smelling. We buried them. Some of them were not pushed down too far. There's two in the yard, six under my window, one officer in the flower garden. The bush closed in. That brought mosquitoes bigger than fowl, rats, snakes. A lot of corpses are in this place."

I asked him what his prayers were like.

"More planes," he said vaguely. "More planes. Bigger planes. More planes." Not far from the mission, there was still a billboard reading, "Pepsi, the Big One."

Ralph Nwokedi's father had trekked all the way from Nimo for a three-week visit to his son. He would also visit Ralph's mother, twenty miles farther on. Although Christian, the elder Nwokedi is a polygamist. The elder Nwokedi, a tall, distinguished man, with long bare feet and a long maroon robe over a faded collarless shirt, ceremoniously broke a kola nut for his family and guests, in their dark living room. Kola nuts are full of caffeine, and are supposed to make water drunk after them taste very sweet. The kola nut, about three inches long, broke into six natural pieces, and the elder Nwokedi sliced these into halves and passed them around. He said a prayer, and then everyone chewed, and drank water from the house's only glass.

"When the first refugees come," the elder Nwokedi said, "we begin to harbor them, begin petting them, say, 'Be quiet, be quiet, peace will come.' Now we have to break off, finished. If I am young, I should go inside the battlefield and fight. Now I see how I try to keep my household together. We take cover each time, and our hearts run each time. I was a big man, but now I shall never weigh ten stone again." He was silent for a very long time. "When I become a Christian as a boy, I get a small book, and when I have children they should learn to read and write. The war breaks in and it turns my heart. It should be college now. Of all the time of my life, this is the misery."

Later, at the dinner hour, in the house of Dr. Ifegwu Eke, commissioner of information, who studied at McGill and at Harvard, where he earned his doctorate in economics, with a dissertation entitled "Study of the Productivity of Water," few of the guests showed up, because of the intensity of the rains. The conversation turned again to the defection of Dr. Azikiwe. "He was with us," Dr. Eke said. "But when Aba, Owerri, and Okigwe fell in rapid succession, he didn't want to come back."

I asked Dr. Eke whether much was known about the history of the Biafran region before modern times, and he said that there was material for research in European libraries but that no one had had time to get at it yet. "I lost all my own manuscripts when Enugu was disrupted," he said. "But Port Harcourt was the saddest fall. People were weeping that they should leave a town they had so long defended. At the last minute, the roads were full, miles of nothing but people trekking."

I asked whether Biafrans heard much of the news outside Biafra, and he said that people listened anxiously to any available transistor radio, that it made them feel they belonged to the world. "Ask a small boy about the moon," Dr. Eke said. "He will rattle off everything." He spoke of the front. "In many places, the mud comes to your waist in the rainy season, so everybody stays where he is." I asked about Biafran guerrilla activity in disrupted areas, and he laughed. "Call it infiltration," he said. "But whatever it is, we are there."

I had been told by several Ibos that Dr. Eke's time in America had not been happy, but he did not speak of it. He only spoke rather skeptically of the Red Cross and starvation ("They always overestimate or underestimate," he said. "When they needed two million dollars, they said two million children would die by February") and of the general indifference of the world. "You know how it is with any tragedy," he said. "After the first two floods, contributions will decline. People will simply say, 'Why don't they move?' "

Before dawn on Tuesday morning, a State House car, which had already nearly run over several hitchhikers who tried, with a kind of limp-wristed motion, to flag it down on the road to Mbano, picked up A. Kalada Hart, the young Biafran secretary of the Ministry of Energy and Mineral Supplies. "I don't seem to have any now," he said. The day was hot and not rainy for a change, and at Angara Junction, of the Okigwe, Owerri, Umuahia, and Orlu roads, there were trekkers who looked particularly desolate. The driver looked rigidly at the road. "Sympathy is such a silly sentiment," he said. At a compound in Mbano, Dr. Bede Okigbo, who was once dean of agriculture at the University of Nsukka, who studied at Washington State University and Cornell, and who is now coordinator of a farming directorate called the Land Army, discussed the problem of raising poultry in the part of Biafra that is left. "First, we have to see how much maize there is," he said. "We must minimize the competition between human beings and poultry for the maize."

Each community in Biafra must now donate a piece of land for farming by the Land Army, and each member of the community must spend a day each week on the Land Army farm. Half the produce remains with the community; the other half must be sold to the government. Land under dispute in the courts is frozen until after the crisis and planted. "Food scarcity here is not new," Dr. Okigbo said. "Before the war, there was often near famine. It is the soil, storage problems, and the insects."

I asked Dr. Okigbo how Biafran farmers reacted to the Land Army.

"The people are very individualistic," he said. "Each little farm used to grow a little of everything—twenty farms for twenty families. It is very hard to mechanize. First, we sent in boys to teach the local people, but the people were not much impressed. Now we are hoping to get them to ask for the experts." All the agriculture experts from Dr. Okigbo's faculty at Nsukka are now in the regular army, except the wounded or people with administrative jobs, who now work on the land. Dr. Okigbo looked at a government memo datelined "Enugu/Mbano." "We are studying plants which will not tempt people to eat the seedlings," he said. "We are studying the wild local vegetables for identification." A member of Dr. Okigbo's staff mentioned a soldier of the Madonna Commandos, who had volunteered to serve as a guinea pig for any vegetation the soldiers were afraid to try. (Biafran commandos, who are among the most respected Biafran soldiers at the front, travel along the roads in trucks with gray skull and crossbones on the windshields, quite unlike the more cheerfully decorated trucks other units travel in.) "We have learned we cannot establish targets for our farms," Dr. Okigbo said. "We have found our local pullets thrive better on less, on kitchen refuse, than imported pullets. But each time we plant, the enemy comes in. No matter how much target you establish, you see, you may not attain it."

On Tuesday afternoon, Moses Iloh, National Secretary of the Biafra Red Cross, sat in his headquarters in the bush at Abba, in a trailer with a broken wheel. "We have been disturbed so often," he said. "I don't see how we can move again." He spoke of people who had died from trekking, mothers who had miscarried, pneumonia, tuberculosis, malaria, orphans too young to know their names found with people moving in the bush. "And so many have lost their minds," he said. "The worst time was last year—May, June, July, August, September. Now the kwashiorkor is beginning again. A child who has had this thing twice shrinks. There is the brain damage. We have lost a hundred thousand people over fifty-five from shortage of bulk carbohydrates. You cannot fly in bulk carbohydrates. What will happen when there is nobody to tell us of the past, nobody to inherit the future?"

Mr. Iloh and I went to a Red Cross orphanage near Abba, where about twenty children were sitting quietly on their beds, which consisted of metal frames and bamboo pallets, some covered with blankets, some not. The children were led outside under a frangipani tree, a baby was placed on the ground in the center, a nine-year-old girl put her hands together in an attitude of prayer, a five-year-old clung to the hand of a matron, and the children began to sing, to the tune of "O Du Lieber Augustin," "When we are together, together, together, when we are together, the happier we will be. On your face, on my face, on your face, on my face. . . ." Suddenly, the children switched to a song in Ibo, and I asked what the words meant. "They are asking Gowon to stop killing them," Mr. Iloh said. The children switched to English again:

> "Solomon the king.
> Solomon the judge.
> Solomon the peacemaker."

And then, very deliberately and grimly:

> "Solomon passes sentence."

Most of the children would stay at the orphanage. A few would be sent to Gabon for the duration of the crisis. Some would be sent to São Tomé, to be fed properly for a while, and then returned to Biafra. And Mr. Iloh, who had already adopted one in addition to his own two children, was about to adopt another. "It is wonderful, wonderful," he said. "You can't tell the difference."

We went on to a World Council of Churches sick bay at Isu. A naked child hunkered outside, with the swollen stomach and utter lassitude of kwashiorkor. Mr. Iloh gently pulled down its lower eyelid. The interior was dead white. "Almost a hundred-percent anemia," Mr. Iloh said. I asked him whether kwashiorkor children were in pain, and he said, "Not unless the liver is affected."

There were victims of kwashiorkor and scabies, all with somehow intensely old-looking faces, on the beds and mats inside. The "severe" cases were separated by a raffia partition from the less severe, although I could not tell the difference. Some were coughing; some did not seem to have the energy. The matron, a young midwife, apologized that some beds had only one occupant. "We used to admit two in a bed," she said, "when we could feed them."

On the road to the Red Cross sick bay at Ezeoke, we passed St. Paul's parsonage of the Church Missionary Society, a thatched shop called the Live and Let Live Volkswagen House (empty), and another shop, which displayed one small wooden coffin. A notice was posted on the hospital wall: "On admission, girls on duty should find out the following facts: (1) If the child is an orphan; (2) If the child is motherless; (3) If the child is fatherless. . . ." It was nap time, but the children, all of whom were dressed in clothes of the same material, were lying, sometimes two or three to a bed for companionship (there was a bed for every child), silent and wide awake.

A refugee camp nearby, in what had been the Holy Rosary School and Church Hall, had few occupants, although there were hundreds of pallets and bundles of personal belongings on the floor of a single room, with rain coming in through windows without panes. Most of the adult refugees were out looking for food. The ones who remained seemed to come from everywhere in Biafra. Some had moved more times than they could remember. On the wall, in chalk, there were still attendance figures for the last day of school, in 1967. Nobody seemed to know where the nearest children's feeding center was, except a girl from the local Red Cross detachment, her hair neatly tied in the nine longish pigtails one often sees in Biafra. "We gave out food yesterday," she said. "So there won't be any tomorrow."

On Tuesday evening, in his car on the road to Emekuku, Dr. R. N. Onyemelukwe, who is Biafra's chief health officer, spoke of his problems when the Biafrans retook Owerri. "Sanitation was a very formidable problem," he said. "It was all littered with corpses and night soil. The water supply, you may have noticed, was disrupted. All equipment was broken. All wires were cut. I think they were at war with books." He said that the bush and the snakes had begun to close in, although he himself had not yet seen a cobra. "Before the crisis, we were developing sanitation-consciousness in our people," he said. "We even anticipated problems of air pollution." He laughed. "Although, of course, the crisis has now reduced the number of vehicles." He spoke of burials, sewage, mass immunization. "There was not a single civilian living in Owerri when it was disrupted," he said. "I had one hundred workers, cleaning up. Of course, there was no market, so I had, ha-ha, to feed them. I imagine the population of night snails was depleted. In two weeks, Owerri was ready for the return of our civilians. Two white Red Cross workers, you know, were shot when Okigwe was disrupted. Every home has lost some-one in this war."

Later that night, at the residence of Dr. Fabian Udekwu, head surgeon of the Teaching Hospital at Emekuku, a game of draughts, on a home-made board, was going on. A chair was littered with cartridge tapes—Bach, Mozart, Stravinsky. Dr. Udekwu, who studied at Johns Hopkins and did his residency at Cook County Hospital in Chicago, had worked for a time in a hospital in Ibadan, in Western Nigeria, fled through the bush when a friend of his, another Ibo surgeon, nearly lost his hands in a massacre in 1965, returned for some months to Ibadan, and, after an-other outbreak of killings, returned at last to Biafra. Since then, he has moved several times, as areas were disrupted. "It is terrible, you know," he said, "to come home and keep on running." I asked a friend of Dr. Udekwu's how the mobs had recognized Ibos in the massacres, and the friend replied that they were better dressed and that there was a distinc-tive Ibo facial structure (Ibos, to me, looked very different from one another). Their names were also characteristically Ibo; to find Ibos in cars, Hausa colleagues often kept checklists of license numbers.

Dr. Udekwu took me on a quick tour of the Emekuku hospital, where six hundred patients, mostly wounded soldiers, lay in kerosene-lamp-lighted wards, on beds and on pallets on the floor. They greeted the doctor cheerfully as he pointed out the results of operations; a Steinmann pin, consisting of a sterilized nail through an injured limb, with a bag of pebbles for traction at the foot of the bed; a splint made of scrap metal and screws for bad fractures. "We are born to improvise," he said. Most of the patients at Emekuku arrive at night. It takes them about forty-six hours' travel from the farthest front. The hospital's four senior sur-geons and twenty doctors perform between fifty and a hundred operations a day.

"We need plastic surgeons, orthopedists, neurosurgeons, pediatricians," Dr. Udekwu said. "Then, of course, there's no sense operating on them if we can't feed them. And storage and malnutrition of donors creates a problem with blood donations. But the worst are the victims of the white phosphorus bombs. Have you seen one? Some of them are still smoking on the operating table." He said that he was able to treat them with hydrogen peroxide, and that he hoped never to see war again.

At Dr. Udekwu's dinner table, with several guests—including Dr. On-yemelukwe; Dr. Anezi Okoro, a dermatologist turned surgeon; and Mrs.

Bede Okigbo, wife of the head of the Land Army (Mrs. Okigbo is in charge of food at Emekuku)—Dr. Udekwu said, "Let us pray." Dinner consisted of vegetable *ukwa* soup (rich, somebody said, in sulfur-bearing amino acids), a paté called *moi-moi* ("Why do we call it *moi-moi?*" Dr. Okoro said. "That is the Yoruba word. The Ibo is *mai-mai*"), and chicken, the bones of which, even in the half-light, were picked clean. Dr. Udekwu was worried about Biafran medical students whose education had been interrupted by the crisis. He favored rotating them for study abroad, in crash programs. "There are already eighty Biafran doctors abroad," he said. "But one must consider the overall situation. Forty-five percent of our population is under fifteen. We don't want to run the risk of losing our students. If we die, they can carry on." Dr. Udekwu began to talk about the work of the Biafra Relief Services, of New York, in resettling two Biafran leper colonies whose area had been disturbed. "The lepers are like the prisoners," he said cheerfully. "When an area is disrupted, they will flee and report to the next prison along the line."

After dinner, over glasses of palm wine, a young guest told a story of trying to get a job with Shell BP, the major oil company in the Eastern Region, before the war. He had been selected, out of hundreds of candidates, for one final interview. They asked him what he thought of Shell BP. He told them he thought the company was taking more out than it was putting into Nigeria. They did not hire him. (It seemed somehow characteristically Biafran to find this funny and surprising.) Dr. Udekwu began to talk about recent studies of starvation. "We used to think that people lived for a while off their fatty tissue," he said. "But now we realize it attacks the vital organs. Brain damage, of course, is irreversible. Mercifully, the worst cases will pass on."

Dr. Onyemelukwe and Dr. Udekwu bantered a bit about peptic ulcers, and Dr. Okoro shyly brought out a sheaf of poems. The first line of the first poem was "It was high tide in casualty." Later, as his guests left, Dr. Udekwu said, "I hope you don't think we eat like this every night. I am embarrassed." His guests thanked him and said they were embarrassed, too.

On the drive back to Owerri, Dr. Onyemelukwe initiated a discussion of the new government recommendations for cooking cassava leaves. Plucking the leaves kills the tubers, which creates problems for the survival of cassava. Boiling the leaves, which are hairy, for only fifteen minutes, as recommended, conserves their vitamin content but does not quite eliminate the cyanide they contain. A dilemma. "Just watch a goat," Dr. Onyemelukwe said, as we passed one. "And whatever a goat eats, you won't die. Pluck it and eat it." Before going to his own home, the chief health officer spent some time pushing a young man's stalled car through the rain.

I spent the rest of Tuesday night, with a flashlight, rereading Frederick Forsyth, and a report by some British anthropologists and diplomats familiar with the Eastern Region very quietly asking that the West reconsider its position on Biafra. I was scared in the dark, not of violence (I had not really seen any) or of disease (I had only a kind of muzzy cold from the rain) but of not being able to get out. I was convinced that there would be no planes, or no room for me on them. I became obsessed, like other journalists and Biafrans, with the question of the Telex. Biafra does have a radio connection with Gabon, and finally access to a real Telex in Geneva, but the insistence that there was one right *there*, in Biafra, was quite comprehensible in the dark, and seemed by its own logic to explain more serious questions: for example, censorship. There is, in effect, no censorship in Biafra, but Biafrans have to give some reason why journalists cannot take their cables directly to the Telex office. They claim they must censor the cables, and then they simply radio them, altering perhaps a word or two, to Gabon. They prefer the idea of censorship to the idea that there is no wire, no solid link to the world outside. So did I. One of the two other reporters left in Biafra that night (two weeks later, there were none), imagining that he heard a snake or a person rustling in his food, had thrown his jackknife, frightening himself more with the sound.

Just before dawn on Wednesday, a small congregation was attending a Mass at St. Paul's in the village of Isu. After Mass, an elderly woman pressed something into the hands of Father Gerard Gogan, a white priest, with the characteristic vagueness and despair about his eyes. "What is this?" he said, apparently startled by being approached or spoken to at all. "It is a letter for you," she replied. "I will read it," he said, more calmly, and put it in his cassock. In a black kettle, over a very smoky fire in a little thatched hut, some workers were boiling ten stockfish to feed over a hundred children. A kettle of medicinal leaves was being boiled for an eighteen-year-old malaria victim who stood nearby.

A little later, in the office of Major General Philip Effiong, an Efik, who is Chief of the General Staff, at Defense Headquarters (a camouflaged location in the bush), a copy of *The Geneva Convention Relative to the Treatment of Prisoners of War* lay on the table. On the walls were pictures of the mangled victims of Nigerian bombing raids. A young government worker was talking intensely about the problems Biafra might face after independence. "It will be freedom won through blood," he said. "There will be this background of sorrow, violence, and hatred. What will be the expectations? There will be a second struggle, for order and the fundamental freedoms. Will the people say, 'Where is it, the goal?' Will they have the energy?"

General Effiong walked in, a humorous, most unmilitary-looking man. He went to a wall map stuck with pins and wood slivers (round or square, orange, red, blue, pink) and gave a short briefing about the front. "Onitsha, active. Okigwe, off and on. Ikot Ekpene, changed hands half a dozen times. Umuahia, static, lots of raids by our guerrillas. At Onitsha, they are trying to break through to Nnewi, His Excellency's hometown, but we are almost inside Onitsha to the Savoy Hotel. Port Harcourt, all these areas must begin to feel the pressure. Many of our men at the front are without boots, but when there are gaps we do go through. At the beginning, we had no artillery and no mortars, not a single piece. We had a few helicopters and our famous B-26 [an old plane, from which a mercenary pilot used to kick bombs through a door]. Mark you, between August and October last year we had our most precarious moment. The fall of Umuahia was very depressing. I think we revived very well. There is optimism, and not without reason. You know, they lost three thousand men on the road to Onitsha. I know they have suffered terribly. It is a colossal war," he said. "It is a very, very colossal war."

I asked General Effiong to what extent the Biafran Army has been forced to resort to conscription.

"In a war of this kind," he said, "our people don't like it. We tried it for three months and found we had to stop. Our people couldn't see the point."

I asked whether the recent lessening of air raids was due entirely to the weather. "This has been puzzling us for some time," he said. "Perhaps it is our little homemade rockets popping. And our air force has been up again, nothing to write home to Mummy about but quite a little baby."

General Effiong showed me some captured military weapons, British antitank guns used against people (Biafra has no tanks), Russian napalm, machine guns from countries all over Europe, and some marked "U.S. Gov't Property/Army."

"If we fail, you see," General Effiong said, "then the black man in Africa is going to fail, and the minority man wherever he is. One would think we had done enough against all this to prove that we deserve to live."

At noon on Wednesday, in the Armed Forces Hospital at Nkwerre, which is run by Colonel Miller Jaja (who was once a Fellow of the Royal College of Surgeons in London, and who is a descendant of the Jaja of Opobo, who led a revolt against the slave trade in the early 1860s), Major Dennis Umeh, a thirty-one-year-old surgeon who enlisted in the army on the day before the war, said the hospital had been twice strafed and bombed by MIGs. "We didn't complain," he said. "This is a military hospital." There are two thousand patients in the hospital, which was once St. Augustine's Grammar School, and five thousand more in a large complex across the road. The matron, Major Mary Onyejiaka, is a thirty-four-year-old nurse who once served in the Nigerian Army. She makes the rounds of the enormous complex twice a week.

"I happen to have had the luck to be in the first unit at Nsukka," Major Umeh said. "We got the wounded well and back to the war zones very quickly." He paused and nodded. "Most who are still alive would agree that this is so." Now, he said, because of the malnutrition, recoveries are slower, but only three or four casualties die per ward per month. "They are a pitiable lot," he said. "But they linger on and they make it. I think it is battalion pride." He laughed. "And the food at the front is better." There are only nine qualified doctors and four medical students at Nkwerre, and only one operating theater, with four operating tables. Quite often, when the hospital has to ease conditions on the heavy fronts, casualties are lined up to wait outside the theater. "It increases the morbidity but not the mortality," Major Umeh said; that is, patients stay sick longer, but they do not die. I asked how families in Biafra receive word of wounded soldiers, and Major Umeh spoke of Noticas (Notice of Casualties), which sends couriers to the parents and the units of the hurt.

Major Umeh took me through the huge wards, named for their ailments, and a few tents of wounded outside. Some people in Fractures were singing; Dental seemed rather miserable. He pointed out delicate makeshift operations like Dr. Udekwu's, and he paused in a little X-ray room to warn a technician not to tell a patient of some harmless mortar particles left in his leg. "They are so sensitive," he said, "that if you tell them they will suffer." But he was most proud of the hospital's pharmacy, in which some young scientists were producing dextrose, extracting pain-killers and tranquilizers from mixed pills (for the tetanus and artillery cases), analyzing native remedies ("It is like deciphering a code," a young scientist said), and making pills in test tubes. The pharmacy cannot pro-duce antibiotics yet, but not, the major emphasized, for lack of knowl-edge, only for lack of facilities. "Give us two years of peace and we will do it," he said. "The lowered resistance of our patients to germs some-times puts us back to square one."

I asked whether the pharmacy could produce enough painkillers for the front, and he said, "Oh, yes. Most of them should be asleep when they get here."

A major from one of the battle zones was in the hospital, visiting his men. I asked what unit he was from, and how many of his men were in the hospital, and then realized he could not tell me. Major Umeh was preoccupied. "The world ought to see us in our goodness," he said. "We value life. We have always done well on exams. We only want to have a peaceful life and contribute something to humanity."

On Wednesday afternoon, in the office of the Directorate of Research and Production, at Isu, Professor Ben Nwosu, tired and angry, asked me to understate the accomplishments of his team of scientists. "In the white world, they would call them inventions," he said. "Because we are black, they call them improvisations. Some time before the crisis, a handful of us just thought, If this thing starts, we want to be ready." Since then, the directorate has produced fuel, soap, rockets, booby traps, armored cars (out of tractors), gunboats, and civilian products of various kinds. People bring all sorts of scrap and spare parts to Professor Nwosu's di-rectorate, but "the supply problem still advances upon us," he said. He was extremely bitter about the world's suspicion of the real intentions of Biafra. "We don't woolly-woolly. We didn't have to come back here. I wonder why people in the outside think we came back here. We are struggling because we want to save our lives as a people, and our chil-dren's lives."

I asked how his mechanics could possibly manufacture sophisticated arms without having centralized factories, which would be subject to bombings. "It is simple," he said, abruptly. "If you have ten lathes, you diffuse them in ten places. The result is the same."

On Thursday morning at seven, Sister Mary Joseph Theresa, daughter of the Eze Dara of Uli and sister of both a lady barrister and an engineer in Professor Nwosu's directorate, left the Ihioma Convent and went to the Queen of the Holy Rosary College, a school she had run at Onitsha (now disrupted) and started again at Orlu, with refugee children from all over Biafra. Sister Mary Joseph had also been a refugee, successively, from Onitsha, Port Harcourt, Owerri, and Nguru. "Running from my friends," she said. "I call them 'my friends.' I have nothing against them. We are all human beings. We are fighting because the Devil is there."

Sister Mary Joseph comes from one of the finest families in Biafra, and looks it—tall, frail, and radiant with intelligence, dressed somehow, in the mud and still-spattering rain, in a habit of immaculate white. Most children in Biafra have lost two years of school now, and Sister Mary Joseph recruited six teachers out of fifteen from her school in Onitsha (two are in the army, one is in the Directorate of Research and Production, and one in the police) to teach in a section of a refugee camp at Orlu. "The children have a long way to trek," she said. "Many have heard of us, and they are coming." Children, some with, some without shoes and umbrellas, were arriving in the chilling downpour of early morning.

I asked Sister Mary Joseph whether the school could give them any breakfast or lunch. "My goodness, what would I give them?" she said. "What would I give?"

I asked whether all her students were Catholics. "Now, we don't ask them about religion," she said. "We just say Biafra."

There was a brief morning assembly, with hymns in English and in Ibo, and Sister Mary Joseph asked her teachers, whom she had called together, whether they had heard the newest Biafran hymn. "I've only heard it in the last two or three days," she said. "It is the best song yet." One teacher remarked that new songs travel quickly, since most of Biafra is within fifty miles. "It's more than that," another teacher said quickly. Sister Mary Joseph was riffling through an attendance book. "I can't believe that so much of Biafra is still in our hands," she said. "They've all learned now that there is a God. They can't deny that."

Classes began, separated from one another by raffia partitions, and the youngest class, from eleven to thirteen years old (depending on the loss of those two years), was learning geometry and French. *"Bonjour, monsieur"* and *"Asseyez-vous la classe"* and Euclid rang through the refugee home, where adult refugees were staring out at the rain from an adjoining room. "Anyone here know a song, any song?" Sister Mary Joseph asked the geometry class, and they sang "God, the Creator, Preserve and Guide Biafra." She asked the second class whether they knew any writers. Jane Austen. Any *Biafran* writers? Chinua Achebe. Had they read him? Yes. They returned to the study of cell structure and the soil.

The third class was learning English expressions ("They don't care tuppence," "A yes-man"), and Sister Mary Joseph asked them whether they knew anyone in America. One had a "senior brother" in Baltimore. One had a sister-in-law in California. One had a pre-crisis pen pal in Greenlawn, New York. All of them, in all classes, were extremely eager to answer questions, but Sister Mary Joseph said the fourth was the keenest class. They were all girls. Boys of fifteen in Biafra are eligible for the army. The fourth class had written essays, on lined paper the school had found for them, on "The Horrors of the Nigeria-Biafra War." ("No place is safe. No one is safe." "We might appeal to God to make both sides see reason." "It was also at night that one once felt safe in Biafra.") Sister Mary Joseph, who served her novitiate in Dublin (she has a trace of an Irish accent), recalled that when she was a child her father, Eze Dara of Uli, had insisted that the whole family learn to read, and so she had learned in the same class with her uncles. She thought that if the loss of schooling in Biafra now continued, there might have to be intergenerational classrooms again after the war. She enumerated all the American representatives who had expressed sympathy for Biafra: Candidate Nixon, Senator Eugene McCarthy, Senator Charles Goodell, Senator Edward Kennedy, Representatives Donald E. Lukens and Allard K. Loewenstein, Ambassador C. Clyde Ferguson—even Senator Richard Russell, of the South. She told the story of a young English lady working in Nigeria who had been caught behind Biafran lines. "The Inspector General detained her," Sister Mary Joseph said. "Mind you, it was right after the Eighteen [fourteen Italians, three West Germans, and one Jordanian arrested as Nigerian spies]. Poor Sally. The Inspector General didn't know what to do about her." Sister Mary Joseph had taken care of the English lady, and accompanied her on the flight to Libreville. Sister Mary Joseph asked me, and even an old friend of hers, to sign the inevitable guestbook. She mentioned another old friend, whom she had not seen in a long time. "I would need about two days to look for him," she said, "since we are all so dispersed now."

At a checkpoint on a particularly bad road full of stalled cars twenty miles from Owerri, an official of State House gave the code word in Ibo for General Odumegwu Ojukwu, and was told by the guard, in English, "He passed here at a quarter to eight." Driving on, the official recalled the circumstances of His Excellency's delivery, on June 1 this year, of a speech on the second anniversary of Biafran independence, in the town of Ahiara. The speech, now referred to as "the Ahiara Declaration," or "Ahiara," or even just "June First," had an enormous impact in Biafra. It is twenty-one dense pages long. It includes thoughts as complicated in their expression, and as characteristic of General Ojukwu, as the dedication to his first book (which will be published in November): "To the many sons and daughters whose fathers toiled and tramped with me, and are gone." Another sort of leader might have said, "To the Biafran orphans." The Ahiara Declaration recounts some of Biafra's recent history and concludes that the reason the two-year war has not won more of the world's unambivalent sympathy is that the Biafran people are black. But it deplores insufficient idealism within Biafra, and its political philosophy might be endorsed by anyone from Thomas Jefferson through Fidel Castro to Senator John Sherman Cooper ("The Biafran revolution believes in the sanctity of human life and the dignity of the human person ... the reign of social and economic justice, and the rule of law"). And yet there is the sense of something new, something genuinely humanist and indigenously African about it. Also pride, religion, and despair.

In a military compound, heavily camouflaged, about fifteen miles from Owerri, several chiefs and elders, in long robes and still engaged in conversation, were coming out of the office of General Ojukwu, past a sentry at the door. In a reception room with a blue rug, flowered curtains, red chairs, green walls, and a little white Madonna on a coffee table (altogether more like a room in an inn, made livable by transients, than like part of a military installation), a few young associates of General Ojukwu were waiting for him. Some of them seemed abject and ingratiating, others full of high spirits and a sense of argument. General Ojukwu himself, thirty-six years old, bearded, not slim, educated at Oxford and, much later, at Warminster, came in and slumped in a chair. He looked sad, ready for a joke, and thoughtful, with a brooding gentleness pushed to an extreme that could make a war leader out of a doubting, nonviolent man. He seemed to have the quality of the sort of person who can make people in a church sit still and be decent when all the exits are burning. His father, Sir Louis Odumegwu Ojukwu, who began in poverty, became a small investment banker, and died one of the richest men in Nigeria, had objected to almost every stage in his son's career, from his two years of work as a lower-echelon civil servant in the Eastern Region to his insistence on going to military school. The Nigerian Army was one of the few regionally integrated institutions in Federal Nigeria. When, after the coup of January 1966, military governors were appointed for all the regions of Nigeria, Lieutenant Colonel Ojukwu was appointed governor of the Eastern Region. After the massacres of May 1966, still believing in a unified Nigeria, he appealed to Eastern refugees from the Northern Region to go back, assuring them that their lives and property were now safe. He has regretted this decision, in view of the massacres that followed, ever since.

I asked him what the meeting that had just dispersed had been about. "It's my regular powwow with the chiefs," he said. "A morale-boosting session." I asked him how often he met with them, and he said as often as he could. I asked him what they talked about. "Everything from air raids to the distribution of salt," he said. "The war situation. The internal situation. Their own personal problems, what the people are thinking, how much of government policy has got down, ways this war has to be fought. Everybody wants to have said something." He smiled. "Chief Mpi held the floor."

I asked how the morale actually was, and he said, "Generally, this is the time for low morale. The rains. The cold. The war usually crawls. People ask, 'What's wrong with the army, is it food they want? Is it possible they enjoy this war? Tell me what they need.' Another position is 'Is there nothing else we can do, is there no other way?' Of course, there are those who are more angry than yourself."

I asked him whether he felt that the returned intellectuals were rediscovering their own people, and he nodded. "They used to look outside themselves," he said. "There was even a conscious effort to obliterate their own origin, looking down on those who stayed at home. Now it's time to come down to earth a bit."

He felt the Ahiara Declaration had expressed the real feelings of the people only as "an articulation in international terms." "I've always been aware of one thing, that I've never really stood an election," he said. When I asked him why he thought the Ahiara Declaration had not had much of an impact, particularly among American radicals, abroad, he said it was not the sort of speech to invite "that sort of dramatic response." He laughed, and said that people had told him they were surprised that "you have managed to mean so much to everyone at the same time." He spoke of the black "secret admirers" of Biafra, who feared the great unknown and could not believe that Biafra might succeed. I asked him how this compared with the white liberal position, and he said he thought white liberals were more openly sympathetic. "They say, 'This would be wonderful if it really succeeded.' They don't say we won't succeed." I asked whether by success he meant the establishment of the first viable black republic, able to compete on an equal basis with white nations of the world, and he said that was exactly what he meant.

I wondered what the postwar politics of Biafra might be in the world, and he said, "There is no doubt in my mind that to survive we must remain uncommitted." He said he believed that little nations either existed as ideological vacuums or opened up to let the two great ideologies flood them, and that he hoped, in sequels to the Ahiara Declaration, to establish a bulwark position that would do neither. "All conflict, of course," he said, "arises from the desire to dominate. The way to avoid conflict is to accept the rights of other men. But I do not believe that another ideology would solve the foreign problem."

I asked him about his book, and he said it was based on "speeches, random thoughts, random subjects, and a frantic period trying to find the underlying thoughts." I asked him what stake the world had in Biafra, and he said, "This is the worst system—this colonial, this neocolonial fraud. It can only yield short-term results. There is no logical case against Biafra. There is no properly argued case against Biafra. There is only fear, and the nuisance of having to reevaluate. They do not know what this phenomenon is." General Ojukwu's stenographer, as in all the general's negotiations and interviews, was writing down each word. When I left, the chiefs who had been talking in the corridor were gone.

———

On the way back to Owerri, the State House driver ran over a chicken, and did not stop. A small boy raised his one arm in a salute. At the airport, a Biafran crew was loading a strange cargo of sacks of cocoa beans and two old English refrigerators on the French Red Cross flight back to Libreville. The car passed a wake, with mourners singing, in Ibo, "He is dead. Got to bury him. He died in a state of courage. We shall all be there sooner or later. May his soul rest in peace."

—1969

BUT OHIO. WELL, I GUESS THAT'S ONE STATE WHERE THEY ELECT TO LOCK AND LOAD: THE NATIONAL GUARD

At six o'clock one recent Saturday morning, a Kharmann Ghia and several other civilian vehicles were parked in the rain outside the Seventh Regiment Armory, at Park Avenue and Sixty-sixth Street. Inside, several uniformed young men were rushing about carrying duffel bags down the carpeted stairs and along wood-paneled corridors to the huge central arena of the armory, where several military vehicles were preparing to move out. A jeep carrying a 105-mm. recoilless rifle was being loaded onto a carrier, and men were climbing into other jeeps and trucks. The First Battalion of the 107th Infantry (New York National Guard) was preparing to join two battalions from the armory at Lexington Avenue and Twenty-fifth Street, one battalion from the armory at Thirty-fourth and Park, and units from armories in Brooklyn, Long Island, Flushing, and (for some organizational reason) Pennsylvania, to undergo—as the Forty-second (Rainbow) Division of the New York National Guard—their two weeks of summer training at Camp Drum. Camp Drum itself, which is in upstate New York, was regarded as too strenuous a trip for a single day, so after rest stops at a racetrack in Goshen and at Whitney Point, the convoy would bivouac just one night at the state fairgrounds in Syracuse. "Inherent in our organization," said Colonel Dominic Pellicio about the Guard convoy's capacity to bivouac, "is an ability to stay out and eat."

Kitchen trucks had set out for Syracuse an hour earlier. To avoid traveling on the Sabbath, an Orthodox Jewish chaplain had gone up the day before. Colonel Pellicio (commander of New York City's Guard units, senior brigade commander during the March postal strike and in his civilian life a contractor) greeted some of his men (another chaplain, a law student, a resident in urology) and made a last-minute check of a long list of hospitals along the convoy's route. "You know, these men drive these vehicles maybe three, four times a year," he said. "In the rain it can be very dangerous." Then, after the first units of jeeps and trucks had left, he set out in his military sedan (complete with a siren, which he did not use) into the rain on Lexington Avenue, across Central Park at Sixty-fifth Street, and onto the West Side Highway toward a "marshaling point" in Teterboro, New Jersey. The reason the colonel had chosen Teterboro, which is not on the most direct route to upstate New York, was to avoid "the traffic density on the New York Thruway" and to "give my men some experience" on a new convoy route to Camp Drum.

There were Guardsmen posted to wave directions at many intersections and at all bridges and toll booths on the way to New Jersey Route 17. The first units arrived on schedule, at 0734 hours, at the marshaling area—a parking lot across from the Teterboro Airport. But by 0816 hours, the colonel learned, two vehicles were already lost (one broke down, one was hit by a station wagon), and more would be lost, with maintenance problems, along the way. Vehicles continued for three hours, desultorily, to arrive at the marshaling area. Meanwhile, the men smoked, caught some sleep in the trucks, or ate sandwiches from the first of their several box lunches. Most were armed with M-1 rifles, while "key" men carried pistols, and one (like Colonel Pellicio himself, an older man and a veteran of World War II) wore a bayonet in a camouflaged sheath at his waist. A lot of the younger men wore mustaches. Maneuvers at Camp Drum, the colonel said, would consist mainly in borrowing a hundred or two hundred tanks, using them, and, at the end of the two weeks, returning them to the regular army. Last summer, a Guardsman had knocked himself unconscious falling off a tank the first day. "But our main concern is the safety of the men in these vehicles," the colonel said. "Getting them up to camp is always the biggest problem." The weather was clearing a bit, and two civilians drove up safely enough, at 0927 hours, to the Teterboro Airport. "Hey," one of them said as they passed the marshaling area. "Will you look at them weekend soldiers."

The National Guard is one of the oldest, most muddled and crisis-ridden lethal forces in our history. At present, it consists of 478,860 men (394,133 of them in the Army National Guard, 84,727 in the Air National Guard), 2,774 local armories, 68 Army Guard airfields, 90 Air Guard flying bases, an annual appropriation slightly in excess of one billion dollars (of which $972,364,000 is paid by the federal government, the rest by the states), several billion dollars' worth of more or less obsolete federal military equipment, one of the oldest, most effective lobbies (the National Guard Association, founded in 1879) in Washington, and long, not altogether tamper-proof waiting lists—one at every Guard armory in each of the fifty states, Puerto Rico, and the District of Columbia. What training Guardsmen actually receive (six months of basic army training, a few drills each year, and two weeks of camp in each of six successive summers) is almost exclusively for war, but of the several hundred occasions on which Guardsmen have been called up since 1945, all but two have been local natural disasters or civil disturbances lasting about a week. National Guardsmen have otherwise remained at home and pursued their civilian careers. Since National Guardsmen are accountable, except in times of declared war or federalization for extreme emergency, not to the federal government but to the governors of their respective states, National Guard units are really State Guard units—a fragmented, fifty-two-part duplicate of the regular army reserve. They are also exempt from the draft.

The National Guard's history—like its present composition and purpose, if any—is a kind of swamp. Nearly every state Guard unit has its own historian. The only attempt at an exhaustive history of the whole National Guard, *The Minute Man in Peace and War*, by Major General Jim Dan Hill, of Wisconsin (published in 1964 by the Stackpole Company, Harrisburg, Pennsylvania), consists largely of obscure grievances against politicians and journalists, from Stephen Crane and Richard Harding Davis to "a young political-science teacher in a Midwestern college," whom the general cannot even bring himself to name, and irate defenses of the Guard against charges of draft-dodging, incompetence, redundancy, favoritism, strikebreaking, snobbery, unpreparedness, patronage, loafing, irresponsibility, boondoggle, cowardice, obsoleteness, and bungling—charges that have evidently been leveled against the Guard throughout its history. The general's style is everywhere idiosyncratically partisan ("The Guard must have seemed Heaven-sent for the role of a whipping boy riding into the desert astride a dejected scapegoat"). Although his research is probably the best there is, a sentence in his preface may explain a lot: Concerning the bibliographical notes with which each chapter ends, the general writes, "Without exception, they are far from all-inclusive."

The contemporary National Guard can trace its origins to the Organized Militia of the original thirteen colonies, who, in various units and capacities, defended their own homes, conducted raiding parties against the Indians, and fought the Revolutionary War in Washington's Continental Army. After the Revolution, to avert the threat to democracy inherent in any professional "standing army" (and with some doubt that the country contained enough paupers to fill such an army), Jefferson hoped that every citizen might be trained to be a soldier, civilian in peace, prepared to defend his country in war. Baron von Steuben, who had been Inspector General of the Revolutionary forces, argued that this was unrealistic, "It would be as sensible and consistent to say every Citizen should be a Sailor." Washington himself proposed a small, paid regular army to protect the country's frontiers and also a larger civilian organized militia in each of the several states. In the end, the Constitution embodied all three ideas: an unorganized Enrolled Militia, consisting of all male citizens eligible for military service only in time of war; a small Regular Army of professional soldiers, accountable first and only to the President as Commander-in-Chief; and a state Organized Militia of citizen-soldiers, "reserving to the States, respectively, the Appointment of Officers, and the Authority of training the Militia according to the Discipline prescribed by Congress." It is this clause in the Constitution (Article I, Section 8, Clause 16, commonly known as the Militia Clause) that leaves us, in a nuclear age, with a National Guard.

Since then, especially as the danger of Indians, state insurrections, or land invasions by way of Canada or Mexico becomes remote, there has been a continual dispute about what the Guard is meant to do—and it is possible that the Militia Clause, together with the later misnomer "National Guard," has somehow maintained throughout our history an uneven, crazy, dangerous collection of state military forces whose purpose is undefinable and which it is impossible either to train for some national purpose or to disband. The misnomer "National Guard" itself dates from a trip Lafayette made to America in 1824. In honor of his visit, a group of New York City peacetime volunteers—young men who had drilled and caroused together quite a bit, designed and bought their own uniforms, elected their own officers, compared horses, paraded, and called themselves the Seventh Regiment—renamed themselves the "National

Guards," after the distinguished Paris corps commanded by Lafayette. In 1832, the regiment dropped the *s*. In 1862, the Volunteer Militia of all New York State adopted the name. The Massachusetts Volunteer Militia, who considered themselves the original citizen-soldiers of Lexington, resisted the change to the last, but in 1903 the National Guard became the federally recognized (and, for the first time, in part federally subsidized) collection of state militias which it is today.

The Guard's post-Revolutionary appearances in American history include participation or evasion of some sort in all the country's wars, including the Mexican, which all the New England states were reluctant to join, and the War of 1812, in which neither Massachusetts nor Connecticut cared to take part. The Guard had its greatest strength in those days, and until the time of the automobile, in the urban centers of the North and East—if only because these areas, being the nation's most densely populated, could most easily muster units to drill and parade. In 1860, the governor of New York State alone could summon more units of infantry, cavalry, and artillery than the entire regular army of the United States. Since most recruiting in the Civil War was done by the states, it could be argued that most of the Union soldiers (all but the United States Army Regulars) and *all* the Confederate troops (led by Colonel Jefferson Davis, of the First Mississippi Rifles, as Commander-in-Chief) were organized militia, and that the War Between the States was largely a war between what might now be called units of the National Guard. But North and South had recourse, in the Civil War, to the draft, and it is more characteristic of the Guard's subsequent anomalous role in our history that New York's Seventh Regiment (the one for which the whole Guard, after all, was named) spent most of the Civil War at home and distinguished itself mainly by suppressing the bloody Draft Riots of 1863.

The National Guard really enters modern history, in anything like its current form and spirit, in the 1870s and 1880s, as a strikebreaking force. Regiments of organized militia had turned out as early as 1794 to crush the Whiskey Rebellion. Southern states, years before the Civil War, had maintained large militias for fear of slave revolts. New York's Seventh Regiment had already killed twenty-two and wounded thirty-six in the Astor Place Riot of 1849 (over the relative merits of a proletarian production of *Macbeth* in the Bowery and a white-tie performance at the Opera House). Militias had been used to suppress industrial disorders in

Missouri and Kansas, vigilante groups in California, striking miners in Colorado. But in 1877, with railroad strikes in Martinsburg, West Virginia, in Baltimore, Chicago, and St. Louis, and, more particularly, with the Pullman Strike and Haymarket Riot of 1886, the National Guard earned a reputation as a business-financed, elitist, repressively antilabor force; and throughout the Depression, until World War II, most unions still banned their members from taking any part in the Guard. It was in the 1880s that the grotesque, turreted redbrick armories were built for Guard cavalry. The Seventh Regiment built its own, the one at Park Avenue and Sixty-sixth, in 1880, and still owns it. Squadron A, an equally upper-class nineteenth-century unit, lost its armory, on Park Avenue and Ninety-fourth, a few years ago and regretfully disbanded, to become just the Squadron A Club, in rented, wood-paneled rooms at the Biltmore Hotel. Businessmen financed the Guard in those years, and wealthy young men joined it, to keep the immigrant laborers orderly, state by state.

A history of New York City's Squadron A, N.Y.N.G. (New York National Guard), includes several journals kept by young Guardsmen of the time. There are proud references to Squadron A as "all millionaires" and as being as exclusive as "any club in New York." There are accounts of breaking a railroad strike in Buffalo in 1892, a trolley strike in Brooklyn in 1895, and a strike at the Croton Dam in 1900. The sort of enemy the Guardsmen thought they were protecting the state against is implied by references to encounters with Italian laborers as "the Italian Wars," cheerful allusions to Central European workers' abject fear of horses with men on them, and in a poem written for the unit as late as 1925:

> ... There's a garment strike on and it's got to be broke,
> So ye lawyers and bankers and salesmen so free,
> Turn out—you're Hussars of the N.Y.N.G. ...
> The strikers are gathered in Washington Square,
> Their war cry "Oi, oi Gewalt" pierces the air. ...

There are also candid accounts of "promiscuous shooting at phantoms" in the Croton Strike (on the way to which the unit's commander was thrown from his horse and broke his leg); pointless racing about, firing of blanks, and cries of "You're dead!" at the Guard Manassas Maneuvers, in 1904; mothers perennially sending caviar and foie gras to their sons on duty; a Guardsman who, in one pistol drill, accidentally blew a hole in the ceiling and, in the next, blew a hole through the floor of the armory; endless showy parades through New York to accompany such visitors as the Duke of Veragua, the Infanta Eulalia, and the Chinese Viceroy, Li Hung Chang; constant explosions, during strike duty, of shells that had fallen from the belts of sleeping Guardsmen into their straw bedding; and accidents, fires, and equipment mix-ups on every maneuver of every kind through the years. In 1939, the year the squadron's history was published, Squadron A of the New York National Guard was arguing passionately that the imminent World War II, despite tanks and other machines, would prove the absolute indispensability of cavalrymen on real horses for the national defense.

In years when there were no wars and there was no strike duty, Guard units tended to languish in their armories, and, even in rural areas, to become social clubs, like the Kiwanis or Elks. They liked to march and to rise in rank, but their preparedness for the two world wars, when they did break out, was problematical. Had it not been for the strength of its lobby in Washington, the Guard might, on several occasions, have been abolished altogether. In *The National Guard in Politics*, a study of "one of the most successful pressure groups in a system noted for the advantages that it gives pressure groups," Martha Derthick, an associate professor of political science at Boston College, says that the major goals of the National Guard lobby in Washington have always been two: federal support of the Guard (regular army pay for Guard drills, federal military equipment, federal money for armories, federal recognition of Guard officers), along with freedom from federal control—that is, state appointment of officers, state control of units, state standards for training, and, in case of war, federal mobilization of state Guard units intact.

In order to gain these federal concessions and subsidies while maintaining states' rights (in the early 1900s, southern and midwestern states'-rights congressmen had become the main supporters of the Guard, the northeastern states having more or less lost interest in it), the National Guard had to argue that it was the nation's principal military reserve force. The National Defense Act of 1916 gave it that status. Guard divisions were renamed and officially renumbered, divisions 26 to 75 inclusive, and sent off to World War I—with mixed results. Some Guard units *were* preserved intact, with their own state patronage-appointed officers. Many of those officers soon had to be replaced for sheer incompetence. Some Guard units were used as "depot divisions," just to supply replacements for casualties among regular army division volunteers and draftees. Out of leftover Guard units from several states, the army created the symbolic, "overarching" interstate Forty-second (Rainbow) Division, in which Douglas MacArthur served as brigade commander in France. The rainbow has since become the division that left with Colonel Pellicio for Camp Drum.

After World War I, the Guard, except for its lobby (led by a Guard officer who was also chief lobbyist for the National Rifle Association), languished again—until the Depression, when drill pay earned by Guardsmen became a new source of patronage for governors, and of bitterness for men on relief who could not get appointed to the Guard. In World War II, the Guard's performance once again was controversial and mixed. The December 1941 issue of *Fortune* said that the National Guard, untrained and unprepared as it was, could not be reorganized, because it had become "a political hornet's nest." Other branches of the military, in any case, were not impressed with it. When New York's Twenty-seventh Division of the Guard, for example, was put under marine command at Saipan, Marine Lieutenant General H. M. Smith found that while his own units advanced about ten miles each day, the Guard division, composed mainly of New York politicians and their friends and relatives, invariably stayed put. The marines would have to drop back each night to maintain a line. Finally, General Smith replaced every single officer of the Twenty-seventh—creating a terrific scandal back home in New York. An entire Guard division from the Midwest, on the other hand, was wiped out at Corregidor, and New Mexico Guard tank units at Bataan were annihilated, leaving towns in the states from which they came bereft of their entire populations of young men. To avoid a recurrence of these regional disasters, and to circumvent the ineptitude of Guard officers, Guard divisions were broken up. Of eighteen National Guard division commanders at the beginning of World War II, only two retained command at the end. One general of the regular army began calling the National Guard Bureau itself "an organizational monstrosity." In 1944 Lieutenant General Lesley J. McNair, commanding general of the army ground forces, said, "The training experience of this headquarters for nearly four years has its most important lesson in the inadequacy of the National Guard in practically every essential. . . . One of the great lessons of the present war is that the National Guard, as organized before the war, contributed nothing to national defense."

General McNair recommended that the Guard be abolished. So did his successor, Lieutenant General Ben Lear. National Guard General Ellard A. Walsh, the adjutant general of Minnesota, who was head of the Guard lobby in 1944, was quick to respond. He spoke of the regular army's "undiluted and undisguised hate of us" and of "a diabolical attempt to destroy a great citizen force." He recommended more, newer, and fiercer lobbying. It worked. In 1948, National Guardsmen became, by law, completely exempt from the draft. (The token Guard units that were federalized for service in Korea required seven to nine months to train—as long as regular draftees who had received no training before.) Although the states had traditionally financed their own militias, until the years when the local businessmen started to, the federal government began to pay 97 percent of the cost of the Guard. A Guardsman now receives, for a half day's drill, the equivalent of a regular army soldier's full day's pay. And despite the existence of a regular army reserve, the fiction is still maintained—in Congress, in the Guard, in the Department of Defense—that the National Guard is the first line of reserve for some future war, and that training its men for war is what the Guard ought primarily to do.

There exist, in Guard archives, fairly riveting accounts of more or less recent Guard tactical maneuvers, like 1960's Operation Big Slam/Puerto Pine ("In this exercise there was a notable 'first,' the movement, on short notice, of a National Guard Artillery Battalion from Utah to Puerto Rico, in 'off season' for the part-time soldiers, and their speedy inauguration of a realistic field training program in unaccustomed surroundings"); Exercise Dixie ("The map problem set up for study involved defense of the Southeastern United States against an Aggressor airborne and seaborne attack in the vicinity of Mobile Bay, Alabama. The first phase consisted of the Aggressor successfully invading the Florida Peninsula by airborne and waterborne units, which were met by XII Corps troops. In addition to the invasion of Florida, Aggressor agents worked constantly to upset the civilian population"); and Operation Vikings Thrive in Arctic Cold ("The purpose was for the Minnesota Guardsmen from the 47th 'Viking' Infantry Division to learn how to ski and to overcome the handicaps of cold weather"). Air National Guard units (which, since Guardsmen almost immediately after Kitty Hawk could afford their own planes, have often predated regular air force units, and which now consist largely of air force veterans, civilian pilots, and men who just like to fly) are allowed to fly brief cargo missions to Vietnam and elsewhere. One recent Air Guard "combat" mission to Vietnam turned out to be Operation Yuletide—a ferrying over of Christmas presents to servicemen.

Sixty-three percent of young Guardsmen in a recent survey acknowledged that they had "joined the Guard because it offered least interference with your personal plans"; 49 percent that they had joined "because you knew you would be drafted if you did not"; 71 percent that "some individuals you know joined the Guard to avoid service in Vietnam." Only 19 percent thought that they might reenlist in the Guard when their time was up or that their second lieutenants were capable of combat leadership. Waiting lists for Guard units, since the Vietnam War began, have been so long that they are often closed, and the persistence of professional athletes, movie stars, relatives of politicians and of people with political influence in Guard units (as well as the reminiscences of young men who have recently completed their service in the Guard) yield the impression that the waiting lists are seldom impartially administered. Despite what was meant to be an intensive program for recruitment of Negroes after the Detroit riots of 1967, the percentage of Negroes in the Army Guard actually went down, from 1.18 percent to 1.15 percent, between 1968 and 1969. The percentage of Negroes in the Air National Guard, it is true, went up—from 0.77 to 0.90.

The adjutants general of the National Guard in all but two states (South Carolina, where the highest Guard officer is elected by the public, and Vermont, where he is chosen by the legislature) are appointed by the current governors. They, like all Guard officers, are meant to meet standards set by the federal government, but as early as 1948 the army's Director of Personnel and Administration complained that "experience since the war has demonstrated that governors will not accept the decision of a Federal Recognition Board." National Guard General Walsh himself complained, in 1948, that Governor Earl Long had fired a Louisiana adjutant general because of political pressure from a Plaquemines Parish constituent, Leander Perez. In six states today, the adjutant general of the National Guard is also the Director of Selective Service.

National Guard officers sit on almost all draft boards—which is a bit like asking the leaders of the draft-avoiders (or, as friends of the Guard prefer to put it, the "draft-motivated") to administer the draft impartially. In a recent *Congressional Quarterly* survey, only twenty-two U.S. senators and representatives actually said they had sons or grandsons in the reserves or the National Guard. But of the 234 draft-eligible sons and grandsons of members of Congress, 118 had received other sorts of deferment since the Vietnam War began. Only twenty-six served at all in Vietnam. None were missing or killed. One—Captain Clarence D. Long III, son of a representative from Maryland—was wounded.

One hundred and twenty-two U.S. senators and representatives (more than a fifth of the members of Congress) currently hold commissions in the reserves or the National Guard, and an organization of young Guardsmen and reservists, called the Reservists Committee to Stop the War, has filed suit against the secretary of defense on the ground that the Constitution specifically forbids U.S. congressmen from holding "any office" bestowed by, or under the control of, the executive branch of government.

In "In Pursuit of Equity: Who Serves When Not All Serve?"—a report prepared in 1967 by the National Advisory Commission on Selective Service, under the chairmanship of Burke Marshall—recommendations for draft reform included something on the order of a draft lottery, which we now have, and the abolition of the National Guard as a draft haven, which may follow of itself, in December 1970, when the draft lottery has gone completely into effect. There may then be National Guard problems of an entirely other kind.

A chronology of domestic duty by National Guard units since World War II reads like a history of the country transposed into a rather special key. In 1945, there were only three call-ups, all local—one for an industrial dispute in Indiana, two for reasons now forgotten, labeled in Guard histories "unknown." In 1946, there were five call-ups, all for nothing much, three of them "unknown." Between 1947 and 1950, there were nine, including five "industrial disputes," one "threat to local sheriff" (Loudon, Tennessee), and, in Puerto Rico, one "uprising against government." In 1951, there was just one call-up, a "race riot" in Cicero, Illinois. In 1952, there were three: two "prison riots" and a "student riot," at Columbia, Missouri. In 1953, there was nothing. In 1954 and 1955, two "crises in law enforcement" (Phenix City, Alabama; Gulfport, Mississippi), three "prison riots," one "industrial dispute," and (in Whiting, Indiana) a "natural disaster." In 1956—two years after the Supreme Court decision to integrate the schools—there were three "integration crises" and one memorable "teenage riot" (on the beach, at Daytona, Florida). There were four "civil disturbances" in 1957 (in Benton, Prentiss, Marion, and Simpson Counties, Mississippi), one "industrial dispute" (in Portsmouth, Ohio), and—from September 6 to September 20—the federalization of the National Guard in Little Rock, Arkansas, with which the first phase of the most recent period of the Guard begins.

In September 1957, Governor Orval E. Faubus called out the Arkansas Guard to prevent the enforcement of school integration. President Eisenhower federalized the state Guard to ensure enforcement and sent in some regular army troops as well. From then on, the Guard was engaged for some years in protecting civil rights, during what Guard archives started calling "racial disturbances," in the South. In 1958 and 1959, the Guard was called up for eight "racial disturbances" (all of them in Mississippi); also for one "prison riot" and three "industrial disputes." In 1960, there was just one call-up: the Rhode Island Guard for a "civil disturbance" (jazz festival) at Newport. In 1961, there was one "teenage riot," one "prison riot," three "racial disturbances," and two mysterious "sabotages of microwave stations" (in Utah and New Mexico).

In 1962 and 1963, there were suddenly three federalizations of the Guard: one each for "integration crises" at the University of Mississippi and the University of Alabama, and one after the bombing of the four young girls in a church in Birmingham. These federalizations of the National Guard in the southern states gave the regular army a chance to shake up and reorganize (as in wartime) some of the most patronage-ridden state units in the country. The Guard reforms were much like the changes that southern offices of the FBI underwent, under pressure from the Justice Department, in the same years. The army officer in charge of Guard federalizations and reform was General Creighton W. Abrams, who is now Commander of U.S. forces in Vietnam. In 1963, too, there was a call-up of Guard troops by the Washington, D.C., commissioners for what Guard archives call simply a "civil-rights demonstration" in Washington—the one in which Martin Luther King's "I have a dream" speech was heard at the Lincoln Memorial. In September 1963, Governor George Wallace called out the Guard, as Faubus had done six years earlier, to prevent compliance with the law in the school "integration crises" at Birmingham, Mobile, and Tuskegee. President Kennedy federalized the Alabama Guard, and General Abrams shook the Guardsmen up again. In 1964, there wasn't much. Nineteen sixty-five begins with a federalization of the Alabama Guard, and the addition of some regular army, for the march from Selma to Montgomery; has a little call-up for a "motorcycle riot" in June (at Weirs Beach, New Hampshire); and ushers in another era in August, with the rioting in Watts.

There followed what might be called the period of the urban disasters—in which, having been for eight years primarily a peacekeeping force, the National Guard was suddenly in the position of killing people. In Watts, 13,393 California Guardsmen were called. Four thousand Negroes were arrested, several hundred were hurt, and thirty-four were killed. National Guardsmen do not have the authority to make arrests, but they do carry arms, and, as the National Advisory Commission on Civil Disorders, under Governor Otto Kerner of Illinois (in a report more valuable for its substantive descriptions of events than for its philosophical generalizations), subsequently put it, of those thirty-four dead Negroes "several . . . were killed by mistake." In July 1966, there was the Filmore race riot in Chicago (4,300 Illinois Guardsmen called out, three Negroes killed, including a thirteen-year-old boy and a fourteen-year-old pregnant girl) and the Hough race riot in Cleveland (2,000 Ohio Guardsmen called out, four Negroes killed, and several children injured, as in Chicago, by "stray bullets"). In state after state, Guardsmen were called out to deal with urban looting and rioting—with tanks, guns, and training designed for waging war against an organized, armed foreign enemy. In July 1967, in Newark, 4,400 New Jersey National Guardsmen were called out. The New Jersey adjutant general, James F. Cantwell, was at the time, and still is, president of the National Guard Association. When order was restored, there were twenty-three dead, twenty-one of them Negroes, two of them children. Later that month, in Detroit, when 10,253 Michigan Guardsmen were called and then federalized, the disturbance ended with forty-three Negroes dead. There began a period of serious deliberation about the Guard. It became as clear as anything about the National Guard ever gets that Guardsmen were performing duties other than those of a "first line of military reserve," and the possibility arose that in civil disturbances much, if not most, of the tragedy and nearly all of the deaths were attributable to forces called out to restore order. Detroit was a crisis in the history of the National Guard.

Looking back on previous urban riots—the "killed by mistake" of Watts, the "killed by stray bullets" of Filmore and Hough—officials of the departments of Justice and Defense began to find the performance of Guard units, state by state, surreal. Guardsmen were in the habit of arriving by tank or truck, weapons loaded, and shooting out street lamps at night, for protection, then deluding themselves that the sound of their own shots in the dark was "sniper fire." Since their aim, moreover, was bad, the rounds of ammunition required to dispatch a single street lamp often injured people in apartments blocks away or in cars on other streets. The first person killed by Guardsmen in Newark, for example, was a small boy in a family car being driven home from a restaurant. In Newark, coordination between the local police and the New Jersey Guard was so bad that Director of Police Dominick Spina told the Kerner Commission, "Down in the Springfield Avenue area, in my opinion, Guardsmen were firing upon police and police were firing back at them."

Police Director Spina, who was tried and acquitted of charges arising out of alleged Mafia operations two years ago, and who was dismissed from his job on July 1 of this year, emerges, in the Newark riots of 1967, as something of a hero, on the order of *High Noon*. According to the Kerner Commission:

> On Saturday, July 15, Spina received a report of snipers in a housing project. When he arrived he saw approximately 100 National Guardsmen and police officers crouching behind vehicles, hiding in corners and lying on the ground around the edge of the courtyard.
>
> Since everything appeared quiet and it was broad daylight, Spina walked directly down the middle of the street. Nothing happened. As he came to the last building of the complex, he heard a shot. All around him the troopers jumped, believing themselves to be under sniper fire. A moment later a young Guardsman ran from behind a building.

The Guardsman said that he had fired the shot to scare a man away from a window, that his orders were "to keep everyone away from windows."

Spina said he told the soldier: "Do you know what you just did? You have now created a state of hysteria. Every Guardsman up and down this street . . . thinks that somebody just fired a shot and that it is probably a sniper. . . ."

By this time, four truckloads of National Guardsmen had arrived, and troopers and policemen were again crouched everywhere, looking for a sniper.

The Director of Police stayed at the scene for three hours. The only shot he heard was the one fired by the Guardsman.

Nevertheless, at six o'clock that evening two columns of National Guardsmen and state troopers were directing mass fire at the Hays Housing project in response to what they believed were snipers.

On the 10th floor, Eloise Spellman, the mother of several children, fell, a bullet through her neck. . . .

Suddenly, several troopers whirled and began firing in the general direction of spectators. Mrs. Hattie Gainer, a grandmother, sank to the floor.

A block away Rebecca Brown's 2-year-old daughter was standing at the window. Mrs. Brown rushed to drag her to safety. As Mrs. Brown was, momentarily, framed in the window, a bullet spun into her back. . . .

And so on, in Newark. The result of calling in National Guardsmen began to seem, in retrospect, frightened Guardsmen, frightened police, and a toll of babies in distant bassinets, grandmothers in distant kitchens, mothers with their backs to windows, idle spectators, and unarmed citizens of every sort. But Detroit was the worst.

Governor George Romney, to begin with, was extremely reluctant to issue an official request that the Michigan National Guard be federalized—although local police, supported by the Guard under state control, were exhausted and had been unable to cope with rioting and looting for several days—because federalization of the Guard implies an "insurrection," which exempts insurance companies from paying damages to holders of insurance policies. Governor Romney repeatedly made urgent, unofficial requests for federal help to Deputy Secretary of Defense Cyrus

R. Vance, who (according to his subsequent report of events in Detroit) felt that he had to reject them on the ground of their unofficial language. Deputy Secretary Vance, Attorney General Ramsey Clark, Supreme Court Justice Abe Fortas (not in his capacity as Supreme Court justice but as friend and political adviser to President Johnson), Defense Secretary Robert McNamara, and others were pacing with President Johnson on the White House lawn, discussing their own reluctance to federalize the Guard, or to send in more competent regular army troops, because they preferred to avoid the precedent of a liberal administration's sending troops to cope with urban rioting, in an action that might be construed as repressive or racist. In response to more urgent requests from Governor Romney, President Johnson sent Deputy Secretary Vance and a team of officials from the departments of Defense and Justice to Detroit, to study the situation and to discuss it with Mayor Jerome P. Cavanagh and other local citizens. While legal and philosophical deliberations concerning federalization were going on, the number of incidents in Detroit continued to climb. At 2310 hours on July 24 (about twenty-four hours after Mayor Cavanagh and Governor Romney had first telephoned Attorney General Clark about the emergency), Deputy Secretary Vance recommended to President Johnson that the Michigan National Guard be federalized and put under regular army command. Ten minutes later, the President federalized the Guard, under the command of Army Lieutenant General John L. Throckmorton, and sent in regular army troops as well.

The Guard's behavior until the President's move, and after, was a revelation and a nightmare. Some of the Guardsmen had traveled two hundred miles and been put on duty for thirty hours straight—most of which they spent firing. Guardsmen in Detroit fired off more than 13,326 rounds of ammunition, compared with 201 rounds fired off by the regular army. Some Guard units got lost in the city, and panicked. Two Guardsmen assigned to an intersection on Monday were still there on Friday. Guardsmen kept pulling up in tanks, shooting out streetlights, scaring themselves with the sound, and then blasting out the walls of whole buildings. At four o'clock one morning, a regular army unit went to the rescue of a Guard troop crouched behind a high school, claiming to be pinned down by sniper fire. The army colonel, hearing no shots at all, ordered all lights in an adjoining building turned on. The residents were terrified and unarmed. The Guardsmen had shot out every window. Mistaking a lighted cigarette in one window for a sniper, two Guard tanks drew up and a machine gunner opened fire, nearly severing the arm of a young woman and killing her four-year-old niece.

General Throckmorton, whose soldiers were doing fine without much shooting, thought tension might be reduced by less firing, and ordered ammunition removed from all weapons. The Guardsmen apparently never received the order. The Kerner Report continues:

> Without any clear authorization or direction, someone opened fire upon the suspected building. A tank rolled up and sprayed the building with .50-caliber tracer bullets. Law enforcement officers rushed into the surrounded building and discovered it empty. "They must be firing one shot and running" was the verdict.

Julius Dorsey, a Negro private guard, was trying to defend a market from looting. He fired three shots from his pistol into the air. The police radio reported, "Looters. They have rifles." Three National Guardsmen arrived and, seeing a distant crowd of fleeing looters, opened fire. They killed Julius Dorsey. The only soldier killed in Detroit in 1967 was Larry Post, a National Guardsman caught in a cross fire between two units of National Guardsmen.

After Detroit, it became clear that something would have to be done about the National Guard. In most states, Guard units—on the "first line of military reserve" theory—received no riot-control training at all, and in states where they did receive it, it was short and not uniform. There seemed, at the time, to be three basic positions about the Guard. One, that it was inevitably a corrupt, ungovernable mess of untrainable incompetents, and that it should be abolished as a peacekeeping force; local police forces should be better trained, and on those rare occasions when civil disturbances became extreme emergencies, the regular army, which has training and discipline, should be called in. Two, that nothing is perfect, that the Guard had done as well as could be expected, and that people in an area where there is rioting (even if they happen to be in their bathrooms or bassinets), though they may not merit the death penalty exactly, are in some sense "asking for" whatever they get. Three, that the Guard should be buffered with some immediate riot-control training, and that since the regular army soldiers, many of whom were Negroes, had done so much better than the Guard, the Guard should immediately recruit as many Negroes as possible.

The history of Negroes in the American army and militia is a kind of absurdist tale of its own. The South drafted some slaves, and the North drafted some freedmen for its 150 regiments of Negroes in the Civil War. But when the North took Louisiana, a southern black unit was caught in the middle and ultimately became the Union's Corps d'Afrique. Black militia briefly terrified some southern states in the early years of Reconstruction; then the black units were disbanded and the white southern militias started terrorizing blacks again. In New York City, Colonel William Hayward started a Negro National Guard regiment, the Fifteenth New York Infantry (Colored), with its own armory in Harlem and tried vainly to get it attached to any American unit in World War I. Finally, the unit simply attached itself to a division in the French Army, and served with considerable distinction throughout the war. In World War II, black divisions were still segregated, and although one of them, the Ninety-second Infantry (Buffalo) Division, took part in the liberation of Italy, most black soldiers were in service or maintenance units. After President Truman desegregated all divisions of the armed services, the black soldier—in Korea and, of course, still more in Vietnam—came militarily into his own. There have been, not surprisingly, hardly any Negro National Guardsmen since the National Guard began.

The group that favored a Guard buffered with some riot-control training and some Negroes won out. Each Guardsman in each state was to receive thirty-two hours of such training, and Negroes were to be recruited intensively. Some administration officials who did not agree with this policy quietly quit. The Guard had become, in their view, a crucial issue that had to be uncompromisingly met. The strength of the country, they argued, had always lain in the ability of liberals and conservatives to police their extremes. Now neither left nor right was willing to cope with the question of the Guard—the right (which was currently out of federal office anyway) because of a belief in states' rights and a feeling that people who got in a Guardsman's way probably deserved what they got; the liberal left, which was in power, out of a fear that facing the issue of law and order in civil disturbances would further alienate the radical left, and also because of a reluctance to tinker with the haven of the draft-dodger. The regular army and the National Guard, in any case, preferred to pretend that civil-disturbance duty was not the major responsibility of either of them but, rather, devolved upon local police officers—who, in turn, preferred to think of themselves as delivering babies and solving ordinary crimes. The civil disturbances were not exactly revolutionary. They were simply anomalous—flash reactions against urban conditions and inequities that had not been resolved.

For a year or more after the crash patchwork job on the Guard, all seemed to go well. The Negro-recruitment program was a failure and the hours of training in riot control went down, in most states, to less than six. There was no uniform procedure from state to state about whether to put ammunition in weapons, or what sort of weapons to use. But the "long, hot summers" never materialized. There were all sorts of civil disturbances (including one, at Grambling College in Louisiana, which Guard archives describe as a "riot for academic excellence"). But in the 1967 march on the Pentagon, Guard units behaved, under heavy provocation, extremely well; and nobody was killed by Guardsmen in any of the urban riots, in April 1968, over the assassination of Martin Luther King, Jr. It looked all right, as far as National Guard behavior was concerned. Even at the Democratic Convention in Chicago (August 1968), nobody was killed.

Guard duty in 1969 began with a blizzard in Pender, Nebraska, and went on through floods, train wrecks, downed planes, tornadoes, ice storms, forest fires, power failures, a hurricane (in Apalachicola, Florida), a "collapsed dam" (in Wheatland, Wyoming), "haul water" (in Berry and Oakman, Alabama), "flood" (in Soldotna, Alaska), "civil disturbance" (in Zap, North Dakota), and "searches for missing persons" (in such places as Rice Patch Island, North Carolina; Tallapoosa City, Alabama; and Tofte, Minnesota). True, there were "college disturbances" at Berkeley and Dartmouth, but the Guard did all right—as it did in the Moratorium March on Washington in October and, for that matter, at a Stamp Dedication Ceremony for the late Dwight David Eisenhower, in Abilene. The National Guard began again to stress its role in the national defense, and National Guardsmen, by 1969, were running 40 percent of the country's (militarily obsolete but still functional) Nike and Hercules missile sites.

A Harvard graduate, class of 1962, came to New York the summer after his graduation and took a job in a bank. His employer asked how he planned to fulfill his military obligation. The young man didn't know. The bank gave him two letters of recommendation. Within a month, he had risen to the top of the waiting list at the Seventh Regiment Armory and begun his six months' basic training, before returning to the bank. A young advertising executive, a friend of whose mother was the wife of a veteran of Squadron A, got into the squadron just before he received his draft notice, and about a year before Squadron A became defunct. "It's a total joke," he said of his Guard training. "It's a farce. It's a stupid movie. It's just one constant snafu after another. At the armory drill, you just get into what they call a 'skirmish line.' Militarily, it's obsolete. The equipment is all bad. They're all badly trained. They're all stupid. At scenic Camp Drum, in your tank, they wait till the end of the afternoon to issue ammunition. There's no way to give it back. You have to get rid of it. So you just keep firing and firing until the gun barrel gets red— shells that cost the taxpayer ninety dollars apiece, guns that will knock down a whole building. Once, somebody made a mistake and started firing his machine gun at us, round after round, before he could stop it. He just said, 'Uh-oh.' "

A Guardsman who participated in what was intended to be the first of sixteen hours of riot-control training at some abandoned army barracks in Southern California said, "It was chaos. It was total confusion. We were divided in half—half 'rioters,' half 'riot controllers.' Nobody knew what to do. We raced around shouting. Then both sides started just destroying the buildings. We kicked in doors and smashed windows. After twenty minutes, the officers started blowing their whistles. They barely got people under control. Even at Guard drills now, discipline is on very thin ice. Every unit has lawyers, and officers know that dissident Guardsmen can make full use of the law. Marksmanship practice is a joke. The unit wants to look good. The rule is: everybody passes. There is a tremendous difference between the troops and the officers. The troops are better educated. The old guys just don't want to know it, but if there were a war now these boys simply would not go."

Right after the shootings at Kent State—when it was still thought that the Guardsmen's tear gas had run out, that they were surrounded, that they had been pelted with rocks, that some were injured, that it was simply a question of panic—friends of the Guard deplored the tragedy, while opponents of the Guard said the Guard had all along been a "farce" and a "scandal." But friends and opponents agreed that the fact that there had not already been many Kent States seemed to them "a miracle."

"No, we're not, we're just not bloodthirsty," Colonel W. D. McGlasson of the National Guard said to a recent visitor, in the National Guard Association's office at 1 Massachusetts Avenue, in Washington. "Why, I remember when you didn't have the draft to send you everybody. There was a time when having horse shows and whatnot was the only thing that kept the Guard together. Harry Truman once said that he used to have to pay twenty-five cents a drill for the privilege of drilling at his hometown armory. Now we have become, in reality, a federal force. They can shift us all the way to the North Pole if they want to. The waiting lists have fallen off a bit in the last two, three months, what with the lottery for the nineteen-year-olds. But these kids that come in for six years and then leave, they're not Guardsmen in spirit. People who liked the hiking and the training, those were always the heart and soul of the Guard. Defense Secretary McNamara wanted to reduce us to a force of three hundred and forty thousand, but when he asked the adjutants general and the governors, state by state—well, we wound up with approximately half a million. Now with this Kent State thing, the newspapers are against us. Probably seventy-five percent of the press are not like that. It's the large-circulation ones, mostly. But then, you know, we never killed a soul in all those April riots over Dr. King, all over this country. And national defense is really the Guard's primary responsibility. As for civil disturbances, nobody has found an ideal solution. In this country, we're so accustomed to the idea that if we have a problem there must be a way to resolve it. Well, there isn't always a solution. And the problem has been"—Colonel McGlasson shook his head regretfully—"just when the racial thing was starting to simmer down, the antiwar movement popped up."

"You know, a Guard unit is not a unit. It's a rabble of men," said Arnold Sagalyn, former senior vice president of the International Criminal Police Organization (Interpol) and now a consultant on urban affairs and a member of the President's Commission on the Causes and Prevention of Violence. "They have no sniper or gas teams, no discipline, no army sequence-of-force procedure—where first you give a warning, then you fix your bayonet, then you load your rifle, and so on. They're forbidden even to carry out civil-disturbance training in summer. In some cities, they've fired at shadows, fired at ricochets. In North or South Carolina, I forget which, Guardsmen were clearing a school, and they went through the doorway too close and started bayoneting each other. What we ought to have is some regular force—it would take just a fraction of what we spend on highways—ready to get to a disturbance fast, trained for it like a firefighter, trained to contain it, every man ready to file a report whenever he fires his weapon. Right now, a few militants making trouble in more than one city could put whole states out of action. The only answer is nonlethal weapons—make people sick, make them uncomfortable. It's better than killing them. When the draft lottery gets so that the only people who join the Guard are the ones who really *want* to be in it, you're going to get the wrong kind of people, the people who like to break heads. When I think of the way it is now, when I just think of the power of death that we entrust to them!"

"Now, Guard procedures vary from state to state," Lieutenant Colonel James Elliott, of the National Guard Bureau, said recently to a visitor in the Pentagon. "Now, in New York State, I believe, the Guard in civil disorders is not issued ammunition. I am not aware of the procedures in all the other states. But Ohio. Well, I guess that's one state where they elect to lock and load."

"I believe that the Guard has no purpose," said Paul Warnke, former Assistant Secretary of Defense for International Security Affairs. "And to the extent that it has a purpose, I don't agree with it. Now, McNamara and Vance, after Detroit, they thought if you have a disturbance you just smother it in people. I think what you do is you train the police to see that it doesn't spread. That's the only function that's essential. Now, if I were a major-league shortstop I wouldn't want to be drafted, either. But if this country has become so Vietnamized that we need Regional Forces and Popular Forces to deal with domestic disorder, well, I certainly don't think it has. And we already have three and a half million men under arms. But if this country is really at a stage where we need a special Guard to deal with domestic disorder, then I don't think we need a Guard anyway, because if we were at that stage, then I wouldn't give a damn."

"The army prefers the police in domestic disorders," said Colonel Dan
Henken, a public-affairs officer of the Defense Department. "Frankly, we
at the Defense Department want no part of it. In Detroit, though, we
had to wean the citizens off the regular army. A lot of our men were
black, and people were bringing them sandwiches and asking them not
to leave. Saying, 'We don't want trouble, we just don't want those trou-
blemakers around here.' But that's a police problem. If you send in the
army, the voters get upset. What we ought to learn, though, is that you
don't shoot. You make people uncomfortable. There was a terrific fuss
when we used eight canisters of tear gas at the Pentagon in 1967. Eight
canisters. The public now accepts the use of tear gas. The National
Guard, you know, is primarily for the national defense. And anyway,
they have a state-to-state jurisdictional problem. I shudder to think what
would happen if there were a civil disturbance on the Belt Parkway
between Virginia and Maryland."

In general, people's despair of the National Guard as a troop of le-
thally armed, untrained state anachronisms tends to correspond with a
fear of extremists, right or left. People who are most sanguine about
the country tend to think the Guard is one more evidence of the kind
of muddling, and mix-up, and loophole, and bungling that makes the
country work.

"Look, they said we couldn't break up the caste system and the Klan
in the South," said a former official of the Justice Department. "They
said, 'You can't turn the FBI around.' The FBI at the time was hunting
Communists. Well, there weren't many Communists in Mississippi, so
it was a pretty sleepy Bureau. The Justice Department started doing its
own investigating for civil rights. And the FBI's pride got involved.
And one day they were sending all their best men down there. The
South got to be the proudest assignment an FBI man could get. Well,
now, you throw yourself at a problem and if you can't break it you
throw yourself at it again, and if you still don't break it—well, the
next guy will. Now somebody's got to throw themselves at this National Guard Bureau. Somebody's got to say, 'I don't care about the patronage, and I don't care about the draft-dodging, and I don't care how

elusive the problem is, I'm going to shake up that Guard Bureau.' And when the Bureau's shaken up and there are some good men in there, they're going to start shaking up the National Guard in every state right along the line and make something of it. After Detroit, nobody wanted to tackle it, because it looked like bad public relations. But now somebody's got to tackle it or we're going to have killings. At least the President's Commission on Campus Unrest has subpoena power. Now somebody has just got to tackle the Guard Bureau in Washington."

"The Bureau is just the purse strings of the National Guard," said Lieutenant Colonel James Elliott at the Bureau offices in Washington. "We just do what the Department of Defense tells us to do, and we are a liaison between Washington and the governors and adjutants general of the states. We think our performance in civil disturbances is adequate, but of course it varies from state to state. In August, when the American Legion held its annual convention in Oregon, the state authorized sixty hours of civil-disturbance training for its Guard, and there was no disturbance. But that was the state of Oregon."

The *New York Times* of Friday, July 24, published an FBI finding that the National Guardsmen at Kent State were not surrounded, had not run out of tear gas, had not been hit by rocks or subjected to sniper fire, and were not in any way injured when they killed four students and wounded thirteen others on May 4. The Justice Department's report found that six Guardsmen might be liable to criminal prosecution. It seemed at first astonishing that there should be an FBI report so rapid, so candid, and so devastating about any branch of the U.S. military. But the agent in charge of the investigation that led to the report was Joseph A. Sullivan, one of two Bureau chiefs who in the early sixties turned the Mississippi FBI to the cause of civil rights.

The Guard having passed, in its domestic duties since World War II, through four not quite discrete phases—civil defense, protection of civil rights, intervention in urban disorders (primarily looting) from Watts through Detroit to the King riots of 1968, and what appeared to be a phase of disturbance on campuses—Arnold Sagalyn, who was becoming less sanguine every minute, had become extremely concerned that the

Guard was taking no interest in nonlethal weapons, particularly the chemical agent CS, which he advocates in lieu of deadly firearms. He pulled out from his desk a report he had prepared for the Kerner Commission two years ago.

"Its effect on rioters in Washington," he had written of CS, "was described by one police official as 'phenomenal.' Those exposed to this nonlethal control agent were strongly deterred from any activity which would risk another dose. Some police officers reported that they found it to be so effective that if they merely tossed an ordinary beer can, which resembled the CS container, a crowd would quickly break up and scatter. . . . It was found that dropping it inside a store that had been broken into immediately deterred future rioters from entering." Mr. Sagalyn put down the report. "When you have half a million Guardsmen armed to the teeth, with no uniform leadership or policy," he said, "and you bear in mind that *civilians*—farmers, hunters, Panthers, vigilantes, extremists, housewives—have more guns than all the other military combined, you pray that the situation isn't as volatile as it looks."

In mid-September, the National Guard Association of the United States, the lobbying group to which virtually all Guard officers belong, held its ninety-second annual convention, at the Americana Hotel in New York. The association, which goes by its acronym, NGAUS, had among its guest speakers General William C. Westmoreland, Chief of Staff of the United States Army; Dr. Curtis W. Tarr, director of the Selective Service System; General Lewis B. Hershey, former Director of the Selective Service System (to whom NGAUS was giving an award); Mayor John V. Lindsay of New York (whom various peace groups had tried to persuade not to speak); and Senator John C. Stennis, of Mississippi, chairman of the Senate Committee on Armed Services. Major General James F. Cantwell, adjutant general emeritus of the New Jersey Guard and still president of NGAUS, was scheduled to open the convention, but since he was currently under indictment in New Jersey (for putting Guardsmen on active duty to work in remodeling his house), he did not attend. Major General Sylvester T. DelCorso, adjutant general of the Ohio National Guard (and a member of the NGAUS executive council), did not attend, either.

There was a bomb scare on the first day of the convention, and some Guard officers discussed the possibility that a convention of the Guard at this time, with these speakers, at the Americana Hotel, might be construed by radicals as a provocation of some sort. But the convention quietly endorsed several resolutions, some military, some having to do with holding next year's convention in Hawaii, where, the adjutant general of Hawaii assured them in a tape-slide travel lecture, they would find "some of our *aloha* spirit, which is so needed now." But the major concerns of the conference were three: how to get less obsolete military equipment from the federal government in what most Guardsmen predicted would be a "weapons fallout" from the reduction of fighting in Vietnam; how to get combat veterans to enlist in the Guard, and six-year enlistees to reenlist for another term; and, most important, how to profit from the "Laird Memorandum," issued in early September by Secretary of Defense Melvin Laird. The Laird Memorandum proposed, in essence, an all-volunteer professional army, a "zero draft," and a better-trained, better-armed National Guard and Reserve to constitute, instead of draftees, the genuine first line of reserve in the country's defense.

Guard officers were dreamy, ecstatic, and characteristically muddled about what the Laird Memorandum would mean in terms of Guard recruitment—but they were unanimously certain that it would mean better arms, M-16 rifles instead of the old M-1s, helicopters, planes, perhaps missiles, the best technology. "We're tickled to see the Laird Memorandum," Major General Winston P. Wilson—known throughout the Guard as Wimpie, and, since 1963, chief of the National Guard Bureau—said on the morning General Westmoreland arrived. "We're going to have progress from the fallout of troop reduction in Vietnam. We're going to get rid of the Korean-vintage equipment. Why, out West, sometimes someone still has to bring their own shotgun. Now we're going to have a smooth escalation."

Asked about equipment for civil disturbances, General Wilson, who has served forty-one years as an Arkansas National Guardsman, twenty of them rising through the Bureau in Washington, said that he thought the Guard's equipment for such duty was adequate. "But we would like to have anything," he added vaguely. "We didn't really wake up at Watts. Now we would like to have batons, water cannons—you know, bulletproof vests, a little better dispensers for gas, bullhorns, bird shot, face masks that go on the helmet." He paused. "But on the local level there still is a judgment factor. There's a lot of sympathy just now for batons, but"—he paused again—"the rifle is still primary."

Asked whether the zero draft might result in zero motivation to join the National Guard, he explained, as Guard officers often explain, that the Laird Memorandum would simply restore the National Guard to the "first line of military reserve" status it held before the draft exemptions of 1948. Asked whether the Guard had opposed the draft exemptions of 1948, he explained that the Guard had in fact supported them. "You see, at the time, we had a recruitment problem," he said. Asked whether it was not precisely that recruitment problem that might now recur, he explained, as Guard officers often explain, that the National Guard was frequently accused of being the haven of the draft-dodger, whereas, on the contrary, it was a place where "draft-motivated" young men could perform their military obligation without being subject to the draft. This line of questioning among Guardsmen is never a productive one, and General Wilson returned with evident pleasure to an anecdote he had been telling all day, about his visit the evening before to the Persian Room of the Plaza, where he had witnessed a performance by Joey Heatherton. "She invited us to her room," he said amiably to anyone in sight, "and she gave me a great big buss . . ."

By five o'clock on the last afternoon of the convention, a small group of demonstrators were quietly picketing opposite the entrance to the Americana on Seventh Avenue. It was rumored, inside and outside the convention, that Vice President Agnew might attend the States Dinner, the formal closing banquet of the convention, that night. General Wilson had flown to Washington, to return with Senator Stennis in time for the dinner. Earnest discussions among younger Guard officers were taking place in the Americana's bars. Whether an army of mercenaries, supplemented by a force of citizen-soldiers, was really what the Constitution had in mind. Whether, as someone suggested, if a "Seven Days in May" situation should arise, with the professional army holding the President captive, the National Guard might prove the country's only defense against its mercenaries, in the Laird Memorandum's terms. Whether, with a zero draft, anyone but rednecks and martinets would join the Guard at all. How curiously characteristic of the American system it is that *no* branch of the military cares to confront civilians in civil disturbances. Whether an army composed in part of draftees was not a greater restraining and liberalizing force than a combination of mercenaries and citizen-soldiers. There was talk of an anecdote from Dr. Curtis W. Tarr's speech of the day before. "A small minority question why they should do anything for their country," the director of the Selective Service System had said. "One young man put his question bluntly: 'If I don't want to go into the armed forces, don't want to try to argue that I am a conscientious objector, don't want to go to jail, and don't want to go to Canada, what can I do?' My answer did not please him one bit: 'Somewhere you must find a society to which you will feel willing to contribute.' "

By six-thirty on the last night of the NGAUS convention, most of the officers were in full-dress uniform—black for Army Guard, white for Air Guard—and their wives were in evening dresses. Many of the older men had medals from World War II, but the invitation to the States Dinner, in a bungle perhaps typical of the Guard in things military, omitted a rather important "hours." "The President of the Association," it said, "earnestly requests all guests to be seated by 1930." Guardsmen and their wives, looking like figures from the antebellum South, occasionally wandered, drinks in hand, onto the steps of the Americana to look at the demonstrators, under police surveillance, across the street. One lady said she preferred to watch through a window. "Come on, Joanie," another lady said. "Don't be chicken." A photographer from the *New York Post* photographed a Guard sentry outside the banquet hall, sound asleep.

The States Dinner itself passed like any other convention banquet in the Americana's Imperial Ballroom. There were speeches, a clatter of butter plates, reunions of old friends, some tipsy conversations. Then, just before Senator Stennis spoke, there was an apparently annual ceremony. The sergeant at arms announced the presentation of "the various flags of our Union, in order of admittance," and the state flags were brought in, with appropriate music ("Maryland! My Maryland!" for Maryland, "East Side, West Side" for New York), one by one. People sang along with the songs they knew, but as the flag-bearers came in (many of them presenting also the first black faces of the convention), the officers from each state rose to their feet or stood on their chairs to cheer, waving their yellow Americana napkins over their heads. Hawaii, which gives the best parties, got a standing ovation from everyone. (So did the chaplain-escorted wife of an Air Guardsman missing in action over Vietnam.) But Mississippi, Ohio, Puerto Rico, Wisconsin, and Oregon were also roundly cheered. Yellow napkins were waving everywhere. Then Senator Stennis spoke, rather hawkishly about Vietnam and rather doubtfully about the Guard's capacity to recruit with a zero draft. The banquet became solemn again. Vice President Agnew did not appear. Outside the Americana, by 11:30 P.M., the demonstrators had long disappeared, but there were an inordinate number of horse-drawn carriages of the sort that go through Central Park. Asked whether so many hansoms were normal even for a convention of tourists at the Americana, a New York cabdriver said they were not. "I've never seen so many of them," he said. "What's going on in there?" Told that it was a convention of the National Guard, he said that explained it.

—1970

CONCENTRATION, SQUARES, JEOPARDY, AND BOUILLON CUBES

It would take only a few hours of watching daytime television to realize that the quiz shows have stumbled into very strange territory, and very far out. Ever since early radio, there has been some variant of what seemed to be the quiz-show principle: knowing or doing something, on the spot, and getting paid for it. The Quiz Kids, in their time, put the emphasis on precocity, on knowing things young; people who were not impressed by Margaret O'Brien and Peggy Ann Garner for being so cute on the screen were meant to be in awe of Joel Kupperman for being so smart on the air. There was also the aged, mellow, omniscient Answer Man, with listeners sending their hardest questions in. It was, anyway, the time of the spelling bee, the *Amateur Hour*, the Eagle Scout, and the 4-H Club. There were "contestants" in everything from playing a tune on a wax-papered comb to recognizing a song from its opening bars, through raising a cow, having total recall, or doing a sum in one's head. It had its own sense.

Now it hasn't. The respect for "answers," for seeing instant information rewarded with grand sums of money, fell apart—a while after the $64 *Question* had escalated to the $64,000 *Question*, and up, and the great quiz-show scandals had hit. The thing went all to pieces, and the scandals of 1959 don't explain it by half. Payola in popular music, after all, surfaced the same year, and though there have been less evident forms of corruption in the pop-music field ever since (bribes of small-time disc jockeys on local radio stations, to affect national hit-record charts; an occasional jukebox-syndicate murder, which gets a few lines in the press; the fact that even big-city radio stations have to guard against attempted payoffs by limiting disc jockeys' contracts to thirteen weeks at a time), the music has flourished. The audience's taste in pop music just turned out to be stronger than the industry's ethical problems.

But the quiz shows. The respect for encyclopedic minds conjoined with limitless money naturally declines when the thing is exposed as a fraud. Very odd scraps remain. What the "questions" are, what the "answers" are, what is the *point* become more peculiar every year. There was until recently a quiz program in which three celebrities were given both questions and answers; the object was for each of the celebrities to guess which of the answers one of the other two, or another celebrity entirely, had given to the questions. It was strange, but one could understand it. The celebrities got publicity. The writers-in, on whose behalf they were playing, got prizes. The prizes, which were explicitly brand-named and described, got under-the-table commercials. The audience got to watch celebrities and prizes. Another show had two teams, each with a "celebrity captain." The object was to give, in a sort of limited free word association, the same answer as your teammates. If, for example, the question was "I screamed when I saw the burglar climbing in the . . ." and you answered "spoon" or "twilight," you were both an eccentric and not a good player. The answer—if the whole thing can be described in terms of question and answer—would more likely be "window," since that's what your teammates' answers were likely to be. Strange, but still plausible. A premium on being the samest. A long way, though, from the really big money and the encyclopedic, rewardable mind.

Now. If you turn on your set at ten-thirty in the morning, you are likely to get *Concentration*, a game on the order of the card game that children are so good at, only easier and with odd additions. In the child's game, fifty-two cards are laid in rows, facedown, on the table. When a child turns up one card, perhaps a queen or a 9, he is supposed to remember where there is another queen or 9, lying facedown, to match it. The more pairs he remembers, the closer he is to winning. In the adult *Concentration*, there is a board of numbers, 1 through 30. Behind each number there is a prize, which matches the prize behind another number. If you choose the number 3, behind which there is a washing machine, and if you try to match it with a 5, behind which there is a toaster, you lose. But if, later in the game, you choose 11, behind which there is a toaster, you are meant to remember the 5, and the toaster is yours. So far so good. One has the feeling that if television could come up with a panel-audience version of slapjack, it would do so. But there is more. First, behind some numbers there are "wild cards," so you get whatever prize there is behind the other number you have chosen. A slight whiff of poker. Then, some prizes are jokes. On a recent show, there were such "prizes" as "two duckpins," "twenty-two duckpins," a "catfish," a "dog-wood," a "horsefly," and a "duck call." Whatever these prizes were, if you matched the two numbers behind which they were, you got them. There are also always two numbers behind which there is the word "Forfeit." If you match two numbers concealing "Forfeit," you have to give up one of your prizes—presumably, in the recent case, your horsefly or duck call. But the final innovation—what is called in the game-show business the Moment—consists of something entirely other. Behind each number, in addition to a prize, there is a line or a component of a rebus. Each time two numbers are matched correctly, two portions of the rebus are exposed. "The Moment" comes when a contestant guesses the whole rebus. On the show that contained the duck call, the portions of the rebus were these: a picture of a toe, the letters *nt*, a picture of a bee, a picture of a seal, and the letter *e*. The rebus, in other words—or in words at all— read "toe nt bee seal e": Don't be silly. Another was *wh*, a picture of an ear, a picture of a shoe, a *d*, a picture of a tie, a picture of a book, and the letters *in*. "Wh ear shoe d tie book in": Where should I begin? All right. Still nearly sane. Ed McMahon, of the Johnny Carson show, was once master of ceremonies on this program. Again, the rewards are not money but prizes—each prize described in the terms of a very dreary but direct commercial for it, quite aside from the commercials for the advertisers who actually sponsor the show.

At eleven-thirty (and also one night a week) comes *Hollywood Squares*, the seventh-most-popular program in daytime television. The first six are soap operas, the best of which are in the afternoon, when there are more viewers and fewer quiz programs of any sort. *Hollywood Squares* is tick-tacktoe, but the differences border on insanity. In each box of the tick-tacktoe grid there sits a celebrity. One contestant has the *x*s, the other the *o*s. The contestant picks a celebrity (Charlie Weaver, Wally Cox, Paul Lynde, *Star Trek*'s Mister Spock, and someone called just Rose Marie have been fairly regular among the nine) in his box. The celebrity is asked a question. He answers. The contestant is asked whether the celebrity's answer is true or false. If he is correct in thinking that the celebrity's answer is true, or if he is correct in thinking that the celebrity's answer is false, he gets the square, for his x or his o. If he is wrong, the other contestant gets it. The object is to be right about three celebrities in three boxes in a row—vertically, horizontally, or on the diagonal. Just so the audience does not lose its grip on the point of the game, the contestant usually announces his intention—say, "Charlie Weaver, to block," or "Rose Marie, to win." There is an added fillip: the Secret Square. One box, with its celebrity in it, is worth a mine of prizes if the contestant is right in believing or disbelieving the celebrity's answer to the question posed. Only the audience at home knows which is the Secret Square. The prizes attached to that box are again described in pure advertising detail, *whether the contestant wins them or not.* The secret ad.

But here is what is oddest: The show used to have the implication that the celebrities answered to the best of their knowledge, and the contestant's problem was to discern which celebrities were best informed—unless, of course, he already knew the answer himself. The show was, in essence, based on a condition of trust. But in the course of time the celebrities, in their boxes, began to make so many ad-lib jokes that the jokes began to be part of the show. Now the ad-libs are written by joke writers in advance. The audience is warned that the celebrity may or may not be trying to mislead the contestant. The honesty—more on the order of sincerity—of the whole program is called into question here, although, of course, sincerity is hard to measure, and impossible to monitor in investigational terms. Even the questions, although they are sometimes on the order of "Do both male and female reindeer have antlers?" often specifically mention a current book, writer, or magazine. On one recent show, there were, among others, the following three questions: whether, according to *Glamour*, there is any difference between jogging outdoors and jogging in place at home; why, according to the *Ladies' Home Journal*, there are so few male secretaries; and what, according to *Cosmopolitan*, the value is of rubbing a frog on one's face. The whole thing has become an utter muddle of trusts, ethics, joking, advertising, and quizzing. Nobody seems to mind.

At noon, there is *Jeopardy*. This show was conceived in 1964, as incorruptible, quiz-disguised comedy; but the audience's disappointed feeling for some combination of mind and money, for getting ahead in some reasonable way, was apparently such that *Jeopardy* gradually did become a conventional quiz show. Except that what is given is the answers, and the contestants are meant to formulate the questions. That was where the comedy used to come in—on the order of: What is the question to which the answer is 9W? "Is your last name spelled with a V, Richard Wagner?" It could not be kept up. The contestants, who used to be stars but are now civilians, go for straight answers, some simple, some extremely difficult, and are rewarded for correctness with money. Not great sums, but money. I don't know who watches *Jeopardy*; surveys show, in addition to housewives, a high proportion of both college students and people over sixty-five. About half the answers for which contestants find the questions are too difficult for, for example, me. *Jeopardy* receives little of television's ethnically bewildered, psychotic, or hate mail, but there was one letter complaining that so many contestants were Jewish the program ought to be renamed "Jewpardy," and another—from someone who apparently misunderstood one of the program's categories, "Potpourri"—expressed a distaste for this reference to "Popery," as "ridiculing the head of one of the great religions of the world, 'The Pope,' the head of the Roman Catholic Church." *Jeopardy* ranks ninth among the daytime programs—slightly ahead of *The Newlywed Game*, *Let's Make a Deal*, and *The Dating Game*. With *those* shows one gets into another world entirely, closer to and yet farther from the Moment and the point.

Daytime television, strangely, accounts for 75 percent of a network's profit. The production costs are low, the addiction tends to be daily, and a single hour of soap and/or quiz can bring in $7 million a year. There used to be two weekend conventional quiz programs: *The College Bowl*, in which college teams answered what turned out to be increasingly difficult questions, and *It's Academic*, in which high-school teams competed. *College Bowl*, after more than ten years, has gone off the air, maybe partly because the students were beginning to answer and behave with a certain radical, or just antic, irreverence, but mainly because the football games were on at the same hour. *It's Academic* remains, and local high-school teams are apparently still quiz kids enough to compete straight. But *The Newlywed Game*, *The Dating Game*, and, most particularly, *Let's Make a Deal* have become (with the possible exception of political press conferences) the most bizarre question-answer sessions in all of television.

The Newlywed Game's appeal to its audience seems fairly clear. Four couples—now usually three white, one black—are slid around on two platforms. The men are asked what their wives would reply to certain questions. Then the wives, who have been out of hearing, are slid forward to reveal what their replies actually are. Then the men are slid out of hearing, and the wives guess what the men would answer, and the men slide back and answer for themselves. If a husband's and wife's answers match, they win points. If not, they don't. The questions, like the name of the game itself, are usually loaded with sexual innuendo. There can also be questions like "Where did your husband eat his last baked potato?" or "What is the steepest hill near where you live?" In fact, on a recent program those questions were asked. But more common are questions about how many parts the bed has, or what the first marital quarrel was about, or what the husband would say was his worst fault or biggest blunder ("Would he say it was something he did, or something he did not do?"). The answers are usually embarrassing in the extreme: somebody mutters something, in terms that seem to him elliptical, about his "wedding evening" or his "manual dexterity." The mysterious thing is why the newlywed couples should choose to appear on the program at all. When their answers disagree, they look at each other with absolute loathing, and often quarrel. (The audience enjoys this, and the announcer looks at the couples as though he had no idea that anything of this sort could occur.) But when their answers agree, about no matter what, they embrace. One has the feeling that if the wife in one of these newlywed couples said that her husband thought his worst fault was impotence, and if he did in fact give that answer, they would be more delighted than if she had said singing off-key in the shower and he had said biting his nails. The prizes—each, again, given an elaborate brand-name commercial—do not seem worth this public wrangling and mortification. Perhaps just being seen by a public seems worth it and blessed.

The Dating Game resembles *The Newlywed Game,* in a crazier key. Three bachelors are separated from a girl, by their anonymity and a wall. She asks them questions and decides, on the basis of their answers, which one she will date. There is a lot of sexual innuendo here, too, and sometimes, among the bachelors, wit. Occasionally, the three bachelors and the girl are black. Sometimes, a star and her daughter appear on the same program. That is, one day one of one set of bachelors got to date the daughter of Gloria de Haven and one of another set got to date

Gloria de Haven herself. "Bachelor Number Two," the daughter asked, "what does 'intimate' mean?" He paused. She said, "Uh-oh." He said, "That's it, 'intimate' means uh-oh." "Bachelor Number Three," her mother asked of the latter set, "how much sex appeal do you exude?" He replied with something about not wanting to know too precisely for fear of "deviating from the paths of rectitude on which I tread." Winning bachelors get a date—a chaperoned trip to a named resort, by means of a named airline. Losing bachelors get prizes, again described in commercial detail. References to race and to color occur on the show. When one of the black bachelors was asked to describe himself, he said he looked like John Wayne, if John Wayne were not missing something. Blackness, presumably. The audience laughed. The only quandary, again, is why anyone would appear on the show, why anyone would watch it, what (resorts being what they are) the black couple were going to do with their chaperoned skiing trip, and what Gloria de Haven was going to do with her twelve-day chaperoned trip to Curaçao.

The Newlywed Game and *The Dating Game*, both on ABC, are in the afternoon, where they are up against NBC's superior soap operas *Days of Our Lives* and *The Doctors*. But at one-thirty *Let's Make a Deal*, known in the trade as LMAD, is up against CBS's soap opera *As the World Turns*, the most popular program in daytime television. LMAD may be the most disgusting but somehow most puzzling and poetic program on the air. It used to be on NBC, but Monty Hall, its announcer, wanted to move to the evenings, to have prime time. NBC didn't give it to him. ABC gave him, in addition to the daily program, one night a week. LMAD moved, leaving, according to an NBC executive, a "tremendous hole" in NBC's afternoon programming, which six or seven successive shows—including an Art Linkletter program and a fine soap, *Hidden Faces*, later known in the trade as "Hidden Ratings"—have tried unsuccessfully, to fill. CBS has its supersoap at that hour, NBC has its hole, and ABC has *Let's Make a Deal*.

Let's Make a Deal is the disintegration of the quiz shows, pure. It moves so fast that it's nearly impossible to follow, but the upshot of the whole thing is a manic conjunction of risk, exhibitionism, and greed, and the whole program is nearly solid with prize-commercials, interrupted only by the commercials of the sponsors themselves. The only "questions" are who will be chosen for the program and whether they will barter what they have been given for something unknown, hidden behind a curtain or in a box. In order to be chosen for the program, the audience dresses in a lunatic fashion, and screams. A recent program began when three contestants—one of them a man fantastically made up and wearing a conical hat, the others women in unmemorable costumes—were asked to assess the value of a shaving kit, whose brand was named. People in the audience were screaming answers, but somehow the lady who came closest to guessing the real price won $500, the man won $150 and a pipe, and another lady won a "consolation prize." Then the lady who had won the $500 was asked whether she would trade her $500 for whatever a curtain concealed. Since what is hidden behind the curtain is often a joke prize, and worthless, there is a little cruelty here. At some point, the whole thing was interrupted by a real commercial, apparently designed to make the Man from Glad's image more male. Then the lady, with screamed encouragement from the audience, did trade her money for the becurtained unknown. She seemed to have won only a collection of food for dogs and cats (brand-named), but then, just as she was getting depressed, a curtain behind the original curtain revealed a living-room set. She jumped and screamed.

At one point in the program, the announcer began offering people a small container of bouillon cubes. They all traded it in. Suddenly, the announcer pointed out that there might be money concealed inside. Somebody soon won, by trading in a paper box that had $150 in it, a kitchen range, hams, and a trash-disposal unit (all brand-named), total retail value $959.59. She screamed. Somebody narrowly missed trading a product in hand for what was behind another curtain: a joke prize—a battered, worthless old wooden station wagon. Then somebody quite outlandish, a woman, began to outscream the rest. The announcer read out her name from a card she was wearing. "I'm not picking you. I'm just looking at you," he said. "But you said my *name*," she said hysterically. "Oh, all right. I'll take her," the announcer said. She shrieked. She was wearing an ABC sweatshirt, homemade, and was otherwise dressed as a cheerleader, and waved pom-poms about. She traded the bouillon cubes for what lay behind the curtain and won American Tourister luggage (American Tourister luggage and items from the Spiegel mail-order catalog appear as prizes, consolation or real, on almost all game shows) and a stereo set (brand-named), total retail value $592.95. "Hi, kids," she screamed, waving toward the camera.

Then the announcer approached a black lady, conventionally dressed, and said it was a relief to have a quiet lady for a change. He offered her the bouillon cubes. She traded them for what was behind the curtain and won a player piano, value $1,281 (brand-named). There were screams and kisses. Nobody seemed to wonder what use a player piano was going to be. What they screamed at was the price. The last person to be offered the bouillon cubes was costumed and screaming. "What am I going to do? What am I going to do? Shall I trade? Shall I trade?" she shrieked, as though the drama of her life were at its crisis. Everyone shouted "Trade!" "I'm gonna keep it," she finally said. The jar contained $50, and behind the curtain she had rejected, there were prizes, all brand-named, whose total value was $1,824. Part of the genius of these programs is the explicit mention of all the prizes, won or lost. Those prizes totaling $1,824 were described as carefully and lovingly as though someone were not actually stuck with her $50 and her bouillon cubes.

Then came the Moment—the "Big Deal"—in which nearly everyone who had won something was asked to trade. A couple who had previously won a trip to Paris stayed with what they had. The man with the pipe and the $150 chose one of three curtains, and got a $33.50 shaver and a $438 sewing machine. The black lady, with much encouragement from the audience, traded her player piano for another curtain, and got $25 worth of olives. While she was coping with her disappointment, the olives slipped aside to reveal what was, after all, the Big Deal—a car, retail value $4,175. The announcer forgot to ask the lady with the original consolation prize, an iron, whether she wanted to trade it. (Some matters are often forgotten on the game shows. The runner-up couple on The Newlywed Game, for example, also wins prizes, but these people are nearly always forgotten as the show comes to an end.) As Let's Make a Deal was ending, and the credit lines were beginning, the announcer was shouting, "One hundred dollars for a bar of soap"—if anyone in the audience had happened to bring one—one hundred dollars for a playing card, two hundred dollars for a lemon." As it turned out, someone had brought a playing card, and was given $100 as the half hour of LMAD came to an end.

The question is what it can mean. In the course of trying to eliminate the corruption of coached answers in the conventional question-answer-money format, the programs have succeeded only in muddying the point of the questions, the point of the answers, and have come up with un-investigatable noncontests of noncash cupidity for prizes that serve as unacknowledged ads. It is bizarre. And not the least bizarre thing is that the contestants and the audiences, too, now seem to prefer prizes, how-ever peculiar, to cash; and exhibitionism, or simply appearing, to dem-onstrated competence of any sort. It may mean something about the economy, but it doesn't seem so. People go off with their unearned, unneeded products, their living-room sets (were their living rooms empty?), their luggage, their trip to Las Vegas, even their electric organ, as though they had hit a jackpot, a grand surprise, more tangible than money, more satisfying than real winning. It is weird. It will probably not go on much longer. The soaps are gaining on the quizzes all the time. But in the hands of some highly austere dramatist, that choice between the perhaps rich bouillon cubes and the perhaps cruel mystery behind the curtain might be life's main proposition. The audience, almost to a man or to a screamer, agrees almost always, and volubly, that whatever is behind that curtain *must* be preferable to the object, or perhaps the life, one already has, and with which one might, conceivably, be content to be stuck.

—1971

AFTERNOON TELEVISION: UNHAPPINESS ENOUGH, AND TIME

You have to tolerate extremes of hatred and loneliness to follow, Monday through Friday every week, through a still unterminated period of months, the story of an educated man so bitter that he kills himself solely to frame another man for murder. Yet there is an audience of at least six million at two-thirty every afternoon New York time (other times across the country) prepared to watch this plot line, among other plot lines, develop on *The Doctors*, a television program of the genre soap opera, or daytime dramatic serial. Whatever else it is, it is no joke. There cannot in all fiction be a purer single act of rage and isolation than this imploded revenge, the carom suicide: no simple murder of somebody else, no murder of somebody else to frame a third, no ordinary suicide that might leave others feeling guilty of some metaphorical murder by neglect. This contriver of his own death to make it look like someone else's literal crime has, in one classic solitary act, detonated incalculable threats in other lives. *The Doctors* plays it out.

For all I know, it happens all the time in life. So many events are quite other events in disguise. But *The Doctors* has a special instance here. It certainly has high tragic possibilities, except that no one writes high dramas now. In times of mass violent death, individuals in drastic personal straits look tabloid. Most fiction keeps its personal crises low profile and small; writers with serious claims upon the desperate dramatic themes seem to have crossed further out of tragedy and into melodrama than writers of soaps have crossed going the other way. The term "pop culture," never of much use or elegance, is empty now. There is almost no culture of any other kind. People with a taste or instinct for the arts are thrown back on the classics or must bide their time. The arts, first-rate, second-rate (the creative enterprise is not a horse race, after all), are just not much in evidence.

Painting is a kind of caricature: ribbons, billboards, commercials are not simply the inspiration—they are *better* than this incessant, humorless joke that passes through museums and galleries in the name of art. In writing, one would never have found a Kafka on symposiums or on the Johnny Carson show. But, in all the modern strategies of fame, it becomes harder than ever to know where to look.

And then there are the soaps. They are pure plot. Perhaps the grand oral tradition rambled on this way, and then we had the *Iliad* and the *Nibelungenlied*. For months, the audience was not told—the characters did not yet suspect—that Dr. Allison killed Dr. Allison. But the audience knew. Everyone knew. It was so in line with the characters and their motives over the last four years, at least, that the only questions were when Dr. Aldrich's murder trial would begin, if it began, and how it would come out. Conviction. Acquittal. Conviction and—perhaps months *later*—acquittal. All this was not conventional suspense. Too much was known. It was more like sustained morbidity and dread. Things were going to get worse before they got better, if they ever did. White housewives, black housewives, children home from school, men unemployed, the aged, the preschool young, the idle, the ladies at the ironing board—there was no telling, even from commercials, who was watching this, except that they were millions, across the country, and that they were, and are, willing to endure what has become the perfected medium of daily, inexorable, and almost unrelieved depression.

It takes about five days to catch on to the plot of a soap opera in apogee. It takes five years for one of these fictions, whose beginnings and ends are as obscure as the first questions of the universe, to capture and maintain an audience. There seems to be no reason for whole generations of adults still to have strong, clear memories of Helen Trent and other characters from the radio soaps. Surely we could not have been sick, or otherwise home from school, on so very many mornings, and "amnesia" need not have been our first word of adult pathology. But the television soap operas (the radio ones are now defunct), in addition to being in the afternoon, have brought their stories far closer to home. "As sands through the hourglass," says a voice, over music, each day at the start of a daytime serial, "so are the days of our lives." The program happens to be called *Days of Our Lives*. In all the years of the program's logo, the top half of the hourglass has never emptied and the bottom never filled. It is yet another Hundred Neediest Cases of the mind. Fidelity, betrayal, rape, murder, amnesia, alienation, misunderstanding, literal misconception (wives pregnant by their husbands' brothers or by the fiancés of their husbands' sisters), hostages, adoptions, suicides, loves, wars, friendships, deceit, insanity, operations, villains, tea—whose sands and hourglass are these? A lot of people's, evidently. The serial *Search for Tomorrow*, which is just now floundering a bit (writers of soap operas burn out, shift programs, lose their touch, endure, go mad, or simply vanish with their own dramatic frequency), has been on television continuously for more than twenty years. The serial *Another World* became so popular and full of plot (also so pressed by NBC's need for another loved half hour) that it split in two: the old *Another World*, at its usual 3 P.M., and *Another World* (*Somerset*)—later renamed simply *Somerset*—with many of the same characters, at 4 P.M. *The Doctors* itself, at two-thirty, is NBC's competitor with CBS's *The Guiding Light*, which was once one of the most-watched programs in daytime television. No more. *The Doctors* was just a better-written, better-acted epic of despair.

My happiest moment on any of the soaps I have watched with anything like constancy occurred some years ago, when Andrea Whiting, of *Search for Tomorrow*, cracked up on the witness stand. Her villainy had been relentless, undiscovered, pathological for years. She had broken the engagement of her son, Len Whiting, to Patti Tate. She had refused to divorce her estranged husband, Sam Reynolds, so that he could marry his true love, Joanne Tate, Patti's mother and the program's heroine. Andrea Whiting had been responsible, many years before, for the death by fire of Len's twin. She had blamed the death on her husband, Sam, thereby estranging Sam the father from Len the son. She had tried to kill several people in the intervening years—most recently Sam—but she had contrived to make it look as though Sam had been trying to kill her. Sam was on trial. He was being defended by Doug Martin, the father of Scott Phillips, who was going to marry Lauri Something, the mother of an illegitimate child. Names have little to do with paternity on any of the soaps; few legitimate children, for the most complicated reasons, have their fathers' names. Doug Martin, Scott Phillips's father,

was about to marry someone else. Doug had overcome a severe breakdown only recently, and his marriage, his confidence, his relationship
with his own son (Scott having just returned from Vietnam) depended
on the success of his defense of Sam. Anyway, under questioning by
Doug Martin, Andrea cracked up. The truth about the fire death came
out, the truth about everything came back, in flashbacks spanning years.
Andrea was carried off. I stopped watching for many months, quitting
while I was just a bit ahead, I thought. Now it turns out that while I
was away Andrea returned. Sam Reynolds is in prison in Africa. Joanne,
having gone blind for a while, and thinking Sam dead, has fallen in
love with her neurosurgeon. Len's wife, Patti, has had a miscarriage, and
his girl, Grace (I can't explain about Grace), had a child and died herself. It is such misery. I'm almost glad the writers are troubled now with
quite other problems I don't care about. Andrea is scheming again.
("Nobody can match Andrea in the scheming department," a CBS plot
summary says. I do see that.) I simply don't understand *Search for Tomorrow* now. Some characters seem to be buying a house.

My second-happiest moment on a soap was a mistake. Several years
ago, a girl named Rachel had, by the most unscrupulous means, ensnared
Russ Matthews, son of one of the most decent families on *Another World*.
They married. Many months later, a very rich self-made young man
called Steven Frame came into town and fell in love with Russ's sister,
Alice. Alice Matthews loved Steve, too, but so did Rachel (by this time
Mrs. Russ Matthews), in her own unscrupulous way. Rachel seduced
Steve. She became pregnant, and claimed that the child was Steve's. Her
husband, Russ, was, naturally, upset, as was his sister, Alice, who im-
mediately broke off with Steve. For several months, I stopped watching.
Then, one recent afternoon (recent in soap terms, that is—around July),
when I was on the telephone, I had *Another World* on, with the sound
off. The scene was a christening. The characters were Lenore and Walter
Curtin (who had a difficult history of their own), a chaplain, a baby,
Alice, and Steve. I thought—I truly hoped—that Alice and Steve had
been reconciled and married while I was away, and that the child was
theirs. All wrong. The baby was Lenore's and Walter's, although Walter
had grave doubts on this very point. Alice and Steve were godparents.

Since then, Alice and Steve have really married. I missed that scene,
but they have passed their honeymoon, and so I know. Russ and Rachel

have divorced. Rachel has remarried—a young man whose business is now being financed by Steven Frame. Russ is engaged to Rachel's new husband's sister. Or he was, until a few sad weeks ago. People have to keep meeting at parties, where there are so many problems about previous marriages and affairs and present babies. Now Rachel's husband has been in a coma and has made sordid revelations about his past. Walter Curtin has vanished, under mysterious circumstances. Lenore has received, by messenger, a scarf. Walter has confessed by phone to the murder, in a jealous rage, of Steve's secretary's former husband, whom he suspected of having slept with his (Walter's) wife, Lenore. Most recently—in fact, tomorrow, as I write this—Walter has died. But on the whole such sudden accelerations of the plot are better on quick, episodic soaps, like *Edge of Night*, which are akin to closed, formed, Aristotelian thrillers, which I never watch.

There are moments when some aesthetic things, all art aside, are simply so. People know it, without any impulse or attempt to argue: Something is on. Such a moment, years back, protracted over many months, was the Moon Maid episode in the *Dick Tracy* comic strip. Long before the slogan "Black is beautiful" appeared in and receded from the news, longer before the astronauts reached the moon, Dick Tracy's son, Junior, returned from the moon with Moon Maid, pleaded with her not to remove her horns or try to conceal them with a beehive hairdo, married her, and delighted in their baby's little horns. The word would not even be *miscegenation* now. Junior was light-years beyond the country's perception of its race problems then. The McCarthy time of *Pogo* was less golden. It was one of those finest hours that *Peanuts*, in another key, has sustained over many years with genius consistency. Something was touched.

The same was true for years of the talk shows on television. They were on. They meant something. Now, regardless of Nielsen ratings, watchers, they are off. One knows it. They simply do not matter in the sense they did. It is also true, oddly enough, of television coverage of the news. It had its years and faces. Then it had the instant things it was perfectly designed for: the shooting through the head of a man by the chief of Saigon's national police; the moon landing. Then it lost its purchase on events and, no matter how many people watched it, faded. The anchorman would mention an event, switch to the local correspondent, who would mention it again, then interview its source, who would mention it in his own idiom. No depth, no time, and lots of waste of time. McLuhanism was wrong. The mind needs print. Perhaps the news as captured by TV will matter again. Maybe tomorrow.

The soap operas, which have endured as long as anything in television, have their own rhythms, fade, recur. It was on *Another World*, some years ago, that there was a moment—or, rather, nearly a half hour—of dramatic brilliance. It was just after Rachel, still married then to Russ, had slept with Steve and spent a weekend searching for her father. Russ naturally knew that she had been away, but not where or with whom. Suddenly, Russ insisted that he and Rachel pay a call that night on everyone they knew in town—to keep up appearances. Rachel resisted, in her usual sulky way, and then gave in. They made the tour. It was a masterpiece of compression. Russ and Rachel acted out their drama in such a way (by concealing it, and pretending that all was well) that all the other dramas on the program—and they were many, and of long standing—were called to mind, as though the audience were going through an Andrea flashback on the witness stand.

They went to visit, for example, Walter Curtin and Lenore. Walter Curtin had been the prosecutor, several years before, in a case in which Missy Fargo was mistakenly convicted of the murder of her husband, Dan. She had married Danny Fargo, in the first place, because Liz Matthews (another unrelenting villainess) had tried to prevent the love match of Missy and Liz's son, Bill. Liz, the mother, had decided at the time that her son, Bill, should marry Lenore, now Curtin but then single and in love with Bill. Bill loved Missy. Lenore loved Bill. Walter loved Lenore. When Danny Fargo was murdered, Liz (the mother), Walter (the prosecutor), and Lenore all had an interest in seeing Missy go to jail. Several years later, Missy was sprung and married Bill. Then Walter, repentant and, anyhow, in love, married Lenore. Liz, the villainess, was hysterically distressed, but she had other lives to wreck, including a long-lost daughter's, and she did.

Russ and Rachel, in their tour, met others—several generations of the Randolph family, for example, and Rachel's mother, Ada, of humble origins but of major significance in solving the Missy case. What had happened since Missy's trial (can I go on with this?) was an interminable riveting episode in which Lee Randolph, a daughter of the Randolphs (who are related to the Matthewses by innumerable ties of blood and

misunderstanding), being in love with Sam Lucas, a relative of the humble Ada's, had, under the influence of LSD, killed someone, whose name
I don't remember, of the criminal element.

This business of not remembering has an importance of its own, although insanity has replaced amnesia as the soap operas' most common
infirmity. The files of the soaps are so sketchy that their history is almost
irretrievable. "Laura comforts Susan, and Scott is surprised by a statement
from Julie," for example, is NBC's plot note for the March 13, 1970,
Days of Our Lives. And "Nick and Althea did make it to the Powers
apartment, and the dinner did not burn" was NBC's summary of two
weeks on *The Doctors* during the AFTRA strike of 1967. The only true
archivists of the whole history of a soap are the perpetual watchers, the
loyal audience, whom, out of a truly decent sense of tradition and constancy, the ever-changing writers try not to betray. This requires careful
and intuitive examination of those files, and an attempt to avoid anything that might violate the truth of the story as it existed before a given
writer's time. Only the audience knows, and yet there are so many Scotts
and Steves and Lees on various programs that even the most loyal audience can get mixed up.

Anyway, Sam Lucas took the blame for Lee Randolph's having murdered, under LSD, a thug. Everyone was acquitted in the end. Of course,
there is no end. But Lee, thinking that LSD had impaired her chromo-
somes, kept far away from Sam, who misunderstood her motives as having
to do with the milieu from which he came. Sam Lucas married a girl
called Lahoma, an earthy character who was meant to appear only briefly
in the plot but who was so good she had to stay. Lee Randolph eventually
killed herself. Sam, Lahoma, Missy (now widowed again), and Missy's
baby by Danny Fargo have all moved to *Somerset*. Strangely, none of the
catastrophes on soaps—and nearly every soap event is a catastrophe—
are set up with much sentiment. I do not think the audience ever cries,
except at Christmas, anniversaries, and other holidays, all of which are
celebrated on their proper day. The celebrations are bleak enough, but
it is the purest gloom to find oneself on December 25 or January 1 watching a soap or, if the football games are on, deprived of one. The other
days are just alternations of being miserable and being bored, or both,
and knowing that the characters are the same.

Well, there were Russ and Rachel, visiting all these people on *Another
World*. To someone who had not been watching, it did all come back.

It is not necessary, technically, to *watch*. Since most of the characters address each other incessantly by name, one can catch it all from another room, like radio. On the other hand, one needn't listen, either. I would have found out my mistake about the christening soon enough. There are the most extravagant visual and aural flashbacks, ranging from "Have I told you what Russ said to me last night?" (answer: "Well, Russ did tell me"; both characters retell it anyway) to visual flashbacks that would do credit to the cinema. In the case of the temporarily misunderstood christening, it was my telephone that had turned the set on with the sound off. The ring of a telephone is often on the same frequency as the remote-control device that operates some television sets; many households have this strange mechanical rapport. A pin dropped on a table will sometimes do it, or the clicking of a belt buckle. One thinks one is alone, and suddenly the room is full of voices, or faces, or both, from *Another World*.

Another moment, this one from *Days of Our Lives*. It takes, as the whole addiction does, some bearing with. Mickey Horton we know—though he does not—is infertile. Tom Horton, Mickey's brother, returned several years ago from Korea, face changed, memory gone. His memory came back. About three years ago, Bill Horton, another brother, made pregnant Mickey's wife, Laura, a psychiatrist. Tom Horton, before he went to Korea, had a ghastly wife, extremely ghastly. When his memory returned, she returned, too. Dr. Horton, the father of Tom, Mickey, and Bill, knows—as Bill found out by accident, as Laura knows, as we have always known—that Laura's offspring cannot be her husband Mickey's. Mickey does not know. Last year, there occurred the following episode: Tom's ghastly wife was at the senior Hortons', trying to be nice. The senior Hortons of *Days of Our Lives*, like the senior Randolphs and Matthewses of *Another World*, or the Tates of *Search for Tomorrow*, are technically known by soap writers as "tentpole characters," on which the tragedies are raised. Anyway, as she set the table for dinner that evening at the senior Hortons', Tom's ghastly wife was singing. The elder Mrs. Horton said that she had a lovely voice, that she ought to make a professional thing of it. The ghastly wife went directly to Dr. Horton's study and made a tape recording of her singing voice in song. She forgot, in her slovenly way, to turn the tape recorder off. Later that evening, Dr. Horton had a chat with his daughter-in-law Laura about her child, her husband's infertility, and her brother-in-law's fatherhood. The tape recorder was still on. Tom's ghastly wife, trying later to recapture her own singing voice on tape, heard all the rest. It was unbearable. Months of blackmail, we all knew. It might have been a lifelong downer. I turned off for several years. The present moment—since July, I mean—as far as I can tell, is this. The tape incident seems nearly over. Mickey Horton, however, was believed by everyone, including himself, to have made pregnant a girl other than his wife. Even I knew this was impossible, unless Mickey's medical tests had been in error—in which case he might be the father of his wife Laura's baby after all—or unless the writers, and Laura and her father-in-law, had forgotten the whole thing. When Mickey's girl's baby was born, it did turn out, through blood tests, that the baby could not have been Mickey's. Of course not. Anybody who had watched even five days two years ago knew that. Meanwhile, a friend of the Horton family, Susan, who has had a terrible life, has been raped in the park, and is being treated by Laura, the psychiatrist. Well.

One thing about a work of art is that it ends. One may wish to know what happens after the last page of *Pride and Prejudice*. Some writers give signs of wishing the reader to abide with a given novel; one of the century's great prose works, after all, ends in such a way that the reader is obliged to begin again. But narrative time in art is closed. The soaps, although they have their own formal limitations (how many times, for example, a major character is required by contract to appear each week on-screen), are eternal and free. One can have a heart attack during a performance of *King Lear* or fall in love while listening to Mozart, but the quotidian, running-right-alongside-life quality of soaps means that whole audiences can grow up, marry, breed, divorce, leave a mark on history, and die while a single program is still on the air. Aristotle would not have cared for it.

The soaps can, and sometimes do, adopt the conventional thriller form, which has a different sort of addict altogether: the solvers, the classicists who demand a beginning, a middle, and an end. There was a superb many-month conventional kidnapping episode on *The Doctors* once, when a trustee of the hospital abducted a nurse, under enthralling circumstances, and the only one who gradually caught on was the nurse's roommate, Carolee Simpson, a character who, like *Another World*'s La-homa, was meant to stay just briefly but has ever since been so good that she is essential to the plot—particularly in the recent matter of Dr. Allison. There was also a young lady physical therapist who thought herself widowed in the Six Day War (her husband had been a correspondent in the Middle East) and who fell in love with the son of the chief of all the doctors. The son was in love with her. Then it turned out that an Israeli girl had been nursing a blind American. He was rude to her for ages. She was kind to him. He turned out, after months, to be the lady therapist's thought-dead husband, and things were resolved. Such episodes do occur. But they are rare. They are too self-contained. Now the wife of the chief of all the doctors, having been kidnapped and returned some months ago, thinks she is going mad. Her paternal uncle was a schizophrenic in his time.

There does not seem to be a single sense in which soap operas can be construed as an escapist form. There is unhappiness enough, and time, to occupy a real lifetime of afternoons. There is no release: not the scream, shudder, and return to real life that some people get from horror films; not the anxiety, violence, and satisfactory conclusion of detective, spy, or cowboy shows; certainly not the laughing chapters of fantasy home lives like *Lucy*, *Bachelor Father*, or *The Mothers-in-Law*. There is no escape, either, from political realities. The allegations that the soaps avoid the topical are simply false: race, Vietnam, psychosis, poverty, class, and generational problems—all are there. One thing soap operas do not do is flinch. They simply bring things home, not as issues but as part of the manic-depressive cycle of the television set. And what they bring home is the most steady, open-ended sadness to be found outside life itself.

No one can look forward to a soap unless he looks forward to the day, in which case he is not likely to be a watcher of soaps at all. Watchers resign themselves. There are seventeen soap operas on television now, some obviously less good than others (a soap that fails is not simply dropped from the air; it is, for the audience's sake, quickly wrapped up: The hero, for example, is run over by a truck), and in their uncompromisingly funereal misery there is obviously some sort of key. Most sentimental or suspense forms—dog, horse, or spy stories, for instance—have a plotted curve: Things are briefly fine, then they're down for a long time, then they rise for a brief finale. There is some reward. The soap line goes almost straight, though inextricably tangled, down. The soaps are probably more true to the life of their own audience than they appear to be; certainly they are truer in pace, in content, and in subjects of concern than any other kind of television is. Not that there is much amnesia or that much insanity out here. Not that each woman's secret fear, or hope, is that she is bearing the child of an inappropriate member of her family. But the despair, the treachery, the being trapped in a community with people whom one hates and who mean one ill, the secrets one cannot expose—except once or twice—in the course of years when changes and revelations occur in sudden jumps: These must be the days of a lot of lives.

This is not the evening's entertainment, which one watches, presumably, with members of the family; not the shared family situation comedies, which (with the important exception of *All in the Family*) are comfortable distortions of what family life is like. Soap operas are watched in solitude. This is the daytime world of the Randolphs, the Matthewses, the Hortons, the Tates—a daily one-way encounter group, a mirror, an eavesdropping or the apparent depression of being just folks for more than twenty years. It is even entering the commercials now—the utter joylessness. There are still the cheery, inane commercials with white tornadoes and whiter wash. But there are beginning to be hopeless underdogs: unpretty, sarcastic Madge, who, as a manicurist, deals with dishpan hands; a moronic young housewife who can scarcely articulate what she is shopping for; the emphasis on cold-water products, with actors who look as though they knew about life in cold-water flats. The view of life as a bitter, sad, dangerous ordeal, with a few seconds' reprieve before the next long jolt to decent souls, cannot be confined to one side of the screen. Not on seventeen daytime dramatic serials. When, for millions, a credible villain is a suicide, dead and well out of it, and a hero is a man compelled to live his drama out, the daylight view of what life is like is far less sunny on television, anyway, than the view by night.

—1972

WHO'S HERE? WHAT TIME IS IT?

Whatever expectations television may have raised at the outset, it is now clear that television is not a medium at all. It is an appliance, with peculiar relationships not only to owners and watchers but to other appliances and devices in, and outside, the house. It is, for example, the enemy of all forms of transportation—in particular, the car. You simply cannot drive while you are watching. Radios, on the other hand, have a strong rapport with cars. In a world of extremes, television would be at odds with much of what it now advertises. Not detergents, air conditioners, food, or deodorants; but tires, gasoline, airlines, even cosmetics. Television competes with most other appliances only for a few minutes of your time, and for the fuse; but there is a shadow world in which product and sheer idleness collide: If the commercial succeeds, and you go out to buy something, it means that a program has failed somehow. You are buying, not watching. In a world of extremes, you could buy a product direct, using some device on the set as you would use a credit card. Certain products bought that way would be in immediate conflict with the set itself: theater tickets, sleeping pills, books. In a world of extremes, television would be the enemy of all these. But it is not at all inconceivable that in some far-from-extreme world we should use our television sets to vote, just press an endorsing button and vote. The link between television and political action becomes daily more intimate. And to have politics thrown onto the screen like oddly selected clothes into a windowed washer-dryer is not good enough.

Whatever television coverage has done to political conventions in the past, this year [1972] it has probably terminated them in the form we knew. There was a time—until 1968, perhaps—when continuous convention coverage had a certain fascination. All those delegates milling about with balloons and interminable speeches, roll calls by state, tallies, making decisions in what appeared to be (still, in its odd way, is) one of the major processes of a free society. But now we've seen it, several times. This year, one party seemed to try to summon, in its speech and its style and its struggles, the America of the early sixties; the other, in its music and its apparent lack of struggle, the America of the late fifties. The two decades saw, and were frightened and repelled by each other. In the end, everyone was dangerously bored. Both conventions were not just subjected to television's scrutiny; they were almost entirely created, and exposed to death, by it—the scripted one and the unscripted one. There will have to be more conventions. Television will have to be at them. But it is unthinkable that we will have this crazy important political process staged in quite this way again.

It was not just the lack of suspense: A sports fan who knows that his team is overwhelmingly ahead will watch with great attention anyway. Nor was it length: A fan hopes for long games, play-offs, extra innings, marathons. Or pace: The chess games at Reykjavik, with their long intervals between moves—and even though they were played by proxy here—were thought by many viewers of Channel 13 to be of so much more immediate interest than politics that when Senator McGovern's pivotal economic speech to the New York Society of Security Analysts lasted beyond 1 P.M., the station's switchboard was jammed with calls demanding instant resumption of the proxy Spassky-Fischer games. It is probably one of the strengths of this country that not so many people are passionately interested in politics. But if the living room is to be brought to the convention floor, or the other way around, something more than a set of infinitely protracted, briefly frightening, briefly reassuring, utterly unenlightening foregone conclusions must be played out.

The Democratic Convention was to such a high degree a convention of the press that reporters meeting in the lobbies of Miami Beach hotels and asking "Who's here?" were inquiring not about delegates or politicians but about other members of the press. (At the Republican Convention, the density of Secret Service agents was particularly high.) The literary people present, as distinct from the professional reporters, knew with the least precision, and felt the least obligation to know precisely, what was going on at any time. For them, the reporter's basic question—

what the story is here, and what the point—was resolved autobiograph-
ically: Story and point were whatever happened to impinge on the author's sensibility. The form is valid, in its way, but it is not true, in the
sense in which news that becomes history is true. The position diamet-
rically opposite to the personal was expressed by Walter Cronkite when
he was interviewed by reporters from Top Value Television, an ad-hoc
collective of twenty-eight young freelance cable-television reporters from
groups called Raindance, Ant Farm, and Videofreex, who, to their own
surprise, received press accreditation to the Democratic Convention; they
then rented a house and, with inexpensive videotape equipment, did
some of the best reporting, including the mirror-within-mirror, intra-
media sort, from both conventions. "All this introspection," Walter
Cronkite said of television reporting, "is not good for a journalist."

Television was true to the story and the point of both conventions
only to the extent of showing, at full length, that the democratic process,
in what are, and probably ought to be, its most dramatic moments, is, of
necessity, a bore, a strain, partly a charade, and a mess. Whom, for example, did the Democratic delegates, some really elected in little pri-
maries, some appointed, some brought in by a quota system that might
in another context be an undemocratic farce—whom did they represent?
Whom have delegates at any convention ever really represented? Who
are they? The answer is probably that they have always been a gathering
of politically interested people, a mixture so large and various that
through it the public will, to the extent that there is a public will, is
expressed to some degree. An inadequate degree, it would seem this year,
when we were so uninformatively saturated with words, faces, and blurred
issues that the public will was, after continuous convention coverage,
actually less informed, less educated, and less clear than before television
came along.

Channel 13's idea of showing mainly what went on on the podium,
as what the delegates themselves saw, was a nice but bad idea. Delegates,
except at relatively crucial moments, pay less attention to the podium
than the network cameras do. Delegates pay most attention to who they
are and what is expected of them. They like to vote as they are instructed
to vote, and they like to cheer when they are supposed to cheer. For the
rest, the problems vary. The Kentucky Democratic delegation, for example, depressed by the accommodations in Miami Beach, commuted to

the convention each day from Fort Lauderdale. What they saw was a lot of the Florida highway system. Others saw familiar faces, like those of Charles Evers and Aaron Henry, from the days when Mississippi was still news. And entirely unfamiliar faces. There was a sense that new and unknown delegates, as representative in their dedication as anyone ever is of anybody else, would be present at conventions after this.

But the best-known faces, the most reassuring in their familiarity, were those of the network reporters, who, with their cumbersome equipment and their special problems, were the princelings of the event. In that strange combination of awe and downright hatred of the press which surfaces now—not just in the administration but in the public, too—the newspaper and magazine reporters were regarded as reviewers, who might, through bad notices, close the show. The television reporters had become very much the stars in the cast. When there was the simplest thing to explain, they tended to blow it. The parliamentary question of the California challenge was explicated as though it were Goedel's theorem, to be communicated, with sympathetic expressions of puzzlement, to subnormal grade-school children. (Top Value Television did much better here, too, in simply eavesdropping—if a reporter with videotape equipment can be said to eavesdrop—on an explanation by a McGovern aide to several delegations. He explained the California challenge, the South Carolina challenge, the relation between them. And then, in explaining the Alabama challenge, which was of no strategic importance to Mc-Govern supporters, he summed up, casually, inadvertently, one of the characteristic dilemmas of the times. "On this one, you can vote your conscience," he said, "or with your union.") The treatment of spokespersons for women's liberation was, on all networks, an uneasy travesty. Just before an interview with Gloria Steinem about the South Carolina challenge, one reporter found himself drawing some sort of analogy between the women's movement and a few out-of-step legs on a centipede. NBC congratulated Catherine Mackin for being the first full-time woman floor reporter at the conventions. She accepted the congratulations on just the right note: coolly.

Centipedes aside, the imagery at the conventions suggested that—and this, too, may be one of our society's great, unlikely strengths—very few Americans seem to be inhabiting the same country. Except for "Four More Years," "Now More Than Ever" was the most popular Nixon slogan of them all. "Now More Than Ever," on buttons, chanted, sung, as though every college graduate in America would not inevitably complete the line not with the "Nixon Now" of the slogan but with "seems it rich to die." Although the Republicans had, in some respects, the stronger women's-rights plank of the two parties, the overt Republican gesture to women's lib, a Women of Achievement brunch, featured not only the brunch's printed menu but its recipes, "low in cholesterol," to be used by the Women of Achievement in cooking for their families. The walk on the beach that ended Nixon's movie biography took a calculated risk of being compared to Kennedy beach-walking films. But the row of medals and ribbons that every delegate and reporter to the Republican Convention got (longer rows for higher degrees of Republican distinction) inevitably reminded everyone of the rows of medals—Sharpshooter, Marksman, and so on—that boys at summer camp used to get from the National Rifle Association. In trying to remember what the last—highest—in such a series of medals had been, or could be, more than one person morbidly thought Assassin. With the view of George Wallace lurching palely forward in his wheelchair toward the podium, and with the possibility that the safest campaign speeches from now on may be the ones made for television screens, television, in a world of extremes, began to seem not just a voting and vending machine but a box with leaders in it and an armed but passively watching electorate outside.

To the extent that television has a memory, the conventions were full of odd coincidences, easy ironies, memory loops. The key figure, for example, that Rockefeller has been: It was Rockefeller who, having failed to inform his chief supporter for the presidency in 1968, Spiro Agnew, that he did not choose to run, turned Agnew to Nixon and, ultimately, to the vice presidency. A respected, conciliatory, liberal Maryland governor had been gradually moved, first by criticism from black leaders of his remarks to them after disturbances in Baltimore, then by Rockefeller's move, and later by attacks from the press, who used to call him "Spiro who?" and a "buffoon"—he thereupon attacked the press—to positions rhetorically much more to the right. At the convention, he seemed to be returning to his conciliatory self. It was also Rockefeller who brought in Kissinger, with all that that implies for foreign policy. (Some members of the press indicated that they'd feel easier if there were a Kissinger of domestic policy as well.) There was Abbie Hoffman, trying to be photographed with that idol of what remains of the radical young: John Wayne. There was Ronald Reagan, now holding the office that Nixon lost to Pat Brown, and having won that office largely through the role he had played in the Goldwater campaign of 1964. On the other hand, there was Senator Tunney, a Kennedy friend, now holding the office he won from George Murphy, a screen actor of the right. There was the oddity that only Channel 13, covering the podium, caught the remarks of that Middle American hero, the quarterback Bart Starr. There was the Missouri Republican delegation casting the votes that put Nixon over the top—in a speech that included tributes to Harry Truman and Thomas Eagleton. There was the wife of the Democratic mayor of Milwaukee, who, having always been a model Democratic mayor's wife, virtually cracked up, calling the press to announce that she was not Martha Mitchell but that, what with one thing and another—the fact that the networks cut away from her husband's ten-minute convention speech, the fact that the committee for the beautification of Milwaukee had never given her a plaque, other things—she had become a Democrat for Nixon. At the Republican Convention, this lady gave a thirty-second seconding speech, which the networks caught, but without filling the background in. Television coverage included several uninformative slurs that passed as commentary: one network correspondent reporting, with an edge of contempt in his voice, that among the Republican VIPs was a "plasterer"; another likening the Nixonettes and the Young Voters for the President, who packed the galleries sometimes to cheer on cue, to the "sewer workers" Mayor Daley used to bring in to cheer. These were liberal-elitist slips and slurs about the ordinary working people. Plasterers, in politics, are not unlikely VIPs. There was Ribicoff again, another strange figure in conventions of the past: the Ribicoff to whom President Kennedy promised any cabinet position he would like, and gave HEW; the Ribicoff of 1968, who elicited from Mayor Daley and his delegation those epithets which so outraged another Illinois citizen, William Singer, that he ran for and became alderman and a leader of the delegation that unseated the Daley slate this year; the Ribicoff who, we were asked to believe, had been offered the vice presidential nomination this year and was said to have declined it. And there was another leader of the Illinois delegation, the Reverend Jesse L. Jackson, who, when the Illinois question was resolved, shouted in triumph "What time is it?" expecting the answering chant "Nation time!" but getting a factual "Four forty-five A.M."

———

At the ugly second session of the Republican Convention, Ronald Reagan and Barry Goldwater (Goldwater in an uncharacteristic tone of spite and bitterness) seemed to appeal to an odd anger in what had not really been such angry delegates. They had had four years; in all likelihood they would have four more. It was unclear what all that sudden anger was about. Reporters, except for those who have made punditry their source of income, do not like to prognosticate. No one wants to risk saying, "I have seen the future and it works." No one quite wants to risk the opposite position, "I have seen the future and I'm scared," either. The television people, with their forecasts of tallies and their buildup of a nonexistent 1976 candidacy for Senator Charles Percy (who seemed to have few supporters, if any, among delegates or elsewhere), limited their predictions to speculations of the most trivial sort. But, besides recording what will become history, journalism has to risk some plausible conclusion about what it all means, repeats, and foretells. Television, perhaps necessarily mining just the surface of issues and persons, clarified nothing of what is before the voter or what will be. Maybe conventions have always had this sense of the muddy and futile. Now that television has so thoroughly and drearily exposed it, conventions will just have to change. Something deeper than images and phrases that mean one thing to people of a given lifestyle and the opposite to people of another lifestyle altogether will have to be presented, and presented in a deeper and more honest way. All of us do, after all, inhabit the same country. We are almost all, one way or another, Middle Americans. Few people, having watched these conventions, have learned anything, changed their minds in any way, felt happier, or cared more about the processes of our society. The conventions, as they were televised, just pushed us all a bit more helplessly apart from any common interest. Now that, by virtue of our sets, we all have floor passes, that is going to have to change. As created this year for television, the shows were awful—presenting to each party an unenlightening window into the other and an unsatisfactory image of itself. Maybe that was what some of the joylessness and anger were about.

—1972

COOKIE, OSCAR, GROVER, HERRY, ERNIE, AND COMPANY

When a seven-foot, yellow-feathered bird who is subject to depression attempts to seat himself upon the letter *h* and fails, it is no longer simply an event in children's television, or even in the media. It is part of the intellectual history of a generation, who are already in important ways the children of *Sesame Street*. There is an idiocy in current discourse, which calls things about which people can be angry or mistaken "controversial." In that sense, *Sesame Street* and its sequel, *The Electric Company*, are controversial programs. It is as though all the lessons of New Deal federal planning and the sixties experience of the "local people," the techniques of the totalitarian slogan and the American commercial, the devices of film and the cult of the famous, the research of educators and the talent of artists had combined in one small experiment to sell, by means of television, the rational, the humane, and the linear to little children.

The human characters of *Sesame Street* live in a brownstone on an integrated urban slum block, where, in the company of cloth figures called Muppets—most of which are brightly colored and furry—they teach, among other things, the alphabet, induction, friendliness, geometric forms, and counting. Oscar, the green-furred grouch who inhabits a trash can, where he collects fish heads, mud, an old sneaker, a petrified brownie, and who makes occasional trips, for the sake of his collection, to the dump, is not just a creature of whimsy, with a tendency to rant; he is something of an expert on ecology. His neighbor is the inexhaustibly obliging blue-furred Muppet Grover, who will run great distances, interminably, to illustrate the concepts "near" and "far," who will patiently deliver to a restaurant customer the letters missing from his alphabet soup, who will dance, sing, and demonstrate in waltz time,

"Around, around, around, around, over, under, and through," and who will be frightened out of his hiccups and into unconsciousness by a not altogether successful creature called the Snuffleupagus, whom all the human members of the cast, black and white, Puerto Rican and Anglo, still take to be a figment of the seven-foot bird's imagination.

Small children from poor or middle-class families who watch *Sesame Street* do better on cognitive tests and in first grade than children who do not watch it. Children who watch it frequently do better than children who watch it rarely. Children who begin to watch it at the age of three learn more rapidly than children who begin at four. Eighty percent of America's twelve million preschool children have watched it. Ninety-seven percent of American households now have television. Yet Joan Ganz Cooney, the founder of the Children's Television Workshop, which created both *Sesame Street* and *The Electric Company*, points out that in a survey of activities favored by preschool children, watching television ranks second from the bottom, followed only by "petting my dog." "They don't dislike petting their dog," Mrs. Cooney says. "It's just not high on the list of their priorities." Neither, evidently, is watching television. It doesn't play with them, or, normally, offer them the pleasure of acquired competence in anything. But lots of children, particularly disadvantaged children, are becoming (in an expression the Children's Television Workshop once used in research but now regrets) "zombies"—riveted, without any discernible reaction, to the television set; getting, within a year or two, beyond the age where they have the natural aptitude of learning to read, for example.

In the first year of *Sesame Street*'s existence, a Muppet, a cartoon, or a famous person from a network program (Bill Cosby, Pat Paulsen, all the Cartwrights from *Bonanza*) would recite the whole alphabet each day, not just for the sake of repetition but out of concern that a child who saw only ten letters in a single program might be misled into thinking he had mastered the whole thing. One day, the research staff discovered what has since been known as the James Earl Jones Effect. Mr. Jones recited the twenty-six letters slowly, in a tone of menace, staring directly into the camera. At the first recitation, children repeated the letters in his pauses; at the second, they were beginning to recognize the letters as they appeared on the screen beside him; after that, they began very quickly and with pleasure to recite the alphabet before him. The alphabet has now acquired, through the prestige the celebrities brought to it at first, and through later developments among the regular live cast, cartoons, and Muppets, such currency in preschool circles that daily repetitions are no longer necessary. Counting, too, has gone up since the first year, from ten to twenty; and when Big Bird persists in believing that the alphabet is a single, beautiful word pronounced "ab-ka-def-gi-jekyl-mnop-ker-stew-uk-zee," which he can sing but not decipher, nobody seems confused, except him.

On *Sesame Street*, there has been an amiable, senile Muppet pedant, Herbert Birdsfoot, who is in the habit of addressing Kermit, the Muppet frog, as "young man," and who, being profoundly devoted to physical education, found himself stuck one day in the middle of a deep knee bend. "Young man," he said, looking pensively at the floor, to Kermit, "do you realize that you have webbed feet?" Kermit himself has given many lecture-demonstrations, among them one that embroiled him with the letter W, that program's sponsor. Every program is "sponsored" by a few letters and numbers, which are given elaborate commercials in graphics and song. "Zap. Zap. Zap. Zap" may not be everybody's description of the four lines of the letter W, but it was Kermit's, and the shaggy blue-furred Cookie Monster ate the lecture's subject anyway, transforming it, with successive bites, into an askew N, a V, a tilted I, and nothing. A substitute W began to wiggle, walk, and wobble—in a kind of visual, extra-prose equivalent of onomatopoeia (the word "path" on *The Electric Company* walks down one)—and ultimately wrestle (a phonemic mistake, unusual on the program) with Kermit until he weakened. Kermit has had other misfortunes with lessons. When he was counting four eggs, for example, they hatched, and the chickens began to walk away, leaving three, and then two, and then one. "All right," Kermit said, "there's only one chicken left, so let's count it." The program is extremely patient with error and frustration.

There is the Muppet Ernie, neurotic, easily moved to tears, particularly by the letter E, with which his name begins. A Muppet salesman, with a green face and a blue nose, dressed in a shirt, tie, trousers, jacket, black hat, and trenchcoat, has repeatedly tried to sell Ernie the number 8. "Hang it on the wall," he suggests at the beginning of his sales pitch. "Next time you wanna know how many legs an octopus has . . . next time you wanna know how many reindeer Santa Claus has . . . next time you wanna know what time you eat your breakfast . . ." and, with each sinister and ingratiating phrase, he flashes the

8 inside his trenchcoat furtively toward Ernie. It costs a nickel. Ernie does not buy it. *Sesame Street's* attitudes toward consumerism are skeptical, except in the realm of learning.

"Our next contestant," says the Muppet master of ceremonies in a little parody of the quiz show *Concentration*, "is a monster from Sesame Street." The contestant is the Cookie Monster, known to some as Monster, to some as Cookie, and to fathers in the world outside, at bedtime, as a difficult creature to imitate the voice of. Cookie is a fanatic, undeviating in the quality of his obsession. He eats things. Many lessons on *Sesame Street* are terminated when something eats them. But Cookie, who has of late been eating mainly cookies, is a junkie. "To me, your nose is a cookie," he once said to another Muppet in a desperate moment. He sees cookies in all things circular: a rubber-tire swing, or a bicycle wheel. Geometric forms are among the program's many subjects. When cookies arrive, he tends to eat the entire shipment, but he is moved to empathy at the sight of a human being temporarily deprived of a cookie. "How sad," he says. "You taking it so well." He has never quite correctly learned the language. Other characters on *Sesame Street* use dialect, make grammatical errors, even speak in Spanish. The black expression "Give me some skin" has now become so common among characters asking for a handshake that Muppets say "Give me some fur." On the quiz show, Cookie won by losing. There were four numbers on the wall, concealing prizes. As in *Concentration*, the object was to name the numbers that concealed matching prizes. Cookie failed to match anything. He lost a jet plane and won a consolation cookie. *Sesame Street* does not overvalue competition.

Herry, a disheveled blue Muppet with a magenta nose (no program is a better argument for color television, which is, unlike color movies, in every way better than black-and-white), once confided his secret, the whole alphabet, with shyness, to Grover, who repeated it to several other Muppets, who repeated it, in turn, with incredulity. It was unlike Grover to betray a confidence, but, as a teaching method, it was an advance over several educational strategies of progressive schools in, say, the forties and fifties. I can remember classes learning to sing, "This is / the symphony / that Mr. Schubert never finished." *Sesame Street* uses the best techniques available, and develops new ones. There is an inspired, unlikely reading song composed of traffic signs: "In, Out, Park, Walk, Yield, Enter, Exit, One Way . . ." The whole program has this sort of odd, useful intelligence. There are beautiful animations: a fakir who counts on his fingers and, since the desired total is twenty, sprouts two extra arms before dissolving into the psychedelic, and doing the whole thing again in Spanish; a bluesy serpent who sings, "I'm Sammy the snake. I go sssss in the morning"; a pride of uncaged, ferocious xs, one of which leaps to take its place in the word "exit"; cartoons by the Hubleys and Maurice Sendak; an instructive appearance by the Pink Panther. There are short films of real wildlife, some of them accompanied by instructions: "Everybody scratch" (which was redeemed by clips of penguins grooming and a baboon daintily scratching his wrist); some of them accompanied by music: a whale having his teeth brushed to the lyrics "I got those I-can't-get-enough-of-brushin'-till-I-make-my-teeth-white blues"; some of them silent.

There are "Moonbird" voice-overs of uncoy, childish voices, and appearances by very small real children, some of whom fail, with the utmost confidence, to follow the instructions for such simple games as "Simon Says." There are little discussions of seasons, weather, sirens, rain, and nightfall. And there are real adults. They are the least interesting characters on the programs, partly because they lack the ingenuity of the fantastic, partly because their lives are meant to be so exemplary, unfrightening, and normal. They are a bit flat. Like other creatures on *Sesame Street*, and even on *The Electric Company*, they often sing off-key. Like the songs of other creatures, too, their songs are often carefully unrhymed, for fear that a child will catch only a too-tight rhyme scheme and lose the meaning.

What happens when an utterly charismatic presence appears on the program was illustrated a month ago. Jesse Jackson, once an associate of Martin Luther King, Jr., and the head of Chicago's Operation Breadbasket, sat on the stoop of a *Sesame Street* brownstone. In cadences very moving and familiar, Mr. Jackson led a mesmerized integrated group of very little children in speaking such lines as "I am somebody. I may be four. But I am somebody. I am black. I am brown. I am white. I am somebody. I can learn anything. I can grow. I can be President. I can be governor. I can be mayor. I can change the world. Beautiful children can grow up and make the whole world beautiful. What time is it? Nation time. What time is it? Nation time," and so on. The performance was followed by Kermit's singing of one of the program's most popular laments: "It's not that easy being green, having to spend each day the color of the leaves." Oscar the grouch soon demanded to know whether the children were listening to him. Oscar told them, characteristically, that he did not care to see their ugly little faces, and unsentimentally slammed the lid of his trash can. There was no sense in which Jesse Jackson's leading the children was controversial. But, for much of the country, the performance, and the integrated life on *Sesame Street* in general, may have been maddening. Nothing but the once apparently token but now vital appearance of black performers on network television would have put many adults in the frame of mind to stand it. The techniques of teaching and of demagogy are never quite distinct; one does learn some things by rote or chanting, because that is the most efficient way to learn them. But the people who run *Sesame Street* have so far been extremely wise about whom they permit to appear on the steps of that brownstone.

Sesame Street and, in other ways, *The Electric Company* are, with lapses, the most intelligent and important programs on television. That is not saying much yet. Their combined annual budget is $13 million—immense in terms of educational television, minuscule in comparison with programs on commercial stations or the cost of reaching an equivalent number of children by conventional teaching methods. The money is drawn from the federal Office of Education, from foundations, and, recently, from sales of products—books, records, toys, Muppets, plastic letters and numbers—designed to help in teaching and to help the two programs become, to some degree, self-supporting. It is a very powerful collaboration of adults for children. Young adults from the Neighborhood Youth Corps, who feel that they themselves were ripped off by the school system through inadequate preparation, are teaching their younger brothers and sisters in local communities, in cooperation with the Workshop, with funds from the federal government. It is very hard for anybody, except the silly and the idle, to argue that learning to read itself is dated or a rip-off. A lot of what the programs create is really art—which is extraordinary, considering that the ideology here, the catechism, the product, is just letters, geometric forms, decency, and numbers.

No one but a few educators, who have argued on both sides of several questions—whether *Sesame Street* is too authoritarian or too permissive, too middle class or too poor, too fast-paced or too unambitious—and one English TV program director, who used all these arguments simultaneously, has taken very strong exception to *Sesame Street* yet. There is going to be a *Plaza Sesamo*, a *Vila Sésamo*, a *Sesamstrase*, and possibly a *Rue Sesame*, in addition to the English version of the program in the fifty countries where it already runs. But *The Electric Company* has higher, later stakes. It was designed specifically for the second-grader who is behind in reading. It teaches only verbal skills. But the audience consists of people who are older and younger than the target children. The younger ones, still also *Sesame Street* watchers, are not a problem. It is common these days to find a three-year-old, who still has trouble speaking, sounding out the brand name on a tea bag or a box of breakfast cereal. *The Electric Company* has a black hippie reading freak, called Easy Reader, who dotes on legible matchbook covers. It has a daily soap-opera parody, called *Love of Chair*, in which almost nothing ever happens. "The boy," the sentence reads, the announcer says, the scene demonstrates, "is sitting on the chair." Or "The chair is sitting on the boy." Accompanied by conventional soap organ music, the announcer concludes, "For the answer to these and other questions (What number are you calling? And what ever happened to Naomi?), tune in tomorrow for *Love of Chair*." For some reason, this feature is extremely popular throughout the country. *The Electric Company* is used in eighteen thousand schools.

There is also an enlightening cooking lesson, given by "Julia Grownup," who once taught the "ill" syllable by producing a grilled dill pickle with chilled vanilla filling. Miss Grownup, played by an excellent moronic comedienne, Judy Graubart, produced her masterpiece when she was demonstrating plurals. Regretfully, as she was making a fresh-fruit salad, Miss Graubart removed ss from her list, as she found herself improvidently with a bowl of grape, a box of raisin—"Can we get a close-up of the raisin? It's a fine one"—and a solitary apple. To her great relief, she had a wheelbarrow of lettuce in her kitchen. She placed the three pieces of fruit upon it, and in dressing her salad she proudly added three plaid children's dresses.

The Electric Company paints letters on everything—on newspapers, balloons, shoe soles, subway turnstiles, rows of medals, hats. It uses syllables as units of sound and units of meaning; it anthropomorphizes and ceaselessly alliterates them, as in two short, beautiful animations by the Hubleys: one featuring a languid nightclub singer who breathes, "Tr ue, bl ue S ue," the other starring a snarled green multilegged snakelike creature who shoots C into *ool* at the billiard table and then produces C *ool, p ool f ool.* A character called J. Arthur Crank regularly telephones to protest the similarity between the "ue" and the "oo" sounds, and other injustices in the language, but he doesn't work out. A tortured horse in an animated cartoon about a cowboy who persists in singing—off-key, as the "ie" sounds don't match—"I could die for a piece of your pie" works better.

There is a frenetic, high-powered quiz program whose object is "The Secret Sound," and whose master of ceremonies, Skip Hinnant, another excellent comic, is simply beside himself whenever anybody makes it. On a day when the secret sound was "ar," the master of ceremonies was ecstatic when the contestant, Bill Cosby, spoke of someone who "gave me my big start." He pivoted a full circle with enthusiasm when the contestant mentioned that he "works very hard." He became totally hysterical by the time he heard the sentence "It's pretty far." The contestant, already loaded down with prizes, had his sleeves, his collar, and his mouth stuffed with money when he asked for a "cart" and went to pieces. The same sort of thing happened on a day when the sound was "th." Bill Cosby appeared as an absentminded fellow with an umbrella in his jacket pocket, said he was too nervous to think, that his age was thirty, that he just couldn't hold another thing, and added a final, fatal "Thank you."

Comparatives are illustrated by the words, by their placement on the screen, by music, or by anything else that will help explain. "High, higher, highest" is a nightmare in semantics, graphics, music synethesia. But there are graceful things, like a fine cartoon with a character who introduces herself as Myrna and then proceeds to name and gather up Myrna's lamp, Myrna's curtains, Myrna's fireplace, Myrna's other possessions, until she falls, by sheer weight, through the floor—and goes on about Myrna's furnace and Myrna's basement until she has altogether thoroughly illustrated the possessive.

There is a talentless but friendly child rock group, called The Short Circus. But there is also a splendid detective and decoder who, with one foot perpetually in a wastepaper basket, puts scrambled messages through a machine that looks like a washing machine with roller dryer. He studies such enigmas as "key's The doormat. the under," looks for capital letters and periods, and comes up with such formulations as "The key's the doormat. There you have it! The key *is* the doormat." He points out this nonpossessive use of the apostrophe, long before the actual message is correctly deciphered, with that tremendous enthusiasm and utter conviction that the entire cast brings to the most elementary spellings and inductions. "Mad" kicking the sinister silent "e" from "made"; a broom sweeping the word "litter" away; a mover unloading the letters "b," "d," and "e" from a van, assembling a word, and going to sleep on it; a cartoon Message Man who is always too slow to sound out instructions to "Run!" "Step back!" "Duck" (in this one, he is actually clipped from the air by a duck) or "Do not bother this giant person"—it is all still very uneven. It is also hard to predict what effects it will have on notions of written prose, which has its limitations.

Rita Moreno demonstrates punctuation with a group in a Latin rock song. There are animated parodies of 2001, in which, with Richard Strauss music and a giant slab with metaphysical overtones, the syllables "oo," "all," "ee," and "alk" are created by seismic disturbance. (It does not seem to matter whether parodies are perceived by children as parodies; they tend to keep the program alive for the creators.) There is a subsequent bit in which a sage speaks of the four basic "alks" of life, and expresses her belief that life is a beanstalk. Minds are constantly kept shuttling between rules and exceptions, jokes and hard sells. The program always ends with a lightbulb being turned off and the phrase "And now, the last word." In the past, it has been "pajamas," "sneeze," "dim," "reach," and "garbage." Next year, for complicated reasons, *The Electric Company* is going to make great use of the rebus.

What all this energy produces is very hard to measure. A lot of adults—veterans, prisoners, migrant workers, other people—watch it. A few weeks ago, in Jackson, Mississippi, Big Bird conducted the seventy-five-piece Jackson Symphony Orchestra. He led an integrated audience of more than ten thousand children and their parents in a passionate recitation of the alphabet. He counted to ten. The audience, including a few retarded adults, clapped and counted with him. Big Bird kept addressing the regular orchestra conductor, whose name is Lewis Dalvit, as "Mr. Dingbat," recalling that other complicated political presence Archie Bunker. A Jackson policeman drove white, black, and Chicano members of the cast to the Jackson airport. The mayor had welcomed them when they came to town. Nation time.

The Children's Television Workshop has seventeen full-time community organizers, working with local groups, parents, teenagers, teachers, anybody, throughout the country. The organizer for Appalachia, Paul Elkins, is based in Clinch Valley, beside the River Clinch, in St. Paul, Virginia, where the biggest local employer is the Clinchfield Coal company. Mr. Elkins was once a school principal, but now he works for *Sesame Street* and *The Electric Company*. When local people suspect the programs of Communism—because there are so many black people on them—Mr. Elkins, who was born and raised in Appalachia, reassures them, and changes the subject. He visits the people in shacks and schools. At the Riverview Elementary School in Clinch Valley one recent morning, three classes were watching *The Electric Company*, in color. The children deciphered the message "ho, Silver." "Hi" with enthusiasm—while the cowboy on the screen was still remarking, "I said it to the horse, and he just looked at me." They were very pleased with *Love of Chair*. At a nearby shack, a four-year-old boy had recently rubbed his eyes with oven cleaner, but his father, who was home on welfare, told Mr. Elkins he could not have watched *Sesame Street* anyway, since the television set, in a local expression for being out of order, had been "torn out" for two weeks. "You can turn the thing wide open and you can't get a sound—not even 'Bonanza,' " he said. The name "Brenda" and the letters "Bre," "Br," and "Bren" were printed all over the sagging front porch of another shack near the rusting fragments of a car, the coal heap, and the garbage in the front yard. A young woman said her four-year-old daughter, Brenda, liked both *Sesame Street* and *The Electric Company*. A grandmother, farther along the hollow, said that one of the seven children of her three unmarried daughters particularly liked *Sesame Street*. "Ain't no such thing as not watching it for Walter," she said. A two-year-old with a bleeding eye walked in. His mother explained that someone had thrown a rock at a chicken the other day, "and he was just coming round the corner." *Sesame Street* was not on the air just then. A soap opera, *Another World*, was. Everyone was watching. At the last shack in the hollow, a mother of three children, who had participated in workshops for mothers of *Sesame Street*'s most regular watchers, was asked by Mr. Elkins whether her four-year-old boy still watched the program. "Nope," she said.

—1972

G. GORDON LIDDY IN AMERICA

"His eyes. They're so cold," one woman said to another, on the sidewalk outside a radio station in Portland, Oregon. "I've never seen such flat, cold eyes. He looks just like a reptile. A *reptile*."

When Frances Purcell Liddy heard, in Oxon Hill, Maryland, that Robert Conrad, an actor, might buy the screen rights to her husband's autobiography, *Will*, she was pleased. She had seen Conrad on television, in *A Man Called Sloan*, and noticed what she called a twinkle in his eyes. She thought photographs somehow never managed to convey the twinkle in the eyes of her husband, G. Gordon Liddy.

Liddy himself had overheard the comment of the lady in Oregon; he knew, as was evident from the lady's tone, that she intended to express intense admiration. At the same time, since the comment was accompanied and followed by a hopeful glance at him, he thought politeness obliged him to reply. "I didn't know what to say," he said, regretfully, some moments later. "I just didn't feel I could say thank you." So he said nothing.

Will, by G. Gordon Liddy, was published in late April by St. Martin's Press. *Time*, in its issue of April 21, 1980 (cover story, "Is Capitalism Working?"), had run excerpts from the book, under the heading "Exclusive: Watergate Sphinx Finally Talks." The excerpts contained five pieces of information which seemed to determine all subsequent coverage of the book, in reviews and by the press: that Liddy, as a small boy in the care of a German maid, had been impressed by prewar Nazi radio broadcasts and even, until his father explained to him what Naziism was, inspired by them; that, as a fearful and neurasthenic child, and later, as a man, in times of stress, he had tested his courage by subjecting himself to physical ordeals, most disturbingly the holding of flames to his arms and hands; that, being less tall and less good at mathematics than he would have liked, he hoped to, and in fact did, marry a tall blond woman who was good at math, a choice which, he wrote, was influenced by considerations of his "gene pool"; that he had apparently been prepared, as a civil servant, if ordered to and for reasons of "national security," to kill the columnist Jack Anderson; and that he had later been prepared, in prison and for reasons that seemed unclear even to him, to kill his fellow prisoner, former friend, and co-conspirator in the break-in at the Watergate, E. Howard Hunt.

Beginning on the Monday of the week in which that issue of *Time* appeared, the switchboard at St. Martin's Press was overwhelmed with local and long-distance requests for interviews. On Thursday, Liddy was scheduled to be interviewed on the morning news broadcasts of two networks—ABC's *Good Morning America* and NBC's *Today*. To talk with Liddy, ABC had invited "a member of our *Good Morning America* family," Jack Anderson; for *Today*, NBC had invited E. Howard Hunt. Liddy and Anderson, who had never met, agreed to appear together. Hunt had accepted NBC's invitation (a book of his own, a thriller, was about to be published); but both he and Liddy had, separately, insisted that they appear on separate segments of the program, that they not actually meet. *Today*'s producers hoped, all the same, to bring about a confrontation on the air.

Within ABC, as it happened, there had already been an angry struggle over Liddy—between the network's entertainment and its news executives. The news branch claimed that he was news and that, as news, he belonged on an early-evening news broadcast. Entertainment claimed him for the mixed format of a morning show. News lost this dispute, but before it was resolved, in the late hours of Tuesday night, ABC news had filmed an interview with Liddy, which was virtually sneaked onto the air at 11:30 P.M., on Wednesday night's *Nightline*, several hours before Liddy's scheduled *Good Morning America* debut. Since this scoop marked a little insurrection, Liddy's name was not listed in newspaper advertisements for Wednesday's *Nightline*. News listed him instead for 20/20, on Thursday, at 10:00 P.M. Viewers of ABC's night news programs thus had two consecutive surprises. On Wednesday night, an unannounced appearance by G. Gordon Liddy. On Thursday night, the following cryptic announcement:

This final note. The interview with G. Gordon Liddy scheduled for tonight on 20/20 was broadcast last night on *Nightline*.

At 6:45 on Thursday morning, G. Gordon Liddy sat in the makeup
room of the *Good Morning America* studios, on West Sixty-third Street
in New York. He was dressed, as usual, in a dark suit and tie; and he
was talking to the makeup people with a combination of formality, at-
tentiveness, and good manners, which seemed always a little to discon-
cert people who met him for the first time. He had signed three copies
of *Will* for members of the ABC crew. A newspaper reporter, one of
several assigned to Liddy that first week, mentioned that a letter Liddy
wrote in prison had recently been sold for $125. "In that case my wife
is sitting on a fortune," Liddy said. Outside in the hall, Jack Anderson
could be heard. "I don't have to shake hands with him, do I?" Anderson
said; "I may have to restrain myself from punching him in the nose."
Some moments later, when they were introduced, Liddy and Anderson
shook hands. They entered the lighted set at the front of a darkened
studio. They took armchairs across from each other, on either side of the
anchorman, David Hartman, who sat on an ample sofa, among plants,
yellow walls, bookshelves, lamps, a coffee table. "It's six fifty-four. Quiet,
folks," a voice said to the people scattered in the dark behind the cameras. "Forty-five seconds, folks. Fifteen seconds. Quiet. Shh." A stillness.
"Good morning," Hartman said to his viewers across the country. "It's
seven o'clock." He introduced G. Gordon Liddy, "the best-known of the
Watergate conspirators." He mentioned Liddy's book, "In it, he reveals
that he had plans to kill Jack Anderson." Then he said, "Good morning,
Jack. And good morning, Mr. Liddy." The program, and G. Gordon
Liddy's eight-week tour of America, were under way.

"Perhaps more than any of the Watergate characters," *Time* had said,
in an obviously bewildered introduction to its excerpts, "Liddy embodied
the principles underlying the scandal that destroyed a President." It
seemed clear, however, not just from the excerpts but from Liddy's conduct in all the years since Watergate, that whatever the "principles"
underlying the scandal may have been, no Watergate character embodied
them less. Ever since the first reports, in 1972, of the events that became
known as Watergate—throughout the trials, the Ervin Committee hearings, the impeachment inquiry, the resignation of Richard Nixon from

the presidency of the United States, the various prison terms, acquittals, memoirs, commutations—the conduct of G. Gordon Liddy, and his alone, had seemed in two respects remarkable. While other participants talked, in truths, or lies, or half-truths, Gordon Liddy kept his silence. And, in the midst of a political scandal never completely understood but obviously in important ways and on an unprecedented scale financial, Liddy shredded cash. The second fact was less widely remarked on than the first. Destruction of cash, from Natasha's burning of rubles in *The Brothers Karamazov* to American millionaires' lighting their cigars with dollars in the tabloids, has always been an imaginatively powerful idea. Amid bribes, hush money, "contributions" foreign and domestic, private and corporate, voluntary and extorted, open and secret, Liddy's first instinct, when the break-in was discovered, had been not to take or to hide dollars but to destroy them. And far from eliciting money for his silence—in a story that consisted so largely of paid silences alternating with testimony designed to exonerate a speaker, implicate others, get a lenient sentence—Liddy was left, after fifty-two months in various prisons, with debts, for fines and legal fees, of more than $300,000. People thought him crazy, or sinister, or honorable, or even heroic; but Liddy was known primarily for his refusals, and in these he was alone.

Silence and, apparently, indifference to money. Apart from that, in a country that was reading, and watching, tales of espionage, detection, mysteries, thrillers, Liddy was known to have been at least twice, on June 17, 1972, in Democratic headquarters at the Watergate; on September 3, 1971, at the office of Daniel Ellsberg's psychiatrist, a conspirator, a burglar, and a sort of secret agent. Before that, he had been a lawyer, a candidate for Congress, a prosecutor in Dutchess County, for five years an agent of the FBI. He seemed to combine, then, in his person several characters in contemporary fiction: the criminal, the policeman, the district attorney, and the spy. In the Ellsberg break-in, moreover, Liddy was a government employee, acting in his official capacity, on the authority of high officials of the government. In the Watergate burglary, he was a private citizen, employed by politicians to act in knowing violation of existing law. Though the personnel and even the objectives of the two events may have been similar, their implications were vastly different. Liddy somehow managed, with these two acts, to pose successively a Nuremberg or Eichmann question (When is a man obliged, in conscience, to disobey what he believes to be a lawful governmental order?)

and the key question of civil disobedience (When does a man have the right, in conscience, to defy certain laws within a legal system on whose basic protection he relies?). One is the problem of a functionary, in a government's abuse of power; the other, almost on the contrary, the problem of a rebel. Both acts occur within a system which the actor regards as, on the whole, legitimate and benign. Both questions were, of course, formulated most precisely and in the greatest depth by Hannah Arendt. But never together—that is, as the predicament of a single spirit. And never, certainly, for a man like Liddy, who took, as Ms. Arendt pointed out a civil disobedient is obliged to take, the legal consequences of his own acts (those years in prison); who never did obey an order at variance with his conscience; and who never, so far as is known or likely, did or caused physical harm to anyone at all. Finally, Liddy had, in his own way and almost incidentally, played out a drama of ex-radicals in the fifties, refusing not just to name names or to extricate himself at the expense of former associates but to invoke any constitutional protection for his reticence.

Throughout the years, and until the publication of *Will*, there was, inevitably, an impression that Liddy's silence must conceal some vital secret, some great fact or explanation to complete the story of events in which he played a part. "You have played a vitally important role in a major historical development," Stewart Alsop wrote to Liddy, in July 1973, "and it seems to me that by now you owe it to yourself, and indeed to history, to say more about that role." *Will* has many qualities, and contains several kinds of information: but one thing clear from it is that Liddy knew nothing quite so broad, even about Watergate. During most of the cover-up, he was in prison. Before that, if one can trust his account of what he knew, and, on the basis of evidence in and outside the book, it is almost impossible not to trust it, Liddy's own pieces of Watergate information, though not unimportant, were few. Liddy knew that he had told Richard Kleindienst, the Attorney General of the United States, in considerable detail about the Watergate break-in, within hours of its occurrence. Kleindienst rebuffed him, and did nothing to further the investigation until April 1973, when John Dean's testimony to federal prosecutors led to Kleindienst's resignation—along with H. R. Halde-man's, John Ehrlichman's, and Dean's. Liddy knew that Robert Mardian, former assistant attorney general for internal security, had taken charge, as early as June 20, 1972, of the initial phases of the cover-up. And he knew that Gordon Strachan, Haldeman's chief assistant at the White House, had known about the break-ins at the Watergate. None of these three men went to prison. The statute of limitations has, in any event, run out on all Watergate offenses, one reason for Liddy's having postponed till now the writing of his book. Kleindienst was never indicted for obstruction of justice. Mardian was indicted and convicted of conspiracy, but acquitted on appeal. Strachan, who like Kleindienst and Mardian persistently and indignantly proclaimed his innocence, was never convicted of anything and was particularly commended for his candor at the Ervin Committee hearings by the chairman, Sam Ervin.

From a strictly Watergate point of view, these may all have been facts of historic consequence—particularly the information about Strachan. There had always been a missing link (specifically, a missing memorandum in a numbered series of twenty memoranda) in the chain of evidence from Watergate to Strachan; as there had always been missing pieces (specifically, just what facts Liddy had told him) in the link to Kleindienst. The information about Mardian, whose indictment rested on quite other evidence, was entirely new. Liddy, of course, had details of many other kinds, but Liddy's allegations about the three men, if he had spoken at the time, would have led, directly and inescapably, to the President; and it is Strachan who would inevitably, by implicating Haldeman, have implicated the President, for having authorized the break-in after all. In that event, on the plane of the historical what-if, if Liddy had, at the time, told all he knew, it is almost certain that President Nixon, immediately after the 1972 election, would have taken responsibility for the break-in, explained it somehow, and gone on to serve out his constitutional term. It was, after all, the cover-up, prolonged, intricate, disintegrating over a period of more than twenty months, that became finally intolerable; it took more than two years of extraordinary events and processes before a mechanism for removal of the President was in place. Of that long disintegration of the cover-up, Liddy, who tries carefully to distinguish what he speculates about from what he knows as fact, has only an impression. A sweep of Jeb Magruder's hand toward a desk drawer which held Republicans' derogatory information about Democrats caused Liddy to believe that the purpose of the break-in was to find what derogatory information the Democrats had about Republicans. Liddy does not dwell at all upon these, his Watergate scoops, such as they are (three historic felonies at the highest level, one sweep of the hand). And in the course of all his travels, no interviewer, Watergate reporter, or reviewer mentioned any but the last, the sweep. And few mentioned that.

What they did all mention, and want to talk about, was Liddy as a Nazi sympathizer; Liddy as a racist believer in genetics; Liddy as a burner of his own hand; Liddy, and this with the greatest fascination, as a man prepared to kill. Also, increasingly and perhaps surprisingly, Liddy as a philosopher about the human condition and Liddy as a commentator on American political affairs. He was asked, everywhere, what he would do in President Carter's place about foreign policy, what were his thoughts on the nature of good and evil, how people ought to raise their children (the Liddys have five, two daughters, three sons, between the ages of seventeen and twenty-two), what is the relation between hope and death, free enterprise and regulation, military preparedness and the democratic system, and so on. Some interviewers addressed him in the most respectful terms, as a kind of statesman. Others seemed to bait him as a dangerous fanatic. Others still to treat him as though there were no distinction, as though statesman, fanatic, writer, presumptive killer were all essentially the same.

"Tell me, Mr. Liddy," a distinctly hostile television interviewer asked him, in Los Angeles, right after the failed helicopter rescue mission to Iran, "if Richard Nixon were still President, would our hostages still be in Teheran?" She spoke with an air of wariness and triumph, as though she had risked the violence of a madman to provoke an item of sensational news. "If Richard Nixon were still President," Liddy replied, amiably and without hesitation, "the *Shah* would still be in Teheran."

All over the country, interviewers asked him who he thought had really killed President Kennedy. "I'm not a believer in conspiracy theories of history," he would say. "Such a conspiracy would have had to be too large. So many people could never keep a secret." He was often asked the identity of Woodward and Bernstein's informant, Deep Throat. Each time, he replied that he was virtually certain, just as any reader of *All the President's Men* would be certain, that there was no single such person, that it was a literary device to cover a variety of sources. And then he would add that since he was in prison during most of the period covered by the book, he could know no more about the matter than anybody else.

Sometimes, in fact quite frequently, in the middle of Liddy's most reasoned and polite replies, there would emerge what Michael Denneny, Liddy's young editor at St. Martin's Press—a friend and student, as it happens, of Hannah Arendt and Harold Rosenberg at the University of Chicago; also, a founding editor of the gay magazine *Christopher Street*— would characterize as the imp. A passage in Liddy's book, for instance, describes a time in his childhood when, ashamed of having wept over a wounded squirrel, he decided to nerve himself for the army, in case that war should last long enough for him to join it, by helping to kill and pluck chickens in a neighbor's chicken coop. "How," an outraged and trembling lady asked him in San Francisco, "can you equate the killing of chickens with the taking of a human life?" "Well, madam," Liddy said, "you have to begin somewhere."

Dick Cavett, who devoted three successive programs to interviews with Liddy, seemed particularly mesmerized by the subject of killing. Exactly how, by what means, he asked within the first minute of the first program, had Liddy planned to kill Jack Anderson? With a knife, Liddy said, or by breaking his neck. Gasps. "Just like that," someone in the audience whispered. In returning constantly to that sort of question ("But aren't you glad you didn't kill John Dean?"), Cavett seemed almost unaware that, at least on the evidence of his autobiography, or of the public record, Liddy was not in fact a violent man. And that if he were, it would be remarkably imprudent to interview him in this way. Having referred, for instance, to "your almost unbearable appetite for violence," Cavett asked, "Can you see how people would be uneasy to have you out on the streets?" "You're so likeable," Liddy said, soothingly. "There's just no problem with you at all." Cavett said he meant other people. "If they're your friends," Liddy said, "then I'm sure they're likeable, too." Even Cavett laughed at this. "See me after class," he said. But on occasions when the lady in Portland, and now, doubtless, the Cavett audience, and the lady in San Francisco as well, saw the reptile, and Frances Liddy would detect the twinkle, Denneny and others thought they saw the imp.

In 1978, Liddy had published a rather good, conventional thriller—in no way related to Watergate, or even to politics. Its hero was of complicated Italian background. His mistress was Chinese-American. Among other plot developments was an inspired alliance, for good purposes, of the Mafia and the tongs. St. Martin's Press had published that thriller, called *Out of Control*, and sent Liddy on a book tour to promote it. Interviewers had inevitably wanted to discuss Watergate. Liddy had refused. With *Will*, which rapidly became, as *Out of Control* was not, a best-seller, there was of course another book tour. There were, at the same time, two other tours: a journalistic circuit, in which one reporter after another tried to find in Liddy's book, and in his person, "news value" of some kind; and a people's tour, in which various groups asked Liddy to address them, and individuals, on the street or even in late-night phone calls (the Liddys' number has never been unlisted), asked Liddy's views, or told him theirs, on the basis of the kind of man they, in the years since Watergate, had thought him to be. In the first week, the week of the *Time* excerpts, the journalistic tour tended, not surprisingly, to predominate. Soon afterward, it gave way to the other two.

"It's twenty-five after seven now," David Hartman said to his *Good Morning America* audience. He still sat on a sofa between chairs occupied by G. Gordon Liddy and Jack Anderson. "In his autobiography, *Will*, G. Gordon Liddy said that he urged that Jack Anderson be killed. Before the break, we were discussing that." *During* the break, Liddy and Anderson had in fact been discussing other matters. Liddy had complimented Anderson for his black belt in karate. Anderson had modestly pointed to his own increasing waistline. Hartman had asked Anderson why he would appear on a program that would almost certainly sell copies of Liddy's book. Anderson had said, "This book must be read." Liddy had said, "I've certainly sold a lot of his columns in the past." "Mr. Liddy," Hartman continued, "what did Richard Nixon know?" Liddy said he had no idea and that he declined to speculate. "I want to ask you something else," Anderson said, dropping for almost the first time in the course of the broadcast the subject of killing, "I wrote at the time that you were an admirer of Adolf Hitler. Is that true?" "No," Liddy said, and began the story of the German maid in his childhood. More conversation. Commercials. "It's seven-thirty," Hartman said. "Most people wouldn't consider G. Gordon Liddy to be a very nice man. . . ." Weather. Commercials. News. Commercials. Time. More weather report. "It's twenty minutes before eight right now," Hartman said. "This is the first time these two gentlemen have met." Anderson told a long anecdote about President Nixon's having embarrassed Henry Kissinger on the yacht *Sequoia*. "Well, what is your question?" Liddy asked. Anderson said that

Nixon's "deep abiding resentment" of the press might have contributed to the notion of killing him, Jack Anderson. Liddy said that, although Nixon reciprocated the press' "deep abiding animosity" toward him, the whole matter had nothing to do with that but with the question of whether Anderson had in fact compromised a CIA source abroad.

"Mr. Liddy," Hartman suddenly said, "what in your opinion is the value of human life?" Liddy said, "The value of human life is sacred." Hartman asked whether Liddy's case had not been a matter of blind obedience. "I don't believe in blind obedience," Liddy said. "I do believe in reason, and you must be answerable to your conscience. Ultimately, it comes down to a matter of individual conscience." "How then," Hartman went on, undeterred and still referring to the idea of killing Jack Anderson, "are you different from those German soldiers who said they were just following orders?" "I wasn't following orders, was I?" Liddy said. "I proposed it."

Anderson left, to return to Washington. Commercials for two ABC soap operas, One Life to Live and All My Children. The program resumed. "You wanted to be a dangerous man," Hartman said. "No," Liddy said, "let me explain to you. When I was a little child . . ." Conversation about childhood fears. Hartman read aloud a passage from Liddy's book: "That sounds like someone who is really desperate." Liddy said, "I was." More conversation. "You really are not afraid to die," Hartman said. "No. I mean we're all gonna die," Liddy said. Talk about the episode of killing chickens. "You don't seem simply to be just willing to kill," Hartman said. "It's almost killing as a celebration." No, Liddy said. Talk about why Liddy had waited to write the book until after statutes of limitations had run out, even for associates he no longer liked or admired. Liddy said he had been taught that "One does not seek to extricate oneself at the expense of friends or associates, whether they are erstwhile or not." More talk. "Thank you, Mr. Liddy. It's four minutes, almost four minutes before eight. We'll be right back," Hartman said. Liddy went off, by NBC limousine, to the Today show.

Immediate mention, by Today host Tom Brokaw, of killing and G. Gordon Liddy. "Killing takes up a very small part of the actual book," Liddy said. Brokaw, who had not read it, continued. "This is a nation, Mr. Liddy, of laws, not of men," he said. "We do not respond to just what our superiors tell us, whether it's here at NBC or even in the government." ["I don't know about *him*," said one of the men looking at screens and flicking dials in the control room, "but here at NBC we do *exactly* what our superiors tell us."] Security for Liddy's appearance on the *Today* show had been so tight that no newspaper reporters were allowed in the studio; a few stood behind the men at the control-room dials.

"Do you have any contemporary heroes?" Brokaw asked. "Let me think a minute," Liddy said. "No. They're all dead." Who were they? "Leonidas, Catherine de Medici, Machiavelli, Caesar, MacArthur, Patton." Conversation. "We have E. Howard Hunt who is waiting offstage here," Brokaw said. "There's a certain tension in the air." ("If there's any flicker in his eyes, stay with him, stay with him," said the director in the control room. The camera was on Liddy. There was no flicker. The camera moved to Brokaw.) "A few minutes ago, we heard some bizarre Watergate stories from Gordon Liddy," Brokaw said, reading from a cue card, "and we'll be talking again with him in a moment. Coming up, our TV critic, Gene Shalit." Shalit appeared on the screen.

"There's a lot of press out in the corridors," he said. "A lot of newspaper reporters. I was interested in Liddy's heroes. The first one, I agree with. When he first said Leonidas, it didn't click. I thought he meant a ballet dancer at the Music Hall. Well, I don't have any heroes in public life. My heroes are in the arts." A brief meditation. "What does *heroes* mean anyway? Edwin Newman said a 'sung hero' was a sandwich in a Chinese restaurant. People are no longer larger than life." Some news, regarding Ezer Weizmann's resignation from the Israeli cabinet, and the acquisition, by Norton Simon and his wife, Jennifer Jones, of a single painting for $3.7 million. Some commercials. "It's eight-thirty, good morning," Brokaw said. Then he asked Liddy what he would say to people, "and I suspect I might be one of them," who thought Liddy's autobiography, his whole story perhaps, might be "a media hype." "Well, I did the fifty-two and a half months," Liddy said. "There's nothing manufactured about that." Brokaw asked whether Liddy thought Charles Colson's religious conversion, in the years after Watergate, had been genuine. "I can't look inside the man's head," Liddy replied. "I have no idea." Brokaw asked, "Would you ask your children to grow up to be like you?" "No," Liddy said. "I want them to grow up to be the way they want to be." More conversation. "Let him out. Get the other guy in," the man in the control room said. As E. Howard Hunt entered the studio to be interviewed, Liddy and two reporters went down in the elevator and out to the street.

On the sidewalk, at Rockefeller Plaza, a young black woman said, "Congratulations. I agree. It all depends on where you stand." Liddy and the reporters crossed Fifth Avenue and walked toward the Westbury to have breakfast. Liddy now said that, in spite of the guards and the tight security, just as he was entering the *Today* studio, a worried man, carrying a briefcase, had approached him. "He said, 'Mr. Liddy, I need your counsel,' " Liddy recalled. "I said, 'I'm sorry. I'm afraid I've been disbarred.' " It turned out that the man had a complicated theory that a popular White House physician who had resigned in a controversy over drug prescriptions, was in fact a Soviet agent. None of the NBC staff knew the man with the briefcase. A guard had finally spotted him and sent him away. "I mean, here's this guy with a theory that the President is the Mongolian candidate," Liddy said, "and *he's* the only one who gets through security."

A passerby waved, and Claire Crawford, a reporter for *People* magazine, which was planning a cover story on Liddy for its next issue, asked Liddy how strangers generally reacted to him. "Some people say, 'I'm proud of you,' and some say, 'I hope your dog dies,' " Liddy said. "Nobody seems to be neutral. Although a lot of people behave as though they know they've seen my face somewhere, but they can't quite place who I am." Ms. Crawford said she knew the syndrome well. She had once been working on a piece about Spiro Agnew, when he was Vice President and at the height of his popularity. A passerby had looked at him intently, puzzled, then brightened and approached. "I know you," he had said, enthusiastically. "You're Ed McMahon."

On Saturday morning, two days after Liddy's New York network interviews, I took a cab from Washington National Airport to the Liddys' house, in Oxon Hill, Maryland. The driver, who was black, said he was going to take the afternoon off to drive to a wedding in Philadelphia. He asked whether I might be going to a wedding in Oxon Hill. I said no. Then, seeing that he had on the seat beside him a copy of the *Washington Post*, opened to a feature story, in the Style section, on G. Gordon Liddy's book, I said I was going to the Liddys' house. He whistled, then paused. "Believe it or not, I was locked up with him," he said. "In the D.C. jail. I wanted to meet him, but I never got to." Another pause. "I admired him for two reasons. Number one, he helped a lot of inmates. And number two, he didn't talk." Then, the driver wrote down his name, address, and phone number, in case his passenger, or Liddy himself, should ever want to call.

Oxon Hill is a quiet, well-kept suburban town where a lot of present and former military people live. The Liddys' house, on Ivanhoe Road, is of wood and brick, with an ivy-covered chimney. A sign in the yard advertised lawn mowing. There were two cats, both in the last stages of pregnancy, and one dog, a hound of some sort, which kept at a considerable distance from the house. The Liddys have four cars, all old and with a lot of mileage on them: a Jeep; an improbably worn and unkempt Cadillac; a Volvo, which their daughter Alexandra keeps at the College of New Rochelle, where she is a nursing student; and a battered Ford. On this Saturday, *People* was paying for Alexandra and the other two absent children, Jim, a senior at Mercersberg Academy, and Tom, a junior at St. Alban's, in Washington, to come home. Grace, who was taking a semester at the University of Maryland, and Raymond, a student at a local public school were already at home. Claire Crawford, the reporter, and a photographer from *People* were expected at noon.

Liddy was pale and rather haggard. For two days he had been unable to eat solid food, on account of a cracked and infected molar. Frances Liddy was tidying up a room off the kitchen, which, piled with magazines, books, and newspapers, serves as a combination study and auxiliary living room. Raymond drove off in the Ford to get mustard and mayonnaise for the sandwiches that his mother intended to serve at lunch. The household had gotten up relatively late that morning. Liddy had been scheduled, early on the previous evening, to appear on a radio show, *Buchanan and Braden*—Patrick Buchanan, the Republican columnist and former speechwriter for President Nixon; Thomas Braden, the Democratic columnist and friend of the Kennedys, more recently author of *Eight Is Enough*. The two-hour radio program had been such a success—although one woman had called in, to say, "The thought of a man like you working in the White House simply makes me want to *scream*"—and Braden, Buchanan, and Liddy had found themselves in agreement on so many issues, particularly the proper conduct of American foreign policy, that the interviewers had invited Liddy to appear on their television program later that night. They kept him so long on the TV show that their scheduled guest, former ambassador to Moscow

Malcolm Toon, had complained and threatened to leave. After the program, Frances Liddy had stayed up in order to complete the family's tax returns, which were more than usually complicated this year, because of the book.

For the past ten years, Frances Liddy, who holds a master's degree in education, has been teaching in downtown Washington, at an elementary school which is almost completely black. "This time of year," she said, pausing to sit down and have a cigarette, "teachers are tired. Children don't sit still; they become hyperactive. Not just in urban schools. Everywhere. They don't read, nobody reads to them. They don't even play house anymore. There isn't the imagination. Except when they're watching television, they don't sit still." She was tired, too, she said, because the past few weeks, when the book and the *Time* excerpts were being edited, had been a strain. "Imagine if *Time* had leaked," she said, "and here we are, a family known for our silence." She laughed. She had read each chapter of the book, she said, as her husband wrote it. "I thought, Now people will know what I've gone through all these years." Then she added, "It's very strange to read it, and realize it's your whole life."

Raymond returned from his errand. His mother put out her cigarette, and started to make sandwiches on a sideboard between the kitchen and the auxiliary living room study. A cab drew up. Sandy, looking like any attractive, well-educated young woman returning from college, walked into the kitchen. "I need money," she said, meaning to pay for the taxi. "Everybody always does," her mother said. When the cab had been paid, Sandy began to help with the preparations for lunch. "I have to be back at school tonight," she said; also, "I'm starving." Frances expressed approval of her daughter's peach-colored suit, then remarked that she was not wearing panty hose. "It's summer, Mom, you don't have to wear them," Sandy said. "That's not my understanding," her mother said.

They both sat down, Frances to smoke another cigarette, Sandy to eat her sandwich. Sandy abruptly mentioned the *Time* excerpts. "I've never been so shocked in my life," she said. "I haven't read the book. I don't know what *else* is in there. We never even had time to sit down and discuss it as a family." Her mother said nothing. "Somebody actually walked up to me on campus and said, 'Are you as crazy as your father?' " Sandy said. Then, with her version of the Liddy twinkle, "I said, 'Yeah, and you better watch out.' "

Ms. Crawford and the photographer arrived, together with Pam

Mason, an undergraduate at Dartmouth, who was spending the year in a "journalism internship" at *People*. The three went with Liddy and Raymond to the main, larger living room, where there was a piano. "We're still two children short," Frances said. Phrases drifted through the open door, reminiscences of the forties, "piano lessons," "recital," "largo," "Master Liddy will now play 'Largo.' " Mother and daughter talked a while longer, in the living room/study. A limousine drove up, delivering Jim. "Why does he get a limousine," Sandy said, laughing, "and I get just a taxi?" She finished her sandwich. Jim walked in. "Go and say hello to your father," Frances Liddy said.

The phone rang. "Raymond," Frances said. "I think it's Mrs. Tower." Senator John Tower's wife was calling to inquire about Raymond's lawn mowing. While Liddy was still in prison, all the children took up various jobs. Sandy, for instance, earned her first year's college tuition by driving a city bus at night. Tom, at the same time, talked his way into St. Alban's, Washington's finest private school, under a special program for minorities and foreign indigents. The front door banged. "Thomas has arrived," Frances said. "Tom has arrived?" Liddy's voice asked from the next room. "Tom has arrived, in his usual splendor. With his laundry bag. Don't you have a clean shirt? And, Tom, your *hair*. It's all right. Just go and get a clean shirt." "I have a laundry bag full of dirty shirts," Tom said. He had just come from the final rehearsal for the St. Alban's production of *The Boys from Syracuse*, in which he played a starring role. He was wearing tattered army pants, a shirt, sneakers. "No. Go and take one of your father's shirts," his mother said. Mild protests. "Thomas, your mother says you're not wearing a clean shirt," Liddy said, amused, "and that your hair looks like a mare's nest. Go and take one of my shirts." "You know, you'll never get it back," Tom said, starting up the stairs. "I know I'll never get it back," his father said.

The *People* photographer began to wander around, looking for a place to set his tripod. "I don't know just what I want yet," he said. "Anything on this floor," Liddy said. "Evidently the second floor is off-limits." The reporter and Pam Mason were in the main living room, interviewing Liddy children. Was there anything they had found odd, as they were growing up, about their father? No. Anything eccentric? Again no. Raymond wandered into the kitchen, and poured himself something that appeared to be chocolate milk from a pitcher on the sideboard. "What's this?" he asked, before taking a sip. "It's poison," Frances Liddy said. "Your mother, of course, is trying to poison you." Raymond drank his chocolate milk.

Only one of the children, Grace, who was apparently in her room upstairs, had not joined the group talking with the reporter. "Do you think you could get Grace to come and sit with us?" her father asked. "Let's get Grace to come down and join us." One of the children started up the stairs. "Be diplomatic now," their mother said. Grace came down and sat with the others. There was laughter, anecdotes. In answer to a question, Liddy mentioned his pride in each of his children. "Of course, I was away during most of their formative years," he said. He went upstairs to get some medication for his tooth. Had their father never embarrassed them? the reporter resumed at once. No, he hadn't. Did the children have habits of which their parents disapproved? Drinking? Marijuana? No. The children, trying obviously to oblige, took up any line of conversation that did not reflect badly on their father or the family.

In the living room study, Frances Liddy had another cigarette, and spoke of her often-disappointed hope that one of the pregnant cats, a calico, would this time produce a calico male. Jim walked in, and began to explain the aloofness of the dog, Hounddog. The hound had strayed into the Liddy yard several years ago, "when Pop was in prison." "We already had two dogs," Jim said. "Hounddog was very shy, very scared. He stayed around because of the other dogs, I think. He would play with them just out of our reach. Finally, we could pet him, then we took the ticks off him. He didn't like it much. Whenever we would touch him, he was shaking and jumping. Pop would always ask about our progress with Hounddog. Then the other two dogs died." One was poisoned. The other was hit by a car. "So of the three dogs we had," Jim said, "the stray is left."

Liddy came in with the photographer, talking of cameras. "You know, a lot of situations I find I cannot use a flash," Liddy said. "I hate a flash," the photographer said; then, "I still don't know just what I want." Liddy asked whether anyone would like coffee. The photographer would. "Can you make me a cup?" Frances asked. Liddy made coffee and passed the cups around. "See, somebody loves me after all," Frances said. The photographer went back, with Liddy and Jim, to the room where the other children were still being interviewed.

"When he was away, the family just had to unify," Frances said. "Everybody learned to cook. Many days, after teaching school, I thought I would never survive. But the children would say, 'Now, Mother.' They were between nine and fourteen. I thought, Either he's going to be released, or he's not going to be released. We have to give it every chance. And I got them swimming. In swimming, there isn't any fussiness about male or female. Most coaches are good strong men kids can look up to. It's not like those other sports, ice hockey, the Little League, which are so competitive, where you have children straining muscles they should not; and where you have fathers, mothers and fathers, who haven't accomplished anything since seventh grade, living through their nine-year-olds. In swimming, you don't have that. It's a good clean sport. It took up a lot of their energy, it was good for their bodies, the environment was healthy. So I thought, I'd better get those boys in the water and keep them out of trouble. The older children made meals, when we came home at nine o'clock at night. Weekends, I would cook like mad. Some days I was so worn out I thought there was no way I could have driven them one more day. Then, they started to get old enough to drive. I thought, I've just got to work to get him out. Because one night it dawned on me, These children were going to be grown up and *gone* by the time he got out.

"So I worked to get him out. There were committees, George C. Higgins was a godsend, television appearances. I used to say, 'Did you watch me? Did you see your mother on television?' They need their privacy at that age. They had usually watched *Saturday Night Live*. But we kept the ties going. And they had to be kept. Gordon is very much a family man. He's always been so interested in his children. They all have their individuality. I encourage that, I guess, because I was an only child. To raise them as individuals. But we talk about everything. Now, we're both running to make up for the upset, because their lives of course were not normal in those years." She paused. "When he's an old man, they will come," she said. "Pretty soon, there'll already be another"—she hesitated—"facet to their view of him. And in five years, they'll see another facet. And when they're thirty, another." Pause. "You work on that, when you build a family. When he is an old man, they will come."

Everyone took a break, and adjourned to the sideboard for lunch. Jim, who would go to Fordham in the fall, and Tom, who had not decided on a college yet, questioned Pam Mason earnestly about Dartmouth. Sandy talked about what she called a major issue in medicine: tension between doctors and nurses. Nurses increasingly competent and well-trained, doctors, ever more diffident, frightened of malpractice suits, and unwilling to acknowledge the increased responsibility of nurses. She mentioned an old patient at the hospital where she works at night, and the efforts by nurses, over a period of weeks, to get doctors to pay attention to his bed sores. Finally, a young doctor had operated on the old man, without anesthetic, right there on the ward. "You'd think they would listen to the nurses sooner," she said, "or at least show some compassion until God took him away."

The photographer, meanwhile, had decided what he wanted. "Mr. Liddy," he said, "would you just hold your hand over a flame for me?" Liddy declined. In that case, would Liddy put on a ring with jagged edges, honed as a weapon when Liddy was in prison, and make a fist? "I just need one zinger picture," the photographer said. "It's unfortunate, but that's the way the magazine operates." In the end, Liddy put on the ring, but declined to make a threatening gesture. The photographer took some pictures of him, and of the whole family standing in the yard. "You got what you wanted," Liddy said as he was taking off the ring, "and I didn't get what I didn't want." The following week, *People* ran a piece several pages long. Lacking a photograph with a flame, however, it was not a cover story.

At 6 A.M. on Monday, a few people sat, with their early morning pallor, coughs, expressionless faces, in the lobby of the Waldorf-Astoria. Some were reading newspapers. A young woman was reading a paperback, *De Votre Inconscient*. All seemed waiting for diverse errands and appointments. A huge Seiko map high up on one wall flashed the time in various time zones of the world. Little black billboards with white plastic letters announced meetings scheduled to take place in the hotel that day: the National Association of Manufacturers, the New York City Central Labor Council, Descente America, Inc., Young & Rubicam, the Knights of Malta. At 6:15 A.M., two maintenance men, one black, one white, carried the hotel's large American flag to the Lexington Avenue entrance, where they unrolled and raised it. At 6:25, the Musak went on; at 6:30, the lobby chandeliers, and the lights in the men's and ladies' rooms. At 6:45, a limousine rented by St. Martin's Press drew up at the Park Avenue entrance. Danny, the driver, and Mindy, a young publicity assistant at St. Martin's Press, met Liddy just inside the hotel door. Liddy was scheduled that day for eight radio and television interviews. In the course of the morning, Mindy and a reporter persuaded the St. Martin's publicity department to cancel two interviews. They took Liddy to a dentist. By that time, three interviews had already passed.

As the limousine set out along Park Avenue, Mindy gave Liddy an envelope containing money for expenses on his trip. "I haven't seen that kind of money since I was giving it to the Cubans," Liddy said. Mindy remarked how "refreshing" it was to have an author who carefully accounted for what he spent in cash. At the corner of Madison Avenue and Fifty-second Street, a car ran into the limousine and crumpled the front fender. Danny and the driver of the car got out. A little contretemps ensued. A police car arrived. Liddy recalled a night in early 1973, when a car had crashed into his jeep. The damage had not been serious. But the driver of the other car, a retired general, who was slightly drunk, had been outraged. "He kept saying, 'Citizen's arrest! I hold you in a citizen's arrest,'" Liddy recalled. "I said, 'No need for this citizen's arrest stuff. Let's wait for the State Police.' He said, 'Citizen's arrest! Do you realize you could get thirty days for this?' I said, 'It's okay. I've already got twenty-one years.' He said, 'My God, are you *him?*'"

"Mr. Liddy, we live under a rule of law in this country," Shelley Henrye began, on the Shelley Henrye radio show, and the interview took a not unfamiliar course. When the listener phone calls started coming in ("Did you know anything about the Kennedy assassination before it happened?"), they were not unfamiliar, either. At a console, separated by a glass panel from Liddy and Ms. Henrye, a young man was fielding calls. The whole switchboard remained lit up. "I'm sorry, I can't take your question," he said. "Good question. Please hang on and we'll get to you"; "I'm gonna take you first. Will you turn your radio down. Okay, gottcha"; "Uh-huh, so what's your question? Well, tell me, because it makes a difference"; "Good. There's a question he can answer in spades"; "I'm sorry. During the commercial break I asked him that question and he said he had nothing to say about it"; "All right. Be as brief as you can because we're running against the clock." Then, a caller who identified himself as Dick Tuck was on the air. Liddy greeted the man Democrats thought of as their merry prankster of the 1968 and 1972 campaigns, with real delight. He saluted him as a practitioner of "world-class dirty tricks," "when we were on the other side of the fence." Tuck laughed. "A prison fence?" he asked. Liddy laughed. "Not anymore," he said.

After Liddy's session at the dentist's, an interviewer at the UPI radio station said, in welcome, "I expected your eyes to be blue." He asked whether Liddy would like coffee or lunch. Liddy asked for yogurt, on account of his tooth. A little refrigerator, in the rather shabby office, turned out to contain five flavors of yogurt. The interviewer asked whether they might begin to tape at once. Liddy asked whether he might eat his yogurt while they talked. "Sure," the interviewer said. "This isn't NBC. This is UPI. Just don't slurp on the microphone." Then, they talked, of "morality or ethics, and the rule of reason," of "free will versus individual responsibility." "What's your highest value?" the interviewer asked. "Country, family," Liddy said, then more softly, "friends." When Liddy emerged from the radio station, the limousine stood empty at the curb. Danny, who had been sent to fill a prescription made out by the dentist, had apparently vanished. So had Mindy. When they came back, it turned out that Mindy had been making phone calls. Danny, in addition to filling the prescription, had bought a copy of Liddy's book.

On *News Center 4*, as Liddy appeared in the studio, Tom Snyder, the host, was interviewing Irving Schiff, the New Haven "tax refusenik," who, on what he says are constitutional and other grounds, has paid "not one dime in income taxes since 1973." "That's kind of a dangerous thing," Snyder said. Schiff reminded him that the American Revolution was provoked by "taxation without representation." He started to give five reasons not to pay income taxes. "One, it's patriotic. Two, it will improve your social life, talking about it. Three, if I were to pay my taxes the government would merely waste more money." He spoke of the "subterranean underground" of people who conduct their transactions in cash, to avoid records for tax purposes. He spoke of the fake "churches, trusts, and charitable clubs" being formed to avoid paying taxes for "the Disneyland on the Potomac." "People are dropping out in droves," he said. Next, Snyder interviewed the actress who played the heroine, Joanna Tate, on the soap opera *Search for Tomorrow*, which had run for twenty-seven years. "It's not everyday life," the actress said, of the program. "That would be boring." Commercials. An announcement that an interview with Liddy was coming up. "First, we're going to cook," a television chef said, and made an omelette. Commercials.

Then, Tom Snyder said, by way of introduction, "Today, Gordon Liddy is not afraid of anything."

By late afternoon, Liddy had two New York interviews remaining, before he left for Chicago and the West: one, with Scott Kaufer and Paul Slansky of the *Soho News*; the other, with Judy Klemesrud of the *New York Times*. The *Soho News* reporters arrived at Liddy's room in the Waldorf. Slansky at once asked Liddy to review Richard Nixon's book, *The Third War*, for the *Soho News*. Liddy thanked him but said that, during the next few weeks, he would have no time "to do so in a scholarly and thoughtful way." "I've not read the *Time* excerpts," Slansky said, "I've just read the book." It became clear at once that these were by far the most competent interviewers Liddy had had so far. They asked him what questions he had been asked the most, and then asked no one else's questions. They asked him when he had decided to write the book. "After it was absolutely clear that nothing could be salvaged at all," Liddy replied, "and I realized that, for historians, my book would have to be a primary source." They asked him whether Maurice Stans, finance chairman of the Committee to Re-Elect the President, and certainly the biggest political fund-raiser in history, had known about the Watergate. And Liddy (in perhaps a strong instance of his credulity) said, "He didn't know. You see, he didn't need to know." They asked whether he liked the press to think him crazy, "just to keep them off the trail." He replied, "To a little extent, I'll have to admit I've exploited it a bit"; and added that a lot had "sprung from the anticipation of my caricature." In answer to a question, Liddy was saying, "People who like to kill are sick people," when, at the door, there was a loud, peremptory knock. There was a startled pause. A voice bellowed, "Room checking!" They asked him, about the Watergate scandal, "Is there anybody who could have been removed who would have stopped it?" He replied, "No. You'd have had to blow away a cast of thousands."

They asked him what he read, whether he helped his wife with "domestic chores," what he thought of a Nixon quote about him on the tape of June 23, 1972 ("just locker-room talk," he said, calmly), whether he cared about the pennant races, "Do you think people draw the wrong conclusion from your fascination with things German?" To the last question, Liddy gave quintessentially a writer's reply. "I think my book is my best shot," he said. Just before they left, Slansky and Kaufer asked him to record the following messages for their home answering tapes: "Hi.

This is G. Gordon Liddy. Please leave your message when you hear the tone. Or I'll kill you"; "Hi. This is G. Gordon Liddy. Please leave your message when you hear the tone. Or I'll break your knees." Curiously enough, though Slansky and Kaufer leaked the contents of these answering tapes to the *New York Times* People column, which published an item about them, they did not use one word of their interview, which was also taped, in the *Soho News*, but ran a brief, friendly item, "Ten Reasons to Like G. Gordon Liddy," instead.

En route to the airport, Danny announced that he was "twenty percent through" Liddy's book. "It reads easily. It's written fluidly," he said. Mindy reported that she had heard a radio interview with former Vice President Agnew, in which he claimed, apropos of Liddy's book, that a high government official had warned him (Agnew) that he must resign from the vice presidency, that he faced "assassination" unless he resigned. Liddy asked whether Mindy had remembered to bring two copies of his book, which he wanted to inscribe to the two dentists who had worked on his teeth. She had. One of the dentists, she said, had called St. Martin's Press to find out how Liddy was, and the switchboard operator, thinking the call was from a crank, had said, "There's a dentist on the line." Liddy signed the books.

Traffic was slow, because, Danny said, it was Earth Day. Liddy mentioned an interview in which he had met Jan Teller, daughter of the scientist Edward Teller. Before Liddy went on the air, Ms. Teller had sewed on a button that had fallen off his jacket. "We had a heck of a good conversation," he said. He recalled an interview with National Public Radio. "A bit adversarial," he said. "Politely so, however." Danny turned on the car radio. "The Casper Citron Show with G. Gordon Liddy." Why, Citron asked, had Liddy waited until the statute of limitations had expired, even for people he did not like. "Otherwise, it's not a matter of principle," Liddy said. "It's a matter of vindictiveness." Why should anyone buy a book by a convicted felon? "Think of O'Henry, Villon, Daniel Defoe," Liddy said. "They all did time."

On Tuesday night, shortly after eight, Gordon Liddy stood outside the doors of O'Hare Airport in Chicago. At nine, he was scheduled to begin a two-hour interview with Dr. Milton Rosenberg, a professor of sociology at the University of Chicago, who happens also to run the city's most popular nightly talk show. Taxis, limousines, and private cars passed Liddy on the ramp. There was no sign of the limousine hired by St. Martin's Press. Liddy stood for some minutes beside his suitcase and his garment bag. Then he went inside, to see whether the chauffeur might somehow have missed him at the baggage claim. A tall dark man, carrying a suit jacket, with loosened tie and open shirt collar, walked up to Liddy, shook his hand, and, addressing him by name, offered him a ride into the city. Liddy thanked him, but explained that he was looking for a limousine that had been hired for him. The tall man offered his own driver and limousine. He was going to the Drake Hotel, he said. Liddy called the agency that should have sent his car. They said they had sent it. Liddy waited another ten minutes under the lights, in the dark outside O'Hare. He looked at his watch. The tall man and his limousine were still there. At his insistence, Liddy and I got into the backseat. The tall man sat, beside the uniformed chauffeur, in front.

"I gotta tell you, you're one of the few stand-up guys in the world, in the entire world," the man said, leaning his elbow over the front seat and further loosening his tie. "And you can use my limousine. I just happen to think that your conduct, okay? regardless of the circumstances, the sacrifices, whatever reasons possessed you, I respect you immensely. Immensely. I respect your family. Whatever you may think of the President, for better or for worse. Out of respect for the man, and on behalf of his office, you made the sacrifice. Not many in the entire world would do the same."

"I hope you're wrong," Liddy said. Then he muttered something about the exemplary conduct of prisoners of war, returning from Hanoi, and that "nobody makes a continuing fuss over them."

"I'm not talking about *groups*," the tall man said, firmly. "I take things on an individualistic basis. I've seen an awful lot. I've known so many miscreants. I'm chairman and chief executive of a company, okay? I have money, a lot of emoluments. But I've seen some terrible, terrible weak links." He paused and looked out of the window. "My business is jukeboxes, vending machines. Also hearing aids, bandages, crap like that. The worst part of business, the most tragic part of business, okay? you make your first mistake and guys start copping out on you. *And they were partners at the time.*" He looked out of the window again. "In any business you sometimes have to cut corners," he said. "In consultation with your partners. I heard that clown Hunt, forgive me for being subjective and personal, but I can tell you, *one man on my team like you . . .*"

Liddy took up the reference to Hunt. "I happen to have been surrounded by the spectacularly weak," he said.

"No," the man said, again firmly. "So many miscreants. Such terrible, terrible weak links. Now a classic example is Joel Dolkart, of Gulf & Western, who's indicted for stealing two million dollars. And then started to cop out on Charlie Bluhdorn. Who built a very fine conglomerate, I might add. And the miserable miscreant plea bargains. Now who pays for that?" Silence. "The shareholders. And this lousy bum walks the streets."

"In the FBI, we knew," Liddy said, taking up the reference to plea bargains, "if a fellow knows something, he'll tell you. If he doesn't, he'll make it up."

"Sometimes I think there's only two stand-up guys in Chicago. That's Adolph," he turned to the driver, who was black, "and me. Tonight, I'm taking a judge, and his girlfriend, to dinner. An impecunious judge. You know what I'm talking about. So many miscreants. Such bad judgment retrospectively." He turned, and again leaned his elbow over the seatback. "There was a man in our organization, okay? I refer to as our John Dean. He talked his stinking guts out. One day I looked at him in the office, I said, 'So help me God, you are our John Dean.' "

Liddy said nothing.

"Look, I mean, I started work, I was eleven, as mail boy for a bank. Then there was a man, the man was an absolute genius, an absolute financial genius. A friend. When I tell you he gave me checks for x, y, and z deal, 'your interest.' And I never even knew what x, y, and z deal was. One day, he said, 'I've made a tender offer. B. F. Goodrich. Two and a half million dollars for each of us. I was scared shitless, to be honest with you. The banker said, 'Will you tell that Jew bastard to get out of B. F. Goodrich, or we'll stop his line at the bank.' So we gracefully withdrew. But there was one half a million dollars, for each of us, in one day. In one afternoon. That's some story."

"It's the American way," Liddy said.

"I don't know if it's the American way or not." Another pause. "My son got married a week ago Saturday. Both sons are in law school. In Chicago. You know, the joy; my greatest aspiration as a young husband and father was the fear How am I going to educate my children. My greatest achievement was to educate my sons. As for my daughter, so far her grades are not good enough. We have this joke, I may have to build or buy a college for her education."

"They can't take what's in your head," Liddy said.

"That. And. Or. Experience." A long silence. "Especially in a community like that. I mean a prison. I think there's a time when people should talk. But when all the other rats jump off the ship, and one man does not, that man has character. I don't say this because you're here, because we'll probably never see each other again. But for you to make the sacrifice you did, for *honor*'s sake. You're, in my opinion, the only good thing that came out of Watergate."

"I'm an educated man," Liddy said. "I was compensated for it."

The limousine stopped at the Drake Hotel. The man gave both Liddy and me his address and phone number, "as a courtesy." He told the driver to take Liddy directly to the radio station. "This is Adolph," he said, earnestly, in farewell. "You should get to know him."

Adolph set out into the nighttime traffic. "Are you taping tonight, or are you going on live?" he asked. Liddy said live. Adolph mentioned the failure of Liddy's own limousine to show up. "Here's our card," he said. "In case you need (chuckle) dependable service."

The radio station building was a two-story yellow-brick structure, in a remote, poorly lighted area of the city, among vacant asphalt lots. A guard just inside the entrance took Liddy's garment bag and suitcase and put them in a supermarket shopping cart. It was not clear to what use the supermarket cart was ordinarily put inside a radio station. A young woman appeared, the *Milt Rosenberg Show*'s producer, and led the way down a corridor to a small, dingy cafeteria. She brought Liddy some coffee, in a paper cup. They sat down at a table.

"You're the cool one," said a friendly, professorial voice from the doorway. Milt Rosenberg. "The last time you were here"—when Liddy had come to promote his thriller—"you never mentioned you were writing this book." "*You're* the cool one," Liddy replied, greeting Rosenberg with obvious pleasure. "The last time I was here, you never mentioned that you have a title. I didn't know you were Professor." They talked a while. Liddy kept addressing his host as "Dr. Rosenberg." "Let's strike a bargain," Rosenberg said. "You are Gordon. I am Milt."

Milt led the way upstairs, down a corridor of offices locked for the night, into the studio. An announcer was just doing the nine o'clock news: "George Bush and Edward Kennedy have slim leads in the Illinois primary." Liddy and Milt sat beside each other at a sort of conference table. They put on earphones. Rosenberg, in introducing Liddy and his book ("A book of multiple value, I think, of compelling value. Excellent autobiography"), turned to Liddy and said, "It reveals qualities in yourself that you may not be aware of." Liddy said that, as a young man unsure whether to become an operatic tenor or a lawyer, he had taken, as did so many of his generation, the Johnson O'Connor aptitude tests. They had suggested that his talents might lie in publishing or in something literary. "It appears, after all these years," he said, "that they were right and I was wrong."

Rosenberg spoke awhile: "My summary of your vita to date includes your years with the FBI, some of them spent just in our backyard. Gary, Indiana," and mentioned the plan to kill Jack Anderson. "But it did not get executed," he said. "*He* did not get executed," Liddy corrected, mildly. Rosenberg spoke of "values that are based on Machiavelli but suggest Nietzsche," of matters of "*Weltanschauung* versus *Uebersicht*," of "Some values perhaps that are of a different modality from those that inform our way of life?" A moment's silence. "My turn?" Liddy asked. He spoke of his perception that the crisis in the country at the time of Watergate consisted not of "gentle little girls in bare feet carrying daisies" but of campus riots, burning cities, and so forth. "In that context, with that perception, always distinguishing between mere protesters and bomb throwers," he said, he had taken the actions that he took. A listener called in to ask how Liddy could possibly justify the break-in at the office of Ellsberg's psychiatrist. "We did not know what we had there in Dr. Ellsberg," Liddy said. Commercials. A jingle: "Crunchies. Delicious. They're everything they're cracked up to be," "Are you aware of anything I have asked you, Gordon," Rosenberg asked, while their microphones were turned off, "that might make you uncomfortable in any way?" Liddy said no, it was always stimulating to talk with Dr. Rosenberg.

"A document of our time," Rosenberg resumed, speaking of *Will*, when he and Liddy were back on the air. He mentioned Liddy's marriage and genetics. Liddy said that Charles Lindbergh had spoken of similar considerations in his marriage to Anne Morrow. (Anne Morrow Lindbergh had appeared that week, on *60 Minutes*, to promote her book about her husband.) They spoke of "Social Darwinism"; then, of spying for political purposes. "It's as American as apple pie," Liddy said. "It's right out of

The Last Hurrah. It's the way the game is played." When the subject of Liddy's childhood interest in Naziism came up, Liddy mentioned that, before the war, the custom in all American public schools was to pledge allegiance to the flag with a straight-arm, palm-down salute. Rosenberg asked Liddy whether he thought his book was "the definitive history" of Watergate; and Liddy replied, "No. I'm probably disqualified from writing the history. I'm too close to it. Where do I get off doing that? I might be wrong. You see what I mean." Liddy made a distinction between the purposes of what he called Watergates I and II. "In the second break-in, the focus changed," he said, "from the spoken to the written word. We were sent to photograph all files." Rosenberg asked, given the uselessness of those files, whether Watergate resulted from "a Matterhorn complex. They had to break in because it's there." Liddy said no. Commercials. When the microphones were off, Liddy asked, "Going well?" Rosenberg replied, "How could it not?"

On the air, Rosenberg alluded to Machiavelli once again. "You might conclude that it's all right to be a good soldier of the Prince," he said, "but you'd better find a Prince who's ruthless enough, as yours was not." "I'd say that's a pretty good summary," Liddy said. Nearly an hour and a half had passed. The program was turned over entirely to phone calls from listeners: "I'm a practicing attorney. I've read only the review in *Time.* I'm a free thinker and a humanist. How many misguided souls like you are still at large in government?"; "I feel you were very seriously used. Knowing your nature to be blunt and brutal, I think you were being used, and I think it's sad." One man called to inquire what Liddy thought of "the Ehrlichman thesis," that McCord was a double agent, sent in to bring the Nixon administration down. Liddy replied that he did not think so, that he was not a subscriber to the conspiracy theory of history. Then, someone asked what he called the "nitty-gritty question," one that prompted considerable speculation in almost every book about Watergate: why the tape on the lock of the door to the Watergate complex had been placed horizontally (so that it was visible even on a shut door) instead of vertically. Liddy explained it very carefully. All maintenance men, he said, taped locks horizontally, for the simple reason that vertically placed tape would not hold. "But try it. Put it on vertically, and see if it holds. You'll find it pops right off." More questions, theories about CIA conspiracies, theories about the death, in an airplane crash, of Mrs. E. Howard Hunt. "Look, what you have here," Liddy said, "is the phenomenon of obsession with the details of enormously publicized events." And that was that. Rosenberg returned to matters of philosophy and statecraft.

Liddy said he thought that, as a result of the Vietnam War, Americans were permitting their foreign policy to be conducted both timidly and as though they inhabited a safe and benign world. "We can no longer afford the luxury of that illusion," he said. Rosenberg said, "You're left with a very dark vision of the future." Liddy asked him to imagine a bad neighborhood, and a man, looking like a wimp, with a fat wallet, walking toward a man with a machine gun. "Let's not be the guy who looks like a wimp," he said, becoming, for the first time in his trip, overtly hortatory. More talk. "You're a very interesting man," Rosenberg said, at the end of the program, "and a totally honest one." Outside, on the sidewalk, he said, "Come back again, and let's talk about prison conditions." Liddy said he would.

The next morning, Liddy left his hotel to shop for suspenders. On account of his tooth, he had by now not eaten solid food in nearly a week. He could not further tighten his belt. A woman walked up to him and said, perfectly amiably, "Death to the CIA." As he walked, with a newspaperman, outside the Commodities Exchange, a man, who identified himself as a commodities broker, shook Liddy's hand and said he admired him. "You're in a riskier business than mine ever was," Liddy said. Suddenly, in a corridor, a young man emerged from an office and greeted Liddy with considerable affection. It was Dwight Chapin, the former White House appointments secretary, who went to prison for a Watergate-related felony. He is now editor of something called *Success Magazine*, which is published by the biggest public contributor to the Nixon campaign, R. Clement Stone. Stone had hoped to be ambassador to London. So had another large contributor, Russell Firestone. According to Ervin Committee records, Firestone had written to Chapin, after a meeting with President Nixon, "Thank you for permitting me to bask in the radiance of his presence." Neither man became ambassador to London.

Liddy's stay in Los Angeles coincided with a Southern California balloon race. Steve Harvey, a young reporter who had for several days been covering the balloon race for the *Los Angeles Times*, was assigned for a day to cover Gordon Liddy. "I do off-beat features," Harvey said, with a little shrug. At eight o'clock in the morning, Liddy and the young reporter set off from Liddy's hotel, L'Ermitage, by limousine for an interview on the Mikael Jackson radio show. "I thought you'd be out there with the balloons," Jackson said, when Liddy introduced him to Steve Harvey. "I had to interrupt the balloons," Harvey said. They entered the studio, a small gray room, with a dartboard whose target was a large photograph of Ayatollah Khomeini, and with various signs (a picture of a cymbal, for instance, captioned "status cymbal") and other *objets* strewn about. On Jackson's desk, beside his microphone, was a book, *How to Live With Your Teenager*. The news was coming through a speaker: "Secretary of State Cyrus Vance has resigned . . . with a 'heavy heart' . . . says he will support the President on other issues." A voice said, through the intercom, "I have that Vance resignation, if you want it on tape." "Thanks," Jackson said. "I've got it live." Then, he turned to Liddy. "Welcome back," he said. "Is it cold out there? Is it raining?" No. "So my forecast here is entirely wrong." A red light flashed, airtime.

"This is really gonna be a wildly busy morning," Jackson said, in English-accented (he was born in England), staccato American slang. "We'll have Dick Gregory calling in, from his fifteenth day of fasting in Teheran. Jack Nelson, calling in from Washington. Also, coming up, our food critic, Elma Dells." Then, his interview with Liddy: "You were dangerous, brave. To what end?"; "Are they all childish games?"; "Was it all worth it? Did it serve any purpose?"; "This is better written than the first book"; "How do you feel about Carter now?" During a break, Jackson sang along with a commercial for Gallo Salami. "Is it going all right?" Liddy asked. "A little tight," Jackson said. "We don't have the rapport we had last time."

On the air again, in reply to a question about Secretary Vance, Liddy was saying, "He's a lawyer." "Liar?" Jackson asked. "Lawyer," Liddy said. They discussed the failed mission in the Iranian desert. Liddy compared it to Dieppe, and other early failures of World War II. "What matters in life, sir?" Jackson asked, abruptly. "Doing one's very best," Liddy said, then recalled Winston Churchill's advice to a class at Eton, "Never give up. Never. Never. Never. Never." "I can see the mail now," Jackson said, drumming his fingers on the desk during another break. "How come you didn't attack G. Gordon Liddy?"

On the air, more conversation. Many listener phone calls. Several hostile callers, attempting to *spring* their angry remarks after some innocuous opening sentences, gave their views away with the sarcastic tone of the first syllable. "He's not much better than other people in government," one caller said, after a fairly long and abstract meditation. "He's nothing but a *pansy*." Liddy called this a "declarative statement," and asked, "What is your question?" "You could never have this on the BBC," Jackson said during the next commercial break.

In Liddy's hotel room, the interviewer for Los Angeles *NewsCenter 4* looked at Steve Harvey, and at me, with some suspicion. "You fancy yourself a hero," she said to Liddy. "But a lot of people went to jail because you remained silent. What would you say to them, Mr. Liddy?" "Who?" Liddy said, genuinely bewildered. The interviewer changed the subject. What did Liddy think of ABSCAM? He said that, as a lawyer, he sensed entrapment in it. "What would you say to the many people who regard themselves as being had by Richard Nixon?" the interviewer asked. "Who?" Liddy said again. "Many people regard you as a morally bankrupt man," she began again. Silence. "Do you see yourself as a morally bankrupt man?" "No," he said. "I do not." Whom did he support for President. Liddy declined to answer. "I might get myself into a position of a gratuitous endorsement, and that would be harmful to the candidate," he said. "Come now, Mr. Liddy, isn't that a cop-out?" she said. "When you're peddling your book, when you're doing a TV interview to sell your book, in effect don't you think it's a cop-out not to react?" "I have just reacted," Liddy said. "I understand that I have not reacted in the way you want me to. I'm sorry." "In all honesty, Mr. Liddy, why should anyone buy a book by a criminal?" Liddy gave his O'Henry, Villon, Defoe answer. The interviewer asked what he thought of "the world situation in the next few months." He said it looked grim. War? "Not in the next few months, but sooner rather than later." What kind of war? "War over natural resources in the Middle East." The interviewer asked the cameraman to stop the camera.

Liddy and the interviewer talked about military preparedness for a while. Liddy spoke of the bad neighborhood, the fat wallet, and the wimp. The interviewer at once asked that the camera be turned on again. "Mr. Liddy," she said then, "do you think Cy Vance is a wimp?" "No," he said. "I think Cyrus Vance did the honorable thing. When you disagree with a policy, you resign over it. A time came when he could not publicly support the President, he resigned." "Is it more fun writing a book than conducting spy missions?" she asked. "It's not fun at all," Liddy said. "Both are hard work." The interviewer asked, "Mr. Liddy, if Richard Nixon were still President, would the hostages still be in Teheran?" Liddy gave his "The *Shah* would still be in Teheran" reply. "Do you think the country's attitudes are changing more in line with the Liddy view of how things should be done?" "I hope so," he said. The interviewer gave up.

As she and the cameraman were leaving, the cameraman turned to Liddy. "I have to agree with you," he said. A friend of his, a reserve officer, had made a trip to inspect a military base, and had told the cameraman, "The equipment out there is all junk." "The skies are black," Liddy said, shaking his head, "with chickens coming home to roost." The interviewer later called both Steve Harvey and me, to ask what sort of pieces we were doing. ("We're keeping them honest," Harvey said to me.) *NewsCenter 4* that night simply reported that the book was out. Of the interview, there were just the lines about Nixon and the Shah.

At noon on the first Friday in May, Gordon and Frances Liddy were due on the playing fields of the St. Alban's School in Washington, D.C., where this year's Track & Field Meet of the District of Columbia Special Olympics was being held. The Special Olympics, which have occurred annually all over the country since 1968, consist of sports events for retarded or otherwise damaged children. At 10 A.M., Eunice Kennedy Shriver, who was one of the most enthusiastic founders of the national program, had administered the Special Olympics Oath. A runner had lighted a special torch. Races and games had begun all over the field. Gordon Liddy was to be one of the honorary judges or, more precisely, awarders of ribbons. The events are so organized that as many children as possible will receive ribbons of some sort. The three top competitors in each of many simultaneous and successive events are encouraged to climb on pedestals in front of a reviewing stand, where an announcer calls out their names through a microphone. Judges, with handfuls of first-, second-, and third-prize ribbons, stand in front of the pedestals. The children naturally are of various heights and ages. Not all of them understand what the ribbons are for or that, given the height of the pedestals and the height of the judges, taller children must lean downward to have ribbons pinned on their

T-shirts. Three judges, one of whom was an army colonel, were pinning ribbons somewhere on the clothing of a very rapid succession of winning children. Since the work of pinning and congratulating is a strenuous and not unathletic business, the adults worked in shifts. Liddy's shift was in the afternoon.

At one end of the field, at the finish line of one of the longer racetracks, Tom Liddy, wearing his army pants, sneakers, and a sports shirt, stood, with six other boys from St. Alban's. Each was carrying a stopwatch and holding on to a section of an often-torn and re-knotted colored string, which served as the finishing tape. "Who's got the guy with the green pants and white shirt?" Tom asked, as children lined up in their lanes at the starting line for the beginning of one race. "I've got the tall guy in blue," one of his classmates said. "Let's do it by numbers," another boy said. They were each timing, and otherwise watching out for, a child in a single lane. The children had numbers pinned to the front of their shirts. A card, with name, age, and school, was pinned to the back. The timers decided to keep track by numbers. "Remember, if someone comes barrelin' down and doesn't want to stop at the finish line," one of the older boys said, "let 'em come. Sometimes they don't like to stop."

"ALL RIGHT! ALL RIGHT! ALL RIGHT!" Tom bellowed, in the hearty way of athletes on playing fields and basketball courts. Then, as the race began, "Way to go. Way to go. Way to go." An extraordinary number of people seemed to be cheering each child and then hugging each child as the races finished. It turned out that adults and St. Alban's students in charge of the meet had been divided into timers, huggers, and runners. The runners accompanied each child, after every race, back to an area near the reviewing stand where there was the group from his own school. In every race at Tom's track, there were stragglers, children who walked all the way, or turned back, or simply stopped running. The seven boys at the finish line would cheer, beckon, wave, smile, and advance slightly toward those children, until the last child had reached the finishing tape, and been given his hug. "Congratulations. Boy! You really moved. You flew," the timers would say. "Is that all right? You pleased? Hey, c'mere, I've gotta get your name and everything." Timers would read the child's name on the back of his shirt and record the time. A hug. For the most part, the children hugged back, or slapped hands, or simply grinned. Some of the larger children came along the track with such force and speed that the seven holders of stopwatches would have to step back a bit, to avoid being bowled over. The finishing tape kept advancing toward small stragglers, retreating before large, pounding racers. "Watson, do you have a class?" a girl student asked one of the timers. He said he did. She took his place.

Gordon and Frances Liddy arrived at the reviewing stand. A student immediately introduced herself to him and set him to awarding ribbons. Frances walked around the field toward where Tom was. She had wanted to talk to him about his grades, but, seeing how busy he was (all the timers, huggers, and runners, by this time, looked as though they had taken part in an athletic marathon themselves), she decided to raise the matter by letter instead. "In first place, *Roulette Taylor!*" a girl student's voice shouted, with hoarse enthusiasm, over the loudspeaker; all the announcers' voices were starting to go. "It's very good for our kids, very important to them," a St. Alban's mother said to me. "It exposes them to a serious, important part of reality." "I'm standing all by myself," a very little girl said, standing next to her. "I'm all by myself. I'm all alone." "Why, I'm all alone, too," the St. Alban's mother said at once, and lifted her up to watch a race.

During a break, Eunice Shriver and Gordon Liddy had a brief conversation. A member of the student organizing committee told Frances that Tom would be in charge of the Special Olympics next year. Somebody was in a bulldog costume (Frances had for years been in charge of the washing of it), and she thought for a moment it was her son. "I almost hugged it," she said, "but then I saw the legs were too thin." The races began again. Tom was by now lifting up every child that came near him at the finish line. So was Ronald Brown, a black student and national champion in the 100 meters, who had been admitted to St. Alban's under the same program as Tom Liddy. Music came over a loudspeaker. A white child, with a number on his T-shirt, stood in front of it, rapt in a kind of ritual dance. Only first-prize ribbons were left; most children in the final races got first-prize ribbons. "I've been sort of encouraging people along," a girl student said, happily, to the Liddys as they were leaving, "and I'm just *dead.*"

After being stranded in Kansas City by an Ozark Airlines strike, Liddy arrived one night in St. Louis, at the Marriott Hotel. He had been looking forward to his stay there, he said, because of the hotel chain's "Rolls-Royce Silver Shadow ads." "Is this your first experience with Marriott?"

he said they asked him at the desk. He said it was. "Everybody's saying 'Hi,' as in the ads," he said, in telling the story the next morning. "All I'm asking for is shelter, and everybody's saying 'Hi.' They call a boy named Charlie to the desk, and say, 'Mr. Liddy, this is Charlie.' Charlie says. 'Hi.' We take an elevator, and walk down a hall. Charlie throws open a door, and says, 'Mr. Liddy, your *room!*' Evidently, it isn't. There's a man in the bed. There's an airline captain's jacket hanging over a chair. Your first Marriott experience. Off Charlie runs. Only one elevator works, so there is a wait. I'm there, outside the room, standing on one foot and then the other. Alone with the baggage cart. Two women walk by. One says, 'I think that's Gordon Liddy.' The other says, 'I don't think he's got a room.' Charlie comes back. We go to another room, on another floor. He throws open the door. 'Mr. Liddy, your *room!*' A man sleeping in the bed. Another pilot's jacket. Even the rank is the same. You know, this is my first Marriott. It's after midnight. Finally, I get a room.

"When I'm in bed, I start to hear this little sirenlike whistle, in the air-conditioning. I think, I'll endure this because Bill Arript [of Marriott] was so good to Sally Harmony." (Ms. Harmony, who was Liddy's secretary at the time of Watergate, is unforgettable to viewers of the Ervin Committee hearings, for at least one line: Asked whether, when she was typing from photocopies with the outline of gloved fingers at their edges, she had not guessed that the work in progress was clandestine, Ms. Harmony replied, "I knew it was clandestine. But to me, Senator, clandestine does not mean illegal. And I can keep a secret." Later, Marriott gave Ms. Harmony a job.) "But I just can't sleep. So I call downstairs. Up comes this maintenance fellow. He checks. Then he says, 'It's the air conditioner. There's dirt in the cones. Sometimes, even when you turn them off, there will be this little whistle.' I said, 'I'm sure your analysis is correct. But can you fix it?' He said, 'Not before tomorrow.' "

At the airport in Minneapolis-St. Paul, there was again no limousine— or rather, there was a mysterious locked and empty limousine. No driver. Liddy took a cab to his hotel. On the flight to Detroit, Republic Airlines lost Liddy's luggage. A day later, they found it. An interviewer for the *Detroit Free Press* said to Liddy, "You are remembered as a second-rate burglar. How would you prefer to be remembered?" Liddy said, "More favorably." When the interview was over, Liddy said, "I think that fellow believed we were having a tough-guy contest in there."

Back in New York for a brief visit, which included three appearances (a breakfast meeting of advertisers and businessmen, organized by the Smith-Greenland Agency; an address at lunch to the Coast Guard Officers Club on Governor's Island; and an afternoon taping of the three interviews with Dick Cavett), Liddy stood on a sidewalk, waiting for a taxi. Finding none, he looked repeatedly at his watch. An off-duty cab drew up. "I disagree with your views, but I like you. Get in," the driver said. Liddy got in. The driver said he was already late. He was going to pick up his wife, in Queens. Then, describing himself as "a moderate Jewish liberal," he began a long disquisition about himself, his background, his politics, his wife, Queens. At an intersection, he saw a man with a briefcase, trying to hail a cab. "Where are you going? LaGuardia?" he shouted. The man said, "LaGuardia Airport." "I'd like to help this other fellow out," the driver said, remarking that LaGuardia was near enough to Queens. Then, having introduced Liddy to the passenger, he resumed his discourse, about politics, his wife, Queens, the quality of city life, Mayor Koch. At a red light he turned, with an interrogatory inflection, to his new passenger for agreement. "Am I right? Or am I right?" "Well," the man said, "I'm from *Ohio*."

During the cab ride Liddy told me that he and Frances had begun a negotiation, which he hoped would be successful. They had put in a bid for a house, on the Potomac, which had originally been built for Alan Drury, author of, among other Washington novels, *Advise and Consent*. They expected to have an answer within the week.

At the businessmen's breakfast, Liddy stood for a moment in silence at the microphone. Then, rather loudly and startlingly, he said, "Boo!" His audience laughed, a bit uncertainly. Previous speakers at these breakfasts had included Harrison Salisbury, Arthur Ashe, Theodore Kheel, Mayor Koch, Pete Rozelle, Martha Graham, George Gallup, William Safire, Jack Valenti. ("We were going to have Princess Ashraf last month," a man told me, as he was putting on his name tag, "but the idea was shot down.") The Smith-Greenland Agency had somehow created the impression, within St. Martin's Press and also with Liddy, that audiences for these breakfasts were limited to members of the Fortune 500 (although actually the guests were mainly advertising people). After his "Boo!" and with a few other equivocal jokes and interjections, Liddy addressed what he had been led to believe were "movers and shakers" with a long, impassioned stem-winder about American politics, foreign policy, and morale. The Founding Fathers, he said, had been wise but tough men, and the world was still and would be a tough place, always. "It is that way, and it's been that way since the mind of man runneth not to the contrary." He was worried, he said, about the country's "post–Vietnam War abhorrence of battle." Not that he believed in battle, except when there was no other choice, but he believed in preparedness for it. He was concerned, he said, when a great democratic country chose to rely on an all-voluntary, and underpaid, professional army. Among peaceful nations with armed, trained citizenry, he mentioned Switzerland, then said, "I think Universal Military Training is the fairest way to go."

He approved, he said, of President Carter's "resolve" in undertaking the Iranian desert rescue mission. He was not of course qualified to appraise its planning. He recognized its difficulty. "A helicopter," he said, "was once defined as ten thousand nuts and bolts trying to fly off in the same direction." At the same time, he worried about the "mind-set" of contingency plans for failure. For this audience, though, no mention of the wimp, the bad neighborhood, the wallet. First, the Founding Fathers. Now, Liddy spoke of the conquistadores, who had no contingency plans for failure. "They burned their ships behind them," he said. "They didn't start their mission ready to say abort, abort, abort." He worried that the country, irresolute, was growing "weaker and weaker." Then, he ended on a ringing, hortatory note, and took questions—of which there were very many. Toward the end, a tall black man got to his feet, and asked, "How do you see your own future?" Liddy said, "Well, let's face it, I had my shot. And I missed." Then, he told of a famous admiral, a man so abrasive that he fell into disfavor and obscurity, until World War I broke out and his country needed him. A correspondent had asked the admiral how he could account for his recall to a post of great importance. "When the shells start to fly," the admiral replied, "they call on the sons of bitches." Liddy paused a bit wistfully.

The chairman of Smith-Greenland finally called the questions short, then made a few remarks about Liddy's "forceful personality." "As evidence," he said, rather oddly, "he has five wonderful children." Liddy said, "I was away during their formative years." Several people gathered around him when he had finished speaking. Several others milled about, muttering to one another that he was "crazy" or "insane."

Some of his remarks this time about where America stood, however, had been so unremittingly bleak that I asked him, when we had left the breakfast, why he usually seemed, by temperament, so sanguine. "I see these problems recognized as problems by serious people in a position to do something about them," he said. Then, he recalled that, after a lot of ineffectual bumbling, the country had pulled itself together for World War II. "Of course this time, the reaction time with missiles makes it unlike World War II. We have less time to protect ourselves from folly, and there is a steeper price. But I measure the price of failure against the great reward attendant to success." He mentioned that we have, after all, a constitutional democracy. "Some might favor having a President answerable to Parliament," he said. "And the White House press corps is a poor substitute."

In the car, a shiny new Mercedes, which had picked Liddy up at the Waldorf for the drive to lunch on Governor's Island, the driver, a Coast Guard officer, described how eager and then how glad he had been to avoid service in Vietnam. "I didn't wanna stop a bullet," he said. "I didn't even wanna slow one down." On the drive downtown and during the fifteen-minute ferry ride, he and Liddy chatted amiably. The officer said his wife had just had a hysterectomy, but was feeling better. Liddy said he was glad she was feeling better. The ferry docked. "Guess you haven't been here since the Korean conflict," the officer said to Liddy. Then he took us on a quick tour of the island's Coast Guard installations: its golf course; its housing; its view of the Statue of Liberty; its nursery school (the Hooligan Haven Day Care Center); its lot for the repair of damaged or rusting buoys. He parked in front of the Governor's Island Officers Club. "Those who enter here," said a sign in the hallway, "shall buy a round of cheer. Those who do not pay with verve, we shall refuse to serve."

During drinks on the terrace, Liddy was introduced to a lot of Coast Guard officers, several of whom asked him to sign copies of his book, and most of whom seemed to be drinking a quantity of Bloody Marys. At lunch, after all visitors, including Coast Guardsmen from other installations, had been introduced, and had acknowledged the introduction by rising slightly in their chairs, Liddy gave another stem-winder. There were no black Coast Guardsmen in the room, and only one Coast Guard woman. Someone at my table remarked that, last year, at the Coast Guard Academy in Groton, "the homecoming queen was a cadet."

Again, there were a lot of questions, most of them decidedly unmilitaristic. An early questioner referred to "your rather Spartan discipline, the Prisoner of Zenda–type stuff." "Let me clear the record," Liddy interrupted. "I have never done time in Zenda. Though I seem to have done time everywhere else." "What level did you have reason to think approval or disapproval of your operations was bucked up to?" "At least to a level that had access to the Oval Office. But we had to leave the President in a position of plausible denial," Liddy said. One questioner mentioned the anomalous appointment of General Alexander Haig to succeed H. R. Haldeman as chief of the White House staff. "Did you ever have reason to think we were in danger of a military takeover?" he asked. Liddy thought a moment. "Never," he said. "Not the military, in their wildest fantasies, never. It's just not in the institutional memory of the military, in this country, to think that way."

Someone asked how, if Liddy had received an order to kill an American civilian, he could ever have reconciled it with his conscience. Liddy said he recognized that any reasonable man might have a moral doubt about any order to kill. "It's only, if you have these problems, get out of that line of work," he said. General Gerard, a retired reserve officer in his middle eighties, got to his feet. "I wonder if this would be correct," he said. "If someone, the President, were to call one of us and say, 'Your country needs you to do something, above or outside the Constitution, to save your country,' wouldn't we do likewise? If you were called in such a situation, would you just say, 'Forget it'?" Silence. Someone asked, "After they were caught, why didn't everyone just say, 'We did it,' and get it over with? Is that simplistic?" Liddy said that, in Washington, cover-up at the highest level was an unvarying custom and an institutional reflex. "It's all a cover-up, in Washington," he said. "I mean, that's what they do down there." The questions continued for three hours.

The next afternoon, Liddy taped his three interviews for the Dick Cavett Show. They began shortly after one o'clock. "Good evening," Cavett said, as usual, at the beginning of the first half hour. The audience, which was aghast at almost every instant of the interview, seemed to find nothing at all odd in being greeted with "Good evening," before two in the afternoon. They applauded dutifully, as studio audiences do applaud, when a sign reading "Applause" flashed. At the beginning of both of the next two half hours, Cavett would say, "Good evening. To-night we're continuing last night's interview with Gordon Liddy." The audience did not seem to find that peculiar, either. With something analogous, perhaps, to the press' incapacity from time to time to for-mulate an issue, the studio audience, while it must have been perfectly aware that three nights could hardly have passed, literally, in a single afternoon, seemed unable to discern what was literal in the rather gro-tesque conversation before them, and what was not. Or perhaps they did know, exactly, and the gasps themselves were not to be taken literally. Or perhaps, again, they had suspended their disbelief so far, that three nights did pass for them early one afternoon.

Later, in a cab on the way to Chelsea, I asked Liddy how negotiations were going for the purchase of the house on the Potomac. He said he had reason to hope that their offer would be accepted. He was not sure. Moreover, as a result of a cutback by the District of Columbia Board of Education, Frances Liddy had received notice that she had lost her teach-ing job. For the moment, apart from his book, the Liddys had no income. We were on our way to a tavern on Nineteenth Street for Liddy's first conversation with Eric Norden, a writer who wanted to do an interview with him for *Playboy*. Norden had told him that *Playboy* interviews were done with tape recorders. Liddy, not surprisingly, had bought a tape re-corder of his own. At the tavern, the bartender greeted Liddy with par-ticular affection. A zealous supporter of the IRA, he had done time with Liddy, for smuggling and unauthorized possession of firearms.

In July, Liddy was inducted, as an Honorary Member, into the Honor Legion of the Police Department of New York. "Composed of members of the police force of the City of New York, comprising all ranks, who, during the last sixty-eight years, have received departmental recogni-tion . . . for deeds of valor performed at imminent risk of life, or who have been recommended for meritorious acts. . . . It holds in one great bond of comradeship the honored men of the department, the bravest of the brave. It recognizes no rank. It is a force within a force, a tower of strength to combat evil, an inspiration from within, a beacon of hope for the weak, a haven for good. . . . Its tenets: self-respect, courage, loyalty, and devotion to duty." He had also become a member of the Association of Platform Speakers, which would book him for speeches all over the country, for a fee. The fees would be particularly welcome. Although Frances, as abruptly as she had been notified that she had lost her teaching job, had received notice that she was rehired, the Liddys had calculated that, with Sandy, Grace, and Jim at college, and Raymond and Tom in private schools, the cost of the children's education alone for next year would be $31,000. Liddy had completed his interviews with *Playboy.* And he had accepted an invitation to speak, on August 22, to the annual convention of the Association of Independent Truckers of America, in Colorado Springs.

Gordon and Frances Liddy arrived at Washington's Dulles Airport for their flight to Denver, just as the airborne mobile lounge for passengers, was leaving the main building for the plane. Liddy told me that, last week, while Raymond was driving the Cadillac, which by now had 200,000 miles on it, "the steering went." "And," Liddy continued, "the fourth gear of the Volvo is no more." The bid on the Alan Drury house had been accepted. The Liddys were now trying to sell their house in Oxon Hill. Frances said that the reason they had been so nearly late for the flight, however, was that she had left at the last possible moment from her zoo course. Zoo course? As soon as she was reinstated as a teacher, she had enrolled, at the Washington Zoo, in a cram workshop for twelve teachers "in teaching children how to appreciate the zoo." She was pleased that zoos weren't just zoos anymore, but were actively breeding endangered species and educating children. "It's good for the kids, of course. And it's good for me, working with people who are so enthralled." She spoke of how glad she was to have been rehired, after "the shock of being rifted." Rifted? "Reduction in force," she said. "When you're suddenly rifted, after ten years, you go through a lot of feelings. You've got to be dedicated to have stayed with it that long. Special programs for the difficult kids are virtually nonexistent. So you have to make a choice. Either I'm going to go crazy, or I'll stay because I really like to teach. There are always one or two kids each year that you know you've helped, two out of twenty-five you really feel you save. About half of them are going to make it anyway. Only two or three are going to go down the drain. And you don't need to put those down a well. They just need special education programs. Now everybody wants to save birds and fishes. Much as I love birds and fishes, they are not our most important natural resource." I asked about her cats. There had not been a calico male, but the local veterinarian had a list of people wanting kittens from each litter. "It's fun to have births," Frances Liddy said. Jim, the Liddy's third child, had been born in Denver, nineteen years ago, when Liddy was with the Denver office of the FBI. Frances had not been back since. "In the FBI, you get restationed so often," she said, "but with seniority, you get a choice. And for a lot of agents, Denver is the office of preference. For their last years." The Liddys were going to stay on a few days, after the truckers convention, "to see Colorado people that we knew." "It says a lot about the kind of people they are," she said, "that we would be friends after those nineteen years."

At the Denver airport, we were met by a policeman, a policewoman, and Bill Scheffer, vice president of Overdrive—an organization which, in addition to sponsoring annual conventions, publishes a magazine, runs a pension fund, gives legal assistance, lobbies in Washington, and performs other services for the Association of Independent Truckers of America. The Independent Truckers, who own and drive their own trucks, are not only distinct from the Teamsters—the Teamsters have tried for years, through legislation and by other, often violent, means to put them out of business. In fact, a combination of political and business interests has made it highly unlikely that Independents, many of whom are husband-and-wife teams, driving a single rig, will manage to survive. Like all drivers, they are particularly vulnerable to rising fuel costs. Like all truckers, they resent the "double nickel," the fifty-five-mile-an-hour speed limit, which of course costs them driving time—and, Scheffer claims, in spite of government pronouncements to the contrary, fuel. Owing to regulations by the Interstate Commerce Commission, however, and pressures by the Teamsters, and the response of politicians to those pressures, the Independents are subject to special rules, and special costs and taxes. They are obliged by law, for instance, to pay 27 percent of the proceeds from most interstate hauls to interstate carriers which are already licensed by the ICC. Independents are unable to obtain such licenses. The so-called trucking deregulation bill, The Motor Carriers Act of 1980, which had just passed Congess, was designed to eliminate such inequities and abuses. Under election-year pressure from the

Teamsters, Scheffer said, as he drove the Liddys and me from Denver to Colorado Springs, the Trucking Deregulation Act had become "just a cosmetic piece of nothing."

Earlier this year, when the Independents succeeded for a time in a protest, a truck blockade of Washington, some Teamsters tried to break it. A few Independents shot at them that time. Scheffer, who had come to Colorado from Washington, where he testified before the Senate Sub-committee on Surface Transportation, said the Independents were plan-ning another such boycott for October 20. "Congress only reacts to a crisis," he said. "So sometimes you have to create one." He mentioned that, in addition to Liddy, the speakers at this convention were Con-gressman Philip Crane, who had run for the Republican nomination for President, and who was one of five candidates said to have been consid-ered by Ronald Reagan for his running mate, and Congressman John Rousselot of California, one of the most powerful and respected House conservatives.

Liddy inquired about the make of car we were in. Scheffer, with mild disgust, said it was "one of the most underpowered cars Ford ever made." Liddy looked at the rather many dials on the dashboard, which resembled an instrument panel in a cockpit. Scheffer pointed to one which read Miles to Destination. "I don't know how it can indicate that," he said, reflectively, "since it doesn't know what our destination is." Then, he told us what we might have guessed, that this was not his car. He drove very fast and well. He spoke of Overdrive's part in the three years of litigation which finally got rid of the kind of speed traps by which Justices of the Peace in small towns used to augment their incomes. "Three years," he said, "to get that overturned." Then he spoke of the present administration's Department of Transportation, and its head, Joan Clay-brook, who was once an assistant to Ralph Nader. "Joan Claybrook is against everything on wheels," he said. "And Carter is probably the most antitrucking President we've ever had." He mentioned a relatively minor matter, a new regulation by which the DOT was trying to force all truck-ers to change their rearview mirrors. "Such a goofy thing," he said, "but a huge financial burden for our industry." He pointed, silently but with obvious disapproval, to a state police car, blue lights flashing, and a trooper giving a summons for speeding to a driver at the side of an oncoming lane.

The highway we were on was broad and uncrowded, four lanes separated by a wide green divider. Scheffer slowed down, just perceptibly, and eased from the left lane into the right. He did not point or even seem to look this time at a police car lurking beside our own lane. "There are a lot of good radar detectors you can buy now, on the market," he said. Then, with considerable satisfaction, he described court cases and public exhibitions in which he (Scheffer was once an engineer and later trained by the army as a radar specialist) and other representatives of the Independent Truckers Association had demonstrated the ineffectiveness of police radar in detecting speeders. "A trooper was going on about how effective and reliable it is, blah, blah, blah. Then we gave our demonstration. They were embarrassed. The *L.A. Times* caught a picture of a trooper, furious, beating on his dashboard. They used our caption: State Trooper Makes a Minor Adjustment to His Radar," Scheffer said.

A car whizzed by us on the left. Scheffer said, "He's really going." Liddy mentioned that in some states, Pennsylvania for example, there are signs reading Keep Right Except to Pass. Scheffer nodded, approvingly. He returned to the subject of the Department of Transportation. "Diesel truck races are now becoming very popular," he said. "Sometimes, of course, you get so much torque that the right-front tires blow. Because of the heat and the weight. Now, Joan Claybrook has done everything in her power to stop those races." No one said anything. "Well, all right. But can you imagine, she came out to one of our conventions. And she brought us a Department of Transportation film called *Underride*. Its message was, You're all potential killers and murderers. I mean, can you imagine? These guys know their profession. They have families. She brings them this audiovisual aid for kids." He dismissed as government propaganda, too, the request that Americans, as an act of patriotic energy conservation, drive less this summer. "We have research proving," he said, "that you use less fuel on a camping trip in the car with your whole family of four than you would have used if you'd spent your entire vacation at home." Suddenly, he turned to Liddy and asked him what reaction there had been to him across the country. "Most people are favorable. Not all, of course," Liddy said. "But most Americans, let's face it, do not like a snitch."

Scheffer arrived in Colorado Springs, and pulled into the driveway of the Four Seasons Motel. Most of the parking lot was covered by a circus tent, which contained equipment of interest to truckers. The rest was

covered with vans and rigs of every size. Scheffer pointed to a converted
city bus, with signs reading Overdrive, Honk If You Want to Save the
American Dream, Truckers for Free Enterprise, etc. Scheffer had told us
that, when the association had inquired of the Four Seasons whether the
truckers might hold this year's convention there, the motel's manage-
ment had written, as managements in such situations customarily do, to
the site of last year's convention, a motel in Nashville, to ask what sort
of guests these independent truckers were. "They told us Nashville's recommendation said ours was the best convention they'd ever had," Scheffer said. From the minute we entered the lobby, it became clear why this
might be true. The convention looked like the sweetest-natured, best-
mannered, grave, friendly, strong, and yet highly varied large group of
Americans I had ever seen. There were few blacks, and I saw no Asian
or Spanish-Americans. Most of the men present had at one time been
Teamsters, when the Independent Truckers Association was not yet
strong enough to make it possible for them not to be. Most of the women,
including the secretaries and copy editors of Overdrive, had at one time
been, or still were, truckers. And the financial and regulatory difficulties
which the Independents have faced in recent years made it remarkable
that so wide a variety of owner-drivers should still have the time, the
money, and the tenacity to attend a convention of this sort, or even to
exist. They did not drink much—I never saw more than three people in
the bar. So they could not have been desirable guests in that big-spender
sense. But I remembered a hotel detective in New York, saying that, of
all conventions, hotels most dread associations of psychologists or psy-
chiatrists, who are forever hiring prostitutes, male or female, and refusing
to pay in full, or having their wallets stolen, or getting hurt, or otherwise
becoming involved with the police. The truckers, from one small, frail
driver who was nearly ninety, to the many couples, with or without well-
behaved but animated children, spent their money in the restaurant and
coffee shop. Teenage sons and daughters, when they were not in the pool
or at the Ping-Pong table, spent their change in a little gallery of pinball
machines. And there was nothing of even Shriner-level mischief in anyone at all.

At the reception desk, Scheffer detached a walkie-talkie from his belt
and, speaking into it, asked where Michael Parkhurst, president of Overdrive and the Independent Truckers Association, was. A voice said, "He's
right here." Scheffer said, "But I don't know where 'here' is." There was

a little static. Then, the voice said that Parkhurst would meet Scheffer and the Liddys in the Liddys' room. The Liddys' room turned out to be a duplex, with a bar on which there was Scotch, bourbon, gin, vodka, Seven-Up, Coca-Cola, a bouquet of flowers, and a bottle of champagne, on ice. There was also, rolled up, a large poster, with a red circle crossed by a diagonal red bar, which to drivers all over the world means No Entry, superimposed on a picture of a peanut. The Liddys laughed. "We also have one of Khomeini," Scheffer said. Michael Parkhurst came in, a large, dark-haired man in his late forties, who looked as though he might have spent his adult years, as he has, in fact, spent them, giving the Teamster leadership their first serious opposition. He apologized at once to Liddy. Congressman Crane, it seemed, had refused to speak at tomorrow's barbecue if Liddy was going to speak there. "I guess he's one of those who thinks once you've put nail polish on your nails, it never comes off," he said. But that, in his view, was the congressman's problem. Liddy was scheduled to speak then, and could do so if he liked. "I don't want to make it difficult for you," Liddy said. "Whatever is easiest for you. I don't want to cause you any problem." Then, as Parkhurst continued, rather dourly, to discuss Congressman Crane's objections, Liddy said, "I don't want to make *you* uncomfortable. I don't mind making *him* uncomfortable." In the end, it was decided that Crane would speak, then leave if he liked when Liddy spoke. Liddy asked how accurate the scheduling would be. "We're always right on the money where time is concerned," Scheffer said. Parkhurst said he had not checked the local bookstores, to see whether they had copies of Liddy's book. "I didn't come out here, to your convention, to sell my book," Liddy said.

It was 7:45 P.M. At eight, inside the motel's only ballroom, there was to be an Ice Cream Parlor, sponsored by the Detroit Diesel Company. Just outside the ballroom, the letters ITA (for Independent Truckers of America) were sculptured in ice. A couple were photographing their baby in front of the letters. Behind them, about two hundred truckers, of all ages, with many children, waited for the doors to open. Many of the adults, and most of the children, were holding the strings of pink balloons. Promptly at eight, the doors did open. People filed in, served themselves with many flavors of ice cream from two large tables, then sat down at small round tables with red-and-white checkered tablecloths. When the little tables were filled, people sat on the floor. Congressman

Rousselot was scheduled to speak at nine. The congressman's legs are severely crippled. At the request of his administrative assistant, a desk had been placed in front of the microphone at which the congressman would stand. Shortly before nine, the congressman looked around the ballroom. He asked that the desk be taken away. He removed his suit jacket and his tie. "These are my kind of people," he said, and hobbled to the microphone. He spoke for more than an hour. He mentioned a small businessman's proposal to HUD for the use of a piece of real estate. HUD had replied that he would require the approval of twenty-eight separate agencies. HUD had also pointed out that he had not, as required, traced the deed of his property (which was located several miles outside Baton Rouge) back beyond the year 1803. The businessman had replied in turn, "Gentlemen: I was unaware that any educated man did not know that 1803 was the date of the Louisiana Purchase." He then went on to trace title to the King of France, to the Indians, to Jesus, and to God, adding, "I hope you're satisfied." The congressman spoke of over-regulation by the federal government, of the country drifting toward "dictatorship by bureaucracy." He spoke of the federal food stamp program, which had been intended to be small, local, addressed to the rural poor, and which had burgeoned from 440,000 recipients in its first year to 22 million in fiscal 1979. He said he wanted to "get the federal government out of your pockets, and off your backs," and so forth. He said, "Thank you for what you do. For your posters and your bumper stickers. You do more good than you might think." He asked them to "educate," by which he meant lobby, or put pressure on, their congressmen. He mentioned that contractors had managed to "reeducate" Congress in the matter of common situs picketing, when the unions thought they had permanently "educated" it to the opposite effect.

When the questions came, their tone was earnest, often sad. Could he help reduce the excise tax on trucks and parts? He hadn't known there was such a tax, but "I'll vote for any tax cuts any time, at the federal level." A questioner said that, as an American, he had always thought and spoken in terms of inches, feet, yards, pounds. Now, on account of "the multinations and the scientific community," who wanted a uniform worldwide system for their own convenience, he was forced to undergo the cost of converting to the metric system. "Congressman," the trucker concluded, "are they going to take our language away from us next?"

Rousselot replied that he understood that the conversion from pounds, feet, inches, etc., to the metric system was "voluntary." "How can it be voluntary," another trucker asked, "if it's on the road signs of the Interstate?" The congressman said that, since he normally traveled by plane, he was not overly familiar with the Interstate highway system. He would look into the matter. When the questions were over, he received a standing ovation. It was clear that the Independents were, as he had thought, "his kind of people." It was also clear that he had not known much about them before.

After the Ice Cream Parlor closed, the Liddys, Scheffer, and I, had hamburgers in the coffee shop, with Walda Abbott, a woman from Los Angeles, in her middle thirties, who is the attorney for the Association of Independent Truckers of America. "Walda," a man named Jack Hurlbutt said, from an adjoining table, "if there are a hundred thousand of us, how come we can't get every one of us in the country together, and get some of the deregulation that we want?" "It's because they're Independents, Jack," Ms. Abbott said. "It's just the nature of the beast." Ms. Abbott turned out to have lived for six years in Singapore, where she had worked on a publishing venture with an attorney I had met when he was still working for the civil rights movement in the South. I asked her how on earth she had happened to become the attorney for the ITA. She and Parkhurst and Scheffer, she said, had known one another when they were growing up in Pittsburgh. She had gone to law school. Scheffer had gone to engineering school, then became a Teamster. Parkhurst had become a Teamster, then founded the ITA. When she had come back from Singapore, where she had gone more or less for the sake of travel, Parkhurst and Scheffer had hired her. That was all. The nearly ninety-year-old trucker walked by. Liddy asked what routes he drove. Scheffer said he hauled fruits and vegetables from Florida to Hunts Point Market, in New York.

The Liddys and I knew Hunts Point, the New York equivalent, in the South Bronx, of Les Halles, though considerably rougher. Trucks of food arrive and depart all night long. Just outside the market, in winter, little bands of people warm themselves over fires in steel drums. There are often fights, inside the market and on its perimeter, in spite of policemen stationed at various checkpoints. Scheffer asked whether we had seen the "lumpers." We had not, did not even know what they were. Scheffer said that the regulations regarding lumpers were among the costly impositions that Independents, and only they, are required to bear. To load or unload his truck, an Independent is required to employ a lumper, forty dollars to load, forty dollars to unload. Moreover, under a tax regulation which Teamster and ICC-licensed carrier lobbyists had pushed through Congress, the IRS does not permit Independents to take a deduction for the use of lumpers. It falls not, as might have been expected, under the deduction for "ordinary and necessary business expenses" but under the "No Deduction for Casual Labor Rule." One night, several years ago, Scheffer, wanting to avoid the eighty-dollar expense, had unloaded and reloaded his own truck. As he drove through the Hunts Point exit, he was shot. He showed us the scar on his arm. No policeman had moved to help him. As we went off to our rooms, the Liddys asked where they might buy some Overdrive T-shirts, like the ones some teenagers were wearing in the hall. The next day, Liddy gave yet another, the best, of his stem-winders. He received a standing ovation far longer than Congressman Rousselot's. Congressman Crane received polite applause.

The last week in August, the Liddy's offer on the Alan Drury house was definitely accepted. In the first days of September, the issue of *Playboy* with the Liddy interview appeared. The interviewer, who had interviewed Liddy in sessions lasting part of each of three days, wrote that he had "spent the better part of ten days with him." Since Liddy had taped the conversations as the interviewer was taping them, and since he had asked to see the transcripts, the interviewer had sent him the transcripts, for his approval. Liddy had been surprised to find not only that his answers were changed, and that other answers, which he had never given, were attributed to him, but that even many of the *questions*, which both real and invented answers and even poorly edited sections of *Will* were set as replies to, had been made up as well. He had been told to make what corrections he liked. He edited out only things that he had not only never said but would never conceivably say, references to "my brutal captors" in the D.C. jail, for example, or sentences like "I have always lived on the razor's edge." He also corrected factual errors. West Cornwall, New Jersey, he pointed out, for example, is not and never was "on the Hudson River." He cut out a few passages from his book, which had been misquoted and used as his answers, in conversation, to questions that had never been put and with which they had nothing to do. The interviewer had thanked him for all these corrections, the one about the geographical location of West Cornwall, New Jersey, along with the rest.

In the issue of *Playboy* that appeared on the stands, not a single one of the corrections was made. Liddy still has his tapes. In one of his earliest radio interviews, he had said, concerning the notion of celebrity, "To some people, it doesn't matter whether you're Liza Minnelli or the Son of Sam." In another, he had said, to an interviewer whom he liked, and who had asked him whether, honestly, he had no remaining fear, "Maybe. The fear of boredom." But when, with the tapes in his possession, he read the issue of *Playboy*, he seemed, only for a moment but for the first time since I have known him, somewhat depressed, and a bit demoralized.

—1980

HOUSE CRITIC

The job of the regular daily, weekly, or even monthly critic resembles the work of the serious intermittent critic, who writes only when he is asked to or is genuinely moved to, in limited ways and for only a limited period of time. Occasionally, a particularly rich period in one of the arts coincides with a prolific time in the life of a major critic; or a major critic—Edmund Wilson, Harold Rosenberg—takes over a weekly column and uses it as the occasion for an essay. After a time, however, even Edmund Wilson no longer wrote frequently and regularly about books. He also wrote, all his life, on other subjects. Harold Rosenberg wrote continuously on subjects other than painting. Normally, no art can support for long the play of a major intelligence, working flat out, on a quotidian basis. No serious critic can devote himself, frequently, exclusively, and indefinitely, to reviewing works most of which inevitably cannot bear, would even be misrepresented by, review in depth.

At most publications, staff critics are cast up from elsewhere in the journalistic ranks—the copy desk, for instance, or regular reporting. What they provide is a necessary consumer service, which consists essentially of three parts: a notice that the work exists, and where it can be bought, found, or attended; a set of adjectives appearing to set forth an opinion of some sort, but amounting really to a yes vote or a no vote; and a somewhat nonjudgmental, factual description or account, which is usually inferior by any journalistic standard to reporting in all other sections of the paper. On the basis of these columns, the reader gets his information and, if he is an art consumer, forms his own judgment and makes his choice.

Serious publications, however, tend from time to time to hire talented people, educated, usually young, devoted to the craft of criticism, at least as it entails fidelity to an art and to a text under review. What usually happens is that such a critic writes for some time at his highest level: reporting and characterizing accurately; incorporating in whatever is judgmental evidence for what he's saying (a sign of integrity in a critic, as opposed to an opinion monger, is that he tries for evidence; in reviewing prose forms, for example, he will quote); and producing insights, and allusions, which, if they are not downright brilliant, are apposite. What happens after a longer time is that he settles down.

The consumer service remains the professional basis for the staff reviewer's job; fidelity, evidence, and so forth are still the measures of his value, but the high critical edge becomes misplaced, disproportionate when applied to most ordinary work. The staff critic is nonetheless obliged, and paid, to do more than simply mark time between rich periods and occasional masterpieces. The simple truth—this is okay, this is not okay, this is vile, this resembles that, this is good indeed, this is unspeakable—is not a day's work for a thinking adult. Some critics go shrill. Others go stale. A lot go simultaneously shrill and stale. A few critics, writing quietly and well, bring something extra into their work. Arlene Croce, a fine ability to describe. John Russell, a piece of education in art history. Hilton Kramer, something in the realm of ideas. A few others bring a consistent personal voice, a sort of chat whose underlying proposition is: This is what happened in my field today; here's what I have to say about it; draw what conclusions you will, on the basis of your familiarity by now with my style, my quality of mind, and the range of my association, in short with who I am. Some staff critics quit and choose to work flat out again, on other interests and in intermittent pieces. By far the most common tendency, however, is to stay put and simply to inflate, to pretend that each day's text is after all a crisis—the most, first, best, worst, finest, meanest, deepest, etc.—to take on, since we are dealing in superlatives, one of the first, most unmistakable marks of the hack.

Movies seem to invite particularly broad critical discussion: To begin with, alone among the arts, they count as their audience, their art consumer, everyone. (Television, in this respect, is clearly not an art but an appliance, through which reviewable material is sometimes played.) The staff movie critic's job thus tends to have less in common with the art, or book, or theater critic's, whose audiences are relatively specialized and discrete, than with the work of the political columnist—writing, that is, of daily events in the public domain, in which almost everyone's interest is to some degree engaged, and about which everyone seems inclined to have a view. Film reviewing has always had an ingredient of reportage. Since the forties, the *New York Times* has reviewed almost every movie that opened in New York—as it would not consider reviewing every book, exhibit, or other cultural event, or even every account filed from the UN or City Hall. For a long time it seemed conceivable that movies could sustain, if not a great critic, at least a distinguished commentator-critic, on the order, say, of Robert Warshow, with the frequency of Walter Lippmann. In the late fifties and early sixties, it seemed likely that such a critic might be Pauline Kael.

Writing freelance, but most often in *Partisan Review*, Ms. Kael seemed to approach movies with an energy and a good sense that were unmatched at the time in film criticism. In France, young people were emerging from the archives of the Cinémathèque to write reverently for film publications and, later, to make the films that became the *nouvelle vague*. Here, movie critics were so much the financial and spiritual creatures of the industry that, in 1962, Judith Crist was counted new and brave for having a few reservations about *Cleopatra*. Magazines had staff movie critics; but no one paid much attention to them. Newspaper movie critics were, in general, writers of extended blurbs for high-budget films. Out in San Francisco, though, there was this person, writing as frequently as she could manage to sell pieces. In 1965, a book appeared, something mildly off in the coarse single *entendu* of its title, *I Lost It at the Movies*, but, as a collection of movie reviews, interesting. Ms. Kael continued to write, freelance. One began to look forward, particularly if one had already read a lot about a picture, to reading what Pauline Kael had to say.

Then, briefly at *McCall's* (where, braver even than Ms. Crist, she panned *The Sound of Music*) and, beginning in 1968, at *The New Yorker*, Ms. Kael acquired a staff critic's job and a strong institutional base. Nothing could be clearer—the case of John Simon comes to mind at once—than that such a change is by no means always fortunate. A voice that may have seemed, sometimes, true and iconoclastic when it was outside can become, with institutional support, vain, overbearing, foolish, hysterical. Instead of the quiet authority of the this-is-who-I-am, and here's-what-I-have-to-say, there is the somewhat violent spectacle of a minor celebrity in frenzy, weirdly intent on what he/she is going to "do to" whatever passes for his/her weekly text. For a year or two, Ms. Kael, however, continued to write fine pieces. If there were many weeks when she seemed far from her best, nothing could be more natural; no writer is always at his/her best. She tended to write rather too long for what she had to say each week, and there was something overwrought in her tone. Here, of course, there was a difference from a serious intermittent critic—whose tone and length reflect, not the rote pressures of a deadline but a real pitch and interval of thought. For some time, however, the effect was only this: One could not look forward, always and to the same degree, to reading what Ms. Kael had to say.

Then there began to be quirks, mannerisms, in particular a certain compulsive and joyless naughtiness. Not just conscious, heavy allusions of the sort that recurred in her titles, *Kiss Kiss Bang Bang; Deeper into Movies*, etc., but an undercurrent of irrelevant, apparently inadvertent sexual revelation. It seemed that editing, especially *New Yorker* editing, would have caught this tendency at its most awkward and repetitive. It was possible that precisely the columns most nearly out of all control were episodes in a struggle against *The New Yorker*'s constraints—not always an unworthy struggle. But there was also, in relation to filmmaking itself, an increasingly strident *knowingness:* Whatever else you may think about her work, each column seemed more hectoringly to claim, *she certainly does know about movies.* And often, when the point appeared most knowing, it was factually false. Ms. Kael, for instance, berated George Roy Hill, at length and in particularly scornful, savvy terms, for having recorded the outdoor sequences of *Butch Cassidy and the Sundance Kid* indoors, in a studio: "Each . . . comes out . . . in the dead sound of the studio. There is scarcely even an effort to supply plausible outdoor resonances." As it happens, Mr. Hill had insisted on recording outdoors, at great expense and over heavy objections from the studio, which had predicted (accurately, at least as regards Ms. Kael) that no one could tell the difference. When informed of such errors, Ms. Kael never acknowledged or rectified them; she tended rather to drag disparaging references to the work of filmmakers about whom she had been wrong into unrelated columns ever after.

Still, there were often fine columns that could be the work of no one else. When one struck a long bad piece, or a lot of long bad pieces, one could consider them off-weeks, lapses. Moreover, as there had once been fan clubs for movie stars, and then cults of directors and authors, there were, by the late sixties (as reflected even in names featured on movie marquees), cults of movie critics; a critic with a cult is a critic under peculiar stress. Ms. Kael still seemed to feel extremely strongly about most films she reviewed. Somehow, particularly in bland movie times, that seemed a kind of virtue. It hardly occurred to one that holding too many very strong opinions about matters of minor consequence might elsewhere be the virtue of hucksters and demagogues. A semblance of passion enlivened a weekly column. It was possible to think of each off-column as an exception. I, for one, continued to believe that movie criticism was probably in quite good hands with Pauline Kael.

Now, *When the Lights Go Down,* a collection of her reviews over the past five years, is out; and it is, to my surprise and without Kael- or Simon-like exaggeration, not simply, jarringly, piece by piece, line by line, and without interruption, worthless. It turns out to embody something appalling and widespread in the culture. Over the years, that is, Ms. Kael's quirks, mannerisms, tactics, and excesses have not only taken over her work so thoroughly that hardly anything else, nothing certainly of intelligence or sensibility, remains; they have also proved contagious, so that the content and level of critical discussion, of movies but also of other forms, have been altered astonishingly for the worse.

To the spectacle of the staff critic as celebrity in frenzy, about to "do" something "to" a text, Ms. Kael has added an entirely new style of ad hominem brutality and intimidation. The substance of her work has become little more than an attempt, with an odd variant of flak advertising copy, to coerce, actually to force numb acquiescence, in the laying down of a remarkably trivial and authoritarian party line.

She has, in principle, four things she likes: *frissons* of horror; physical violence depicted in explicit detail; sex scenes, so long as they have an ingredient of cruelty and involve partners who know each other either casually or under perverse circumstances; and fantasies of invasion by, or subjugation of or by, apes, pods, teens, bodysnatchers, and extraterrestrials. Whether or not one shares these predilections—and whether they are in fact more than four, or only one—they do not really lend themselves to critical discussion. It turns out, however, that Ms. Kael does think of them as critical positions, and regards it as an act of courage, of moral courage, to subscribe to them. The reason one cannot simply dismiss them as *de gustibus*, or even as harmless aberration, is that they have become inseparable from the repertory of devices of which Ms. Kael's writing now, almost wall to wall, consists.

She has an underlying vocabulary of about nine favorite words, which occur several hundred times, and often several times per page, in this book of nearly six hundred pages: "whore" (and its derivatives "whorey," "whorish," "whoriness"), applied in many contexts, but almost never to actual prostitution; "myth," "emblem" (also "mythic," "emblematic"), used with apparent intellectual intent, but without ascertainable meaning; "pop," "comic-strip," "trash" ("trashy"), "pulp" ("pulpy"), all used judgmentally (usually approvingly) but otherwise apparently interchangeable with "mythic"; "urban poetic," meaning marginally more violent than "pulpy"; "soft" "(pejorative); "tension," meaning, apparently, any desirable state; "rhythm," used often as a verb, but meaning harmony or speed; "visceral"; and "level." These words may be used in any variant, or in alternation, or strung together in sequence—"visceral poetry of pulp," for example, or "mythic comic-strip level"—until they become a kind of incantation.

She also likes words ending in "ized" ("vegetabilized," "robotized," "aestheticized," "utilized," "mythicized"), and a kind of slang ("twerpy," "dopey," "dumb," "grungy," "horny," "stinky," "drip," "stupes," "crud"), which amounts, in prose, to an affectation of straightforwardness.

I leave aside for the moment Ms. Kael's incessant but special use of words many critics use a lot: "we," "you," "they," "some people"; "needs," "feel," "know," "ought"—as well as her two most characteristic grammatical constructions: "so/that" or "such/that," used not as a mode of explication or comparison (as in, for example, he was so lonely that he wept) but as an entirely new hype connective between two unrelated or unformulated thoughts; and her unprecedented use, many times per page and to new purposes, of the mock rhetorical question and the question mark.

Because what is most striking is that she has, over the years, lost any notion of the legitimate borders of polemic. Mistaking lack of civility for vitality, she now substitutes for argument a protracted, obsessional invective—what amounts to a staff cinema critic's branch of est. Her favorite, most characteristic device of this kind is the ad personam physical (she might say, visceral) image: images, that is, of sexual conduct, deviance, impotence, masturbation; also of indigestion, elimination, excrement. I do not mean to imply that these images are frequent, or that one has to look for them. They are relentless, inexorable. "Swallowing this movie," one finds on page 147, "is an unnatural act." On page 151, "his way of pissing on us." On page 153, "a little gas from undigested Antonioni." On page 158, "these constipated flourishes." On page 182, "as forlornly romantic as Cyrano's plume dipped in horse manure." On page 226, "the same brand of sanctifying horse manure." On page 467, "a new brand of pop manure." On page 120, "flatulent seriousness." On page 226, "flatulent Biblical-folk John Ford film." On page 353, "gaseous naiveté." And elsewhere, everywhere, "flatulent," "gaseous," "gasbag," "makes you feel a little queasy," "makes you gag a little," "Just a belch from the Nixon era," "you can't cut through the crap in her," "plastic turds."

Of an actress, "She's making love to herself"; of a screenwriter, "He's turned it on himself; he's diddling his own talent." "It's tumescent-filmmaking." "Drama and politics don't climax together." Sometimes, one has the illusion that these oral, anal, or just physical epithets have some meaning—"*Taxi Driver* is a movie in heat," for instance, or "the film is an icebag." But then: "*Coma* is like a prophylactic." One thinks, How, how is it like a prophylactic? "It's so cleanly made." Or a metaphor with a sadistic note that defies, precisely, physical comprehension. "The movie has had a spinal tap."

The degree of physical sadism in Ms. Kael's work is, so far as I know, unique in expository prose. What is remarkable, however, is how often, as a matter of technique, she *imputes* it. She writes, in one review, that a female character regards another female character as "a worm for squishing"; in another review, that a male character sees another male character as "a trivial whitey to be squished"; in a third review, of a female character, that "she'd crunch your heart to clean a pore"—without perhaps being aware that all the squishing and crunching attributed to characters, actors, anyone, is entirely her own idea.

"You half expect her to shove that little bug away and stamp on him," she writes, in yet another review, of Candice Bergen. More in a moment about who that "you" might be; but the tactic is perfect. "You" have a violent expectation. Ms. Bergen would "shove" and "stamp on" the "little bug" (another actor). While Ms. Kael is just out there, writing it all down.

"You want to wipe it off his face." "You want to kick him." Your "guts are squeezed." Guts appear a lot, in noun, verb, or adjective form: "The film's discreet, gutted sensitivity," for instance, "is self-sufficient." What?

"You are caught up emotionally and flung about the room." Thirty pages later, "we" are caught "by the throat" and "knocked about the room." All this, of course, is standard, blurb copy. What is less usual is the attention to a specific limb or organ: the "maggot in his brain"; the filmmakers who "should stop lighting candles in their skulls, they're burning their brains out"; the "punishment in the sinuses," "punched too often in the vocal cords," "vocal cords . . . you might think . . . had survived a rock slide." All right, still in the realm of the usual, routine. But then, a pure Kaelism. Having described a scene in which a character "holds her hand over a fire until it is charred and bursts," still apparently unsatisfied, Ms. Kael adds this joke: "(Did Altman run out of marshmallows?)"

I do not mean to suggest that this style, this cast of mind, is pathological—only that it is not just idiosyncratic, either. It has become part of a pattern, an instrument to a purpose—quite remote by now from criticism or even films. Another such instrument is the mock rhetorical question, the little meditation with the question mark. In this book, there are literally thousands of them, not just of the jokey, marshmallow sort, but of every sort, in tirades and fusillades, in and outside parentheses. An apparently limitless capacity to inquire:

> Could it be that he's interiorizing his emotions, in response to Schrader's conception of the emptiness of Jerry's life, and doesn't realize how little he's putting out?

> Has he been schooling himself in late Dreyer and Bresson and Rossellini, and is he trying to turn Thackeray's picaresque entertainment into a religious exercise?

> Yet can we be meant to laugh at his satisfaction with his own virulence after we've seen Florence Malraux's name on the credits as assistant to the director, and remembered that Resnais is the son-in-law of Andre Malraux, who died a few months ago after a long illness?

(Is Cimino invoking the mythology of Hawkeye and the great chief Chingachook?)

Is it just the pompadour or is he wearing a false nose?

How can the novelist have pain in his bowels when *Providence* has no bowels?

Have you ever bought a statue of a pissing cupid?

Were these 435 prints processed in a sewer?

Didn't Alda recognize that his material is like kapok?

Why doesn't he hear her voice first . . . and be turned on by it? And wouldn't he then look to see whom it belonged to? And does she know who he is when she bawls him out? And if she does wouldn't this affect how she speaks to him? And if she doesn't when is the moment she finds out?

Why are we getting these union speeches now? Were the outsiders directing the strike? Were the pros working out strategy? Have we been conned? Have people become so accustomed? . . .

Why didn't anyone explain to him that he needn't wear himself out with acting?

Why is Doc in an unholy alliance with the Nazi villain, Szell?

Shouldn't the movie be about *why* he imagines what he does?

Who is this hitchhiker on the road of life?

Allied Artists and Bantam Books, why are you doing this?

(Is it relevant that Bertolucci's father's name was Attilio?)

How can you have any feeling for a man who doesn't enjoy being in bed with Sophia Loren?

How can the Count's arrival and his plea for a hasty marriage have any vibrations?

Why then does it offend me when I think about it?

And what is Sally doing when she holds out her arms to her husband?

Where was the director?

Does the cavalry return?

Who—him?

You shouldn't risk losing thoughts like that. Has the tape recorder been stored in a safe place?

But, oh, God, why isn't it better? Why isn't there the daring and the exaltation that our senses fairly cry out for?

And so on.

It is difficult to convey the effect of hundreds of pages of these questions. Those that have answers—Yes. No. What? I don't know, sweetie; you're the one who saw the movie—badger the reader, who is courteously inclined to *think* when addressed with question marks, into a mindless, degrading travesty of colloquy or dialectic. Others are coy, convoluted displays of erudition. Ms. Kael wants us to know, for instance, that she knows that Resnais is related to Malraux, and that Malraux is dead; also, that she knows the first name of Bertolucci's father. Others still, addressed, like script-margin annotations, to the film itself ("Shouldn't the movie be about *why*, etc.?"), are proprietary, prescriptive. Ms. Kael, having lost any notion of where the critic sits, wants to imply that she was at the story conference, that the film is somehow hers. And others still, in particular the outcries—to God, and Allied Artists and Bantam Books—are meant to demonstrate that she *cares*, cares more than anybody. It is overwhelmingly clear, however, from the reviews in this book, that one thing Ms. Kael has ceased to care about is films.

She hardly praises a movie any more, so much as she derides and inveighs against those who might disagree with her about it. ("Have you ever bought a statue of a pissing cupid?") And, like the physical assaults and sneers, the mock rhetorical questions are rarely *saying* anything. They are simply doing something. Bullying, presuming, insulting, frightening, enlisting, intruding, dunning, rallying. The most characteristic of these questions, in its way, is the one about Alan Alda and the kapok. Had it been phrased declaratively—Alda doesn't recognize that his material is like kapok—it would still be uninteresting; but it might raise a question of its own. How, in what sense, is it like kapok? (In the same way, perhaps, as *Coma* is like a prophylactic?) Or if the question had been, at least, addressed to Alda—Alda (God, Bantam Books), didn't you recognize that your material is like kapok?—it would be clear what is being asked. I would point out, however, that the question (which permits only a yes or no) is still so framed as to compel assent: Yes, I did recognize; No, I didn't recognize, etc. But to address the question to the *reader* effectively conceals what is being said (namely, nothing), and attempts to enlist him in a constituency, a knowing constituency—knowing, in this instance, about Alda's ignorance about this nothing. The same with "Why didn't anyone explain to him that he needn't wear himself out with acting?" and all the other trivial, inane interrogations. They express what are not views or perceptions, but blunt devices to marshal a constituency—of readers, other reviewers, filmmakers if at all possible—which has, in turn, no views but a coerced, fearful, or bemused falling in line.

I do not mean for a moment to imply that every Kael review is in the vituperative or inquisitional mode. There are meditations of all kinds and, quite often, broad cultural allusions:

> The images are simplified, down to their dramatic components, like the diagrams of great artists' compositions in painting texts, and this, plus the faintly psychedelic Romanesque color, creates a pungent viselike atmosphere.

A word heap, surely. The quality of observation may be characteristic of people who insist that films be discussed in *visual* terms. I am not certain that Ms. Kael has a clear idea what a "Romanesque color" might be, particularly in the "faintly psychedelic" spectrum, and even in the most "pungent, viselike atmosphere"; but I'd like to stay for a moment, in two simpler sentences, with the visual, the cinematic eye.

On page 398, there is an "upper lip pulling back in a snarl" to reveal "yellow teeth like a crumbling mountain range." On 436, on the other hand, there are "jagged lower teeth that suggest a serpent about to snap." Now, the vision, it's true, is consistent. But surely the mouths are peculiarly observed, or both the mountain range and the serpent are upside down.

There are allusions as well to literature. Ms. Kael likes to mention Dostoevsky, Tolstoy, and Shakespeare's fools. "It's like a classic passage in Tolstoy," she writes, and before one can wonder Really? Which? she has dropped the subject. "We're given the components of a novel at a glance," she writes elsewhere, and fortunately drops that, too. But then:

> It's true that one remembers the great scenes from the nineteenth-century Russian novels, not the passages in between; but . . . there's a consistency of vision in Turgenev or Dostoevski or Tolstoy.

One pauses. Can it be that there is actually a thought coming? Yes. It's this:

> We're told what we want to know.

I'll spare you further references to literature and Tolstoy. I'll skip most of the recurrent, indescribable reflections on "art" and "artists": "When artists are raging, straining to express themselves," or "If De Palma were an artist in another medium." Their intellectual content ranges from "An artist can draw a lot of energy from obsessive material"—unarguable, certainly, and not carried further—to this baffling Kaelism: "They are not plagued by the problem of bourgeois artists. They have loose foreskins."

Historically, it is hard to know what to make of the little italicized *eureka* in "Truffaut is romantic *and* ironic"; "romantic irony" occurs so early and often in any liberal education. But even in the cultural province she claims most confidently as her own, Ms. Kael can go puzzlingly astray. When she calls *King Kong* "marvelous Classics-comics," for instance, it seems almost pedantic to recall that Classics Comics were, in fact, condensations of classic books, the Bible, say, or her beloved Tolstoy, not at all the genre that she seems to have in mind. As for allusions to racial or social developments, they tend to take a jokey form. "He's an equal opportunity fornicator."

There are also, however, ruminations of the highest order:

> For those who are infatuated with what they loathe the battle with themselves never stops.

Too true. Several reviews later:

And when your slavemaster is your father and he wants to kill you for your defiance that defiance must kill everything you've ever known.

Perhaps less true.

I'd like to say here that I didn't expect to find this, and I wasn't looking for it. I now think that no one has looked at the *meaning* of these sentences, or at their intellectual quality, in many years. I have also postponed, in some ways I would rather have avoided, Ms. Kael's critical characterizations of specific performers and specific films. These are always largely matters of personal taste. In addition, the mere mention these days of a specific movie can distract moviegoers, with the sheer vehemence of widely held opinions, from what is actually being said, and by what methods and techniques. That situation is only partially a result of Ms. Kael's efforts. Most writing about films now contains a degree of overstatement, meaninglessness, obfuscation. I won't dwell on the advocacy, if that is the word, of Peckinpah, De Palma, Coppola, but turn to very quiet ground:

In repose, Lily Tomlin looks like a wistful pony; when she grins, her equine gums and long, drawn face suggest a friendly, goofy horse.

I'm not sure this is an insight worth restating, or amplifying, three times in a single sentence ("pony," "equine," "horse"). I am quite sure it is not an insight, it is wrong, to write of the characters in *The Deer Hunter*, that "they're the American cousins of hobbits." Then:

George C. Scott has to be dominating or he's nothing.

It's hard to know what to respond—except *Petulia*. Maybe Ms. Kael thought he was "nothing" in that film. Certainly, he was not "dominating" in it. Or:

In *Nashville*, Keith Carradine's voice insinuates itself; that tremolo makes it seem as if he were singing just to you.

This, I submit, is no longer a matter of doubt. The whole point of what was probably the most beautifully thought-out and acted scene in *Nashville*, and perhaps in any movie since, was that Carradine could have been singing to nobody but Lily Tomlin. Each of the female characters who mistakenly believed that he was singing to her—not, however, because of any tremolo, but because he had slept with her—was portrayed as smugly but touchingly obtuse. Each soon recognized that he was singing to somebody else—again, not on the basis of his tremolo but from the direction of his stare.

The only reason this matters in the slightest is that if any "you" would be led by Carradine's voice to the mistake made by specific female characters in that scene in *Nashville*, then there is no reason why those specific characters, and they alone, should have made it. The scene utterly loses its point.

About *Coming Home*:

> Later, we watch her face during her orgasm with Luke; this scene is the dramatic center of the movie. The question in the viewer's mind is, What will she feel when her husband comes home and they go to bed? Will she respond, and if she does, how will he react?

No one, I think, would disagree with Ms. Kael that the scene is the dramatic center of the movie; but it seems just as clear that one question that is *not* in the viewer's mind is the one (or the two) Ms. Kael suggests. The question, if any, is another one, which has persisted almost from the movie's start, and which Ms. Kael would have seemed uniquely designed, by temperament, to spot: What is it that Luke, the paraplegic, does in making love? This essentially clinical question is one that the movie deliberately suggests and then, I believe, dishonestly blurs throughout. Be that as it may, I don't think a viewer in the world has in mind in that scene the question Ms. Kael ascribes to him. I happen not to have liked the movie, either. But, given the physical circumstances, I don't think even Ms. Kael could have taken a cheaper shot, or one less apposite, than the last line of her review: "Are liberals really such great lovers?"

Let's leave all that. Let's leave her unusually many uses of the form so/that, such/that—from "so haughty that her name should be 'Anastasia,'" "so endearing . . . that he should be billed as Richard 'Cuddles' Dreyfuss," "so grasping that the film should be called 'Tentacles,'" through this sort of meander-hype connective:

> . . . so eerily sensitive that your mind may easily drift to the terrible (true) accounts of how people on the street sometimes laughed at Virginia Woolf.

... so lusciously, ripely beautiful in her peach-blond wig that her trained, accomplished acting suggests an intelligent form of self-respect.

Let's leave aside her humor: "you feel she needs a derrick to lift her lids"; "each repositioning of her features requires the services of a derrick"; "you fight to keep your eyes open"; "people were fighting to stay awake"; "but after a while I was gripping the arms of my chair to stay awake"; "the audience was snoring"; "the only honest sound I heard . . . was the snoring in the row behind me," etc. Let's leave even her favorite deep/surface dichotomy, or paradox, or whatever she thinks it is: a director, "deep on the surface"; a film, "deep on the surface"; "deep without much surface excitement"; "rough on the surface but slick underneath." Let's leave aside, in short, all the relatively harmless mannerisms and devices.

A more important, related stratagem recurs constantly in her work, and by no means in hers alone. I don't know how to characterize it, except as the hack carom—taking, that is, something from *within* the film and, with an air of triumph, turning it *against* the film or a performer. "Gere looks like Robert De Niro without the mole on his cheek," for instance, "but there's more than that missing." More than the mole. About a scene with a burning candle, "someone should have taken a lighted wick to [the scenarist's] ideas." About an actor's expression within a role, "His face is stricken with grief and humiliation; that should be [his] face for what [the writer and director] do to him." About a scene of begging for absolution, that the writer and director "ought to be the ones kneeling in penance." Ms. Kael revels in this sort of thing. The only reason the device has any significance is the unpleasant, even punitive overtone—the notion that a film or a performer is not merely undistinguished, or unimportant, or untalented, but actually *guilty* of something. The image of filmmakers penitent is particularly congenial to her work. She speaks often, in this carom mode, of being "betrayed" and of what she (or "we") can or cannot "forgive." ("A viewer could probably forgive everything that went wrong"; "the script seems like a betrayal, of them, and of us.")

Films and performers may be guilty. They may or may not be absolved. Audiences are also at risk. People who do not share, for example, her infatuation with the more extreme forms of violence are characterized as "repressive," "acting out of fear, masked as taste," "turned philistine," "trying to protect themselves from their own violence," "surely with terror and prurient churnings underneath?" "What may be behind all this," she actually writes at one point, "is repression of the race issue." An occasional film may be forgiven (really) as "not the sort of failure you write an artist off for." But those fearful, repressive, philistine, secretly violent, racist, prurient people in the audience are not going to be forgiven until they come around.

Which brings me to the "we," "you," "they," "some people"; "needs," "feel," "know," "ought"—also to a structural mechanism I have seen in no other writer's work. The structural mechanism first. Although it is true that Ms. Kael can hardly resist a restatement, or a repetition, or a meaningless amplification ("ditsey little twitches," "ruthless no soul monsters"; "incomprehensible bitch," "obnoxious smartass"); although she seems at times to have a form of prose hypochondria, palpating herself all over to see if she has a thought, and publishing every word of the process by which she checks to see whether or not she has one; it is also, equally, true that she can hardly resist any form of hyperbole, superlative, exaggeration: "poisonously mediocre," "wickedest baroque sensibility at large in America."

These predispositions—to restate and to overstate—make it all the more curious structurally that Ms. Kael withholds until the sixth long paragraph of one review the words "it's Jack Nicholson's best performance"; to the middle of the third paragraph of another the claim that Sophia Loren "has never looked more richly beautiful or given such a completely controlled great-lady performance"; to late in the fourth paragraph of yet another that Laurence Olivier "has the power to find something he's never done before, in any role"; and to so unobtrusive a place that I could hardly find it when I looked for it again, the word that Paul Newman "gives the performance of his life—to date." Now, it's true, as I have remarked, that Ms. Kael rarely spares us an afterthought, or a forethought. But the structural reason for reserving these superlatives until so late in a piece becomes clear from the last example. Paul Newman's "performance of his life—to date" was in *Slap Shot*. A film directed by George Roy Hill (whom she had mistakenly accused of failing to trouble to record *Butch Cassidy and the Sundance Kid* outdoors). What is operating here is the structure of spite.

"We" and "you" can occur, of course, in any writer's work, in moderation. For the first two hundred pages, it seems that Ms. Kael means a sort of scolding nanny "we," or a flirting schoolmarm's, or a nondirective therapist's, or a tour guide's, or a prison matron's. Consistent with the nanny, miffed, are remarks like, "She consented, but I was offended for her"; "I can't help feeling that the audience is being insulted, although the audience doesn't think so." Also the repeated threats of what will happen "if" an actor, or a director, or a film "doesn't pull" him or itself "together." But then, there is something so pervasive and remorseless in that "we"—"we want," "we resent," "we feel," "we're desperate for," "we don't know how to react," "we know too well what we're supposed to feel," "we want it, just as we wanted," "we all *know*"—that the "we" becomes a bandwagon, a kangaroo court, a gang, an elite, a congregation, which readers had better join, or else be consigned to that poor group of deviants, sissies, aesthetic and moral idiots who comprise "some people," "many people," "a lot of people," "those people," "they."

"You," normally, is the individuated "we." "You may wonder, Are these boys being naughty because they're old enough not to be?" "You feel that some of your brain cells are being knocked out." "You want the director to stop all the nonsense." Sometimes, the "you" seems the subject of a hypnotist: "You feel that you understand everything that's going on"; "You don't feel embarrassed by anything that Clint Eastwood does." But "you" is most often Ms. Kael's "I," or a member or prospective member of her "we." As for "feel," "needs," and "know," Ms. Kael uses "feel" variously, but most fervently in the emotional sense. She has, however, an odd view of what "emotion" is: "the one basic emotion he needs to show—sexual avidity." So I'm not always certain what she means by "feel." "Needs": "He needs a little Terry Southern in his soul." "Jimmy needs to be an exciting, violent, emotional man . . . the pianist/gangster split as a heightened, neurotic metaphor for Everyman—a Dostoevskian Everyman." "Know": A film "doesn't seem to know that that's its theme"; a director "doesn't seem to know what actors are for"; but "we all know" quite a lot of things; and "James Mason knows. God, does he know." "Know" also often goes with a sort of culinary "needs"; "The film doesn't seem to know that it needs a little playful sado-masochistic chemistry." I think I'll just skip "ought."

Ms. Kael's work has been praised as "great . . . a body of criticism which can be compared with Shaw's" (*Times Literary Supplement*). She has won a National Book Award. So far as I know, apart from a personal statement by Andrew Sarris, which appeared in the *Village Voice* as this piece was going to press, the book has received uniformly favorable reviews. *The New Republic* describes it as consisting of "all peaks and no valleys." A Kaelism, surely. None of this is Ms. Kael's fault. It is only symptomatic. The pervasive, overbearing, and presumptuous "we," the intrusive "you," the questions, the debased note of righteousness and rude instruction—the whole verbal apparatus promotes, and relies upon, an incapacity to read. The writing falls somewhere between huckster copy (paeans to the favored product, diatribes against all other brands and their venal or deluded purchasers) and ideological pamphleteering: denouncings, exhortations, code words, excommunications, programs, threats. Apart from the taste for violence, however, which she takes to be a hard, intellectual position, there is no underlying text or theory. Only the review, virtually divorced from movies, as its own end:

> If there is one immutable law about movies it may be that middle-class people get hot and bothered whenever there's a movie that the underclass really responds to.

No matter that the sentence is clearly false. (Think of *Shaft*, for instance.) No matter even that "one immutable law" manages wonderfully to combine Kaeline authoritarianism with Kaeline hype. The sentence is plainly inconsistent with what Ms. Kael writes elsewhere—when it is the elitist mode that suits her: the "mass audience" she derides frequently; the audience she "couldn't help feeling . . . was being insulted, although the audience doesn't think so"; the "many people," of whom she writes, in yet another piece, who "resist quality" because "they're afraid of being outclassed." All that the one immutable law about movies amounts to is that Ms. Kael will not brook disagreement. Personally. And not just with her enthusiasms—which might be a form of generosity in a critic. Also, more vehemently, with her revenges and dislikes. "Did these people stand up and cheer to get their circulation going again?" she writes of even the smallest film she fears might become a hit. She likes to ban.

Three last quotations, as another kind of symptom:

> It's quite possible that [he] . . . wasn't fully conscious that in several sequences he was coming mortifyingly close to plagiarism.

It's as crude as if [he] had said, "Things were really bad in Berlin in '23," and, asked "How bad?," he had replied, "They were so bad even a black man couldn't get it up."

Paul Schrader may like the idea of prostituting himself more than he likes making movies. . . . (For Schrader to call himself a whore would be vanity: he doesn't know how to turn a trick.)

Now, it doesn't matter whom these quotations are "about"—although the middle one concerns Ingmar Bergman. They are not "about" anything. Each marks a kind of breakthrough in vulgarity and unfairness. Look at the "It's quite possible" in the first, and the "mortifyingly." Look at the "as if" in the second, and the "even." Consider, in the third, the "would be." All three involve a perfectly groundless imputation to another (plagiarism, racism, corruption) and a pious personal recoil (mortifyingly, crude, vain). The strategy is characteristic of Ms. Kael's work. I can hardly imagine a reader who would sit through another line.

Cumulatively and in book form, these reviews have an effect different from anything that was even intimated on a weekly or desultory basis. It occurred to me when I had read a few hundred pages that the book assumes an audience composed partly of people who know nothing about the movies, and partly of people who read only film reviews. Accept the claim that she *cares*, and/or remember that it's only a movie; and there's no need to pay attention to the rest. But what I think has happened is this: an extreme case of what can go wrong with a staff critic. Prose events that would, under ordinary circumstances and on any subject other than movies, have been regarded as lapses—the sadism, slurs, inaccuracies, banalities, intrusions—came to be regarded as Ms. Kael's strong suit. Ms. Kael grew proud of them. Her cult got hooked on them. Readers generally skipped over them. There was always the impression, unfounded but widely held (I held it), of liveliness. And it was not clear how radical an imposition each mannerism and device would become when the reviews appeared weekly, and with a strong institutional base.

The New Yorker, as it happens, is an institution of unique civility and patience, dedicated absolutely, although it may not always look that way, to leaving writers free to write what, and at what length, they choose. In recent years, it was having insuperable problems with its other movie critic. Editors of weekly magazines, moreover, work—no less than staff critics—under the pressures of a deadline. The result is that, of practical though not spiritual necessity, staff critics have special institutional support. *The New Yorker* could not devote its energies, every week, to a bitter struggle over movie columns—which, incidentally, were growing so long that other pieces, on which serious intermittent writers had worked for years, were being overwhelmed.

With intermittent writers, when there is a disagreement, a piece can always be postponed. In this way, of course, editors can exert strong, legitimate pressure. It may be your piece; but it's their magazine. With a staff critic, that mild form of blackmail is reversed. Editors cannot, professionally, often postpone a weekly piece. So *The New Yorker* had either to fire Ms. Kael (which would, for many reasons, including the problems with the other critic, have been a mistake; anyway, *The New Yorker* doesn't fire people) or accommodate her work. The conditions of unique courtesy, literacy, and civility, of course, were what Ms. Kael was most inclined by temperament to test. The excesses got worse.

Then an odd thing happened: Ms. Kael went out to Hollywood. For a critic preoccupied with metaphors for selling out, this seemed an extraordinary move. The *New York Times*, for instance, is so acutely aware of the possibilities for conflict of interest in film reviewing that it forbids its critic to write screenplays. When Ms. Kael returned from Hollywood, I, among others, felt strongly that *The New Yorker* should take her back. I hadn't read this collection. She was the critic people knew and talked about. I believed she was lively and that she cared. Anyway, in her absence, it had become clear that nobody else at *The New Yorker* wanted to be the staff movie critic. She did come back.

She writes as she has written these past five years, but at least her column is no longer weekly. Criticism will get over it. Once the tone and the ante, however, have been pumped up to this awful frenzy, it becomes hard—even in reviewing Ms. Kael's work—to write in any other way; or, in the typographic clamor, to detect and follow a genuine critical argument. What really is at stake is not movies at all, but prose and the relation between writers and readers, and of course art.

—1980

A COURT OF NO APPEAL

In January of this year, Simon & Schuster published my book *Gone: The Last Days of The New Yorker*. I had been at *The New Yorker* since 1963—with an absence of about fourteen months, during which I was Bosley Crowther's successor as the film critic of the *New York Times*. Though I had written for other publications, I thought I knew the magazine pretty well. *The New Yorker*, I wrote, is dead. I did not expect everyone to agree or to welcome my account of what happened to the magazine. Perhaps not surprisingly, the colleagues whom I had loved and admired through the years tended to share my views. Those of whom I thought less highly, and whom I portrayed less admiringly, did not.

Throughout the book, I referred to matters in the outside world, politics, travels, issues, assignments taken and not taken, discussions with William Shawn, the great editor, who, over that period of more than thirty years, naturally grew old, declined, and lost control of his magazine. A young editor whom I met in January said he thought I had treated *The New Yorker* as though it were the proverbial canary in a mineshaft. Its death meant something about the capacity of any living creative enterprise to survive within the culture. The thought had not crossed my mind. It has crossed my mind now.

On November 11, 1999, when my book was still in galleys, Charles McGrath, the editor of the *New York Times Book Review*, wrote to Simon & Schuster. Mr. McGrath had for many years been an editor at *The New Yorker*. I had described his tenure there in less than admiring terms. I had also raised questions about what seemed to me an inherent conflict of interest in his having assigned to himself, when he became editor of the *Book Review*, the review of another book in which he figured. "The other day," Mr. McGrath now wrote, "I received the galleys of Renata

Adler's forthcoming book," and "as is my custom, I read through it prior to assigning it for review." He described as a "complete fabrication" an account of a lunch at which he had speculated to his cousin Laura ("who is not my cousin but, rather, my cousin-in-law") that he was, at that very moment, being designated successor to the editorship of the magazine. The lunch had, in fact, been described to me by several people. My account of it was harmless; it certainly had no legal implications. (Mr. McGrath's letter had ended with "cc:" to an attorney.) But I had also written that "no one, at least no writer in his right mind, wants to antagonize the *Book Review*." I thought, what the hell. I wasn't *at* the lunch. I had written, several times, about my distrust of journalism that relies, in quite this way, on "sources." So I replaced the passage with an account of a conversation in which Mr. McGrath spoke directly to me. I framed his letter, and hung it on my wall, as a little distillation of what I thought an editor of a major publication ought never to do.

The *New York Times* subsequently published no fewer than eight, arguably nine, pieces about my book. The first four (on January 12, January 16, February 6, and February 13, 2000) appeared in four sections: Arts, Sunday *Magazine*, Sunday Letters, and Sunday *Book Review*. They were unfriendly, but, apart from their sheer quantity, not particularly striking. The Arts piece, by Dinitia Smith, did mention Mr. McGrath's letter in approving terms ("The material to which he objected," Ms. Smith wrote, "was removed"), but added that Mr. McGrath said "he had decided to distance himself from reviews about current *New Yorker* books." What form that distancing would take, Ms. Smith did not say.

The next four pieces (April 3, April 5, April 6, and April 9, 2000) were dispersed among four more sections (Business/Media, Editorial, Op Ed, and Week in Review), treated as serious news, in other words, from Monday through Sunday of a solid week. It might have been, even as an episode of institutional carpet bombing, almost flattering. It seemed unlikely that the *Times* had ever devoted four, let alone eight, polemical articles to a single book before. There is perhaps an explanation and a story here for both waves of articles. Let me begin with the second wave.

In mid-February, Jack Sirica, a reporter at *Newsday*, wrote a letter to Simon & Schuster, calling attention to a sentence, at the end of a passage on page 125 of my book, in which I wrote about having been assigned, by Mr. Shawn, and deciding not to review, *To Set the Record Straight*, the autobiography (published in 1979, by Norton) of Judge John

J. Sirica, Jack Sirica's father. The sentence in question said I had found that "contrary to his reputation as a hero, Sirica was in fact a corrupt, incompetent, and dishonest figure, with a close connection to Senator Joseph McCarthy and clear ties to organized crime." Jack Sirica challenged me to produce "any evidence whatsoever" that his father was a "corrupt, incompetent, and dishonest figure" or "had clear ties to organized crime." He demanded that Simon & Schuster "issue a public, written retraction" and "remove the references" from all future editions of the book. He distributed his letter widely to his colleagues in the press. A reporter from the Associated Press called me and asked, in highly professional and neutral terms, whether I planned to document my remarks in any way. I said I did. The reporter asked when. I said soon. The reporter asked where. I said in any place that seemed appropriate.

Some days later, I had a call from Felicity Barringer, a media correspondent of the *New York Times*. Ms. Barringer, I knew, is married to Philip Taubman, a member of the *Times* editorial board and an assistant editor of the editorial page. From the outset the conversation had nothing of the tenor of an "interview." Ms. Barringer did not even pretend to any interest in Sirica, only in "ethics in book publishing." Would I give her my "sources"? "Come on. Yes or no. Up or down?" Her deadline: forty-eight hours. No. Why would I not disclose my evidence, if any, to her? Because, as the AP had reported, I was writing a piece of my own. Why wait? I was not waiting; I was writing.

Had I no concern meanwhile, she asked several times, about what I had done to Judge Sirica's reputation? I said I didn't think most people relied for their information about Judge Sirica on a sentence in a book about *The New Yorker*. In fact, none of the reviews, in the *Times* or elsewhere, had so much as mentioned the passage. Before Jack Sirica's letter, no one had apparently noticed it. "Well, that raises the old question, if a tree falls in the forest and no one is there to notice," Ms. Barringer said. A think piece, evidently.

If I did not wish to "disclose" my "sources" to her in an interview, Ms. Barringer said, "Why don't you post it on the Internet?" "You post a lot of your own pieces on the Internet, do you, Felicity?" It must be said that, although I was not, as far as I know, discourteous, I was not particularly deferential or awestruck, either. This was, it was true, the *Times*. It was also an unusually repetitive and mindless interrogation. The game, and its rituals, anyway, are fairly set. The reporter will write what she chooses—not infrequently regardless of what is said. It is one of the many reasons I have always preferred to work with documents, including depositions. They can be verified and checked. Ms. Barringer had a final question: Was my source G. Gordon Liddy? No.

The following Monday, April 3, Ms. Barringer's piece appeared on the front page of the Business section. On Wednesday, April 5, a piece, by Eleanor Randolph but unsigned (I had mentioned Ms. Randolph unfavorably in my book), appeared as an editorial. On Thursday, April 6, there was an op-ed piece, written by, of all people, John W. Dean. On Sunday, April 9, the *Times* published the last (at least so far) of these pieces in its Week in Review.

Ms. Barringer's article was, in its way, exemplary. In my "off-handed evisceration of various literati," she reported, not many people had noticed "Ms. Adler's drive-by assault on the late Judge Sirica." She deplored the lack of "any evidence" and managed to convey her conviction that none existed. Ms. Barringer's own "sources," on the other hand, were the following: Jack Sirica (whom she did not identify as a *Newsday* reporter); John F. Stacks, who co-wrote Judge Sirica's autobiography (and who said Sirica "didn't have the imagination to be anything but straight all his life"); "those who have read just about all books about the Watergate" and "those most steeped in Watergate lore" (whether these "those" were coextensive was not clear); two lawyers, who confirmed that "the dead cannot sue for libel"; an editor, who did not claim to know either me or anything about Sirica, who "explained" (not, for Ms. Barringer, "said"), in five paragraphs of a bizarre fantasy, what I must have said to my editor and he to me ("It is, 'Love me, love my book.' If that's what she wants to say . . . it's either do the book or don't do it"); and Bob Woodward, coauthor of *All the President's Men*, who "absolutely never heard, smelled, saw or found any suggestion" that Sirica had ever had "any connection whatever" to organized crime.

An impressive roster, in a way. I had once, as it happened, unfavorably reviewed, on the front page of the *New York Times Book Review* itself, a book by Mr. Woodward, but he was certainly the most impressive of Ms. Barringer's sources in this piece. Mr. Woodward could of course have crept into Judge Sirica's hospital room, and elicited from him on his deathbed the same sort of "nod" he claimed to have elicited from CIA Director William Casey on *his* deathbed, and then claimed, as he did with Casey, that to divulge even the time of this alleged hospital visit would jeopardize his "source." And when asked, as he was in an interview, what color pajamas the patient was wearing, he could, as he did in the instance of Casey, express a degree of outrage worthy of the threat such a question poses to the journalist's entire vocation. That is evidently not a kind of "sourcing" that raises questions for a media correspondent at the *Times*.

Ms. Barringer, in any case, did not conceal her views or quite limit her account to a single issue. "The attack on the basic honesty and decency of the judge," she wrote, "is of a piece with the whole work." Then came a memorable line. "What she writes and when she writes it, she said," Ms. Barringer actually wrote, with all the severity of the bureaucrat deep in a Politburo, "is for her to decide." Who else, I wondered, at least in our society, could possibly decide it? Her essential formulation, however, was this:

> As it stands, Ms. Adler and Simon & Schuster, a unit of Viacom, are either cheaply smearing Judge Sirica—with legal impunity—or they have evidence. But neither the publisher nor the author shows any urgency about resolving the issue, either by retracting the accusation or establishing its accuracy.

Jack Sirica merely demanded "any evidence whatever." Ms. Barringer wanted evidence (to her standards, presumably, and Mr. Woodward's), with "urgency," and "establishing accuracy." Otherwise, in spite of that lamentable "legal impunity," a retraction. An interesting position, from a reporting, First Amendment, or even a censorship point of view. I will return to that, and even get to the evidence about Judge Sirica. But first a bit more about conditions in the mineshaft.

The editorial, two days later, entitled "A Question of Literary Ethics," ran immediately below a slightly shorter piece, "Justice in Bosnia." "In an irritable little book published late last year about The New Yorker," it began. Why the *Times* would address an entire editorial to a "little book," "irritable" or not, was not entirely clear. One might have thought that, almost thirty years after the Watergate and more than sixty years after some of the events in question, the country really does turn for its information about Judge Sirica to a passage in a book about *The New Yorker* magazine. "Since Judge Sirica is dead," the editorial again pointed out, "he is unable to sue for libel." True enough. "But that does not lift the ethical burden from Ms. Adler to support her charges with evidence that she says exists," but "that she and her editors at Simon & Schuster, for some unfathomable reason, omitted from her book." Then, a new standard, not just "evidence" but a cognate of "proof" crept in. "If Ms. Adler was referring to allegations about Judge Sirica's father . . . she will need to document that unproven contention and show how it relates to the judge himself."

It was interesting to learn what I needed to document and show. I found it difficult, however, to see in what sense my "burden" was (as Ms. Randolph, writing anonymously for the *Times,* put it) "ethical"—or how the passage in my book could have raised an issue of "ethics," "literary" or other. Professional issues, perhaps. Issues of fact, history, judgment. Ethics, no. I was either right or I wasn't, and I either had evidence or I hadn't. (The questions were, by no means, the same.) The *Times,* as it turned out, had not the slightest interest in Sirica or his history. No reporter for the *Times,* or as far as I know any other publication, made any effort to investigate the nature of the connection with Senator Mc-Carthy—let alone the basis for an assertion of clear ties to organized crime. This lack of curiosity seemed to me extraordinary. The sole preoccupation was with a kind of meta-journalistic question—not what happened, but what were my sources and my obligations. As to what was, however, "for some unfathomable reason omitted," the *Times* had only to look at its own op-ed piece the following day.

That piece, entitled "A Source on Sirica?," consisted of John Dean's speculation about something the *Times* had reason to know not to be the case: that my "source" was Dean's old enemy, and current adversary in an embittered lawsuit, G. Gordon Liddy.[1] What was remarkable, however, was less the content of the piece than the words with which the *Times* identified its author. The caption, in its entirety, read as follows:

> John W. Dean, an investment banker and the author of "Blind Ambition," was counsel to President Richard M. Nixon.

If this is the way Mr. Dean will enter history, then all the *Times* pieces in this peculiar episode have value.

That Sunday, April 9, there was the Week in Review section. A single sentence, in an "irritable little book published late last year," had now become part of the news, perhaps more accurately the meta-news, of that week. The word "evidence" was entirely abandoned, replaced by "proof." My book had "announced without proof"; "Ms. Adler told a *New York Times* reporter that she would publish proof when she pleased," and so on. I had, of course, said nothing of the kind. In repeating what had long been a *Times* characterization of Judge Sirica as "a scrupulously honest jurist," the piece surpassed even the op-ed page in the brevity of its identification of John Dean. It described him simply as "former Nixon counsel." The laconic formulation was apparently designed to lend him credibility, in contrast to G. Gordon Liddy, "whom Judge Sirica sent to prison for his role in Watergate." Under other circumstances, this might have been simply a howler. (Dean, of course, was also sentenced to prison by Judge Sirica "for his role in Watergate." One might as readily characterize Liddy as a "former FBI agent and candidate for office in Millbrook, New York"). By now, however, these descriptions of Dean had gone beyond inadequacy. They relied upon and actively perpetuated the ignorance of readers. The *Times*, for some reason, was publishing disinformation.

I have always read the *Times*. In a day of perhaps more distinguished and exigent editing, I even worked for it. On the day Ms. Barringer's piece appeared, I wrote a letter objecting to certain demonstrable errors. I said I hoped Ms. Barringer had made a tape of our conversation, so that my claim of inaccuracies could be verified. No dice. No acknowledgment, even, of the question of a tape. On April 6, I received a phone call from the secretary of the deputy editor of the editorial page. "They have decided not to run your letter," she said, in a very cheery voice. They have? I said. Did they give any reason? "No. They just asked me to call and tell you they have decided not to run your letter." April 6 was the day they ran the op-ed piece by John Dean. On April 7, Jared Stern, of the *New York Post*, ran a piece quoting from my letter—which had been given to him by Blake Fleetwood, a friend of mine and for years a reporter for the *Times*. A spokesman for the *Times* told Stern, what was plainly untrue, that my letter was still "being considered for publication." That very afternoon, an editor called to ask whether I would like to submit another letter.

One of my adventures in this mineshaft had already been to learn that, as a matter of policy, the *Times* does not publish letters that question, or criticize in any way, the work of its reporters. Any claim of inaccuracy or unfairness must be made to the department of Corrections or the Editor's Note. In these departments, however, the reporter, in consultation with her editor, decides the issue—which, I suppose, is why the Corrections in particular always seem to consist of rectifications of middle initials, photo captions, and remote dates in history. (In one recent week, the corrections column pointed out that the correct spelling of Secretary of State Madeleine Albright's "given name" is "Madeleine, not Madeline," and that the middle name of William D. Fugazy, "the chairman of the National Ethnic Coalition of Organizations," is "Denis," "not Dennis.") There *are*, as a rule, no genuine corrections. These departments are cosmetic, a pretense that the paper has any interest in whether what it has published is, in some important or for that matter unimportant way, false.

This, I would say, raises issues, fundamentally, of ethics. So does covering up conflicts of interest: unsigned editorials by writers mentioned unfavorably in books the editorials disparage; quotations, without any acknowledgment of conflict, from "sources" whose work, whose very methods, have been attacked by the person under discussion, in the pages of the *Times* itself. So does the concealment of undeniably relevant information: the fact that Jack Sirica was not just the son of Judge Sirica but a reporter at *Newsday*, a journalist, a colleague (imagine the *Times* coming to the defense, against a single passage, of the father of anyone who was not a fellow journalist); even the omission of virtually defining facts about John Dean. And finally, the bullying, the disproportion, in publishing eight disparaging pieces (seven in nonreviewing sections) about what was after all one little book. The *Times*, clearly, was cross about something. But there are ethical issues, I think, raised even by this sort of piling on.

To turn, then, at last, to Judge Sirica. More than twenty years ago, when I read Sirica's book, I noticed what seemed to me astonishing discrepancies and revelations. I did some research, gave the matter thought, and decided not to review the book. I was sure newspaper or magazine journalists would pick up these anomalies and write about them. By the time I published my book about *The New Yorker*, I assumed other journalists *had* found and written about them. It turned out they had not—had, it seemed, no interest in these matters, apart from the recent questioning of my right to address them, even now.

Contrary to his reputation as a hero, Sirica was in fact a corrupt, incompetent, and dishonest figure, with a close connection to Senator Joseph McCarthy and clear ties to organized crime.

There can scarcely be any question that this sentence is true. One major source for almost every element of my characterization is Sirica's own story, as told in interviews and in his book. That Sirica had a "close connection to Senator Joseph McCarthy" is not in dispute—although, as far as I know, I was the first reporter to call attention to it. Certainly no major piece, book, newspaper, or magazine article—about Sirica, or the Watergate, or Senator McCarthy for that matter—mentions the connection. Certainly not (until its recent reaction to Jack Sirica's reaction to my book) the *New York Times*.

Sirica's own account of the connection is as follows. In 1952,

> While in Chicago, I ran into Senator Joe McCarthy. We had been friends for several years, double-dating once in a while and going to the racetrack together from time to time. I liked Joe a lot in those days. . . .
>
> Then in 1953, Joe McCarthy offered me the job of chief counsel to his Senate subcommittee which was investigating Communist influence in government.
>
> I must say that I found the offer very attractive . . . I wasn't especially excited by McCarthy's charges about Communist infiltration, but it seemed to me at the time to be an important matter that needed further examination. By the time McCarthy made his offer, I had moved over to Hogan & Hartson and was finally earning a decent living. But I was still intrigued by his proposal.
>
> Lucy [Sirica's wife, whom he had married the year before, at the age of forty-seven] . . . was strongly opposed, feeling that since I was now a partner in a good firm, I would be foolish to leave. Joe stopped by our apartment one evening and I told him I felt I had better stay where I was. He agreed that it would be a mistake to leave a good firm like Hogan & Hartson. He told me that since I wasn't going to take the job, he was probably going to hire a young New York lawyer named

> Roy Cohn. . . . I would never have become a federal judge if
> I had taken that job with Joe McCarthy. I'm sure, looking
> back, that had I been single, I would have done so. Thank
> God for Lucy Camalier Sirica.

There is something almost stunningly preposterous about this story.
Sirica devotes less than a page to it. The friendship between Sirica, by
his own account an obscure, impoverished, unsuccessful lawyer who had,
for the "several years" in question, not even managed to earn a living,
and Senator Joseph R. McCarthy, one of the most powerful and feared
senators in Washington, makes no sense. How did they meet? What
views, interests, or other friends did they have in common? How did they
come to double-date? McCarthy had made his first famous speech ("I
have here in my hand a list of two hundred and five names known to
the Secretary of State as being members of the Communist Party"), in
February 9, 1950, to the Republican Women's Club in Wheeling, West
Virginia. In the intervening years, he had attacked, as virtual or outright
traitors, not just the Secretary of State, Dean Acheson, and General
George C. Marshall, but countless others, at every level of public and
private life. By 1953, the McCarthy Era (what Senator Margaret Chase
Smith called the "Four Horsemen of Calumny: fear, ignorance, bigotry,
and smear") was already at its height. Judge Sirica's position ("I wasn't
especially excited by McCarthy's charges about Communist infiltration,
but it seemed at the time to be an important matter that needed further
examination") is not just inherently equivocal and inane. It is also ir-
reconcilable with the intemperate, opinionated man Sirica and his admirers have always admitted him to be. Leaving aside his lack of
professional qualifications, Sirica has entirely omitted from this account
any ideological basis for McCarthy's offer of this job to him. Roy Cohn,
after all, had credentials of a sort. His agenda, his methods, and his
ideology were clear. In Sirica's account, nothing—neither the politics
that produced the offer nor the social circumstance that fostered the
friendship—is revealed.

The rest of his story, as he describes it, and as his legend would have
it, turns out to make no sense either. Born in 1904, in Waterbury, Connecticut, Sirica is the impecunious, poorly educated, and for many years
unsuccessful son of Ferdinand (Fred) Sirica, an Italian-American barber,
who also seems to fail at everything. Between 1910 and 1918, for ex-

ample, Ferdinand takes the family "on a sad sort of odyssey, from city to city," Dayton, Jacksonville, New Orleans, Jacksonville again.

> In each place the story was the same. My father would try to earn his living with one kind of business or another. Each time he would fail. In several cities he purchased small enterprises, only to discover that the income they produced was much less than had been promised by the seller.

In 1918, "uprooted again," they move to Washington, D.C.—where they are so poor they can hardly find a place to live. Somehow, in this "continuous uphill struggle against poverty," Sirica manages to attend two nonparochial private high schools, Emerson Preparatory, "for a year or so," and then Columbia Preparatory. In 1921 he enters George Washington University Law School, where, within a month, he finds himself out of his depth ("I couldn't begin to understand what the professors were talking about") and quits. The following year, he goes to a better law school, Georgetown University, but again, within a month, fails to understand his courses, and quits again. It is not clear why Sirica went to private schools, or what "small enterprises" his father "purchased" in all those cities, or how, having failed "each time," his father managed to purchase *any* enterprises, let alone "one kind of business or another" at all. Sirica does not account for any of these discrepancies.

He starts boxing professionally. "I was pretty good, or at least I thought so." As early as 1921, between his first law school and his second,

> I boxed almost every day with local professional welterweights and middleweights. I had begun boxing at local clubs in exhibition bouts with the professionals. I thoroughly enjoyed my new life as an athlete and felt I had finally found something at which I could excel.

In 1922, however, his father has another contretemps:

> By this time, my father, in another of his attempts to better himself, had bought a small poolroom with two bowling alleys and a snack bar. He had spent all his savings on the business, and soon realized that he had sunk his money into a very rough place. He wasn't making any profit to speak of and didn't like the type of people who frequented the establishment. I used to

help out in the evenings, racking up balls for the pool players and setting pins for the bowlers. But my father was again in despair. As he had so often before, he had trusted someone only to be deceived. We lived in rooms above the place. I remember Dad coming upstairs one night after closing. He poured himself a drink as the tears rolled down his face. He was again facing the fact that his hopes were being dashed.

I guess my father wanted to hold on long enough to sell the place and recover his money. But things just got worse. One evening a particularly unpleasant group came in. Many of them had been drinking, even though this was during prohibition.

I don't think my father owned the place quite a year. He knew that a lot of gamblers and bootleggers came in, but he also knew that if he threw out all the undesirables, he'd be without enough customers to make any money at all. Men from the Government Printing Office, just down North Capitol Street, would come in from work, order a soft drink, and then mix in a little hard liquor from the pints in their pockets. The low point in that whole experience came one night when the city police, aware of the kinds of people who visited the establishment, made a search of the premises. Stashed in the men's room, they found a small quantity of bootleg liquor, apparently left there by one of my father's customers. The police took my dad to the police station and charged him with violation of the Volstead Act. He was not locked up, and the next day, when he appeared in police court with his lawyer, he explained that the liquor must have belonged to a customer and that he didn't even know it was there. No charges were filed, but the incident embarrassed the whole family.

There is perhaps no need to parse this account too thoroughly. How, having in the past, as we know, "failed each time," did he have "savings" to spend "all of," or "money" to have "sunk" into such a place? Why does Sirica find it necessary to point out that many of this unpleasant group "had been drinking, although this was during prohibition," when his father, just five lines before, had "poured himself a drink" (without any comment from Sirica) in his "despair" over having, "as he had so often before . . . trusted someone only to be deceived"? What was the deceit?

"He knew that a lot of bootleggers and gamblers came in"; also "men from the Government Printing Office," who bought soft drinks (from the snack bar, presumably) and then mixed in "a little hard liquor from the pints in their pockets." It seems almost unfair to go on. Even the elaborate formulation "one night . . . the city police, *aware of the kinds of people who frequented the establishment,* made a search of the premises." One can understand not wanting to say *aware of the nature of the establishment,* but why put in a qualifying phrase at all? Why not just: "One night the police raided the premises"? Similarly, why a "*small* quantity of bootleg liquor, *apparently left there by one of my father's customers.*" All these clauses and qualifiers. The next day, when his father, not having been locked up, "appeared in police court with his lawyer" and "explained that the liquor must have belonged to a customer and that he didn't even know it was there," any reader of ordinary intelligence and understanding realizes that the object of the story is—as it was in the McCarthy story—not to tell but to conceal something. How, as the *Times* editorial put it, this incident "relates to the judge himself" is not hard to fathom. Sirica was living in his father's apartment above the poolroom, and he was employed "racking up balls for the pool players" and also as a bouncer there.

To go back, however, to the career trajectory of John J. Sirica as he tells it. In 1926, on his third try, Sirica did manage to complete and graduate from law school. By this time, "I was tempted by the idea of becoming a professional boxer," he writes, "since I felt more confident of my ability as a fighter than as a lawyer."

> On the morning the bar exam was to be given I had breakfast with Morris Cafritz. I had pretty well decided to skip the bar exam and head for Florida to see my father and mother. . . .
>
> [Morris] knew that I was thinking about becoming a professional boxer. "Don't be foolish," he told me. "Even if you're not prepared, take the exam."

He has already described Mr. Cafritz as a "man who advised and encouraged me a great deal," while he was struggling through law school, and as "at the time becoming one of the most prominent and successful real-estate developers in Washington." It is true that Morris Cafritz went on to become immensely successful in real estate in Washington—and a highly respected citizen and generous benefactor of charities of every kind. At the time he was advising, encouraging, and having breakfast with Sirica, however, he was already very wealthy. Again, one wonders, what can have been the basis of this friendship between the poor and unpromising young law student and this highly influential figure. What Sirica does not mention is that Cafritz, too, at the time he "took a liking" to young Sirica, had an establishment involved with liquor and, like Sirica's father's, bowling. In his early twenties (according to Leslie Milk, in an article in the *Washington Magazine* of October 1996), Cafritz had borrowed $1,400 from his father and, a few years later, "bought a saloon."

> But not just any saloon: Cafritz' was across from the Washington Navy Yard. . . . Saloonkeeping was a rough business. . . . Cafritz was his own bouncer. He slept over the bar and kept a gun under his pillow to protect the profits. Cafritz soon moved from barkeeping into a safer game. By 1915, he was known as the bowling king of Washington.

All of this is a bit more raffish, and in some ways more appealing, than what Sirica describes. In the event, after his breakfast with Cafritz, Sirica, who has not even taken the bar review course, does take the bar exam, and goes on to visit his parents in Miami. While he is down there, he finds out, by telegram and to his surprise, that he has passed. He is unable to find work as a lawyer in Miami. He goes back to Washington, finds no legal work, goes back to his family in Miami. To earlier questions about his story is added another: Where, failing as he constantly does to find a job, does he get the money to keep traveling back and forth to Miami? And what was his family doing there?

One source of income, for Sirica, has always been, although he never quite acknowledges it, professional boxing. In Washington, as early as 1921, we know, he has been boxing "almost every day" with local professionals, and "at local clubs in exhibition bouts with the professionals." In 1926, in Miami, after "a local promoter needed someone to box in a semi-windup at Douglas Stadium," Sirica prepares for the fight not just by weeks of sparring but by "running every day at a golf course in Miami Beach"—under whose sponsorship he does not say. Perhaps, in those days, Miami Beach had a public golf course. Sirica's opponent, at Douglas Stadium, is "a six-foot-tall welterweight who was known for having fought one of the roughest bouts ever staged in Miami." ("Back in Washington, I had fought about thirty exhibitions . . . but nothing I ever did worried me as much as that oncoming fight.") Sirica beats him.

> The write-ups in the newspapers the next day were all good, even though they didn't spell my name correctly. I was on my way as a professional boxer.

His mother, he says, "heard about the fight," and objected. He had, of course, as he has already told us (and as his mother must have known), been fighting professionally for years. He would also organize and promote professional boxing matches. What he does not mention, does not perhaps remember or think important, is that professional boxing in this country was at the time, and had been since at least 1903, controlled by organized crime.

That professional boxers, and particularly *organizers* and *promoters* of professional boxing, had such ties was established, for example, in the Kefauver Hearings (U.S. Senate Special Committee to Investigate Organized Crime, May 1950 through August 1951). As the syndicated sportswriter Bob Kravitz recently put it:

> In the mid-fifties, a politician named Estes Kefauver chaired hearings on the sad state of the game, hoping to reform the sport and get it out of the hands of the Mob. When it was over, he realized the corruption was too deeply imbedded, too systemic.
>
> The only way to get rid of corruption in boxing is to get rid of boxing. At a meeting of Mob bosses and boxing managers in 1957, Mafia operative Binky Palermo worried about his boys losing their grip on it. Palermo had nothing to worry about.

As for the boxers themselves, in Washington, D.C., as it happens, *all* professional boxing was illegal—not just in 1921 when Sirica began but throughout the years he was boxing there—until 1934, when Congress finally legalized it in the District. Professional boxing in Washington, in other words, was a violation of the criminal statute. That Sirica knew this is beyond doubt. All the years he boxed professionally in the District before 1934 (including the years 1930 to 1934, when he was actually an assistant in the U.S. Attorney's office), he used, although he does not mention this either, fictitious names. It is, of course, possible to be a criminal without ties to organized crime—a pickpocket, say, or a burglar. Illegal boxing, however, requires payoffs, for the arena, the police, the referee, the promoters, and so on. You simply cannot do it freelance or on your own. It requires a syndicate—notoriously hostile to encroachments on its turf. So that's two sets of "clear ties to organized crime": through professional boxing—as an organizer, boxer, and promoter in various cities at a time when mob control of the sport was essentially complete—and for more than thirteen years in the District, boxing professionally when it was still illegal there.

Is that all? Well, no, it isn't. But it is all I said. It was not I, but the *Times* and its acolytes, who made a sensation of this. I wrote a little sentence, in a specific context, which is all I meant to write. The documentation for it is ample. Ms. Barringer, her "sources," and her colleagues could have found it, if her agenda had really been journalism: the gathering, that is, and publishing of firsthand information. Judge Sirica, as Ms. Barringer and the *Times* kept pointing out, is dead. But if he were alive and he sued for libel, as the *Times* in all its pieces seemed to suggest he might have done—imagine the preposterousness of a federal judge, even Judge Sirica, suing for libel—he would lose.

And that is not all. To resume his own story, in 1926, after being turned down by law firms everywhere, he does get a job as a "sort of messenger" at a criminal law office on Fifth Street. "It wasn't much, there was no regular pay, but it was a start." Meanwhile, he has made another early, implausible, and apparently lifelong friendship with a rich and powerful man, Morris Kronheim, a wonderfully interesting figure—and later, like Cafritz, an extraordinary citizen and a generous benefactor of every sort. Kronheim became, through several administrations, one of the most influential and beloved figures in Washington. In 1903, at the age of fifteen, Kronheim, whose father owned a tavern, started his own liquor store. By 1985, he had the largest wholesale liquor distributorship in Washington and one of the largest in the country.

During his three years at the Fifth Street criminal office, Sirica lost thirteen of fourteen felony cases assigned him by the court. The first case he was allowed to handle involved a "violation of the prohibition laws."

He lost. In 1930, however, Sirica was appointed (on what professional basis is unclear) to the U.S. Attorney's office—whose major responsibilities, in those years, included prosecutions under the Volstead Act. Sirica says he got "valuable trial experience" as Assistant U.S. Attorney, but he mentions no specific prosecutions, certainly none of bootleggers, or of promoters of professional boxing. In fact, he devotes only a single sentence to the whole four years.

In December 1933, Prohibition was repealed. Within two weeks, Sirica resigned from the U.S. Attorney's office, "to start my own practice." The practice was not a success. He entered what he calls "my starvation period," from 1934 to 1949, *fifteen years*, when he says, "I really lived from hand to mouth," it "seemed the phone never rang," and "I nearly had to quit the law altogether." He lived in his parents' house in Washington, and "without that free lodging I would have gone under."

Sirica traveled, in those years, not just to Miami but to "New York for weekends," to visit Jack Dempsey, whom he met in 1934. He does not explain how he paid for these travels. He says he earned a fee by "successfully defending Walter Winchell against a defamation case." What? Walter Winchell? Who brought the case? He does not say. The case he means, at least according to his obituary in the *New York Times*, was brought by Eleanor (Cissy) Patterson, the Chicago publisher. But that didn't sound quite right. I looked it up. It turned out that Cissy Patterson was in fact the owner of the *Times-Herald*, which published Winchell's column. The lawsuit was part of a long feud between them. Cissy Patterson dropped the case. Sirica may have played some part in the defense; but Winchell's attorney of record was Morris Ernst.

According to Sirica, this period, "when I nearly had to quit the law altogether," lasted "essentially until 1949, when I joined the firm of Hogan & Hartson." He was not a success there either. On April 2, 1957 (again, it is unclear on what professional basis), he became a federal judge. By 1970, he had become the most reversed federal judge in Washington.

In 1971, on the basis of seniority, he became chief judge of the circuit. In June of 1972, he read about the Watergate break-in and assigned himself the first of the Watergate cases. He ultimately tried the cases of both the break-in and the cover-up, with the results we know. Or thought we knew.

But wait a minute. To return for just a moment to 1930, and Sirica's situation at the time of his improbable appointment to the U.S. Attorney's office. In 1930, Sirica writes,

> my parents had moved back to Washington from Florida. My dad was barbering again and his financial situation had improved somewhat. He had managed to buy a little house on Fourteenth Street, N.W., and I lived there during my years in the U.S. attorney's office.

The years of Fred Sirica's apparently constant business failures, and Sirica's own inability to find a job, had not been Depression years—only, beginning in 1920 throughout the country (three years earlier, in 1917, in Washington, D.C.), years of Prohibition. The 1930s, however, *were* Depression years—yet the "financial situation" of Sirica's father, "barbering again," had "improved somewhat," to the degree in fact that "he had managed to buy a little house on Fourteenth Street."

Not such a little house. According to the Washington City Directory, the house at 6217 Fourteenth Street, N.W., was large enough so that both John J. Sirica and his brother, Andrew, had apartments there. The place where his father was "barbering again" (called, according to the directory, the Empire Barbershop) at 523 Ninth Street, N.W., was not small either. It held fourteen chairs. The reason Fred Sirica and his wife traveled so often to Miami was that they spent part of their winters there. The Siricas were buying property in Miami. Hard to account for, in the heart of the Depression, even with fourteen chairs, on the proceeds of haircuts at 25 cents per customer.

According to William Emmons, Jr., the son of Fred Sirica's partner in the Empire Barbershop, the barbers were salesmen, selling liquor to customers who could afford it. Packages were stored in both the backroom and the basement. Fred Sirica himself handled the whiskey, splitting the proceeds with his partner, William E. Emmons, Sr. Sirica, living in his father's house and working in the U.S. Attorney's office, can hardly have been entirely unaware of his father's business. Ninth Street in the 1930s had five motion picture houses within a block and a half of the barbershop. The Gayety Theater was only three doors away. There was bookmaking in the back of the shoe store at 519 Ninth Street. The whole neighborhood, in other words, was not so far removed, in its look and its patronage, from the poolroom that had so seriously disillusioned the impecunious barber and his son the law student more than ten years before. Nowhere in his autobiography, *To Set the Record Straight*, does the author so much as mention the name of the barbershop or the address of the "little house" on Fourteenth Street. Both can be found under "Sirica, Fred" (and also under "Sirica, John J. atty" and "Emmons, William E.") in the city directory for at least the years 1930 to 1934. There were no embarrassing misunderstandings, as there had been at the time of the poolhall, at any police station. According to Emmons, the police of the First Precinct were paid off—and there was whatever protection was implied by a son who had become an assistant in the U.S. Attorney's office.

Even 1934, when one thinks about it, was not just the year when Prohibition ended, and Sirica quit the U.S. Attorneys office—and Congress at last legalized professional boxing in Washington. It was also a year *deep* in the Depression, a particularly odd time for a young lawyer to leave a government job and start his own practice. It was the year as well when Sirica says he met Dempsey, and when he tried to start and promote a boxing arena with a "local prizefighter," Goldie Ahearne. It goes by now almost without saying that Goldie Ahearne could not, any more than Sirica himself, legally have been a "local prizefighter" before 1934.

There are countless peculiarities in Sirica's story. His professions of patriotism, for example, coupled with his lack of military service, in any capacity whatever, in World War II. He was, after all, a bachelor. The whole war took place during what he called his "starvation period." The *Times*, in its unusually fulsome obituary of August 15, 1992, which described Sirica as "indisputably . . . a hero," "a great scholar" (and "by seemingly unanimous agreement, an honest man"), particularly stressed that he was "patriotic," "unabashedly patriotic," and added to its repeated characterizations of Sirica as "an authentic American hero" a military component.

> In World War II, he tried to get a Navy commission, but failed for physical reasons. . . . So, during much of the war, he toured the country with Mr. Dempsey on bond-selling drives.

The "for physical reasons," at least on the basis of *To Set the Record Straight*, seems unlikely, considering Sirica's account of his superb physical condition—and of course there are other capacities in which a bachelor, sitting idly in his office "waiting for the phone to ring," might serve in the military. In his book, Sirica never so much as mentions the possibility of military service. But the *Times'* claim that "during much of the war, he toured the country with Mr. Dempsey on bond-selling drives" is beyond description. Here is the relevant passage from *To Set the Record Straight*:

> Jack and I had some great times together. In 1942, he was touring with the Cole Brothers Circus and wanted some company. I met the circus in North Carolina and spent three days with Jack on the circus train. I'll never forget Jack charming the ladies. . . .

In 1942, the Cole Brothers Circus was Clyde Beatty's circus, with no connection to war bonds or a war effort of any kind. In 1945, in other words *after* the war, it is true, when Dempsey went on a tour selling "savings bonds," Sirica went with him. "While thoroughly enjoying myself," Sirica writes, "I also felt I was doing something important for my country." Perhaps he was.

Among Sirica's unlikely, and in this book and his legend unmentioned, friends and correspondents is FBI Director J. Edgar Hoover. Why would a judge of Sirica's renown *not* have become friends with the FBI director? Because Sirica was not yet at all renowned. Hoover died in May 1972, a month before the break-in at the Watergate. His friendship with Sirica dates from the fifties—overlapping, for all one knows, with the friendship with Senator Joseph McCarthy—when Hoover, fighting the Communist menace, was still denying the very existence of organized crime. There must be a true story here somewhere, but so far no one has told or apparently even looked into it.

> Contrary to his reputation as a hero, Sirica was in fact a corrupt, incompetent, and dishonest figure, with a close connection to Senator Joseph McCarthy and clear ties to organized crime.

That is all I said or wanted to say about the subject. If a reader were to read this sentence, at least as quoted and discussed in the *Times*, to suggest that while Sirica was presiding over the Watergate cases he was taking payoffs from the mob, that is not a plausible reading. I was writing, after all, about Sirica's autobiography. "A close connection to Senator

Joseph McCarthy"—in the phrase that directly precedes "clear ties to organized crime"—would necessarily have ended on May 2, 1957, when McCarthy died. Sirica had not yet even assumed his position on the bench. If I had meant that Sirica was taking such payments on the bench or at any other time, I would of course have said so.

But enough. I do not need and never did intend to investigate the story of John J. Sirica. At the time I read his book, I had already written extensively about Watergate. I had also worked, until the day of President Nixon's resignation, for the impeachment inquiry. It only became clear, from the book itself and then in retrospect, that the legend, the accumulation of clichés, received ideas, and bromides—the "scrupulously honest man," the "hero," who rises from humble beginnings to confront "the most powerful man on earth" and to find (if need be in disregard of the rules of evidence) "the truth for the American people"—had almost no basis in reality.

The legend of Sirica as a "scupulously honest man" and a "hero" rests, of course, on the Watergate trials. The conduct of those trials, criticized at the time, raises questions of all kinds. It is by no means clear, for example, why Judge Sirica assigned the cases to himself. There is evidence that, far from seeking to expedite the Watergate investigations, Sirica may have sought for several crucial months to delay them. In putting off the first trial until after the election, he says he was determined to have "a fair trial, not a quick one." Look at that phrase a moment. The fairness of his conduct in those trials has always been precisely the matter most in dispute. In October, on account of "back pain," he postponed the trials again, until January. It may also be that, in spite of the legend, Judge Sirica was less interested in getting at, as he put it, the "truth for the American people" than in some entirely other agenda—for example, in frustrating the investigation of the House Committee on Banking and Currency, the Patman Committee, which was the one investigative body that would have known where to look for the deeper truth about the Watergate—not the burglary or the cover-up but the sources of the cash. The Patman investigation concerned President Nixon so intensely that he sent then-Congressman Gerald Ford to persuade the committee Republicans to deny Patman the subpoena power. He sent Attorney General Richard Kleindienst, an old friend of Sirica's, to persuade the judge, in the name of "protecting the defendants' civil rights," to issue an unusually broad "gag order," forbidding anyone (government officers, witnesses, defendants, lawyers) from making statements about "any aspects of the case" to anyone, including congressional committees. The gag order, as even Sirica acknowledged, "strengthened the hand of the administration in stonewalling Patman." Patman protested, in a five-page letter, to Sirica. By the time Sirica agreed to modify his order, Congressman Ford had persuaded the Republicans. Subpoena power for Patman's Committee on Banking and Currency was denied.

A great deal has been made of what Sirica himself seems to consider the crucial break in the Watergate case: a letter from one of the convicted Watergate burglars, James McCord, alleging that perjury had been committed, that persons higher up than the original burglars were implicated, that "pressure" had been applied to the defendants to "plead guilty and remain silent." McCord himself was a mysterious figure, formerly CIA and formerly FBI, as well as former guard of John Mitchell's loquacious and frequently inebriated wife. On Friday, March 13, 1973, Judge Sirica read McCord's letter melodramatically in open court. Ever since, that reading has been regarded as a turning point in the entire case. This seems highly improbable for two reasons: McCord did not *know* (or at least did not divulge) anything either important or admissible in the case; and he had sent a copy of his letter to the *Los Angeles Times*, so that it would have become public in any event.

The accepted chronology of Sirica's life was always mystifying, and as a career pattern it is almost incomprehensible. It may even be that the real progression in Sirica's life was not as the legend would have it, but rather this: first, the man of Prohibition and illegal boxing, in the U.S. Attorney's office; then McCarthy's man and even J. Edgar Hoover's, with whatever politics that implies; then perhaps just the Republican Party's man, its emissary to Italian communities (mostly, in those days Democratic); then a federal judge, the worst on the Washington bench; then Nixon's man, an irascible figure who repeatedly expresses disdain for the rules of evidence; then, in his unprecedented use of "provisional sentencing" as a form of coercion, a vain sort of bully, who is concerned not "to sit like some nincompoop" while the defendants, under appropriate sentences, are "laughing at us"; then, a sort of obsessed prosecutor, who does not really discover any "truth"; and finally, in his vanity and posturing, a man, a "hero," for the press.

A judge, after all, is not meant to be a hero. The only judges in our times who could legitimately be described as heroes were Frank Johnson, Elbert Tuttle, John Minor Wisdom, and the other judges of the Fifth Circuit, who took genuine risks, and suffered for them, for justice in the South. And judges, under the Constitution, are not meant to ascertain, least of all to prosecute or to coerce by sentencing, the "truth," "for the American people," or even for the jury. They are to preside fairly, under the adversary system, over cases presented by lawyers for the plaintiffs and the defendants before them. Anything else, whether it is posturing for the media, or coercing defendants with outrageous "provisional sentences," or working on behalf of some party not before the court, undermines the system. Far from demonstrating that "no man is above the law," it suggests that the judge himself is above it. We do not, under the Constitution, have a system wherein judges are inquisitors. In any event, though there may be material for a real biography of Judge Sirica, there is also this inescapable and awkward truth: Even in the Watergate investigations, he made no important contribution, except to the lore.

For the moment, almost as a housekeeping matter, just two relatively minor instances of dishonesty, corruption, incompetence—instances where they seem to overlap. In the matter of *voir dire*: Judge Sirica, having promised, at the request of both prosecution and defense, to interview prospective jurors individually, and in chambers, did not do so. As a result, when one juror was reported, at a crucial moment in the trial, to have violated the sequestration rules and spoken at length by telephone with his wife, Sirica interviewed that juror to ascertain whether he had obtained information from the outside world, and perhaps communicated it to other jurors. It turned out that the juror had in fact obtained such information. It also turned out that the juror knew only Spanish, and neither spoke nor understood English. To cover for this error—the juror could understand neither the testimony about the burglary nor instructions in the law—Sirica dismissed the juror and simply *sealed* this embarrassing portion of the record. The incident involved incompetence, surely, followed by a substantial lapse of integrity.

More serious was his use of "provisional sentencing" and outright dishonesty in at least one instance of it. Having imposed "temporary sentences" of unprecedented severity on the five defendants who pleaded guilty, Sirica told them that their actual sentences might depend on their cooperation with subsequent investigations. This was, in itself, a highly improper use of provisional sentencing—widely criticized, as "extortion," "abuse of power," and "the torture rack," by two presidents of the American Bar Association and scholars ranging from Monroe Freedman to Philip Kurland. Provisional sentencing is a procedure to make sentences contingent on reports about the defendants' character, and not a device for judges to coerce testimony when the adversary system (which is, after all, the American system) has already run its course. Far from demonstrating the bromide that no man, not even the President, is above the law, Judge Sirica proceeded as though one man, the judge himself, were above it.

The outright falsification was as follows. On March 23, 1973, Judge Sirica said that the sentences for the five defendants who had pleaded guilty would depend on their cooperation in implicating people higher up.

> Other factors will of course be considered but I mention
> this one because it is one over which you have control and I
> mean each one of the five of you.

By 1975, the President had resigned. John Dean, John Mitchell, Bob Haldeman, and John Ehrlichman, government officials higher up than any of the first seven Watergate defendants, had all been tried, convicted, and sent to jail. In denying an appeal for reduction of sentence by a defendant who had not pleaded guilty, had not received a provisional sentence, and was not one of the original five, Sirica simply "quoted" the last sentence of his March 23, 1973, Memorandum of Opinion and Order, as follows:

> Other factors will, of course, be considered but I mention
> this one because it is one over which *you have control* and I
> mean each and every one of you.
>
> —397 F. Supp. Pp. 949 and 963

There is no doubt that Judge Sirica altered this passage deliberately. About "you have control," he even notes "italics added." The key alteration, however, is from "I mean each one of the five of you" to "I mean each and every one of you." The latter would have included the defendant, G. Gordon Liddy, among those who had pleaded guilty and whose sentences were contingent on their "cooperation." Liddy was never one of them, and Liddy's sentence was never contingent on any cooperation. The falsification was crucial. It enabled Judge Sirica to keep Liddy in jail, in worse conditions and for a far longer term than any other Watergate defendant, including those far higher up in the administration— on the pretense that Liddy had not accepted an offer that Sirica never made to him. The D.C. jail to which Sirica sent him was ancient, dirty, overcrowded, rat-infested, with temperatures that reached 104 degrees. Liddy was for a long time the only white prisoner there. (The D.C. jail has since been closed.) On April 12, 1977, when President Jimmy Carter commuted Liddy's twenty-year sentence to eight "in the interests of justice," Judge Sirica complained to the press.

Why, then, was the *Times* so heavily committed to the received idea that Sirica was "an authentic hero," "by seemingly unanimous agreement an honest man," even "a great scholar," and so forth. Part of the reason is that the *Times* itself has said so, in its obituary—an accretion of myth, clichés, received ideas, and self-serving fables recounted by the subject himself, unusually fulsome even for obituaries. Partly because a relatively recent, complacent kind of sloth on the part of many reporters—sitting at a desk, phoning around, either repetitively badgering or, more commonly, passively receiving quotes from anonymous, self-interested, possibly lying, or even nonexistent sources—tends to welcome and to perpetuate every sort of conventional wisdom and cliché. Partly because the *Times* is committed most profoundly to a certain notion of itself. In the past, this commitment took a highly honorable form. The publisher and his family, one knew, were devoted, financially and in almost every other way, to the quality of the newspaper. Now, much of the paper is devoted to itself in quite another sense—as a bureaucracy, a complacent, unchallenged, in some ways totalitarian institution, convinced of its own infallibility.

As for what it was that made the *Times* so very cross about my sentence, nothing could be clearer than that it was not concern about Judge Sirica's reputation. The most distinguished First Amendment lawyer I know said that the *Times* did more damage to Sirica's reputation in three days than I could ever do. The reputation they were concerned with was, oddly, mine. Virtually every sentence in Ms. Barringer's piece gave that much away: "You could say this is a churlish, lowdown thing Renata

Adler has done," for example, and "You could take the position that it says more about the writer than about what she's writing." There it is. These, and other examples of prose in this series of pieces—"smear," "cheaply smearing," "off-handed evisceration of various literati" (imagine, if you will, an off-handed evisceration), "veering from her literary prey," "cavalier," "even more irresponsible," elsewhere "despicable," "Iago," "lacking a conscience and a soul"—were not, whatever else they may have been, the prose of journalism.

I have friends who have said jokingly, and some not so jokingly, that they fear retaliation from the *Times*. As well they might. I am not entirely lacking in experience in the writing of polemical pieces. I have always found that it is not that easy. It requires some thought, and some familiarity with the material under review. On the other hand, honorable polemic, I would have thought, does not call in reinforcements, attacks rather than joins mob journalists. Here we find almost a parody—journalists not addressing underlying fact but interviewing *one another* about what they "heard" or "smelled." The *Times* editorial said that my "charges" had "startled some of the nation's best investigative journalists who had covered Watergate and found Judge Sirica to be a principled jurist." "Startled" them! The herd, advancing bravely not as single spies but in battalions, thinks the real world consists of received ideas they share with colleagues.

It is true I had criticized, sometimes directly, sometimes by implication, not just Mr. McGrath and the *Book Review* but the *Times*. I had written a book, *Reckless Disregard*, that was largely a criticism of the press. There may even have been implicit criticism, in pieces I wrote over the years. In recent articles, for example, in *Vanity Fair* and the *Los Angeles Times*, I had found, in writing about the Starr Report and its accompanying volumes, proof that Linda Tripp had not required, as the *Times* kept reporting, a set of "elves," under the direction of the literary agent Lucianne Goldberg, to make her way, surreptitiously and at the last minute, to the Special Prosecutor's office. She had, in fact, been working for that office for almost four years.

But that did not account for it either: the eight pieces, the alternately derisive and punitive tone, the pressure to recant. And the prose itself—there can be no clearer indication than this sort of writing that there is no news, no information, no substance there. I had written a sentence. Someone, offended, had asked me to document the sentence. I had said

I would do so. Not much of a story, one would have thought. In the days when there was still a standard of reporting, and of editing, "those who have read just about all the books on Watergate" and "those most steeped in Watergate lore," whoever they might be, would have been utterly unacceptable, in the *Times*, as sources. If the reporter had any genuine interest in the matter, she would have "steeped" herself in "Watergate lore" and read the "books on Watergate" (beginning perhaps with Judge Sirica's book) herself. But no. Here's what it was. At one point, in answer—not, as Ms. Barringer would have it, to the question "Why wait?," to which I gave, repeatedly, the answer that I was not waiting at all—but to a repetition of yet another ad personam question, I said, "How can you be a working journalist and phrase a question as silly as that?"

This is not the way you are supposed to talk to the *Times*. I knew that. But here obviously was the core of the offense, and so seriously did Ms. Barringer take it that she attached it to the wrong question, and so seriously did the *Times* take it that the editorial was virtually based on this intimation on my part that a *Times* reporter could phrase a deeply silly question. "Even more irresponsible," the editorial went on, was a line, inaccurately quoted, in which I asked Ms. Barringer whether she worried "that much about reputation." "Of course we do," the editorial actually said. (Of *course*.) "And so should she."

I have always known, and even written, that the strongest, perhaps sole remaining taboo on freedom of expression, in this country, is any criticism of the press. But here I had not only questioned a received idea cherished by the *Times* but I had not been sufficiently deferential to this *Times* reporter—and the whole *Times* bureaucracy, instinctively, needed to *stamp out this disrespect*. It would, of course, have gone without saying, until the *Times*, through Ms. Barringer, cited it with indignation, that a writer does choose what to write and when to write it. Now the matter had come to this: If you do not accept some cliché, bromide, or myth of theirs, and are not sufficiently deferential to them, this is not just insubordination. It is a *breach of ethics*.

You must be admonished. You must be taught a lesson, so that other people may learn from it. Not only is your own reputation affected. You must, above all, recant. And this, this last issue—retraction—is where the question is inescapably, dangerously, altered. And why the whole series of attacks addresses something more serious than my little book. Look again at Ms. Barringer's formulation:

As it stands, Ms. Adler and Simon & Schuster, a unit of Viacom, are either cheaply smearing Judge Sirica—with legal impunity—or they have evidence. But neither the publisher nor the author shows any urgency about resolving the issue, either by retracting the accusation or establishing its accuracy.

This is nothing if not a coercive formulation, pressure not just on a writer but on her publisher, and even her publisher's owner, "Simon & Schuster, a unit of Viacom," to retract. Whenever—and I think this is true without exception—you find a publication, or a journalist, calling for a retraction or a recantation by, of all things, a single writer (and actual pressure on her publisher, "cheaply smearing"), you know what sort of realm you are in. It is a realm where received ideas are not just propagated but enforced—and it is an unmistakably totalitarian realm. What "issue," after all, could be "resolved" by a retraction? Nothing about Sirica, certainly. The only issue would be the power of the *New York Times*, in the person of Ms. Barringer and other writers, to coerce retractions. What this whole series amounted to was a show trial, with serial accusers, disinformation, designed to end, as show trials do, with recantations.

Well, it nearly worked. The *Times*, of course, is still drawing on trust and respect well earned some years ago. In the course of this recent episode, Joseph Lelyveld, the executive editor, told me as early as April 3 that he had no idea the *Times* had published so many disparaging pieces about my book. He would look out for this sort of thing. Later, he said he would, if it had been his call, have run my letter (revised, of course, to conform with *Times* policy), but he had no jurisdiction over the Letters column. I knew he had no jurisdiction over the editorial page or the op-ed pieces. (Either John Dean is inspired, and writes, submits his work, and is edited with extraordinary speed, or his piece was solicited right after I told Ms. Barringer, to her evident disappointment, that my source was not G. Gordon Liddy.) The editorial board, of which, as we know, Ms. Barringer's husband is a member, does have jurisdiction over both pages. Mr. Lelyveld is, however, in charge both of Corrections and the Editor's Note. On April 7, he sent me a fax. "I try to lean over backwards in matters of corrections and editor's notes," he wrote. He, and Ms. Barringer and her editor, had considered my note. "At this point the only solution I can see," he concluded, "is for us all to give the matter a rest." This was wonderful. The *Times* had attacked me eight times (only the last four of them had even the pretext of Judge Sirica), citing (perhaps this goes without saying) exclusively hostile "sources." These pieces had directly impugned my "ethics." They would not print a letter, an Editor's Note, or a Correction. In fairness he now felt that the only solution "for all of us" was to let the matter rest. Of course, the paper did not let it rest. Two days later, there was the news item in the Week in Review.[1]

Other journalists—in solidarity and taking their cue from the trusted and venerated *Times*—checked in. Some were apparently under the impression that I had used the Sirica passage as a sort of headline, to "hype" my book. Why else, after all, would the *Times* have devoted so much space and so many pieces to it? Piece after piece, in one medium after another, accepted as fact John Dean's speculation that my source was Liddy. One spoke of my "trying to sell" my book with a libel that "shames all caring, responsible journalists." That sort of thing. A media reporter for the *Daily News* wrote, on the basis of the *Times* editorial, that my book had been "plagued by" a series of "forced retractions." In a novel use, by a media reporter, of the formula, she wrote, "Ms. Adler was unavailable for comment"—on the basis, perhaps, of having made no effort whatsoever to reach me. Perhaps the most surprising instance of this herd of indignant *Times*-inspired colleagues occurred on April 8, on CNN's *Capital Gang*. Mark Shields, not usually, I would have thought, so orthodox a member of the guild, said, "And now for 'The Outrage of the Week.' " I had "defamed," he said, Judge Sirica, who was (in the by now altogether obligatory mantra) a scrupulously honest hero. "Renata Adler owes the family John Sirica loved and the nation he served so well an immediate and public apology."

Owing the nation an immediate and public apology does seem a bit much. But the *Times'* campaign began, I suppose, with that first letter from the editor who subsequently "said he had decided to distance himself." I should have left the galleys as they were. There followed the whole set of pieces, right through the almost laughably disingenuous characterization of John Dean. Disinformation. Show trial. Confession. Retraction. Not just yet. The *Times*, financially successful as it may be, is a powerful but, at this moment, not very healthy institution. The issue is not one book or even eight pieces. It is the state of the entire cultural mineshaft, with the archcensor, still in some ways the world's greatest newspaper, advocating the most explosive gases and the cutting off of air.

—2000

AFTERWORD

When I first wrote this piece, many journalists seemed to go more or less berserk. Without realizing it, they conceded that every word of my original sentence about Judge Sirica had been borne out. The ground, however, had shifted. The criticism now was that Sirica's dishonesty, incompetence, connections, and ties were not sufficiently grave, or sufficiently recent, or sufficiently "hot" to justify my having referred, however briefly, to them. There seemed no doubt, however, that if the *Times* itself had discovered any element of the story, especially the reference to Sirica's closeness to Senator Joseph McCarthy, it would have treated each element as a major scoop. Instead, the *Times* ran two more pieces, raising the total to ten, before my *Harper's* piece even hit the stands. One, by Alex Kuzscinsky, was the only one of the ten that could not have served as an example of execrable work in any sophomore journalism class. Another, by Martin Arnold, cited in my Introduction, assured readers that there was nothing in the *Harper's* piece; Martin deplored what was apparently his impression, that neither books nor magazines could meet the checking standards of newspapers like the *Times*. Ms. Barringer said, in an interview, that nothing I said about Judge Sirica could not be said equally about the heavyweight champion Joe Louis— which would be true, I suppose, if Joe Louis had ever fought, under fictional names, in districts where boxing was illegal, or if he had organized and promoted boxing, and served as Assistant U.S. Attorney in a district where his father ran an illegal liquor business, and so forth.

What seemed most to infuriate those journalists who reacted angrily was that I had based my passage mainly on evidence in Sirica's own book. I should, apparently, have claimed an "anonymous source." As it happens, I did have other sources, and other facts, which I would have thought Judge Sirica, or at least his co-author, John F. Stacks of *Time*, would have thought worthy of inclusion, and which the *Times* and its acolytes might have found with a modicum of research. In 1927, in Chicago, for example, John J. Sirica himself (not his father) was indicted, along with several co-conspirators, for fixing a prizefight and for income tax evasion. The indictments were sealed. The case never went to trial.

In his fine biography of Jack Dempsey, Roger Kahn writes that, in looking at a video of the second Dempsey-Tunney fight, with its famous "long count," "I am looking at a crooked referee." Perhaps. Perhaps not, or not just the referee. Kahn, like most other experts on boxing history, writes that Al Capone was very eager to back Dempsey in that fight but that Dempsey, man of honor that he was, firmly rebuffed him. Something seems amiss in the underlying logic of this story. Mob bosses approach fighters and (as in the Black Sox scandal, which also took place in Chicago) baseball players not to *win* matches but to lose them. Winning is what the fighters, or the players, want naturally to do, when they are not bribed to do otherwise. Dempsey, of course, did lose. The fight-fixing for which Sirica and others were named in the sealed indictment of 1927 was the Dempsey-Tunney fight. (No referee is mentioned in the sealed indictment.) My source for the information about Sirica's inclusion in the indictment (for fight-fixing and consequent tax evasion) was the Criminal Investigation Division of the IRS—which published its own historical study for internal use.

In my *Harper's* piece, I confined myself to matters that virtually sprang off the page of Sirica's own autobiography, the book I chose not to review. It was not my intention to address anything more sensational than the literal meaning of a few words on page 125 of my own book. Suddenly, these heroic defenders of reputation (not the reputation, perhaps, of a single scientist, like Wen Ho Lee, in solitary and in shackles, on the basis largely of their institution's coverage) emerged, one after another, as though there were an honor roll: ten within the *Times* alone, to be followed by hundreds more. It was as though the press, self-important and self-righteous as it is, seems entirely unconscious of its own weight against any single, let alone dissenting, individual, or of its own role in the events it claims to cover. I thought this a more interesting and more important subject, than the details of Sirica's status. In view of the astonishing aftermath of the piece itself, however, just for the record, a bit more about what any genuine biography of Judge Sirica would include.

Though Sirica describes Dempsey, at least after 1934, as "my best friend," and although Dempsey, far more openly than Sirica, managed to avoid military service (after World War I, Dempsey was actually indicted and tried for draft evasion), there is, oddly, no mention of Sirica in the index of any Dempsey biography. Or for that matter, in the index of any biography of Senator Joseph McCarthy, or of Walter Winchell—at least two of whom, it may be remembered, had their own involvements with organized crime: Dempsey with Capone, and Winchell of course with Louis Lepke and Frank Costello.

By "organized crime," incidentally, I never for a moment meant the Sicilian Mafia. The interests in question were for the most part Jewish and even Irish. I did leave out one Italian connection: Al Capone. That connection was Neapolitan. Al Capone's father, Gabriel, had immigrated from Castellammare di Stabia, in the Bay of Naples, where he had learned his trade. Like Fred Sirica, who emigrated from San Valentino Torio (also in the Bay of Naples, a few kilometers from Castellammare di Stabia) Gabriel Capone was a barber. The two men were friends.

I leave aside any number of utterly incomprehensible omissions from Sirica's autobiography. Senator Hiram Bingham, of Connecticut, for example, is introduced to Sirica by "a cousin," who "happened to be active in local politics in Waterbury," so that Bingham will "endorse" Sirica for the job of Assistant U.S. Attorney. It is not surprising that we hear no more about the "cousin." Hiram Bingham, however, not only was one of the very few senators ever to incur a vote of censure by the full Senate (in 1929, for putting a lobbyist on the Senate payroll as his clerk). He also had been educated at Groton, Yale, Berkeley, and Harvard; served as lieutenant governor and then governor of Connecticut; written more than a dozen books, and, as a distinguished scholar and explorer, actually discovered the ruins of Machu Picchu. *That* Hiram Bingham.

Some readers seemed bewildered by what I could have meant, in the piece, by "totalitarian." They seemed to think that it meant "totalizing" or something. What I meant by a totalitarian reaction to a piece of writing was this: not debate (particularly not "the free, robust, and wide-open debate" envisioned by the First Amendment); not even invective, or mockery, or expressions of rage, scorn, indignation, disdain, or argument of any sort. But advocacy of *retraction, eradication, silencing.* Not "I disagree with what you say," but "I will attack to the death your right to say it, as well as the forum (book publisher, magazine) in which your work appears." Eradicate, in other words, not just a book or a piece but, if possible, the author and eliminate future outlets for this heresy. This view of what writing is, and the appropriate response to it, is nothing if not totalitarian.

Supposing, however, just supposing, what was not the case: that I had been mistaken. That Sirica had been brilliantly competent on the bench and in his conduct of the case, that he had never so much as heard of Senator Joseph McCarthy or of any form of organized crime, that his book and his life had been models of rectitude and forthrightness. What then? Nowhere, in any of the *Times* attacks, was there the slightest indication that my reputation did not rest entirely on this single sentence on page 125 of my sixth book. If they had misspelled Sirica's name, of course, or mine, they would have felt bound in fairness to run an Editor's Note or a Correction.

People forget things. Everyone forgets. I keep forgetting, for example, to mention that the Starr volumes are in their way a masterpiece that, quite apart from any prosecutorial or political matter, is full of fascinating incidents and characters. It ought to be published with type large enough to read.

—2001

NOTES

Searching for the Real Nixon Scandal: A Last Inference

1. Among the members of this group were Dorothy Shelton, Robert Shelton, Owen Fiss, Robert Owen, Burke Marshall, and the author.

Reflections on Political Scandal

1. *Presidential Campaign Activities of 1972, Hearings Before the Select Committee on Presidential Campaign Activities of the United States Senate*, Book 6, pp. 2,636–2,638.

2. *Hearing Before the Committee on Banking and Currency*, House of Representatives, *Legal and Economic Impact of Foreign Banking Procedures on the United States* (December 1968).

3. By late fall of 1972 it was obvious that Nixon did not need peace in Vietnam for his reelection. He might nonetheless have liked to have it. Certainly Kissinger, though not Haig, did want it. The South Vietnamese government, however, very clearly did not want it. To prevent it in 1968, they had only to stall the negotiations in Paris; by 1972, they had to pay. See more generally "Searching for the Real Nixon Scandal."

4. The residue of that unit, in fact, still exists, as the Drug Enforcement Administration, with 4,000 employees (320 of them abroad) and an annual budget of $182 million. It is now doubtless becoming one of the entrenched bureaucracies, established alongside those that fought it.

Monica's Story

1. The case ended in a mistrial.

A Court of No Appeal

1. Mr. Dean's suit, though neither the *Times* nor any other newspaper I know has called attention to it, has since been dismissed.

COPYRIGHT ACKNOWLEDGMENTS

Previously published essays by Renata Adler first appeared, in slightly different form, in the following publications:

"Searching for the Real Nixon Scandal: A Last Inference" first appeared in *The Atlantic Monthly*, December 1976.

"Reflections on Political Scandal" first appeared in *The New York Review of Books*, December 8, 1977.

"The Justices and the Journalists" first appeared in the *New York Times Book Review* (front page), 1979.

"The Extreme Nominee" first appeared in *The New Yorker*, August 3, 1987.

"Coup at the Court" first appeared in *The New Republic*, September 14 and 21, 1987.

"Decoding the Starr Report" first appeared in *Vanity Fair*, December 1998.

"Monica's Story" first appeared in the *Los Angeles Times Book Review*, March 14, 1999.

"Letter from Biafra" first appeared in *The New Yorker*, October 4, 1969.

"But Ohio. Well, I Guess That's One State Where They Elect to Lock and Load: The National Guard" first appeared as "A Reporter at Large" in *The New Yorker*, October 3, 1970.

"Concentration, Squares, Jeopardy, and Bouillon Cubes" first appeared in "The Air," *The New Yorker*, December 25, 1971.

"Afternoon Television: Unhappiness Enough, and Time" first appeared in "The Air," *The New Yorker*, February 12, 1972.

"Who's Here? What Time Is It?" first appeared in "The Air," *The New Yorker*, September 16, 1972.

"Cookie, Oscar, Grover, Herry, Ernie, and Company" first appeared in "The Air," *The New Yorker*, June 2, 1972.

"House Critic" first appeared as "The Perils of Pauline" in *The New York Review of Books*, August 14, 1980.

"A Court of No Appeal" first appeared in *Harper's Magazine*, August 2000.

INDEX